Recovering Scottish History

For Rita-Gabriele, Ruaridh, Sebastian and Corin;
and in memory of my mother who passed on *le patrimoine*

Recovering Scottish History

John Hill Burton and Scottish National
Identity in the Nineteenth Century

Craig Beveridge

EDINBURGH
University Press

Edinburgh University Press is one of the leading university presses in the UK. We publish academic books and journals in our selected subject areas across the humanities and social sciences, combining cutting-edge scholarship with high editorial and production values to produce academic works of lasting importance. For more information visit our website: edinburghuniversitypress.com

© Craig Beveridge, 2022

Edinburgh University Press Ltd
The Tun – Holyrood Road
12 (2f) Jackson's Entry
Edinburgh EH8 8PJ

Typeset in 10.5/13pt Sabon by
IDSUK (DataConnection) Ltd

A CIP record for this book is available from the British Library

ISBN 978 1 4744 9146 4 (hardback)
ISBN 978 1 4744 9148 8 (webready PDF)
ISBN 978 1 4744 9149 5 (epub)

The right of Craig Beveridge to be identified as author of this work has been asserted in accordance with the Copyright, Designs and Patents Act 1988 and the Copyright and Related Rights Regulations 2003 (SI No. 2498).

Contents

Acknowledgements	vi
Abbreviations	vii
Introduction: Recovering Hill Burton	1
1 Perspectives on Scottish History in the Nineteenth Century	5
2 Burton in Aberdeen and Edinburgh, 1809–49	27
3 Turning to History, Edinburgh, 1850–70	58
4 Utilitarian History	97
5 Romantic History	115
6 Gothic History	146
7 History as Theatre	174
8 On the Pedestal, 1871–81	193
9 History and Heritage: The Revival of Scottish National Identity	259
Epilogue	271
Bibliography	273
Index	290

Acknowledgements

I have benefited from many works, too numerous to mention, which evidence the increasing scholarship devoted to Scottish history and literature in recent decades. However, in the course of researching this book I read Dr Richard A. Marsden's study, *Cosmo Innes and the Defence of Scottish History* which seemed to me to offer a signally fresh approach to attitudes to the past, including the national past, in nineteenth-century Scotland and it is appropriate to recognise my debt to the insights I found there. Professor David Finkelstein's work on the influence of *The House of Blackwood* I also found illuminating.

I am particularly grateful to Cairns Craig, Glucksman Professor of Irish and Scottish Studies in the University of Aberdeen and to Richard B. Sher, Distinguished Professor of History Emeritus, New Jersey Institute of Technology, for their generous assistance in advising on the development of this book. The content is of course entirely my own responsibility.

I should also like to thank the staff of the National Library of Scotland, which houses the John Hill Burton archive, including those in the Special Collections Reading Room where I have frequently required to consult material. They were invariably courteous and helpful.

Finally, I am grateful for the support of family and friends who patiently endured over some years, recurrent and, I fear, importunate appeals for their thoughts on aspects of what follows, in which they had perhaps less compulsive interest than I had myself.

Abbreviations

PERIODICALS

Aber M	Aberdeen Magazine
BM	Blackwood's Magazine
BQ	British Quarterly Review
Ecl M	Eclectic Magazine of Foreign Literature, Science and Art
Ecl R	Eclectic Review
EHR	English Historical Review
ER	Edinburgh Review
FQR	Foreign and Quarterly Review
LQ	London Quarterly Review
MM	Macmillan's Magazine
NBR	North British Review
SHR	Scottish Historical Review
Tait's	Tait's Edinburgh Magazine
Q Rev	Quarterly Review
W Rev	Westminster Review

JOURNALS

Athen	Athenaeum
Chamb J	Chambers's (Edinburgh) Journal
Exam	Examiner
Lit Rev	Literary Review
Lloyd's	Lloyd's Weekly Newspaper
Sat Rev	The Saturday Review

NEWSPAPERS

Aber J	Aberdeen Journal
Banf J	Banffshire Journal
Dund Adv	Dundee Advertiser
Dund C	Dundee Courier
Falk H	Falkirk Herald
Fife H	Fife Herald
Glasg Ev Cit	Glasgow Evening Citizen
Glasg H	Glasgow Herald
Gr Adv	Greenock Advertiser
Inv C	Inverness Courier
Pall M G	Pall Mall Gazette
Sc	Scotsman
Stand	Standard (London)
Times	The Times (London)

REFERENCE WORKS

ODNB   *Oxford Dictionary of National Biography*

BOOKS

APS (1814–24)   Thomas Thomson, ed., *The Acts of the Parliaments of Scotland II–XI* (London: House of Commons, 1814–24)

HOS (1853)   John Hill Burton, *History of Scotland from the Revolution to the Extinction of the Last Jacobite Insurrection, 1689–1748*, 2 vols (London: Longmans, 1853)

HOS (1873)   John Hill Burton, *The History of Scotland: From Agricola's Invasion to the Extinction of the Last Jacobite Insurrection*, A New Edition Revised in Eight Volumes (Edinburgh: Blackwood, 1873)

Introduction: Recovering Hill Burton

JOHN HILL BURTON (1809–81) was one of the great intellectual figures of nineteenth-century Scotland. Originally an advocate by profession who served as secretary (then manager) of the Scottish Prison Board from 1854 to 1877, he distinguished himself as an author and a scholar in a wide variety of fields. He wrote on political economy both in the leading periodicals of the age and in book form, engaging with the great social and economic issues arising from the rapid industrialisation of the mid-century. He published a pioneering study of the life and correspondence of David Hume (1846) and played a leading part in bringing the first edition of Jeremy Bentham's *Collected Works* (1838–43) to publication. He composed a *Manual of the Law of Scotland* (1839), which was respected at the time and went through two editions. Later he became a familiar name to a wider readership through successful, more popular books such as *The Book-Hunter* (1862) and *The Scot Abroad* (1864).

Above all, Burton wrote history, especially Scottish history, and that aspect of his remarkable intellectual achievement is the focus of this book. His profile in historical scholarship was first raised through editorial work for the book clubs, which played a leading role in recovering and publishing source texts across the middle decades of the century. This began with the *Jacobite Correspondence of the Atholl Family [. . .]* (1840), which he edited from manuscript for the Abbotsford Club; and he later searched out and edited an important archive of the *Darien Papers [. . .]* (1849) for the elite Bannatyne. In between he wrote a joint biography of the *Lives of Simon Lord Lovat, and Duncan Forbes of Culloden: From Original Sources* (1847). This focus on Scottish history intensified from the mid-century both in his regular periodical contributions – almost invariably as time went on in *Blackwood's Magazine* – and in book publications.

The first fruit of this sustained effort was his two-volume *History of Scotland from the Revolution to the Extinction of the Last Jacobite Insurrection (1689–1748)*, published in 1853 and covering a relatively limited period. There was then a substantial gap, during which he continued to research and publish on Scottish history in a sustained relationship with Blackwood's publishing house, before the appearance in two tranches of his *History of Scotland from Agricola's Invasion to the Revolution* (7 vols, 1867–70). Burton subsequently added much of the 1853 material to the later work to produce a revised and consolidated eight-volume *History of Scotland from Agricola's Invasion to the Extinction of the Last Jacobite Insurrection* (1873). As the later volumes appeared, the work was positively received and widely welcomed as representing the first complete and well-evidenced account of the nation's past. The present study will build toward an in-depth analysis of that eight-volume work as well as its critical and public reception, and the significance of both for established historiographic perceptions of the period.

Yet history has not been kind to this historian of Scotland. Today the man and his works attract little attention. His reputation began to falter, at least within academic circles, with the increasing professionalisation of historical scholarship at the turn of the twentieth century. It is unsurprising that the first serious criticism of his multi-volume *History of Scotland* appeared in October 1903, in the inaugural number of the *Scottish Historical Review*. W. L. Mathieson, near the start of a respected scholarly career, contributed a critical assessment to the *SHR* listing a series of mistakes of fact and noting a general looseness in parts of the narrative. Nevertheless, the opening sentence of Mathieson's critique is notable: Burton's *History* 'has been so long before the public' and 'has been so widely read' that it would be a waste of time – other presumably than for the limited readership of the *SHR* – to elaborate on its defects.[1] He was correct. For approaching forty years and for some time to come, it was Burton's *History* from which the Scottish reading public had absorbed a sense of their past and of that past as a national history. The work of John Hill Burton was indeed widely read and admired and had a determining influence on how Scottish history was perceived for close to half a century from the 1860s.

The present study has two broad purposes. First, it offers a revision of predominant historiographic perceptions of nineteenth-century Scotland, and of Scottish historical consciousness and national identity as the century

---

[1] W. L. Mathieson, 'Hill Burton in Error', *SHR* I (1903), 48–54 (pp. 48, 52–54).

progressed. Second, it seeks to provide a reassessment of Burton, a significant figure in nineteenth-century Scottish thought who has been largely lost to view. The account of Burton's broader life experience eschews a traditional and comprehensive biographical narrative of all that befell him. While the main events have of course been addressed, particular attention has been devoted to the surviving evidence of exceptional and revealing aspects of his private and public life, foregrounding those that shaped his personality and sensibilities, and informed his historical works. The approach to the historiographic revision, besides a careful exegesis of the text of Burton's national *History*, places emphasis on the contemporary reception of his historical *œuvre* as revealed in a wide range of contemporary print media and manuscript sources.

In what follows, Chapter 1 outlines the views on Scottish identity and historical confidence in the period advanced over recent decades by a number of prominent writers; but also explores what features Burton's contemporaries themselves had come to expect in an account of the nation's annals. Chapters 2 and 3 focus on Burton's biographical development and trace the unusual diversity of his involvement in prominent features of the social and cultural world of nineteenth-century Scotland. This, it will be argued, enabled him to compose an account of the nation's past with which the Scottish reading public who shared that world could identify. Chapter 2 commences with the social and cultural influences that shaped his character and sensibilities as a youth and young adult before his move to the Scottish capital in 1830, and proceeds to describe through the subsequent two decades the wide spectrum of political and cultural relationships that his personality and sociability engendered. Chapter 3 addresses the factors bearing on Burton's increasing preoccupation from the mid-century with Scottish history, both in terms of his own life experiences and in regard to the increasing attention devoted to the Scottish past by publishers, book clubs, records scholars and the new breed of 'archaeologist'.

In Chapters 4 to 7, the book's focus shifts to Burton's *magnum opus*, the eight-volume *History of Scotland*, considered in terms of a number of prominent themes or discourses that are perceived to emerge from the text. It is proposed that these can be captured in the terms of Utilitarian History, Romantic History, Gothic History and History as Theatre. However, though these chapters deal primarily with such textual analyses, in a final section of each the relation of historiography and biography is maintained in tracing the origins of these discourses in Burton's life experience and his immersion in the social and cultural world of his time. Chapter 8 provides an in-depth analysis of the critical issue of the reception and public response to Burton's historical efforts.

The assessment deals first and separately with the impact of his initial 1853 volumes since these were published at a particular juncture – the height of the 'Scottish Rights' agitation of the early 1850s – and functioned, it is suggested, to charge that contemporary discontent with a new historical dimension centring on the 1707 Union; this is followed by an extended analysis of the highly positive reception accorded to his later, multi-volume *History of Scotland* as a legitimate narrative to be cast as a national history, whose characteristics are then set in the context of comparable developments across nineteenth-century Europe. The final chapter summarises the book's conclusions and suggests that, taken together with associated developments in the second half of the century, they evidence a revival of national identity founded on a new engagement with the nation's past.

1

Perspectives on Scottish History in the Nineteenth Century

MODERN HISTORIOGRAPHIC INTERPRETATIONS

FOR OVER FIFTY YEARS there has been controversy over Scottish national identity in the nineteenth century. Unsurprisingly this has often involved interpretations and reinterpretations of the Scots' attitude to their past. In his relatively recent general history *The Scottish Nation*, the country's most prominent modern historian sought a balanced view. T. M. Devine recognised that some social developments appeared to support the judgement, which he associated with G. E. Davie and Tom Nairn, that the Liberal hegemony of 1832–1914 was 'one of profound crisis in Scottish nationhood'. The benefits of Union and Empire were worth 'the heavy cost of anglicization and cultural assimilation'. However, Devine also noted the 'broad argument' emerging from the works of Richard Finlay, Graeme Morton and Lindsay Paterson in the 1990s, which he viewed as 'a radical reinterpretation' suggesting that Scottish national identity had simply 'adapted to new circumstances'. The period had therefore seen 'the reinvention of Scotland, when new or refurbished icons continued to provide the nation with crucial symbols of identity and distinctiveness within the union'. This appears to refer to the periodic enthusiasms for commemorative events, statues and other memorials to celebrated individuals like William Wallace, Robert Bruce and Robert Burns that Graeme Morton has associated with an ideology of 'unionist-nationalism'; as well as with the appropriation of a romantic 'Highlandism'. Devine drew attention to the increasing coverage of Scottish folklore and social history in working-class papers towards the end of the century but his references to Scottish narrative history relate to examples earlier in the century and at the latest Patrick Fraser Tytler's *History of Scotland* published between 1828 and 1843.[1]

The issue has perhaps inevitably been drawn into the broader debate concerning Scotland's 'missing' nineteenth-century nationalism. This was originally driven by the presumption that an explanation was required for the failure of the Scots to develop the type of nationalist reassertion that in this period became characteristic of many small European countries drawn or forced into union with larger states and empires, and evolved into movements for political independence. Early suggestions in the 1960s and 1970s conceived of a cultural 'crisis' affecting the elites unable to sustain the cultural achievements of the Scottish Enlightenment in the previous century and in any case bent on exploiting the opportunities of Empire. For them, it was argued, the rationale for assimilation was powerful. For Nairn, the bourgeois elite's participation in the country's uniquely rapid economic modernisation rendered it disinterested and unable to grasp the expected (and normal) nationalist moment.[2] The situation resulted for Davie in a 'failure of nerve', bringing with it a rejection and devalorisation of traditional Scottish institutional and cultural practices, indeed of Scottish history itself:

> at the very time when other neighbouring countries were becoming increasingly 'history minded', the Scots were losing their sense of the past, and their leading institutions, including the Universities, were emphatically resolved – to use a catch phrase fashionable in Scotland of the early twentieth century – 'no longer to be prisoners of their own history'.[3]

The elites' disinterest in the assertion of national identity and the cultural 'failure of nerve' that incorporated a disestimation of the national past appeared to support the same historiographic interpretation; they were complementary features of a loss of national confidence.

---

[1] Thomas Martin Devine, *The Scottish Nation: A Modern History* (London: Penguin, 2012), pp. 285–7, 292; Richard J. Finlay, *A Partnership for Good?: Scottish Politics and the Union since 1880* (Edinburgh: John Donald, 1997); Graeme Morton, *Unionist Nationalism: Governing Urban Scotland, 1830–1860* (East Linton: Tuckwell Press, 1999); Lindsay Paterson, *The Autonomy of Modern Scotland* (Edinburgh; Edinburgh University Press, 1994).
[2] Tom Nairn, *The Break-Up of Britain* (London: New Left Books, 1977), pp. 105–19.
[3] George Elder Davie, *The Democratic Intellect: Scotland and her Universities in the Nineteenth Century*, 3rd edn, ed. Murdo Macdonald (Edinburgh: Edinburgh University Press, 2013), pp. 337–8.

The writers whom Devine associated with the 'radical reinterpretation' were in part still responding to and reworking those earlier interpretations. At the outset of his analysis, Richard Finlay made a point of dismissing Nairn's views as anachronistic and sought a 'new perspective' on how the Scottish elites sought to accommodate their historical understanding with an increasing participation in the British state. However, his analysis tends to underscore the notion that their sense of history constituted a set of fragmented, almost contradictory beliefs, unreconcilable and unusable in ideological terms or to fashion any coherent historical synthesis. On the one hand the adoption of Scott's Highlandism, and from the mid-century the Wallace/Bruce/Burns commemorations, provided the middle class 'with a heavily romanticised and hazy past which bordered on the mythical'; while in an overlapping 'reinvention' or 'manufacture' of Scottish identity, contemporary values of laissez-faire liberalism were 'thrown back on the Scottish past'. Ultimately, Finlay concluded, this hodgepodge, which distilled 'the essence of Scotland into symbolic representations that were located in a quasi-mythical past' while presenting 'the norms of Victorian values as essentially Scottish values', could only 'paper over' the divisions in Scottish society and weaken the traditional foundations of national identity. Like many other recent historians, Finlay proceeded to emphasise nineteenth-century Scottish identity as derived increasingly from its involvement in the Empire and associated with history post-dating Scotland's 1707 Union with England.[4]

Graeme Morton was also to an extent responding to Nairn's views, which he noted relied on the perception that 'Scottish culture in the nineteenth century is deemed to have failed, and to have been left wallowing in the parochial'. Morton argued that through local civic structures the Scottish middle class had, at least in the period 1830–60, maintained a form of national identity for which he coined the term 'unionist-nationalism'. However, this required that they adopt 'what seems a perverse use of the symbols of Scotland's past, by arguing that the independence of Scotland's civil society could only be guaranteed by greater Union with England'. Morton rather unusually made some effort at a serious analysis of the Scottish Rights movement in the 1850s, then considered, in terms of Anthony Smith's etho-symbolist thinking, the materials available for articulating the Scottish *ethnie*: they remained fragmented and unconvincing.[5]

---

[4] Finlay, *Partnership for Good?*, pp. 20–5.
[5] Morton, *Unionist Nationalism*, pp. 54–60, 133–54, 155.

In recent decades, a number of other historians have explored nineteenth-century Scottish historiography in some depth, developing particular, to a degree complementary and certainly influential interpretations: they include Marinell Ash, Colin Kidd and Michael Fry. In her seminal study, *The Strange Death of Scottish History* (1980), Ash argued that the achievements of Walter Scott and his associates in bringing history centre stage in Scottish cultural effort in the first half of the century – through historical fiction, records scholarship and book club publishing – had thereafter gone off the rails. It had produced, indeed at Scott's direct prompting, P. F. Tytler's *History of Scotland*, which Ash argued had changed Scottish historical work 'in a profound way' by founding 'arguments upon facts', as Tytler had put it himself. For Ash this 'meant that for the rest of the nineteenth century no historian was able to dispute his claim to have written "the *only* history of Scotland"'. By the 1860s and 1870s Scottish historical effort had 'split into many channels', partly under pressure of social changes giving the new middle class 'an essentially British – or even imperial outlook', and partly as a consequence of the fierce political and especially religious rivalries dominating many Scottish historical works. For the middle and upper classes,

> Scottish history had little to offer. And any vestigial feelings they might have had for the history of their country was dealt a mortal blow by the publication in 1861 of the third volume of Henry Thomas Buckle's History of Civilization in England: On Scotland and the Scotch Intellect.

And that was that. For the rest of the century, further cultivation of the past would bring only 'a succession of historical kailyards'.[6]

Starting from the surmise that Ash's 'basic argument [. . .] seems destined to endure', Colin Kidd returned to the 'Strange Death' thesis nearly twenty years after it first appeared, in an article which further developed the argument that 'Scottish history had little to offer' the nineteenth-century middle and upper classes. This was an extension of the thesis previously set out in his book *Subverting Scotland's Past* (1993). There he had identified ways in which the 'historical sociologists' of the Scottish Enlightenment subjected pre-Union Scottish history to critical scrutiny, emphasising institutional failures that rendered it incapable of 'contributing some contemporary inspiration and recognisable structure to the revitalisation of a patriotic historiography'. For

---

[6] Marinell Ash, *The Strange Death of Scottish History* (Edinburgh: Ramsay Head Press, 1980), pp. 123–4, 146.

instance, the unicameral Scottish Estates had been viewed as weak and unrepresentative especially in comparison to England's parliament and biased towards the interests of monarchy, and at other times powerless before a rapacious feudal aristocracy; while the progress of liberty had been retarded by oppressive features of the Scottish legal system including the survival into the eighteenth century of the 'heritable jurisdictions', which allowed the aristocracy untrammelled local power. For Kidd, these and other criticisms constituted a series of 'fault lines' that rendered the Scottish past 'unusable' for the construction of a coherent national narrative, and favoured the adoption of an Anglo-British identity.[7]

In 'revisiting' Ash's argument in his later article, Kidd again placed a good deal of emphasis on perceptions of constitutional arrangements. The histories of Scotland produced in the early part of the century by the likes of Malcolm Laing, George Chalmers, George Brodie and Robert Chambers were held up as devalorising pre-Union Scottish institutions including the parliament and other pre-1603 legal/constitutional arrangements. Kidd proceeded to draw attention to the increasing historical significance accorded to different racial identities in the mid-nineteenth century and suggested that it had reinforced the difficulty of Scottish history providing any basis for a sense of unified national historical consciousness. There had long been debate about whether the origins of the nation lay in Celtic or 'gothic' peoples. What was new was the belief that only certain racial strains carried characteristics that would lead the advance to civilisation. Kidd highlighted the tendency for some historians in Scotland (including Burton) to emphasise the Saxon qualities and origins of the Lowlanders contrasted with the feckless 'savagery' of those beyond the highland line. Just as 'dark age' Scotland had been abandoned in the critiques of Buchanan, these ideas precluded any conception of a unitary medieval Scotland that could support the historical consciousness of the later nation.[8]

Kidd made brief mention of how 'the appearance of intellectual and cultural history suggested alternative ways of celebrating Scottish cultural distinctiveness'. However, it was implied that this had been

---

[7] Colin Kidd, *Subverting Scotland's Past. Scottish Whig Historians and the Creation of an Anglo-British Identity, 1689–c. 1830* (Cambridge: Cambridge University Press, 1993), pp. 129–204.

[8] Colin Kidd, 'The Strange Death of Scottish History Revisited: Constructions of the Past in Scotland, c. 1790–1914', *SHR* 86 (2007), 86–102 (pp. 88–90).

eclipsed by the impact of the works of Henry Thomas Buckle, accorded similar significance by Ash. Buckle's *History of Civilization in England* (1857–61) had indeed included an account of the Scottish past conceived as a history of conflict eventuating in a nation in thrall to an intolerant theocratic spirit – though its supposedly devastating effect on Scottish history hardly accords with the reality that for the rest of the century Buckle's work was widely criticised from a variety of perspectives: it 'flashed like a meteor across the firmament and disappeared'; while in Scotland 'historians took very little notice of him'.[9] Kidd did recognise that there were a few protesting voices resistant to the further development of Whig historiography, though most of these are dismissed as adherents of 'a toryism of regret', 'spectral Jacobitism' or romantic eccentricity. Only at the very end of the century could a single example be found of a Scottish historian able to celebrate 'the preservation of Scottish "nationality"'. Otherwise, in contrast to the 'unbroken evolution' of English history, 'Scotland's past seemed to be a history of discontinuity, conflict, underdevelopment and institutional deformation: an illiberal descent'.[10]

Michael Fry's perspectives on Scotland's cultural development in the nineteenth century are reflected in his recent general history of the period, *A New Race of Men: Scotland 1815–1914* (2013), and (more specifically on historiography) in an earlier contribution to a collection of essays on *The Manufacture of Scottish History* (1989). In that earlier essay, Fry's account of the Scots' perception of their past accorded with many of the assessments discussed above: an extensive adoption of 'The Whig Interpretation of Scottish History' (the title of the piece) had involved a fundamental devalorisation of the national historical experience. Scott had failed 'in creating a historical consensus with which all his compatriots could identify', and the field had been left to Whiggery and the adoption of an Anglo-British historical view that saw little value in pre-Union Scottish institutions and culture. Fry identified the expression of such views in the works of George Brodie and T. B. (Thomas Babington) Macaulay in the first half of the century, with only the 'light relief' of Dean Ramsay and his 'couthy anecdotes' thereafter. He saw little change in the perspectives and impact of more substantial figures like H. G. Graham, James Mackintosh and P. Hume Brown towards its end. Like Ash and Kidd, Fry

---

[9] Ibid., p. 95; H. J. Hanham, 'Editor's Introduction', in Henry Thomas Buckle, *On Scotland and the Scotch Intellect* (Chicago: University of Chicago Press, 1970), xiii–xxxviii (pp. xxxiv–xxxvi).
[10] Kidd, 'Strange Death', pp. 96–9.

gave some prominence to H. T. Buckle, viewing the Scots writers who disagreed with him as not seriously opposing his analysis: they 'merely claimed that he had been uncharitable in doubting the Whigs' official view that they had solved, or could solve, all Scotland's problems'. At the conclusion of the essay, Fry observed that the best recent historiography of nineteenth-century Scotland had emerged from figures like Tom Nairn and G. E. Davie.[11]

Fry's views in the *New Race*, like those of Marinell Ash, also appear to reflect the influence of George Davie whose groundbreaking work he celebrates in the Preface. In the book Fry detects a significant weakening in the nation's cultural self-confidence as the century progressed. He had observed that earlier in the century the Scottish Enlightenment's conjectural and stadial approaches to the past may have provided a fertile background for the Scottish trailblazers in sciences like geology and in evolutionary thinking. However, by the 1870s, his account gives a good deal of attention to the persecution of William Robertson Smith by Free Church zealots. This seemed emblematic of the breakdown of that accommodation between religion and secular culture that had obtained since the eighteenth century. From this point, for Fry, almost the only figure suggestive of any domestic cultural innovation and confidence was Patrick Geddes, while through the second half of the century it appeared symptomatic that it had been necessary for the likes of Carlyle, Robertson Smith, R. L. Stevenson and Charles Rennie Macintosh to take a 'Scottish way into exile'. The decline is also seen as associated with the retreat of native generalist education and scholarship in the face of greater specialisation, recalling Davie's explanation for Scottish cultural hesitancy as the century wore on.[12]

Other recent contributions seem broadly to accord with this explanatory framework. In his recent general history of Scotland from 1880 to the present, Ewan Cameron declared an intention to focus on political and socio-economic issues; however, in his coverage of the later decades of the nineteenth century the scene is set with what he presumably considered a determining 'cultural point' for the era, and one that recalls Ash's notion of the Scots sense of the past as 'historical kailyard'. The

---

[11] Michael Fry, 'The Whig Interpretation of Scottish History', in *The Manufacture of Scottish History*, eds Ian Donnachie and Christopher Whatley (Edinburgh: Polygon, 1992), 72–89 (pp. 79–85, 88).
[12] Michael Fry, *A New Race of Men: Scotland 1815–1914* (Edinburgh: Birlinn, 2013), pp. 323–95.

reading public, reacting from the harsh realities of the industrial present, seemed to cleave to an idealised historical identity conceived as rural idyll and evidenced in the popularity of parochial, 'kailyard' literature. In Cameron's account this reflex seems to recur in the nation's response to criticism of its parochial educational tradition: given its 'centrality to national identity' this resulted only in the adoption of 'a mythic history [. . .] to mask the failure and marginality of the parochial system in modern conditions'. Compared to the rapid progress earlier, by the later century a cycle of decline and emigration 'seemed to combine to sap national vitality', leaving even the economically dynamic middle classes with a vulnerable and 'fragile' sense of national identity founded on a culture of 'enclosed' societies and clubs with intermittent 'set-piece public occasions designed to project, even inflate, their identity'.[13]

In his examination of the teaching (or lack of it) of Scottish history in the universities from 1862 to 1914, Robert Anderson set out by rehearsing the traditional historiographic perspective that he recognised as traceable to the Davie–Nairn view of 'a collective failure of nerve' and to Marinell Ash's subsequent elaboration of its devastating consequences for Scottish history. Writing over thirty years after *Strange Death* first appeared, Anderson judged that on balance 'Ash was probably right to diagnose a general slackening of historical interest' in Scotland by around 1870. In another contribution, Catriona MacDonald did suggest that Colin Kidd had 'somewhat underestimated' Scottish historical confidence in the later nineteenth century, though found evidence only at the close of the century for 'a new national historiography' based on social history breaking free from 'constitutional obsessions'.[14]

James Coleman has recently argued that the 'master narrative of Scottish nationality' for the nineteenth century was based on a Presbyterian historiography that viewed the Glorious Revolution of 1689 as the providential consummation of the national annals. As evidence, Coleman draws on analysis of narrative historical works by a number

---

[13] Ewan A. Cameron, *Impaled upon a Thistle: Scotland since 1880*. The New Edinburgh History of Scotland, Vol. 10 (Edinburgh: Edinburgh University Press, 2010), pp. 4–5, 9–11, 23, 29–34.

[14] Robert Anderson, 'University History Teaching, National Identity and Unionism in Scotland, 1862–1914', *SHR* 91 (2012), 1–41 (pp. 10–15); Catriona M. M. MacDonald, 'Gender and Nationhood in Modern Scottish Historiography', in *The Oxford Handbook of Modern Scottish History*, eds T. M. Devine and Jenny Wormald (Oxford: Oxford University Press, 2012), 602–19 (pp. 604–7).

of Presbyterian writers in the first sixty years of the century and of the commemorations held to mark anniversaries of the Scottish Reformation and persecution of the seventeenth-century covenanters. Coleman makes a persuasive case for the strength, in the first half of the century, of this narrative of Scottish Presbyterian history as central to securing 'civil and religious liberty' and ultimately a providential union with England. The Presbyterian inheritance was certainly a powerful strand in Scottish identity and the analysis accords with current thinking on the importance of collective 'memory' and its manifestations, as well as with recent emphasis on Presbyterian sensibility as a 'banal' or 'everyday' identity for many in nineteenth-century Scotland.[15] Yet many of the historians Coleman refers to were associated with the evangelical churches, and their writings viewed as scholarly but partial, though he maintained that from the time of the Disruption (1843) there was a process of 'nationalising the covenanters'. He argued that commemorative events, perhaps particularly reaching a height around 1859–60, and the tercentenary of the Reformation, were widely attended; although there is some evidence that by the time of the effort to celebrate the 1880 bicentenary of the Sanquhar Declaration repudiating allegiance to Charles II, things were rather running out of steam.[16]

However, as an explanation for how nineteenth-century Scots viewed their history, Coleman's perspective necessarily remains highly exclusivist. The impact on history and historiography of the range of other social and cultural developments that emerged through the century appears negligible. Colin Kidd's emphasis on the continuing impact of the eighteenth-century devalorisation of the Scottish past resurfaces here. For Coleman, perhaps the greatest figure in nineteenth-century Scottish culture, was so rooted in such views that it 'undermined Scott's efficacy as an author of Scottish nationality', leading him to conclude, unusually, that 'Scott was not in a position to inform the present by means of the past'. The great momentum of Scottish romanticism that influenced more than one continent is viewed as eventuating at home only in

---

[15] James J. Coleman, *Remembering the Past in Nineteenth-Century Scotland: Commemoration, Nationality and Memory* (Edinburgh: Edinburgh University Press, 2014), pp. 30–2, 88–110; Trevor Griffiths and Graeme Morton, 'Introduction', 1–22 (pp. 4–5, 11–13) and Graeme Morton, 'Identity Out of Place', 256–87 (pp. 259, 263) in *A History of Everyday Life in Nineteenth-Century Scotland, 1800 to 1900*, eds Trevor Griffiths and Graeme Morton (Edinburgh: Edinburgh University Press, 2010).
[16] Coleman, *Remembering the Past*, pp. 130–40.

facile historical narratives and commemorations centred on 'sentimental Jacobitism', or the controversies and 'contested memories' surrounding Mary Stuart. Just as for Marinell Ash the Scots' perception of their past as the century wore on descended into a facile 'bens and glens romanticism', Coleman could detect beyond the thread of Presbyterian providentialism only the depredations of 'the great tartan monster'.[17]

While the case for a Presbyterian 'master narrative' governing Scottish national identity may appear strong earlier in the century, even strong enough for its momentum to carry on for a time beyond the Disruption of 1843, it could not long survive the sectarian divisions following that event. The 'banal' crystallised out into the noticeable, and its appearance was seen to be conflicted and fragmented: the fissure in the unity of Presbyterian conviction was soon highly visible in the construction of rival church buildings in almost every town and community. Thereafter Presbyterian historiography was unable to present a credible teleology of the nation's unity and destiny and was therefore ultimately unusable as underpinning a cohesive national identity. In terms of national historiographic narrative, this functioned to bring Scotland into line with developments elsewhere in Europe. Religion might continue to be a respected historical element, but as the nineteenth century advanced a new pattern emerged in national histories:

> traditional religion – typically a once privileged confession or church – was 'disestablished' and placed in a subordinate position to the 'real' master narrative of the nation, which now claimed to be more universal in scope than the mere 'sectarian' character of confession.[18]

The shift was typically associated, particularly among the liberal historians of Protestant northern Europe, with increasing respect for 'scientific' approaches to history, which valorised above all else 'impartiality' and objectivity.[19]

At the broadest level, Coleman's interpretation shares an assumption in common with a number of the historians discussed above, to the effect that the Scottish nineteenth-century experience was somehow odd and at

---

[17] Ibid., pp. 27–30, 154–73.
[18] James C. Kennedy, 'Religion, Nation and European Representations of the Past', in Stephan Berger and Chris Lorenz, eds, *The Contested Nation: Ethnicity, Class, Religion and Gender in National Histories*. Writing the Nation Series (Basingstoke: Palgrave Macmillan, 2008), 104–34 (pp. 105–6).
[19] Ibid., pp. 109–11.

variance with European developments. Whereas 'the broader phenomenon of nationality across Europe was capable of combining the political rationalism of the Enlightenment with romanticist historicism', the Scots had to settle for a much more limited 'synthesis' of Presbyterian providentialism and Whig constitutionalism – a variant of that Whig interpretation of history which for many of these modern commentators largely monopolised how nineteenth-century Scotland viewed its past.[20]

Introducing a recent fresh perspective, Cairns Craig observed that in much of the past twenty years Scottish historiography had become 'profoundly reshaped by our increasing knowledge of what has come to be known as the "Scottish Diaspora"'. Craig's own analysis proceeded to challenge the notion that the emigration of many Scots should be accounted simply in terms of a loss of the nation's 'cultural capital'; and to trace how, though physically located within the territory of the British Empire, those involved had established an immanent 'Xenitean empire' that 'would project, institutionalise and embody specifically Scottish values' in a range of social, religious and educational structures across the world.[21] Nevertheless, is not difficult to understand how an emphasis on Scotland as a nation casting its people of drive and ability abroad might sustain the historiographic assumptions discussed above: the nation 'at home', drained of talent and ambition, declined from previous levels of achievement and at the same time failed to adopt those forms of national assertiveness widely adopted by other European nations at this time – including the celebratory reclamation of the national past.

TYTLER FOUND WANTING

Sir Walter Scott had intended to compose a scholarly history of Scotland firmly based on the national records, but one that 'by interspersing the narrative with romantic anecdotes illustrative of the manners of his countrymen' could be made appealing to them. Ultimately unable to commit to the task, he famously urged his young friend Patrick Fraser Tytler, scion of a distinguished family of Scottish historians and jurists, to take it on.[22]

---

[20] Coleman, *Remembering the Past*, pp. 31–2.
[21] Cairns Craig, *The Wealth of the Nation: Scotland, Culture and Independence* (Edinburgh: Edinburgh University Press, 2018), pp. 53–90.
[22] [Anon], 'Biographical Sketch', in Patrick Fraser Tytler, *The History of Scotland from the Accession of Alexander III. To the Union*, 4 vols (Edinburgh: Nimmo, 1882), I, v–xxiii (pp. xv–xvi).

As already noted, Marinell Ash, followed by many others, considered that the resulting work, Tytler's multi-volume *History of Scotland* (1828–43), marked the end of efforts in the nineteenth century to provide a coherent and widely accepted account of the nation's past. As Tytler's volumes were published, many (including Hill Burton) welcomed the work as an account of the national annals that was founded on thoroughly up-to-date standards involving the use of authentic source materials. However, with the appearance of the final volumes dealing with the Reformation and its aftermath, concern was increasingly expressed that the work had failed to maintain a proper impartiality. In the polarising atmosphere after 1843 the episcopalian Tytler's work was brought to the bar for its treatment of respected Presbyterian icons and of Protestant history generally, and found wanting. It was something of a rerun of the rejection in the 1820s by a number of historians of Scott's portrayal of the covenanters in *Old Mortality*. The protest initially centred on the suggestion in Tytler's seventh volume that John Knox had been implicated in Rizzio's murder. There was a hostile public exchange in which Dr Thomas McCrie, the son of Knox's widely admired biographer of the same name, attacked Tytler as biased against the Presbyterian reformers.[23]

A much more comprehensive rejection of Tytler's work emerged in reviews published in the *North British Review* in 1845, which subjected his *History* to pulverising criticism on a range of issues. The articles, which were subsequently developed further and published in book form in 1848, were written by a young advocate, Patrick Fraser. Although at an early stage in his career at the time, Fraser would rise to prominence in the ensuing decades through his contributions to Scottish legal literature, as the Dean of the Faculty of Advocates and finally as a judge of the Court of Session, the supreme court of justice in Scotland. Fraser was of unusually lowly origins for an advocate and was an evangelical Christian who had joined the Free Church. Running through his articles was an increasingly ill-concealed fury at the way the patrician Tytler had presented figures and events related to Presbyterian history. In addition, his critique offers illumination on what, for a young and rising cultured professional not yet part of the establishment, should be expected of a history of the nation for the second half of the nineteenth century.[24]

---

[23] Ash, *Strange Death*, pp. 133–5.
[24] [Patrick Fraser], 'Tytler's History of Scotland', *NBR* 3 (1845), 345–86, and 'Mary Stuart and Her Times', *NBR* 4 (1845), 1–54; Patrick Fraser, *Tytler's History of Scotland Examined* (Edinburgh: W. P. Kennedy, 1848).

Fraser had little time for Scotland's other 'modern' historians – many 'the hacks of booksellers'. It was to be welcomed that a 'taste has arisen for a better instruction than the extinct ephemeral literature of annuals, or the light trifling of novels'. This dismissal of fiction could not of course extend to Scott:

> to the great Novelist is his country indebted, for the disclosure, in his varied publications, of the interesting world of poetry and romance, which slept forgotten in the chronicles of elder days, or were fast fading away in the increasing obscurity of oral tradition.

Fraser initially acknowledged Tytler's scholarship in similar terms, particularly his account of the medieval period, where he had rejected the improbable tales of chroniclers like Hector Boece but incorporated what might 'throw a hue of rich romance upon the dull page of ordinary narrative'. Nevertheless, and heralding what was to come, at an early point Fraser suggested that 'passionate prejudice' lay hidden behind Tytler's gentlemanly liberality and that the 'Episcopalian historian of a Presbyterian country, has few kindred sympathies with its people'. The critique comes to focus on Tytler's account of the forty-five years from 1560 to 1605, a period that was 'crowded with incidents' available to prompt political and moral lessons; at the same time Fraser continued:

> (f)or men of softer natures, there will not be found a page of history, so calculated to rouse the contending emotions of admiration and astonishment, or to wound sensibility by horror and indignation [. . .]. It is a noble theme for a historian who can estimate its spirit. It affords him scope for his highest powers of graphic narrative, or his profoundest reach of philosophical reflection.

Imagination could not have greater opportunity. 'All the wonders are here that imagination would have created, had it left itself untrammelled to create a story[.]' But Tytler's mind had not been untrammelled and Fraser suggested that his 'rash conclusions' had encouraged the plethora of books that had appeared in 1843–5 on Mary, many attacking 'the departed worthies of our country'. One of those whom Fraser considered particularly traduced was Mary's half-brother, the Earl of Murray, but his hostility rose to a pitch when he came to Tytler's presentation of John Knox.[25]

For Fraser there had been no better illustration of Knox's 'unflinching character' than his encounters with Mary Stuart. He judged Tytler's account of their first meeting as so misleading as to have no place in 'the sober pages

---

[25] Fraser, *Tytler's History of Scotland Examined*, pp. 1–3, 11–13, 111–16, 154–9.

of veritable history', and his overall presentation as little improved on that of David Hume's *History of England*, which had conveyed 'the grossest caricature'. Fraser proceeded to refute Tytler's narrative identifying various insertions that had no basis in the records but presented the reformer as an intransigent, bullying tyrant. To support his character assassination of Knox, Tytler had excluded evidence of the reformer's kindly side. This was as typical of 'the one-sided pamphleteering character of this history' as the 'perversions of fact with which it abounds'. In an elegantly written critique punctuated by a dry caustic humour, Fraser then embarked on a lethal dissection from a top legal mind of the assertion that Knox had been 'privy' to Rizzio's murder. Tytler merely 'serves up the old rinsings of forgotten virulence, distilled in the alembic of an affected impartiality'. Fraser was further incensed that Tytler had tried to associate the entire 'Reformed party' with political exploitation of the murder. This was not just some theoretical point of historical dispute, but was 'verging on the confines of national dishonour'.[26]

Fraser's critique was rather dismissed by Marinell Ash as a mix of sectarian prejudice and a reactionary effort to re-establish philosophy or religion as the primary purpose of writing history. But this failed to detect the elements that he was arguing were required to encompass a national history. As he built towards his conclusion, Fraser argued that Tytler had not just suborned individual 'departed worthies' like Murray and Knox, but had distorted the greatest period in the history of the nation: '[H]e gives us a few biographies, and forgets the history of a people', whose social and religious history he could have written instead of 'all this rubbish of quotation from the letters of Lord Mighty and the Duke of Craft, and the Queen of Policy'. So much for all those years in the bowels of the State Paper Office. The development of legal and 'government' institutions was missing, as was the history of 'the commons', of agriculture, the towns, the Highlands. There was virtually nothing of literature, or of 'the gude and godly ballads'. There was hardly a mention of Sir David Lindsay, 'one of the most illustrious men of letters of ancient Scotland', or Gavin Douglas, who had left 'descriptive poetry equal to that of any language', or William Dunbar. They and others 'have all been left contemptuously in the obscurity of their antiquated phraseology, and their country's historian will not condescend to tell us anything of their language and ours'. And if there was little of the Scots tongue there was certainly no appreciation of the stirring and portentous language of the

---

[26] Fraser, *Tytler's History of Scotland Examined*, pp. 168, 181, 186–214, 216.

great Reformation preachers – rather 'solemn denunciations of the coarse vulgarity of Presbyterian ministers'.[27]

For Fraser and for many of those who made up middle-class Protestant Scotland, Tytler had failed to deliver the task that he had been set by Walter Scott.

A SCOTTISH HISTORY FOR THE NINETEENTH CENTURY

For most modern historians, John Hill Burton's greatest work is portrayed as a classic illustration of Whig historiography with an added spice of Teutonism. There is no doubt that Burton adopted the increasing mid-century emphasis on the significance of racial origins and the notion of the Saxon race as particularly well equipped to deliver the progress in economic prosperity and civil liberty that Whig history conceived as having reached a contemporary zenith in nineteenth-century Britain. William Ferguson identified Burton as 'the great chef d'école of the Scottish Germanist historians'. He was 'virulently anti-Celtic' in his approach in much of his *History*: 'the Teutonic peoples were characterised by tenacious, if barbaric, courage, and possessed of a high sense of purpose, quite unlike the feckless Celts[.]'[28]

More generally, in the perspective of Colin Kidd for example, it was to a substantial extent 'from standard nineteenth-century histories of Scotland by the likes of Tytler and Hill Burton' that '[t]he Victorian political nation in Scotland imbibed the negative verdict on the Scottish past'. That verdict, he argued, had been sustained by the 'ubiquitous critique of Scottish feudal institutions, which had done so much damage to the national self-image and had proved so influential in the rise of an Anglo-British identity'. In the more recent past, 'Hill Burton welcomed the Cromwellian conquest of Scotland' and 'denounced the grinding tyranny' and 'practical slavery' experienced by eighteenth-century Scotland prior to the remedial legislation of 1747.[29]

There is a great difference, however, between this modern perception of Burton's work and the response of those who read and reviewed it in his own time. The recent perception of Burton as chiefly significant

---

[27] Ash, *Strange Death*, pp. 118–21; Fraser, *Tytler's History of Scotland Examined*, pp. 235–44.
[28] William Ferguson, *The Identity of the Scottish Nation: An Historic Quest* (Edinburgh: Edinburgh University Press, 1998), pp. 286–8.
[29] Kidd, *Subverting*, pp. 272–4.

through delivering such 'damage to the national self-image' does not explain the acclaim with which his *History* was received on its completion, or comprehend the reasons why, for decades to come, it was so widely admired. As the final volumes appeared in two tranches in 1867–70, the *History* was widely reviewed in articles of substantial article length in the main newspapers both in Scotland and in London, as well as in many provincial Scottish papers. More extensive review articles were published in the major periodicals that had become a central cultural reference point for much of the nineteenth-century Western world. It was almost universally hailed as a triumph. Analysis of this response begins to reveal the modalities through which a successful Scottish history could be written for the second half of the nineteenth century and to identify the themes and subject matter that would convey the 'history of a people', the components necessary for constructing an acceptable and convincing national story. What were the chief characteristics necessary to compose a national history to satisfy critical opinion and provide the nation with an appropriate and acceptable consciousness of its past?

First of all, commentators wished to be assured that the work had been completed according to thoroughly modern standards and methodologies. In the words of one reviewer, Burton's *History* had all the hallmarks of 'modern research and criticism'.[30] It was widely commended for its foundations in empirical scholarship and a cool scepticism regarding any previously treasured shibboleths, preconceptions and mythologies that must be swept away in the process. All of this ensured that the history had been written in a thoroughly objective and dispassionate manner. It was clear from the judgement of many on Tytler that any effort at a national history for the second half of the nineteenth century required to be convincingly impartial – it must not be history written in the interests of the present, of some specific personal or sectarian conviction. Quite apart from the intense religious loyalties felt across Scottish society, the country's history had been ill served by writers pursuing particular issues in what seemed obsessional and biased ways. These were identified on the one hand as the credulous 'antiquarian' writers of the previous two centuries who, famously satirised by Scott in the encounters of Jonathan Oldbuck and Sir Arthur Wardour, had compulsively pursued through lengthy volumes subjects

---

[30] [H. S. Fagan], 'Burton's History of Scotland', *BQ* 53 (1871), 161–76 (p. 162). Wellesley Index has Fagan as 'probable' reviewer.

like the origin and language of the Picts or the roles and religion of the Druids. On the other hand, there were more contemporary authors engaged in still-burning fires of controversy over the personalities and reputations of prominent figures such as the Marquis of Montrose or 'Bonnie Dundee' (otherwise 'Bluidy Clavers') and, perhaps especially, Mary Queen of Scots.

A second expectation concerned the need to supersede out-of-date eighteenth- and early nineteenth-century efforts, which were fragmented and discontinuous. Since William Robertson dismissed the value of studying the early history of nations, historians of Scotland had dutifully confined themselves to various periods post-dating the reign of Alexander III (1249–86). Robertson's own *History of Scotland* was largely confined to the reigns of Mary Stuart and James VI up to 1603. Lord Hailes had gone further back, but his *Annals of Scotland* covered only the eleventh to fourteenth centuries. Of the best-known nineteenth-century writers, George Brodie and Malcolm Laing were largely concerned with the later sixteenth and the seventeenth century, while P. F. Tytler's *History* centred on the three centuries from the reign of Alexander III to 1603.[31] Lesser known figures like James Aikman produced what appeared to be comprehensive works. However, Aikman's original work was limited to the seventeenth and eighteenth centuries, prior to which his volumes were no more than translations of George Buchanan's long-outdated sixteenth-century text. The two-volume *History of Scotland* published by John Struthers in 1827–8 was largely devoted to the first half of the eighteenth century.[32]

The accolades for Burton's volumes were often associated explicitly with critical comments on the efforts of the most prominent Scottish historians since the eighteenth century. Even the greatest figures were

---

[31] William Robertson, *The History of Scotland [. . .]*, 15th edn, 3 vols (London: Cadell, 1797), I, p. 1; David Dalrymple, *Annals of Scotland, from the Accession of Malcolm III to the Accession of the House of Stewart* (Edinburgh and London: Murray, 1776–9); George Brodie, *A History of the British Empire, From the Accession of Charles I. to the Restoration; [. . .]*, 4 vols (Edinburgh: Bell & Bradfute, 1822); Malcolm Laing, *The History of Scotland, from The Union of the Crowns [. . .]*, 2 vols (London: Cadell and Davies, 1800).
[32] James Aikman, *The History of Scotland, Translated from the Latin of George Buchanan; with Notes and a Continuation to the Present Time*, 6 vols (Edinburgh: Thomas Ireland, 1829); John Struthers, *The History of Scotland from The Union [. . .]*, 2 vols (Edinburgh: Blackie Fullarton, 1827).

seen as having limited themselves to addressing fragments of the national past. For instance, the reviewer in the *Aberdeen Journal* directly contrasted Burton's achievement with that of William Robertson, whom he observed had gained an initial, perhaps overrated reputation, but in any case had provided 'only a history of the reigns of Mary and James VI', which therefore was 'no more a history of our country' than Macaulay's account of two reigns had been a history of England. The writer went on to complain that Pinkerton, Hailes and Malcolm Laing had all managed only parts of the story. Tytler's work was admirable but was 'incomplete, both at the beginning and at the end'. There was a thirst for a 'complete' history of Scotland.[33]

The 'completeness' was partly about this temporal extent of the work, but also concerned the range and depth of aspects of the Scottish past that required to be incorporated. There was a growing realisation that the national annals should encompass much more than the focus on political and constitutional development that still dominated history-writing in England, where it served that teleological Whig notion of history as demonstrating the triumph of British liberty. Elsewhere in Europe, a romantic interest in a spectrum of aspects of the past had grown alongside a fascination with the peculiarities and difference of past times with their particular spirit and manners. Many of the Scots *literati* were in close touch with intellectual developments on the continent; and in any case, this was a conception of history coming home, given the pervasive influence of Walter Scott's *œuvre* in its emergence.

Some Scots did share the Anglo-British Whig perspective, but many were developing their own 'teleology' and there was a growing anticipation that their history should trace and incorporate a range of specifically Scottish institutional and cultural components including literature and language, architecture, antiquarian survivals, educational and urban institutions and legal-constitutional development. This expectation was closely related to a growing public awareness of the mass of written, visual and physical material that had been recovered and accumulated by the great effort in records scholarship and in the publication of source editions over recent decades, much of it made more generally available by prosperous Scottish publishing houses and broadcast even more widely by the burgeoning print media to a much-expanded reading public. It offered a fertile repository on which to draw for a re-conception of the narrative history of the nation.

[33] *Aber J*, 22 May 1867, p. 6.

A central figure in this reclamation of sources was a man who would become not only a close friend and confidant of Burton but later also his father-in-law, Cosmo Innes. The appearance of Richard Marsden's recent book on Innes and his work has presented the opportunity for a broader and richer understanding of the Scots' attitudes to both the past generally and their own past in the nineteenth century. He demonstrated that the growing interest in the source work and publications was, like Innes himself, increasingly embedded in influential sections of the Scottish elite; and that in addition, as the middle decades of the century wore on the new interest in and awareness of the Scottish source materials were no longer confined to a few members of elite book clubs and antiquarian societies as they had been earlier in the century. Finally, Marsden showed that both among records scholars themselves and across a broader readership, a sensibility was arising that encompassed both an Enlightenment respect for empirical methodologies tracing social progress and a romantic fascination with the past conceived in and on its own terms.[34] A Scottish history for the nineteenth century would require to reflect this combination.

The mass of words released from the sources was of course seldom couched in the standard English that had been aspired to by most educated Scots nervous of their 'Scotticisms' over the previous century. It extended from the vernacular Scots of different periods to the sonorous religiosity of the historical accounts left by Presbyterian divines and early modern church historians. The recovery or republication of texts expressed in these idioms was accompanied by the issue of new collections of both the formal, more classical poetry of the medieval Scots 'makars' but also of what was viewed increasingly as a peculiarly rich Scottish ballad and song tradition. Interest in such traditional Scots literary material extended from more romantically minded Tories like W. E. Aytoun to the many establishment-oriented Whigs associated with the book clubs; and to the scholars occupying the 'alcoves' of Burton's beloved Advocates Library where he was well acquainted with the likes of John Jamieson, author of the highly successful *Scots Dictionary*. It is clear from the responses to Burton's *History* that it was thought right and appropriate that a national history should recognise and incorporate the nation's characteristic forms of linguistic and religious expression.

---

[34] Richard Marsden, *Cosmo Innes and the Defence of Scotland's Past* c. 1825–75 (Farnham: Ashgate, 2014), pp. 27–37, 234–8, 41–4, 289–95.

Patrick Fraser had pointed out in his critique of Tytler that the use of these new sources to produce a national history founded firmly on accurate research, impartiality and a focus beyond high politics, did not require the abandonment of a romantic sensibility and imagination: although the 'sober pages of veritable history' should not be confused with the text of *The Monastery* or *The Abbot*, Fraser had admired the ways in which Scott had revealed the 'poetry and romance' in forgotten sources and oral traditions and appreciated how the chroniclers themselves could 'throw a hue of rich romance upon the dull page of ordinary narrative'. His aspiration for a proper history was not only to reassert Presbyterian truths but also to realise the potential for a 'graphic narrative' calculated 'to rouse the contending emotions of admiration and astonishment, or to wound sensibility by horror and indignation '. In Fraser's perspective – and the response to Burton's *History* confirmed that many shared it – looking beyond the mid-century Scottish history worthy of the name still needed to 'create a story' filled, at times at least, with romance and even horror.[35]

This was hardly surprising. Despite admiration for Burton's scepticism, empirical reasoning and sober and careful research, even by 1870 it was impossible to escape the expectations raised by Scott's influence and that of the other literary figures who had graced the first half of the century. In that period and for some time thereafter the Scottish literary imagination had drawn inspiration from and almost overwhelmed the narrative history of the nation. The process had conjured up romantic historical novels and poetry and had invaded and partially 'nationalised' gothic literary traditions, producing tales of psychological terror, supernatural encounter and demonic possession. Many of the contemporary expressions of appreciation of Burton's volumes referenced such sensibilities, recognising that he had incorporated the 'romance of history' in the places where it should be.

If anything, since Scott's own day it was the elements of 'gothic' and the otherworldly that had become more prominent. Some of this had to do with the enquiries into darker aspects of the past, which formed one strand of the German romantic literature influential in Scotland, though it was also firmly rooted in early nineteenth-century explorations of Scottish folk tradition. In the same year as Scott published his *Tales of Demonology and Witchcraft* (1830), George Moir, soon to be Professor of Rhetoric at Edinburgh, wrote a lengthy periodical review of C. G. Horst's *Zauber-Bibliothek*, which had recently been published

---

[35] See pp. 226–7.

in Germany. The full translation of the title is *The Magic Library; or, of Magic, Theurgy and necromancy; Magicians, Witches, and Witch-Trials, Demons, Ghosts, and Spectral Appearances*. After reviewing the traditions of such phenomena in different European countries, Moir was clear that Scottish history was their greatest repository: 'From the earliest period of the Scottish annals, "All was bot gaistis, and Eldritch phantasie"'. Burton would later echo this receptivity to the otherworldly in Scottish history when commenting on the story of Macbeth and its supernatural associations, which were 'powerfully characteristic to those accustomed to the spirit of past Scots life and history.'[36]

As the nineteenth century progressed, the Scots (and those in other nations) were increasingly attuned to this vein in Scottish literature and history. Its particular contemporary locus was in the pages of *Blackwood's Magazine* and in works by some of the figures associated with the periodical, including John Galt and James Hogg. As will become clear, Burton is highly attentive in his volumes to elements of terror and the supernatural. Commentators on the *History* welcomed the attention he devoted to 'mysterious' episodes like the Gowrie Conspiracy, the malevolent and opaque plan of vengeance hatched in 1600 by the Earl of Gowrie and his brother to kidnap James VI. Similarly, there was extensive admiration for his lengthy, numinous account of the circumstances surrounding the murder of Archbishop James Sharp on Magus Moor for his part in the 'Killing Times', the seventeenth-century persecution of the 'covenanted' Presbyterians.

While Burton's elaboration of these elements of gothic were appreciated by several contemporary reviewers, there was also recognition of his 'theatricality'. From the 1820s until the 1850s and 1860s, Scottish history as conveyed to the imagination of his readers by Scott was recreated in the scenes presented in theatrical performances of what has been termed the 'National Drama', as well as in the images produced by visual artists in historical-genre paintings (indeed some of the artists were also scene painters in the theatres). For Scottish history, this established an expectation of iconic, dramatic scenes and visual 'portraits', and underscored the importance of capturing what was 'picturesque' in different historical settings and periods. Since these picturesque instances often signified what was peculiar to and characteristic of that particular setting, it complemented the romantic historiographic shift towards a view

---

[36] [George Moir], 'Demonology and Witchcraft', *FQR* 6 (1830), 1–47 (p. 25); Burton, *HOS* (1873), I, pp. 343–4, footnote 1.

of past times as deserving to be considered and where possible visualised in their own terms. The reception of Burton's volumes suggests that his readers recognised these forms of historical narration and that the *History* could not have attracted the attention and gained the acceptance that it did without reflecting such sensibilities.[37]

The present study will argue that, for contemporaries, the *History of Scotland* was a striking success because it combined a range of characteristics that to modern perceptions appear to be contradictory and irreconcilable. The work was viewed as thoroughly 'modern' in its commitment to impartiality, anti-sectarianism and the abjuration of historical and antiquarian controversy. Associated with this was an admiration for its adherence to the methodologies of 'nineteenth-century research' – scepticism on sources and a reliance on induction from the 'facts', which were increasingly available through the great efforts in records scholarship. These underpinned a new historiographic appreciation extending to the early centuries and the Scottish medieval world that did not accord with the eighteenth century devalorisation and dismissal of the Scottish past.

At the same time, there was a widespread appreciation of the way Burton had maintained in their rightful places the associations and tropes of the Romantic and Picturesque, of gothic sensibility and theatrical drama, which were expected to adhere to the Scottish historical story and which had, in reality, continued to be exemplified in national cultural life through the mid-century. To a degree these had been kept in their proper place and adjusted for consumption in the later nineteenth century – Scotland was advancing beyond the age of Scott. Still, if sometimes delivered with a warning of apocryphal hazard, they were almost all there, and now with the added ballast of Burton's incorporation of Scottish historical achievement in poetry, vernacular ballads and songs, architecture, universities, scholarship and, not least, identifiable legal and constitutional traditions. A particular strain in modern historiographic thinking has grasped at the notion that such a range of responses to Scottish history cannot be, and in their day could not have been, reconciled and must have brought about a fragmentation of Scottish historical consciousness and national identity in the nineteenth century. John Hill Burton's *History of Scotland* and its reception challenges this analysis.

---

[37] Barbara Bell, 'The Nineteenth Century', in *A History of Scottish Theatre*, ed. Bill Findlay (Edinburgh: Polygon, 1998), 137–206 (pp. 143–71); Cairns Craig, 'Scott's Staging of the Nation', *Studies in Romanticism* 40 (2001), 13–28 (pp. 13–15); Duncan Macmillan, *Scottish Art: 1460–1990* (Edinburgh: Mainstream, 1990), pp. 186–7, 203–4.

2

Burton in Aberdeen and Edinburgh, 1809–49

ABERDEEN AND THE NORTHERN *NOCTES*

JOHN HILL BURTON WAS born in the northern Scottish city of Aberdeen on 22 August 1809 and would spend most of his first twenty years there. It was an urban environment commencing a period of 'perpetual redevelopment'. Expansion and change in the cityscape were initially focused on the central area, in which he spent his boyhood and youth. Burton's family were never so close to poverty as many of their neighbours huddled in the dilapidated quarters, which would gradually be swept away as the century advanced. Much of the old burgh would have gone by the time, decades later, he recalled his early years there. But it was the place he came from and he looked back to it without rancour, indeed with some pride that he could count himself among 'the last of the Gallowgate bairns'.[1]

Through the years of his boyhood and youth, all of this must have contrasted starkly with occasional visits to his grandfather's country estate just four miles out of the city near the village of Dyce, and offering glimpses of a quite different world. Grandholm House, a small baronial mansion dating from the seventeenth century, stood in rural tranquillity on a bend of the Don with a perspective across the river towards the distant Cairngorm mountains. But this was a world from which his mother Elizabeth (familiarly Eliza) Paton and her own family came in

---

[1] John S. Smith, 'The Growth of the City', in *Aberdeen 1800–2000: A New History*, eds W. Hamish Fraser and Clive H. Lee (East Linton: Tuckwell Press, 2000), 22–46 (pp. 22–6); Katherine Burton, 'Memoir of the Author', in John Hill Burton, *The Book-Hunter*, new edn (Edinburgh: Blackwood, 1882), i–civ (pp. i–ii).

effect to be expelled. Eliza's father, John Paton, the laird of Grandholm, had an unpredictable and obdurate personality subject to extremes of emotion that were manifested not least in his behaviour toward his immediate family. Understanding and flexibility then were unlikely to be the response when Eliza fell in love with a young and largely penniless lieutenant, William Kinninmont Burton, whose regiment had recently been posted to Aberdeen. Their second son retained a strong sense of how harshly his parents' romantic attachment had been resisted, much later describing his grandfather and aunt Mary 'in the darkest colours as having constantly interposed between the two lovers', who 'in spite of all advice to the contrary', soon married. Their union however was blighted by William's increasing ill health, and Burton was just ten years old when his father died in 1819.[2]

Eliza's accomplishments were not limited to firmness of purpose and courage in the face of adversity. She was evidently familiar with and sympathetic to the writings of two of the most controversial and radical figures of the age: Burton's sister Mary recalled how she had been educated at home by Eliza, 'who imbued her with admiration for the ideas of Jean-Jacques Rousseau and Mary Wollstonecraft'. Although Burton followed, for the time and his social position, a fairly typical course of schooling and university education, he recalled that he too had received his education partly in person from his mother. She would have been well aware of Rousseau's warning, when setting out the educational development of *Émile*, not to rely only on books and second-hand instruction: 'make your pupil attentive', he had urged tutors, 'to natural phenomena, and you will soon make him curious [. . .]. The living spectacle of Nature is in the heart of man; and to see it, it must be felt.' Such thinking accords with Eliza's evident encouragement of the long treks into the wilds that Burton undertook throughout his teenage years.[3]

Whether in the country or the town, Burton's childhood and youth would have been steeped in the vernacular culture of the northeast of Scotland. Almost all the voices he heard would have spoken in the abrupt cadences of 'the Doric', the distinctive Scots tongue of Aberdeen

---

[2] Katherine Burton, 'Memoir', pp. ii–iii, vii.

[3] 'Mary Burton', in *The Biographical Dictionary of Scottish Women: From the Earliest Times to 2004*, eds Elizabeth Ewan, Sue Innes, Sian Reynolds and Rose Pipes (Edinburgh: Edinburgh University Press, 2006), pp. 54–5; Jean-Jacques Rousseau, *Emile*, transl. Barbara Foxley (London: Dent, 1993), pp. 156–60, 171–3, 448–9; Katherine Burton, 'Memoir', p. xv.

and Aberdeenshire; and he shared the contemporary literary enthusiasm for the collection and preservation of the vernacular traditional ballads in which the area was particularly rich. Burton's early familiarity with these aspects of a vibrant popular culture would have been acquired largely outside his formal education at the city's grammar school. There, though periodically subjected to severe corporal punishment, he did greatly appreciate the teaching of one master, James Melvin. David Masson, later a distinguished professor of English Literature in London and Edinburgh and another of his pupils, recalled Melvin as a late exemplar of the tradition of 'Scottish Latinity' that stretched back to Thomas Ruddiman, Arthur Johnston and George Buchanan. Burton may also have benefited, as Masson is judged to have done, from the broader cultural characteristics of this tradition: besides the parsing and construing, Scottish education 'introduced aesthetics and criticism into Latin classroom instruction [. . .] and provided Masson with the critical tools that he used in studying English writers'.[4]

In common with many of his fellow pupils, Burton proceeded to Marischal College where his further education was founded on the philosophical and methodological approaches characteristic of the Scottish Enlightenment as Alexander Gerard had envisaged when, as principal, he reformed the curriculum half a century before. His framework reflected Enlightenment commitment to the study of Nature, including human nature, founded on careful inductive reasoning from the observation of known facts. It abandoned the traditional foundation in scholastic logic, in favour of a reformed philosophical approach which, Gerard wrote, should reflect,

> an image, not of human phantasies and conceits, but of the reality of nature and truth of things. The only basis of Philosophy is now acknowledged to be an accurate and extensive history of nature, exhibiting an exact view of the various phenomena for which Philosophy is to account, and on which it is to found its reasonings.

---

[4] Irene Maver, 'Leisure and Culture: The Nineteenth Century', in *Aberdeen 1800–2000*, eds Hamish Fraser and Clive H. Lee (East Linton: Tuckwell Press, 2000), 398–421 (p. 399); NLS MS 9391, fol. 29; NLS MS 9402, fol. 11; David Masson, *Memories of Two Cities: Edinburgh and Aberdeen* (Edinburgh: Oliphant, Anderson and Ferrier, 1911), pp. 251–3; Katherine Burton, 'Memoir', p. viii; G. G. Smith, revised by Sondra Miley Cooney, 'Masson, David Mather', in *ODNB*, accessed 21 March 2021.

This was realised through a four-year curriculum commencing with a year of Greek to which in the second year, were added Latin, mathematics, natural and civil history, as well as 'the elements of geography and chronology, on which civil history depends'; the third year's study was to include mechanics, the physical sciences, including 'magnetism', and criticism and belles-lettres; and a final year incorporated 'natural philosophy', including 'the doctrine of the nature, faculties, and states of the human mind', followed by jurisprudence, politics, the ancient moralists and logic.[5]

By Burton's time, the standard of teaching varied. For David Masson, who attended a few years later, William Knight, Professor of Natural History, was still the brightest light amongst the professoriate, providing 'glimpses of new wonders of knowledge' and of mental activity that went beyond classical erudition or mathematical problem solving. His teaching offered 'a notion of what *thinking* or *speculating* might be'. On the other hand, the professor of moral philosophy, though once of some power, had by Masson's time become rather decrepit, so that 'his diluted dictations from Reid and Beattie were poor nutriment for our young powers of speculation'. Worse still, the *Pro Bono Publico* Club, constituted of four or five students, would:

> disappear during the lecture into the hollow space underneath the rising tiers of benches, and there hold secret meetings with bottled porter and mutton pies, bobbing up now and then to see that all was right, and the Moral Philosophy going on as usual.[6]

Thomas Reid and James Beattie had been Aberdeen-based writers associated with what had become widely known as the 'Scottish common sense' school of philosophy, which was believed to have provided an effective response to David Hume's sceptical and 'infidel' writings. However, there is good evidence that Burton soon moved beyond the 'diluted dictations' of such thinkers and developed a more profound engagement with contemporary debates and tendencies in philosophical discourse. A number of his manuscript essays and study notes survive from the mid to late 1820s and reflect the increasing attention over the preceding decades to inquiries based on associationist theory, aesthetics and literary criticism. While those he considered required reading included one or two English figures including Richard Payne Knight, most were among the

---

[5] R. S. Rait, *The Universities of Aberdeen: A History* (Aberdeen: Bisset, 1895), pp. 300–3.
[6] Masson, *Memories*, pp. 282–4, 287–92.

savants of the later Scottish Enlightenment like Lord Kames, Gerard, Archibald Alison, Dugald Stewart and Francis Jeffrey.

Much in these early literary efforts evidences an independent mind uninspired by the tired and conservative efforts of the senescent philosophy professor at Marischal. This is particularly indicated by his enthusiastic admiration for the thought of Hume himself as well as for the more recent work of Thomas Brown: 'Mr. Hume, whose eye covered at a glance what required the minute investigation of others, has given a Theory of Association worthy the first philosophical genius of his age[.]' Although in this particular essay Burton tentatively offered critical comment on two of Hume's three principles of association, when he turned to the principle of cause and effect – 'one of the most deeply complex operations of our thoughts' – he was effusive in his admiration for Hume's account: he could not, he wrote, pretend to combat 'the glorious Theory of Mr Hume [. . .]. Indeed I look on Mr Hume's classification as one of the most complete which human genius has produced in any mental science.' Proof against the 'feeble reasoning' of James Beattie, it was even more impressive that it had withstood testing by 'a far more illustrious mind' that of Thomas Brown, whose work Burton admired on a range of philosophical issues.[7]

Brown had been Professor of Moral Philosophy at Edinburgh from 1810 until his early death at the age of forty-two ten years later. His writings, particularly the *Lectures on the Philosophy of the Human Mind* published posthumously in 1820, were widely admired and read in and beyond Scotland in the years after his death, not least by 'college students and the general public'; and the work ran to many editions for some decades. Nevertheless, both before and after Brown's death his work was controversial. Burton was clearly open to this serious challenge to the established tradition of the 'Scottish philosophy' stemming from Reid, whom Brown argued had taken principles of intuitive belief too far and had over-elaborated in his analysis of the mind and its faculties. Brown's thinking did indeed lean far more towards Hume than Reid, developing a philosophy of mind that 'expressly advances a version of psychological associationism strongly reminiscent of Hume' (though Brown preferred

---

[7] NLS MS 9418, fols 44–5; Burton had clearly read the defence of Hume's views on causality set out in Brown's *Inquiry into the Relation of Cause and Effect*, 3rd edn (Edinburgh: Constable, 1818), originally written in 1805 during a controversy over a professorial appointment; J. C. Stewart-Robertson, 'Brown, Thomas', in *ODNB*, accessed 21 February 2020.

the term 'suggestion' and was unimpressed by more recent 'mechanical theories' of association).[8]

Brown's approach has been assessed as 'one of the first and most sustained treatments of the "emotions" as a coherent psychological category', subsuming the range of previously established mental categories; and he has been recognised as original and almost unique among nineteenth-century moralists in defending an 'ethical emotivism'. His intellectual proximity to Hume thus also appears evident in his ethical system: for Brown moral judgement itself was

> a kind of emotion. We might detect here an echo of Hume's famous dictum that 'Reason is, and ought only to be the slave of the passions'. [. . .] For Brown, our moral approval of an action is identical to a particular kind of feeling.[9]

More generally, Burton's early literary efforts suggest that in his admiration for Thomas Brown across a range of issues, and of Payne Knight and to a degree Dugald Stewart on aesthetics, Burton was responding to thinking that had its origins in Humian conceptions and anticipated a mental philosophy freed from eighteenth-century rationalism and 'faculty psychology' and open to an emotions-based sensibility. In any case his admiration for and familiarity with the works of David Hume and Thomas Brown constituted an appropriate preparation and signifier for his sympathetic presentation of Hume's life and thought a decade and a half later.[10]

Towards the end of his time at Marischal, Burton's involvement with a particular group of college friends provides further evidence of this

---

[8] Gordon Graham, 'Scottish Philosophy after the Enlightenment', in *Scottish Philosophy in the Nineteenth and Twentieth Centuries*, ed. Gordon Graham (Oxford: Oxford University Press, 2015), 1–22 (pp. 5–8); Thomas Brown, *Lectures on the Philosophy of the Human Mind*, 4 vols (Edinburgh: Tait, 1820), I, pp. 287–90; II, pp. 424–5; Thomas Dixon, *From Passions to Emotions: The Creation of a Secular Psychological Category* (Cambridge: Cambridge University Press, 2003), pp. 107, 109–13.

[9] Thomas Dixon, 'Revolting against Reid: The Philosophy of Thomas Brown', in *Scottish Philosophy in the Nineteenth and Twentieth Centuries*, ed. Gordon Graham (Oxford: Oxford University Press, 2015), 23–46 (pp. 24, 40).

[10] NLS MS 9430, fols 1–134 particularly fols 110–11; NLS MS 9418, fols 44–5; NLS MS 9430, fols 41–3; Dabney Townsend, 'Dugald Stewart on Beauty and Taste', *The Monist*, 90 (2007), 271–86 (pp. 273, 277, 283–5).

intellectual curiosity and, at this point at least, an openness to views that ran counter to the thought-world of the rising Whig establishment. From his mid-teens he consistently associated with a number of fellow students who subsequently participated in a structured and aspirational Society of Writers, which was evidently formed in 1825–6. All had attended the College, commencing with Burton in the 1823 session or in the previous year or two. A number became respected authors by the mid-century: Joseph Robertson as a records scholar; William Spalding, as a professor in literature and philosophy at Edinburgh then St Andrews; George Grub, as a leading ecclesiastical historian of Scotland; and John Stuart Blackie as a classicist. Burton later referred to 'a revival of literary interest in Aberdeen' at this point, with these associates 'fired perhaps by the influence of Wilson and Lockhart in Blackwood's Magazine'. Many of their literary efforts subsequently found an outlet in the *Aberdeen Magazine*, a monthly publication that had a short run in 1831–2 and has been seen as modelled on *Blackwood's*.[11]

Burton recalled his closest friend Joseph Robertson as 'the leader of this school' and it is difficult to avoid a comparison of Robertson's personality and role with that of John Wilson, Professor of Moral Philosophy at Edinburgh: a friend of the Lake Poets, Wilson was also, in the ebullient persona of 'Christopher North', the dominant figure in the scabrous, satirical tales regularly published at this time in *Blackwood's Magazine* as the *Noctes Ambrosianae*. Robertson too was a boisterous, highly opinionated, rather larger-than-life figure, much at home in the convivial atmosphere of the tavern or a well-oiled collective repast. He was 'a Conservative of generous sentiments nourished on poetic ideals' whose sympathies 'were with the high-spirited and knightly cavaliers of the olden days'; and had a love of long walks and days on the hills (when Burton would often have been a companion). A close friend recalled his Toryism as 'chiefly derived from a careful study of the writings of Coleridge and Wordsworth, and an ardent admiration for the

---

[11] Peter John Anderson, ed., *Fasti Academiae Mariscallanae Aberdonensis: [. . .]*, 3 vols (Aberdeen: Spalding Club, 1898), I, pp. 444–59; John Hill Burton, 'Life of Professor W. Spalding', in William Spalding, *A Letter on Shakespere's [sic] Authorship of The Two Noble Kinsmen*, new edn (London: Trübner, 1876), xiii–xxii (pp. xvi–xvii). Burton does not name Blackie, who was still alive, but is clearly alluding to him as the later 'Greek scholar and Homeric critic'; W. Hamish Fraser, 'The Press', in *Aberdeen 1800–2000*, eds W. Hamish Fraser and Clive H. Lee, 448–65 (p. 450).

poems and romances of Scott'. But his fulsome romanticism was balanced by 'slashing criticism' in his book reviews.[12]

It has been observed that the Edinburgh Blackwoodians gave 'especially potent expression to the Blackwood's marshalling of cultural nationalism against Whig political economy' through 'hybrid works of serial fiction and cultural criticism' like the *Noctes* and J. G. Lockhart's *Peter's Letters to his Kinsfolk* (1819). To these literary forms, in the case of those involved in this northern *Noctes*, could be added a renewed focus on Scottish historical and ethnographic subject matter. Robertson's correspondence with Burton at the time reflects their enthusiasm for subjects related to the vernacular ballad tradition, popular superstitions and their origins, and includes discussion of proposed essays for the Society on Scottish medieval history and the 'Constitutional History of Scotland'. What appear to be Burton's earliest contributions to the group in 1825–6 are highly patriotic, even Jacobite. Many of Robertson's articles for the *Aberdeen Magazine* were focused on Scottish history and ethnography.[13]

LAND OF MOUNTAIN AND FLOOD

In the autumn of 1829, a year before he left Aberdeen, Burton decamped on the last and probably longest of those summer treks into Aberdeenshire and the mountains beyond that had been an annual feature of his teenage years. He kept a brief record of the things he saw and how he reacted to them. It is worth spending some time with him on the journey and listening to his asides in this private diary for what they reveal of the character and sensibilities of the man who had just reached his twentieth year. After an early breakfast on Friday, 4 September 1829,

---

[12] John Hill Burton, 'Life of Professor W. Spalding', in William Spalding, *A Letter on Shakespere's Authorship of The Two Noble Kinsmen*, new edn (London: Trübner, 1876), p. xvi; [Anon],'Biographical Memoir', in Joseph Robertson, *Scottish Abbeys and Cathedrals* (Aberdeen: Wyllie, 1891), v–xxxix (pp. viii–x); NLS MS 9402, fols 1, 7, 18; George Grub, 'Editor's Preface', in *Illustrations of the Topography and Antiquities of the Shires of Aberdeen and Banff: The First Volume* (4 vols) (Aberdeen: Spalding Club, 1869), I, i–ixix (pp. iv–vi).

[13] Ian Duncan, *Scott's Shadow: The Novel in Romantic Edinburgh*. Literature in History Series (Princeton: Princeton University Press, 2007), p. 27; NLS MS 9402, fols 24–6, 31; NLS MS 9429, fols 25–6, 36–9; George Grub, 'Editor's Preface', p. v.

Burton climbed aboard the Star Coach which left 'every lawful morning at 8 o'clock' from Melvin's Hotel on Union Street, Aberdeen heading for Inverness. Burton was no doubt relieved to alight about halfway, in Huntly. He then commenced a walk of around two hundred miles, which over three weeks would take him across some of the roughest and most isolated terrain in the country. To add to the challenge, it was almost the worst week in the nineteenth century to contemplate a trek across Morayshire and the central Highlands. Shortly before, seagoing vessels had set off across the Moray plain to try and save those stranded and in danger of being swept away by what came to be known as the 'Great Moray Floods of 1829'.[14]

These extreme circumstances appear only to have heightened Burton's responses to both ravaged or exceptional natural scenes and to manmade ruins and antiquities, often expressed in terms that resonate with the aesthetic thinking evidenced in his *juvenilia* and student essays. They are responses that articulate a romantic subjectivity expressed through a senses-based aesthetic in accord with his preferred sources in philosophy and criticism. So, after negotiating a first set of obstacles of broken bridges and inundated, scarred landscapes, he finally sat down to view the ruined Elgin Cathedral and recorded his first enthused impression: 'the finest feeling is derived from looking at the whole broken & desolate mass'. However, he was anxious to clarify, even to his private diary-self, that this refined emotional response was different from some traditional notions of taste: if such ancient, gothic remains were 'not tasteful (as some will hold)', they possessed 'that which mere cold taste can never effect – the faculty of overwhelming the senses'. It was, he judged, the combination of the ruined forms and the 'solemn and striking mysteries' of the original religious purpose, 'which so fills the mind of any one gazing on a gothic Pile'.[15]

Yet he was also attuned to phenomena in the natural world, which are appreciated in not dissimilar terms. After visiting Inverness, he turned southwest down the north side of Loch Ness, attentive to the effects of the unusually pellucid atmosphere, and responding with a

---

[14] [Anon], *A Directory for the City of Aberdeen and its Vicinity: 1829–30* (Aberdeen: Gordon, 1829), p. 142; Thomas Dick Lauder, *The Great Floods of August, 1829, in the Province of Moray and Adjoining Districts* (Elgin: Stewart, 1830).

[15] NLS MS 9418, fols 9–10.

Wordsworthian enthusiasm to this solitude in nature: '[t]here was a peculiar clearness & lightness in the air w[hich] rendered my spirits quite elastic, & I never was happier than when rambling perfectly alone by that wild path[.]' As the sun set, 'the peculiar clear light w[hich] it threw behind the west hills, appeared to surround them with a warm haze', and rendered the loch 'clear & smooth as glass'. Two small boats on the water 'looked peculiarly picturesque with their white sails gleaming in the moonlight'.[16]

He then crossed by a small ferry in decidedly choppy conditions to the mouth of a river on the opposite side. These were areas that had been particularly badly affected by a secondary flood at the end of August, and all rivers in the area were in a dangerous state due to the outflow from the Monadhliath range. Despite or because of this, he began an ascent to visit a waterfall on the river keeping as close as possible to the roaring water, having declined an offer from the boatman to guide him 'as I wished to enjoy it alone'. A waterfall he judged the least disappointing of all 'remarkable objects', in the 'sensation' elicited by 'the indefinable dread w[hich] surrounds it':

> A fine sight to stand on the edge of the precipices & look at the foaming stream below, alternate black & white [. . .]I felt the rocks shake – the eternal moving mass seemed as if it were [. . .] to swallow me up – A slight – but not disagreeable dizziness passed over me, & I felt the full effect of the place.[17]

Capturing, as he did throughout his account, the atmosphere of the ensuing scene, he proceeded under a 'dark & lowering' sky 'saving one curious red spot like a volcano', for a further fifteen or sixteen miles over mountainous terrain, with bridges swept away by the recent floods, to finally descend to Fort Augustus. Over the ensuing few days he crossed the Corrieyairack Pass, turned south at Struan to Bridge of Tummel thence to Fortingall and along Loch Tay. As he advanced beyond the wildest high country, his asides reflect a modified but still pictorial sensibility. He marked the erstwhile home of the poet Anne Grant of Laggan as 'a sweet place – saw a piece of beautiful water at the foot of a black rock, forming itself into circles of islands among green meadow(s), wh[ich] [I] am certain is what she describes as the abode of fairies'.[18]

---

[16] Ibid., fols 18–19.

[17] Ibid., fol. 20. Burton was almost certainly on the Foyers, not the Ness as he assumed, and admiring the 'Falls of Foyers'.

[18] NLS MS 9418, fols 20–1; Burton had remembered the description in [Anne (née MacVicar) Grant], *Essays on the Superstitions of the Highlanders of Scotland: [. . .]*, 2 vols (London: Longman, 1811), I, p. 281.

In similar terms he admired the hamlet of Killin at the end of Loch Tay as 'a sweet village'; and as he carried on towards Callander, though the hills were no longer very striking, the country was 'yet beautifully green below, & a sweet sedgy brook makes its appearance, winding away like a serpent among green grass'. His cleaving to solitude in nature recurs in his description of the rest of his walk through the glen, in which the stream 'still continues to wind, & at last almost imperceptibly increases into a soft Glassy Lake'. Romantic sentiments were perhaps inevitable as he thus approached the Trossachs, though he found them rather disappointing, 'as all scenes are about w[hich] the imagination is previously raised'. Scott associations were everywhere, but so already were the tourists, which meant 'no getting into a lonely nook with any sort of comfortable feelings'. He noticed that a lady in one group setting off on a 'water trip' was clutching *The Lady of the Lake*. Perhaps taking a cue from this, once he reached Loch Katrine Burton tried to get back in the mood by swimming to 'the lonely Isle' (known as 'Ellen's Isle' after the success of Scott's poem). Sadly, romantic aspiration was deflated by the harsh realities of a Scottish loch in September and he 'found the water too cold'.[19]

Along the south side of the Ochil Hills – 'much more lofty & picturesque than I imagined' – he then visited various places of interest, including Castle Campbell, which he judged 'very romantically situated'. Here again he sought out experiences laced with a *frisson* of fear, placing himself in danger in attempting to cross the Calder Lynn – 'an awful place – A mass of pure white foam, tumbling over rocks as black as ink'. As elsewhere, he made some effort to appreciate the scene by adopting the proper perspective: it was 'difficult to get the whole fall at a glance, a circumstance wh[ich] adds to its Picturesqueness'. Finally, he turned north again to Perth, where he had arranged to meet Joseph Robertson. The two visited various early historical sites, Robertson already making some detailed notes and sketches, reaching Cairn o' Mount on 25 September, exactly three weeks after Burton set out.[20]

It is not difficult to trace in many of the passages of Burton's journal both a romantic, literary sensibility and characteristics of the aesthetic theorising of previous decades. By the early nineteenth century the three major conceptions through which taste could be experienced and described were conceived as the Sublime, the Beautiful and the Picturesque.

---

[19] NLS MS 9418, fols 24–5; Walter Scott, *The Poetical Works of Sir Walter Scott*, ed. J. Logie Robertson (London: Oxford University Press, 1921), pp. 217–28.
[20] NLS MS 9418, fols 26–8.

The most dramatic and awe-inspiring phenomena in Nature elicited, at least in men of taste, the 'emotion of the Sublime'. Around this period, perhaps for a university course, Burton wrote an essay on the subject that evidences his familiarity with conceptions of the sublime in more recent works by Lord Kames, Dugald Stewart and Richard Payne Knight as well as the earlier though still influential *Philosophical Enquiry* by Edmund Burke. Despite an initial critique of Burke, in his essay Burton ultimately agreed that many objects in Nature 'produce an idea of the Sublime from the feeling of danger connected with them'.[21] It seems likely that this was why, in order to properly experience and convey his response to 'remarkable objects' like the waterfall on the Foyers, he manoeuvred to the most dangerous and 'dizzying' vantage point he dared, seeking the sensation of 'indefinable dread' it offered, and so 'felt the full effect of the place'; and later why he sought to experience the 'awful' and 'fearful' Calder Lynn.

By contrast, in responding to scenes and experiences of a calm and tranquil character, which Burton still judged aesthetically pleasing, his appreciation is expressed in the terms of the Beautiful. Stretches of water are attractive when they are 'clear & smooth as glass', or 'a soft Glassy Lake'; or a burn that 'goes winding away like a serpent among green grass'. Aesthetic theory held that 'smoothness' and curvilinear, serpentine lines were indicators or qualities of what was beautiful. An area of water was not pleasing when, as Burton encountered Loch Tay, it is merely ruffled by the wind. This unremarkable roughness held no aesthetic interest, offering neither the sublime nor the beautiful: it was, as he put it, 'the most disagreeable way to behold lake scenery – it is best either in storm or calm'. Similarly, the 'piece of beautiful water' amid green meadows at Laggan was a 'sweet place', the Lochearnhead inn 'very sweetly situated', Killin 'a sweet village', and the stream at Callander 'a sweet, sedgy brook', because aesthetic theory was, to a degree, conceived in analogy with the human senses; and in particular (at least in the early formulations) taste, so that appreciation of sweetness indicated 'good taste'.[22]

However, it is the emergence over the previous half-century of the Picturesque that is attested most clearly in Burton's journal. He uses the term itself several times, less often than 'beautiful'. Yet the entire composition and purpose of the journal is redolent of the influence and

---

[21] NLS MS 9430, fols 39, 41, 48–9, 57.
[22] Ibid., fol. 23; Edmund Burke, *A Philosophical Enquiry into the Origin of our Ideas of the Sublime and Beautiful* (London: Dodsley, 1757), pp. 98–9, 152–7.

sensibility of 'the picturesque eye'. The conception of the Picturesque had emerged from theorising on how painting and poetry might represent and reveal Nature. At every turn, Burton 'painted' the scenes through which he was passing and that he wished to remember: the sky and 'air' were regularly depicted in all the variety of atmospheric effects and weathers he encountered. Similarly, on the way to Lochearnhead he supplemented his description of the landscape – 'the wildest tract I ever saw' – with appropriate atmospherics, which, as it were, completed the picture: '[t]he air was at this time particularly gloomy, & well suited to the scene'. Backgrounds of (often distant) hills and mountains are sketched throughout his narrative ('distance' was an increasing feature in the perspectives of picturesque art). In addition, Burton periodically called on his knowledge of romantic poetry to illustrate or enhance a description or observation. Besides allusions to Scott's *Lady of the Lake* and Anne Grant's fairy grotto at Laggan, Burton's descriptions of particularly intense experiences called up and incorporated poetic lines from Byron. In his enthusiasm for the remains of Elgin Cathedral, he thought it 'a Noble wreck in ruinous perfection' – the response in Byron's *Manfred* as the hero contemplates the Colosseum by moonlight. Similarly, the 'ferocious torrent' of the engorged and debris-strewn Findhorn, 'whose breast of waters proudly roll', called up this (slightly misremembered) description of the Rhine in *Childe Harold*.[23]

However, painting and poetry were not alone in advancing a picturesque perspective on the observer's surroundings. It was also 'influenced by the development of the subgenre of travel writing and scenic description. The terminology and expectations of tourists parallel the written descriptions that depend on evocative language.'[24] Burton's account of his journey is very much in accord with that literary form, and he actually alludes to two such publications in the course of the journal – Boswell's *Tour to the Hebrides* and the Reverend Charles Cordiner's *Remarkable Ruins, and Romantic Prospects, of North Britain [. . .]* (1788–95), composed by the grandfather of one of his close friends from Marischal. It is rather ironic that in the midst of an era when, through such literature,

---

[23] NLS MS 9430, fols 9, 12–14, 18, 24–5; *Byron: Poetical Works*, ed. Frederick Page, new edn, corrected by John Jump (Oxford: Oxford University Press, 1970) p. 405; the fully accurate wording regarding the Rhine is in Canto III of *Childe Harold's Pilgrimage*, p. 217.
[24] Dabney Townsend, 'The Picturesque', *Journal of Aesthetics and Art Criticism* 55 (1997), 365–76 (p. 371).

'the picturesque eye' would segue into 'the tourist gaze', Burton was so disdainful of the party preparing for their sailing trip and armed with their Scott edition, who so interfered with his hopes of romantic solitude. In truth the emergence of the Picturesque can be said to have played a significant role in generating the romantic yearnings of both the group eager to 'gaze' on Scott scenery and the young Aberdonian seeking a quiet corner and solitary reflection. Earlier eighteenth-century aesthetic theorising had been concerned with Nature as 'a carrier of allegorical meaning' and the potential to reveal its 'ideal forms'. The rise of the Picturesque

> shifts the aesthetic paradigm from ideal beauty that is embedded in the lesser forms of actual nature available to the senses to natural feeling that is located in the response of the sensitive viewer. The basic shift is from idealization to sensibility, and it signals a new priority of sentiment as an end and arbiter of taste.[25]

Burton could be quite self-conscious of his participation in this shift and of his responses as a man of taste: as he enjoyed his solitary walk by Loch Lubnaig under the harvest moon, contemplating the 'picturesque hill' above, he resented the intrusion of hunger overcoming his appreciation 'of this fairy scene', and vitiating 'my sentimental propensities'.[26]

The elaboration of picturesque sensibility also helped to change the perception of the surviving signifiers of the past – abandoned ancient buildings, ruined castles, ecclesiastical remains. It drew antiquities away from their identification in the seventeenth and eighteenth centuries with fusty and obsessive old antiquarians and brought them 'into the picture' as conductors of fine feeling and associational reflection on past times. Earlier aesthetic thinkers like Edmund Burke and Hogarth, with their emphasis on smoothness and the curvilinear, could not conceive dilapidated and broken objects or images as beautiful. But the Picturesque was 'never shiny and new'. More recent commentators – as for instance Dugald Stewart in his *Philosophical Essays*, which Burton knew well – took issue with the earlier perception. Stewart refuted Burke's view and was 'inclined to admit asperity, sharp angles, and irregularity (when introduced in their proper places), among the constituents of Beauty'. It

---

[25] Ibid., pp. 366–7; NLS MS 9418, fols 12, 19; James Boswell, *The Journal of a Tour to the Hebrides, with Samuel Johnson, LLD*, 3rd edn (London: Dilly, 1786); Reverend Charles Cordiner, *Remarkable Ruins, and Romantic Prospects, of North Britain [. . .]* (London: Mazell, 1788–95).
[26] NLS MS 9418, fol. 24.

seems clear from his comments on settling down to admire the broken remains of Elgin Cathedral that Burton was aware of the debate and very much on Stewart's side. Other writers Burton particularly admired, like Payne Knight, reflected the changed perception: 'Ruined buildings, with fragments of sculptured walls and broken columns, the mouldering remnants of obsolete taste and fallen magnificence, afford pleasure to every learned beholder[.]'[27]

For Burton, there is no sense in which this was about melancholic reflection on decay, but it was rather an associational empathy with the features of past times. As his other essays at this time make clear, Burton's view of 'authentic history' was expressly conceived in terms of associationism. Only antiquarians dealt in 'detached facts': the historian identified 'their connection of precedence & consequence'. The events of one age 'affect the immediately succeeding' and the principles thus established are 'stored up in the national habits'. It is notable that, in his perception, 'any one gazing on a gothic Pile' like Elgin Cathedral was not only responding to the broken forms that could be 'finely united to please the sense' of the observer, but was also drawn back to the medieval religiosity it represented by 'the connection we form between the building & the solemn and striking mysteries' of that other age. Indeed, the response brought to mind not only associations with the forms of worship of the priests and monks but also with the skills and mental world of the 'artificers' and architect-masons who created the structure: 'the mind in such places feels greater than itself, & falls into the current of the master minds' which conceived 'these beautiful houses where our fathers worshipped.' Burton felt drawn out of his own time, and 'amalgamated into the mysterious enthusiasm of the place'.[28]

This empathy with the picturesque past, incorporating a fascination and 'enthusiasm' for aspects of its romantic and gothic forms and mysteries, never left Burton and it would colour his treatment and depiction of a range of features in his later accounts of the history of Scotland. At the same time, as the century wore on, on large numbers of his fellow citizens within Scottish literate society would also become attuned and attracted to a number of modes of cultural appreciation that depended

---

[27] Townsend, 'The Picturesque', p. 374, 367; Dugald Stewart, *Philosophical Essays* (Edinburgh: Constable, 1816), pp. 296, 304; Richard Payne Knight, *An Analytical Inquiry into the Principles of Taste* (London: Payne, 1805), p. 192.
[28] NLS MS 9430, fols 2–3, 10, 114–15. The poetic quotation is from the Gospel of Isaiah 64:11, lamenting the reduction of the Temple of Jerusalem to a ruin.

on picturesque survivals, pictorial representations and visual re-creations of the nation's past.

WRITERS AND RADICALS

Burton arrived in the Scottish capital towards the end of 1830. As is manifest in his first letters home, he was immediately drawn to the romance of old Edinburgh and not particularly taken with the spacious avenues, sweeping crescents and classical facades remorselessly swallowing up the fields and hamlets from Princes Street, the main thoroughfare, northward: 'Of the Old Town I think far more than of the New, it is so majestic and magnificent, and I am resolved, if I can, to live in it' – which he did, pleased to find accommodation close to 'Heriot's Hospital and the old city wall [. . .] the West Port and the Grassmarket'. Having settled into these lodgings, he then did not sleep for the first half of December, 'living almost entirely on strong tea and coffee'. He had come to Edinburgh primarily to qualify as an advocate, the title conferred in Scotland on lawyers who plead in court, and to escape from what he regarded as a stultifying apprenticeship in Aberdeen. His mother had sold her house there to help pay the fees involved. When he discovered that he must take the necessary examination by 14 December and so had two, not four, weeks of preparation, he decided he would just have to stay awake. Afterwards, he slept for two days, 'sustained no injury to health, and became entitled to style himself Advocate'.[29]

Such dogged determination to succeed remained characteristic of Burton for much of his life. It was not however the kind of hard-edged, driving, egotistical ambition that can alienate others and limit social connections. On the contrary he seems to have behaved in ways that drew people to him and engendered feelings of appreciation and friendship. Soon after he arrived in Edinburgh, he became involved in a remarkably wide range of social, political and literary circles and activities. This commenced almost immediately when, after his legal qualification, he enrolled in John Wilson's moral philosophy class at the University. Burton approached Wilson with a query at the end of a lecture and, rather to his surprise, Wilson addressed the matter with some respect and attention. Even more surprisingly, the professor asked him to dinner, the other invitees including well-known figures like the rising sculptor Laurence Macdonald (the 'Scottish Canova')

---

[29] Burton, 'Memoir', pp. xxiv–xxvii, xxxix–xl.

and Thomas De Quincey. It was the first of 'many a cordial welcome within these hospitable doors'. Burton later recalled Wilson's lectures as 'alive with brilliant and powerful eloquence'. Another student described his approach to moral philosophy as incorporating stirring anecdotes, and praised his lectures for their 'tendency to engender free thought, and to encourage large and liberal-minded study of the works of all the greatest authors'. Many parts of the course drew on literary sources including Burns and Shakespeare, as well as the Lake Poets.[30]

Other contemporaries would have been less inclined to associate Wilson with 'free thought', as he was the leading figure in the group of Tory authors including J. G. Lockhart, James Hogg, R. P. Gillies and at times Thomas De Quincey, who were associated with *Blackwood's Magazine*, and whose alter egos figured in the *Noctes Ambrosianae*. The memoir that Burton contributed to the biography of Wilson, published just after his death in 1854, is warm and admiring. Given some of the similarities in politics and literary performance between the Society of Writers gatherings in Aberdeen and those at Ambrose's tavern, it might have seemed inevitable that Burton would be drawn fully and exclusively into Wilson's coterie and world-view. However, at an early stage, he also struck up what would become a close and sustained acquaintance with another of the leading Edinburgh literary figures, Sir William Hamilton, who had become the 'leader' among the advocates, particularly those who combined legal and literary aspirations and frequented the faculty library. Just as occurred following his introduction to John Wilson, Burton was soon being invited to Hamilton's new home in Manor Place, one of a select group who were regular visitors there. Not for the only time in the ensuing two decades, he thus quickly gained entry to the society of a group of older men of greater social standing and literary reputation. Hamilton's biographer recorded that around 1830–1, 'Mr J. W. Semple, the translator of Kant's "Metaphysic of Ethics", Mr J. H. Burton, Mr George Moir, and Mr Patrick Fraser Tytler, were frequent visitors at Manor Place'.[31]

---

[30] NLS MS 9402, fol. 1; Mrs Mary Gordon, *'Christopher North': A Memoir of John Wilson [. . .]*, 2 vols (Edinburgh: Edmonston and Douglas, 1862) II, pp. 12–17, 21, 32–6, 39, 43–4.
[31] [John Hill Burton], 'Veitch's Life of Hamilton', ER 131 (1870), 193–221 (pp. 201–2); John Veitch, M. A., *Memoir of Sir William Hamilton, Bart.: [. . .]* (Edinburgh: Blackwood, 1869), p. 141.

Beyond the scholarly quiet of the Advocates Library and the literary *soirées* hosted by Wilson and Hamilton, Edinburgh was in turmoil. Burton's arrival coincided with the most extensive political agitation seen in the city for decades, sustained throughout the two years leading to the Reform Bills of 1832. The impact on Burton's political views was rapid and profound, and for over two decades he became deeply involved in the drive for reform. This would include activism in the varied associational structures that developed to achieve change in different areas of reforming endeavour; but also extensive literary effort in support of these campaigns in newspapers and periodicals. Many of the radicals he came to know well were associated with the publisher William Tait and his new periodical *Tait's Edinburgh Magazine*, launched in 1832. Besides Tait himself they included Erskine Murray of Aberdona and William Weir, editor of the liberal-leaning Glasgow paper, the *Argus*. He was soon involved with Tait, Erskine Murray and Weir in the increasingly well-organised agitation for repeal of the Corn Laws, and these Scots radicals developed a set of political tactics that anticipated the later successful approach of the Anti-Corn Law League in the 1840s.[32]

More immediately, Burton took full advantage of the literary opportunities presented by the rapidly expanding range of publishing ventures. While still in Aberdeen he had initiated correspondence with Robert Chambers, offering ballad material for one of his books. Chambers had been quickly responsive to the market for encyclopaedic collections of the lives of illustrious figures and Burton's earlier contact brought an invitation to cover a number of those to be included in *Chambers's Universal Biography of Eminent Scotsmen* (1834). However, many of his literary endeavours appeared in periodicals like *Tait's* and the Benthamite *Westminster Review*, which reflected his growing social and political convictions. His involvement with the editors of these journals led to an invitation from John Bowring, Bentham's literary executor, to take a central role in the effort to publish a first edition of Bentham's *Collected Works*. By the end of the 1830s his articles in the radical journals, together with his activism in the anti-Corn Law agitation, had brought Burton to the notice of the leading English reformer Edwin Chadwick: their relationship was sustained throughout life, but they were in particularly close

---

[32] Pam Perkins, 'Tait, William', ODNB, accessed 27 April 2020; Kenneth J. Cameron, 'William Weir and the Origins of the "Manchester League" in Scotland, 1833–9', *SHR* 58 (1979), pp. 70–91.

touch over the next fifteen years in efforts to secure reform on a variety of issues.³³

Besides the collection of writers and radicals gathered around *Tait's Magazine* and the select coterie invited to Hamilton's intellectual *soirées*, Burton was associated with another identifiable social group from the mid-1830s. In his memoirs James Hedderwick, who returned from London to Edinburgh in 1837 to join the *Scotsman* newspaper as assistant editor, recalled Burton as a member of a recognisable social 'set', some of whom would figure as opinion-makers and corporate power brokers in Edinburgh for decades to come. It included Duncan McLaren, future Lord Provost and MP, who was 'rapidly mounting the ladder of municipal preferment, and constituting himself a power in the city'; the 'gifted brothers Combe, George and Dr Andrew'; their nephew Robert Cox, editor of the *Phrenological Journal*; and J. R. Findlay, future editor of the *Scotsman* and great nephew of its proprietor John Ritchie. Also involved were Ritchie himself, the incumbent *Scotsman* editor Charles Maclaren, Cecilia Combe and the aspiring novelist Catherine Crowe. It seems likely that Burton became involved through Robert Chambers, who also moved in this circle and was a convinced supporter of phrenological claims but also of Combe's broader theorising.³⁴

The writings of George Combe were certainly central to this set of relationships, although not only because of his advocacy of phrenology. Combe was indeed widely known as the chief British proponent of the subject, which posited that the brain was made up of a number of 'organs' controlling behavioural attributes and that study of the cranium could reveal much about an individual's psychological make-up. He and his brother Andrew had been collaborators in seeking to transform the subject, which had originated in theoretical form in France and Germany, partly by seeking a more scientific approach emphasising the need for physiological investigation of the brain. This, it was argued, would open up the potential for a 'practical philosophy of mind', replacing the approach of previous speculative thinking with an inductive science. However, it is increasingly recognised that Combe's significance for the nineteenth century was much

---

³³ NLS MS 9391, fols 82–3, 100, 118–20. On Burton's collaboration with Bowring and Chadwick, see pp. 104–5, 110–12.

³⁴ James Hedderwick, *Backward Glances: or, some Personal Recollections* (Edinburgh: Blackwood, 1891), pp. 58–63; Robert Chambers, *Vestiges of the Natural History of Creation and Other Evolutionary Writings*, ed. James A. Secord (Chicago: University of Chicago Press, 1994), p. xx.

broader than the arguments over phrenology, and rested on the influence of his *Constitution of Man* (1828), which aimed at nothing less than a systematic account of the relation of man to Nature. There is no evidence as to what Burton thought of phrenology, but his involvement with the group confirms an openness to the range of new ideas being explored there.[35]

Combe's *œuvre* placed particular emphasis on the 'organic' laws of nature, and Robert Chambers' involvement with the Combe circle has been associated with the exploration of evolutionary thinking reflected a few years later in his own *Vestiges of Creation* (1844). In accord with aspects of recent, particularly French, continental thought, Combe viewed nature 'in organic rather than mechanistic terms', so that 'society was conceived as an organism, analogical to the human body'. The work has been described as a medium for transferring to a nineteenth-century mass audience the ideas characteristic of eighteenth-century naturalism, but with a 'crucial difference':

> [t]he central motif of the *Constitution* was that all societal relations were analogical to those of a living organism. That is, it took a set of assumptions about the laws governing a living organism and applied them analogically to society. Just as the constitution of man was governed by a set of immutable causes and effects so was the constitution of society.[36]

Those in the circle around Combe were self-conscious modernisers and referred to their ideas as the 'new philosophy', in contrast with the 'old philosophy' associated with establishment figures like Francis Jeffrey and Sir William Hamilton, both of whom attacked phrenology in print.

WHIG GRANDEES AND NEWSPAPERMEN

Despite this association with the Combe modernisers and his reputation for radicalism, Burton became increasingly embedded in the Scottish political and social establishment. As the 1840s progressed, besides being the favourite *protégé* of its intellectual leader, Sir William Hamilton, Burton

---

[35] John van Wyhe, 'Introduction', in *Combe's Constitution of Man considered in Relation to External Objects [. . .]*, ed. John van Wyhe, 3 vols (Bristol: Thoemmes, 2004), I, v–xix (pp. viii–x, xiii–xiv); Combe, *Constitution*, in *Combe's Constitution of Man*, ed. Van Wyhe, p. 12.

[36] David Stack, *Queen Victoria's Skull: George Combe and the Mid-Victorian Mind* (London: Hambledon Continuum, 2008), pp. 34–5, 86–8; David Stack, *Nature and Artifice: The Life and Thought of Thomas Hodgskin (1787–1869)* (Woodbridge: Royal Historical Society, 1998), pp. 183–5.

consolidated and extended a network of relationships among men who figured prominently in both Scottish and Westminster politics. He not only remained on good terms with leading figures like Duncan McLaren and Adam Black, who were (at this point) local political players but began attracting the attention of major figures amongst the Whig elite. Since almost all were lawyers, this may have been aided by the publication in 1839 of his *Manual of the Law of Scotland*, which reached a second edition in 1847. Sending complimentary copies to the great and the good was a common tactic to achieve notice, and Burton used it effectively.

The presentation copy sent to Lord Murray, who had been Lord Advocate since Jeffrey was raised to the bench in 1834, was probably the start of an acquaintance that grew into a genuine and affectionate respect on the part of the much older, established figure. The Lord Advocate was the most senior lawyer in Scotland but had a wide range of other governmental responsibilities, in effect becoming the Scottish political manager of the party in power at Westminster. John Archibald Murray had been involved from an early stage with the cadre of lawyers and critics who, in the first decades of the century, sowed the seeds of the cultural and political ideology that triumphed in 1832. Murray was therefore a friend of Henry Cockburn, as of Francis Jeffrey and the other leading figures who had challenged the 'Dundas Despotism', the lengthy period of conservative rule identified in Scotland with the ascendancy of the Viscounts Melville.[37] By the 1840s, these triumphant Whigs had retired to the bench of the Court of Session or were enjoying the fruits of political appointments and pensions. As the decade wore on, both Cockburn and Jeffrey seem to have adopted Burton as a potential member of the next generation of the Whig elite, Cockburn sending him ebullient dinner invitations. In early summer 1852 the writer and newspaper editor Robert Carruthers wrote to thank Burton for a book and commented that he had recently breakfasted 'with your friend Lord Cockburn: [. . .] I may say, without indelicacy, that he spoke of you in the very highest terms & evinced a deep interest in all your plans, literary and professional'. At the time of Jeffrey's death in 1850, a friend wrote that Burton could at least take comfort in having enjoyed the friendship of such a figure who had 'shown such true interest in you!'[38]

Burton also became acquainted with Jeffrey's friend James Abercrombie shortly after the latter ended his political career as Speaker of the House of

[37] Fry, *New Race*, pp. 243–6.
[38] NLS MS 9392, fol. 195; Gordon F. Millar, 'Murray, Sir John Archibald, Lord Murray', in *ODNB*, accessed 10 June 2020; NLS MS 9394, fols 31–3, 38, 151; NLS MS 9395, fols 27–8, 35, 93, 104, 151, 154.

Commons in 1839 and was created Baron Dunfermline. Burton's relationship with Abercrombie – 'a man at the heart of the new political establishment' – strengthened over the ensuing decade through collaboration around various reform issues, as was also true of his connections with Sir James Gibson-Craig, one of the most liberal of the older Whigs. Such reformist engagement also helps to explain Burton's close relations with a number of other figures in the political and legal elite, including John Cunninghame, who had been the Scottish Solicitor General from 1835–7 and then became a Lord of Session. However, in many of these instances there is evidence of a personal warmth extending beyond political collaboration. Both Cunninghame and his wife Nina wrote to Burton in April 1851 offering congratulations on an article that had appeared in the *Edinburgh Review* on sanitary reform. It was, Nina wrote, an example of his always 'useful and benevolent' public writings and had 'much interested Lord Cunninghame [. . .]. We both feel gratified that we possess your friendship[.]'[39]

Such close relations extended to the younger generation of Whig leaders. By the mid-1840s, Andrew Rutherfurd, Lord Advocate in 1839–41 and 1846–51, was writing to Burton sharing current Whig political concerns in parliament. James Moncrieff, Rutherford's Solicitor General from 1850 and his successor as Lord Advocate for much of the next twenty years, also became a friend. Early in his tenure, in 1853, he commissioned a report from Burton to assess the effectiveness of legislation governing the payment of wages and potentially exploitative practices by employers. With hindsight, how searching it was may be doubted, but at the time Moncrieff wrote warmly to Burton on how his labours would bring 'incalculable benefit to the working classes [. . .] and great credit, I trust, to yourself'.[40]

Since he was still reliant for income on the productions of his pen, one of the benefits of Burton's participation in the late-1830s' Combe circle was his introduction to the owner and editors of the *Scotsman*. He became a lifelong friend and collaborator with John Ritchie, J. R.

---

[39] Fry, *New Race*, p. 270; Emma Vincent Macleod, 'Craig, Sir James Gibson, first baronet', *ODNB*, accessed 4 April 2020; NLS MS 9394, fols 208, 210; See also NLS MS 4257, fols 126–30, where Burton later recalls being 'an integral member of a circle of men far older than myself' who had been 'in close intimacy with [Henry, Lord] Brougham in his early career'.

[40] G. F. R. Barker, revised by H. J. Spencer, 'Rutherfurd [formerly Greenfield], Andrew, Lord Rutherfurd (1791–1854, judge and politician', *ODNB*, accessed 8 April 2020; NLS MS 9392, fol. 250; NLS MS 9395, fol. 123; [John Hill Burton], *Report on the Arrestment of Wages [. . .]* (London: House of Commons, 1854).

Findlay and Alexander Russel, who would oversee the development and expansion of the paper and its influence through the mid-century. As Russel settled in to the editor's chair at the *Scotsman*, he and Burton developed a close association, which lasted into the 1870s. By the later 1840s, the Whig grandees tend to bracket them together. When Lord Murray sent a social invitation to Burton, he added he would be obliged 'if you will induce Mr Russel to come also'. Similarly, Henry Cockburn sent a dinner invitation to them both directly to Burton, assuming that he needn't write separately to Russel. Besides his close relations with the coterie around the *Scotsman*, Burton developed regular and friendly relations with a range of other newspaper editors. William Weir at the Glasgow *Argus* and James Hedderwick at the Glasgow *Citizen* have already been mentioned. Others in Scotland included Robert Carruthers at the *Inverness Courier* and James Adams of the *Aberdeen Herald*. In London, amongst others, he was in contact over many years with Albany Fontblanque and John Forster, successive editors of the *Examiner*, and with Weir again after he moved to the *Daily News*.[41]

From the late 1830s into the 1850s, Burton was involved in a range of campaigns to advance the cause of reform, and he drew on these connections with the establishment Whigs and with the newspapermen in seeking to orchestrate the progressive efforts, often through articles in the *Scotsman* and London papers: the issues included poor law reform; the challenge to rising sectarianism; the campaign for free trade; sanitary reform; and the drive to introduce 'industrial schooling' and a non-denominational national education system in Scotland. Burton's active role in these campaigns cannot be pursued in greater detail here. However, the recognition and admiration engendered within the Whig establishment and the 'fourth estate' by his prominent participation helps to explain why, from both, his publications on the nation's past would attract a proportionate respect and attention.[42]

---

[41] NLS MS 9393, fols 104, 111, 149–50, 211, 259; NLS MS 9394, fols 38, 119; NLS MS 9395, fols 93, 104; NLS MS 9407, fols 199–206.

[42] For Burton's activities already recorded by scholars see I. G. C. Hutchison, *A Political History of Scotland, 1832–1924: Parties, Elections, and Issues* (Edinburgh: John Donald, 2003), pp. 70–4; Peter Mackie, 'The Foundation of the United Industrial School of Edinburgh: "A Bold Experiment"', *Innes Review* 39 (1988), 133–50 (pp. 135–7, 145–6); for evidence in his manuscript papers of his 'networking' on reformist efforts, see for instance, NLS MS 9412, fols 3–4; NLS MS 9392, fol. 175; NLS MS 9394, fols 105–6, 119–20, 121, 191–2, 204; NLS MS 9407, fols 211–20.

Indeed, there is evidence that from the later 1840s, beginning with his *Life of Hume*, the leading Whigs were showing increasing interest and admiration for Burton's literary efforts on Scottish history and culture. For instance, they began to find 'instruction' in his 1853 *History* on issues pertinent to contemporary politics. Lords Dunfermline and Moncrieff expressed particular interest in how the *History* illuminated the increasingly contentious issue of the Lord Advocate's over-burdened role: Dunfermline wrote appreciatively of how Burton's account had demonstrated that with the abolition of the post of Secretary of State for Scotland in the mid-eighteenth century,

> Scotland was left to the L[or]d Advocate [. . .] because the management of Scotland was difficult & disagreeable to English Statesmen. Such has been, with perhaps some exceptions, [the case] ever since & the evil has never been more felt than during the last 10 or 12 years, of which the blame I am sorry to say, belongs chiefly to Whigs.

More generally, he was particularly taken with Burton's account of '[t]he treaty for the Union, the events which followed & the influence which they exercised over the feelings & opinions of the people of Scotland'. As will become clear, this refocusing on the Union and the surrounding events was in accord with many other, more public responses to the work.[43]

Despite an active social life through the 1830s Burton seems to have had no sustained romantic involvement. This changed from early in 1842 when Isabella Lauder came to visit Edinburgh for 'the season'. Isabella was the daughter of Captain David Lauder of Flatfield, Perthshire, an officer in the Perthshire Militia. Her letters to her mother recounted the delights of the social round including a supper party attended by 'a great many new people and clever too – but Mr Burton by far the cleverest'. Shortly after 'Mr Burton' had escorted her to the Advocates Library 'to see some old Thomson p(rin)ts', and on to the Signet library and Parliament Hall. It was perhaps some relief to Isabella that they subsequently

---

[43] Alan Bell, 'Cockburn in his correspondence', in *Lord Cockburn: A Bicentenary Commemoration, 1779–1979*, ed. Alan Bell (Edinburgh: Scottish Academic Press, 1979), pp. 16–17; NLS MS 9392, fols 284–7; NLS MS 9409, fols 157, 188; NLS MS 9393, fols 60, 219, 251–2; NLS MS 9395, fols 27–8, 91–2; NLS MS 9403, fols 105–6; Moncrieff asked for further information on the coverage in Burton's *History*, of the abolition of the Scots Secretary, in preparation for a debate in Parliament on the question of a 'Secretary for Scotland'. NLS MS 9395, fol. 250; Burton, *HOS* (1853), II, pp. 237–9.

'took a walk through the Princes Street Gardens'. There is no doubt that the two fell quickly and deeply in love. Isabella was in the habit of writing poetry and her surviving, somewhat effusively romantic and sentimental verses and letters convey an impression of a sensitive if conventional young woman of her social class.[44] If Isabella's literary accomplishments were rather lightweight, she clearly did appreciate intelligent conversation, and Burton's marriage to her in July 1844 brought increased opportunity for social engagement and reception in Edinburgh polite society, cementing his relationships within the establishment. His second wife, slightly bitterly, recalled that Isabella

> was fond of society, and her husband had not then become positively averse to it. His acquaintance in Edinburgh gradually increased. It included Lord Jeffrey and his family, Lord Murray, who remained a fast friend during his life, and all the remaining members of the old Edinburgh circle.

In the years following their marriage the couple were often invitees to supper parties and soirees in the city. One of Isabella's female friends wrote jealously from the provinces: 'You must enjoy your parties at Lord Jeffrey[']s very much – there is not you know any at least very little intellectual society in Dundee'.[45]

ODDITIES AND ARTISTS

There is however a kind of descent to the swelling tune of Burton's social life in the 1840s, which can be traced in his acquaintance with some of the city's more outlandish characters. He appears to have been regularly in the company of some well-known though rather unconventional cultural figures, including Charles Kirkpatrick Sharpe, Thomas De Quincey, the popular novelist Catherine Crowe and the controversial artist, David Scott. They were not scandalous figures, though De Quincey and Crowe did have their moments, but many in mainstream Edinburgh society would have regarded them as having a distinct notoriety.

Burton knew Charles Kirkpatrick Sharpe well enough by June 1840 to write him a 'laddish', jocular invitation to visit him at the small cottage he had taken for the summer with his mother at Portobello on the coast near Edinburgh. Sharpe by this time however was no lad but approaching his seventh decade, with a reputation as a respected antiquary who had carried out high-quality editorial work for the Bannatyne

---

[44] NLS MS 9413, fols 46, 60, 67, 80.
[45] Katherine Burton, 'Memoir', p. xlix; NLS MS 9413, fol. 113.

Club, the most prestigious of the book clubs that from early in the century had been established and patronised by the Scottish elites. He had collaborated with Walter Scott himself, as well as prominent figures in records scholarship like Thomas Thomson and David Laing. Burton's correspondence suggests he was a fairly frequent visitor to Sharpe's home drawn partly by his first-rate collection of antiquarian books, paintings and *objets d'art*, said to be finer than Scott's. Sharpe also had an extensive knowledge of sixteenth- and seventeenth-century Scottish history.[46]

But he was odd. In *The Book-Hunter*, Burton later painted a picture of his antique style of dress and gently lampooned him as 'Fitzpatrick Smart', one of the obsessive bibliophiles of earlier decades. Reviewing Sharpe's extensive correspondence much later, David Masson commented on his penchant for 'descriptions and imaginations of the physically nasty', as well as a tendency to refer 'in a most inordinate degree, to sexual allusions and to all scandals and speculations of the sexual order'. This louche tendency seems to be confirmed in one of Sharpe's letters to Burton, which did not in fact make it into the published correspondence. It is an invitation to lunch but it suggests he knew Burton well enough to couch the invitation as an elaborate and somewhat *risqué* literary joke. He proposed to receive Burton 'and the ladies', at 1 pm, but suggested that

> we ought to convene with *the popular authoress* in character – alas I am too antique for Oroondates! – so I relinquish him to you – I select the Grand Cyrus – will your mother accept of Clelia? – of course Susan Crow must be Cassandra. [. . .] I recently heard something about Susan Hobbly, which shocks me – it seems, in-spite of many texts in the gospel, she hath repudiated her lawful spouse! fi doric, unfeminine Susanna! – the tail against the head! – never will I play Elder to thee even should I behold thee as bare as a water lily – dixi – and so goodnight, dear Mr Burton.[47]

The letter is not dated, but the occasion was probably just before Burton's marriage in August 1844. The 'ladies' were Burton's mother and the increasingly successful novelist Catherine Crowe, who was then living in Edinburgh

---

[46] Alexander Allardyce, ed., *Letters from and to Charles Kirkpatrick Sharpe, Esq.*, 2 vols (Edinburgh: Blackwood, 1888), II, pp. 525, 574; NLS MS 9394, fols 96, 98; Patrick Cadell, 'Sharpe, Charles Kirkpatrick', in *ODNB*, accessed 20 April 2020.

[47] John Hill Burton, *The Book-Hunter etc.* (Blackwood, Edinburgh, 1862), pp. 18–23; David Masson, *Edinburgh Sketches and Memories* (Edinburgh: Black, 1892), p. 369; NLS MS 9392, fols 235–6, emphasis in original.

having, unusually for the times as Sharpe implies, separated from her husband. Sharpe offers strained jokes on her name: 'Susan Crow' and 'Susan Hobbly' are almost certainly plays on Crowe's most successful novel up to this point whose title was *The Adventures of Susan Hopley, or, Circumstantial Evidence* (1841). Sharpe's biblical reference is to the story (from the apocryphal gospel of Daniel) of Susannah and the Elders, where an innocent and virtuous woman is falsely accused, then surprised while naked and bathing by two lustful older men.

Crowe's work had a serious underpinning founded on a 'strong conviction that her contemporaries needed to be receptive to evidence of a spiritual dimension in nature, in apparitions, and in psychological experiences giving the imagination free rein'. This was partly evidenced in her mainstream novels, but around the time she came to know Burton, her literary activity took a decided turn towards a deeper exploration of that 'spiritual dimension' and receptiveness to 'apparitions'. She seems to have continued to be part of Burton's social acquaintance into the mid-century, when her interest in the spirit world brought her trouble in the material one, and in a way that adds irony to her identification by Sharpe with the apocryphal Susannah. Early in 1854, while preparing a collection of supernatural stories, she was found naked one night in Edinburgh convinced that spirits had told her she would thus be invisible. It came to the ears of Charles Dickens (for whose journal *Household Words* Crowe had written articles), who described the story in a letter of March 1854:

> Mrs Crowe has gone stark mad – and stark naked – on the spirit-rapping imposition. She was found t'other day in the street, clothed only in her chastity, a pocket-handkerchief and a visiting card. She had been informed, it appeared, by the spirits, that if she went out in that trim she would be invisible.

Crowe recovered, though later resumed her exploration of spiritualist phenomena in print.[48]

James Hogg, the son of the novelist, came to know Thomas De Quincey well and later published a collection of memoirs of the writer. One recorded that when De Quincey returned to live in Edinburgh in 1828, among the new friends he made was Catherine Crowe, and that

---

[48] Joanne Wilkes, 'Crowe [*née* Stevens], Catherine Ann', *ODNB*, accessed 22 April 2020; Graham Storey, Madeline House and Katherine Mary Tillotson, eds, *The Letters of Charles Dickens: Volume Seven 1853–55*, Pilgrim Edition (Oxford: Clarendon, 1993), pp. 285–6.

around the time De Quincey began to contribute to *Tait's Magazine* – the early 1830s – a friendship had also developed with Burton, perhaps not surprisingly given that both were close to William Tait, who himself became 'a liberal editor and warm friend' to the Opium-Eater. In fact, De Quincey – like Burton – was in the unusual position of writing for both the Tory *Blackwood's Magazine* and the radical *Tait's*. Burton's lengthy character sketch of De Quincey in *The Book-Hunter* as another of Edinburgh's 'bibliomaniacs' attests to their subsequent sustained relationship.[49] There, 'Thomas Papaverius' is presented as a 'quite peculiar and abnormal case', a fragile and boyish figure 'wherein, however, resided one of the most potent and original spirits that ever frequented a tenement of clay'; and Burton proceeded to describe De Quincey's strange and unpredictable behaviour. Amongst his Edinburgh acquaintances, De Quincey would appear and disappear without warning and he seems to have known Burton well enough to drop in unannounced on his early married life: 'travel-stained and foot-sore, he glided in on us one night like a shadow, the child by the fire gazing on him with round eyes of astonishment[.]' He recollected being guided back into town late at night by De Quincey, who had been loaned a 'wideawake', a large, flat hat:

> Roofed by a huge wideawake, which makes his tiny figure look like the stalk of some great fungus, with a lantern of more than common dimensions in his hand, away he goes [. . .]. Surely, if we two were seen by human eyes, it must have been supposed that some gnome, or troll, or kelpie was luring the listener to his doom.[50]

Burton maintained the association after De Quincey moved to a cottage at Lasswade, some miles south of the city in 1840. In 1852, when J. R. Findlay of the *Scotsman* was keen to meet the author, whose writings he admired, it was Burton who took him out to Lasswade for an initial introduction, which brought an invitation to dinner shortly after. Findlay recalled that Burton, 'was well acquainted with the family'.[51]

To draw attention to Burton's acquaintance with such outlandish characters as Sharpe, Crowe and De Quincey is not to suggest contact with some kind of demi-monde concealed from respectable Edinburgh

---

[49] Alexander Japp, 'Thomas De Quincey: His Friends and Associates', in *De Quincey and his Friends:[. . .]*, written and collected by James Hogg (London: Samson Low, 1895), 1–70 (pp. 55, 58).
[50] Burton, *Book-Hunter*, pp. 32–46. Quotations at pp. 32, 35, 37–8.
[51] John Ritchie Findlay, 'Personal Recollections', in *De Quincey*, ed. Hogg, 122–68 (pp. 127, 131).

society: all of them were also acquaintances of Jeffrey, the leader of polite society, and a range of other respectable figures. What may be more notable is the extent to which they were able to hold their place in such society, indeed be sought out as originals. Still, they had in common a significant strain of the bizarre shading into the otherworldly which is explored further in Chapter 6.

Apart from his eccentric character traits, Kirkpatrick Sharpe was probably best known for his extensive collection of books, antiquarian pieces and paintings. From the 1820s, Edinburgh's middle classes seem suddenly to have come to a realisation that the city, now styling itself the 'Modern Athens', would be deficient in its public cultural aspirations if it remained unable to display evidence of a collective taste in the visual arts. It was appropriate that the Royal Institution, the building that was to provide a new cultural focus for the city, should incorporate its first public exhibition space. Publishers with commercial antennae that would soon enable them to rival and even outstrip the London houses became aware that the embellishment of their books using illustration, at a quality achieved through improved processes of etching and engraving, sold more books. Since historical novels constituted a large proportion of their output, the subjects chosen as illustrations were frequently picturesque Scottish historical figures and episodes often as portrayed in Walter Scott's volumes.[52]

Dinner parties and other social receptions began to include artists and sculptors. When a dinner was organised in 1842 to mark James Hedderwick leaving the *Scotsman*, with Charles Maclaren in the chair and Burton as 'croupier' (or assistant chairman), the editors, lawyers and academics were joined by a number of artists. Burton's young wife shared his interest in the visual arts. In the same year as the Hedderwick dinner, when visiting Edinburgh before their marriage, she made a point of visiting the annual Royal Scottish Academy exhibition in the Royal Institution. Most of those in polite society would no doubt have done so, though as an amateur painter herself she appeared particularly enthusiastic in writing home about the works she had seen: she was impressed by Thomas Duncan's *Entrance of Prince Charles into Edinburgh after the Battle of Prestonpans*, while 'time would fail me to go over Wilkies, Allans, Lauders'.[53]

---

[52] Richard J. Hill, *Picturing Scotland through the Waverley Novels: [. . .]* (Abingdon: Routledge, 2016), pp. 75–6, 113–19.

[53] Hedderwick, *Backward Glances*, pp. 127–8; NLS MS 9395, fol. 52.

A number of Burton's close friends were deeply involved in the developing interest in the visual arts. They included his old school and college friend William Spalding and James Dennistoun, an advocate more interested in painting than in law, whose impressive collection was nearing completion when he invited Burton to a viewing in early 1852 – 'our pictures are now better hung than in our former house'. Burton recalled how Spalding had initially believed that his friend David Scott had the makings of greatness in painting. Scott was the brother of the poet and painter William Bell Scott, whose work was innovative in a rather different direction, and he came to be associated with the Pre-Raphaelite Brotherhood. David Scott's work had notoriety partly because it diverged from the norms of a Scottish painting scene that was just beginning to be a source of some pride. Into this perhaps rather fragile confidence irrupted Scott's work, which was later compared to the visions of William Blake. He exhibited regularly in the Academy exhibitions from 1830 until his early death in 1849. Burton was well aware of his work and of the controversy it could engender. In the summer of 1837 Scott wrote to Burton, evidently providing 'holiday cover' for Maclaren at the *Scotsman*, full of artistic pique at a review that had appeared in the paper. Nevertheless, no doubt through their shared friendship with Spalding, Burton seems to have become a periodic visitor to Scott's studio in Mary's Place, Stockbridge.[54]

For many of the Whig elite, this reflex to promote the arts was emblematic of their aspiration to establish a polite society whose cultural characteristics might bear comparison with the literary achievements of 'the last age' of the Enlightenment. In March, 1838 a great celebratory dinner was held to mark Sir William Allan's second presidency of the Royal Scottish Academy. Recalling the event in his *Life of Jeffrey*, Cockburn acknowledged Allan's personal achievement but viewed the gathering more broadly as honouring 'that extraordinary rise in art, which, both in the native artists we have retained, and in those we have given to England, has distinguished the modern progress of Scotland; and on account of which the Academy had been recently established'. The laying of the Foundation Stone of the new National Gallery building in 1850 was 'the culmination of plans which Cockburn

---

[54] G. C. Boase, revised by Christopher Lloyd, 'Dennistoun, James, of Dennistoun', *ODNB*, accessed 24 April 2020; NLS MS 9395, fol. 5; Burton, 'Life of Spalding', pp. xv–xvi, xviii; Macmillan, *Scottish Art*, pp. 205–8; NLS MS 9391, fol. 279; NLS MS 9393, fol. 204.

and others had long been making for the formal recognition of the artistic community in Scotland'.⁵⁵

Burton's personal enthusiasm for the visual arts reflected this collective aspiration for display of the nation's sophistication in an institutional form. However, it was only one of the ways in which his experiences and intellectual development were moulded by the broader social and cultural world in the two decades since his arrival in Edinburgh. He had become an active and recognised participant in a wide spectrum of social and cultural settings, and in political spheres of influence. These had included the 'set' of self-proclaimed modernisers around George Combe, yet also extended to the inner circle of Sir William Hamilton, the personification for the Combeians of 'the old philosophy'. He had been a prominent member of the group of radical writers and politicians associated with William Tait and the heirs of Jeremy Bentham and a related network of like-minded contacts in the newspaper press; while at the same time a figure increasingly respected and socially engaged with the Whig grandees like Jeffrey, Cockburn and Murray. While he shared the elite's aspirations for public patronage and recognition of the arts, he also remained throughout the period engaged with idiosyncratic figures who espoused unconventional, even outlandish, ideas and habits.

Some were partially overlapping, but in general these engagements represented a strikingly heterogenous range of settings and experiences exposing Burton to the leading social and cultural leitmotifs of the age. Indeed, as will be fully explored in the following chapter, he became involved in a further range of cultural associations that accorded with interests and sources in his earlier life and that he had continued to cultivate, but that he embraced in a much more sustained way from the early 1850s. These instances were centred on a variety of forms of reclamation of the Scottish past; and they would come to rely more on deepening individual friendships than social circles and 'sets'. Yet, for the future historian of the nation, the shift only deepened the extent to which he was attuned to and could later reflect the social and cultural world of his time.

⁵⁵ [Henry] Cockburn, *Life of Lord Jeffrey: [. . .]*, 2 vols (Edinburgh: Black, 1852), I, pp. 373–4; Bell, 'Cockburn in his correspondence', p. 22.

3

Turning to History, Edinburgh, 1850–70

THE WILD MAN AND THE SAVAGE

BURTON ENTERED THE SECOND half of the nineteenth century 'spinning', on a number of counts.

Early in the previous year he had used the term in a letter to a close friend conveying his reaction to events in France, where a revolutionary movement had overthrown the government of the 'bourgeois monarch', Louis Phillipe. What he had perceived just across the Channel was a revolutionary breakdown of social and economic order that would soon after be associated with a regime headed by a Bonaparte. The threat posed by Napoleon I was no distant memory to many, including Burton whose father had fought in the wars that ended at Waterloo. But it was losses in his private life that struck him most immediately and deeply: first in early June 1848, the death of his much-loved mother and in the following year the sudden loss of his young wife. Isabella's symptoms of 'quinsy', an infection of the throat, probably began to give serious concern no earlier than the beginning of October 1849. By the tenth, she was dead. After a brief interlude of outward self-possession, he was thrown into a reaction far beyond the controlled and almost resigned mourning of the Victorian middle class.[1]

He soon displayed acute feelings of grief accompanied by almost chaotic behaviours for a considerable period. Part of his reaction was to seek comfort by throwing himself into the kind of long, sometimes very long, solitary expeditions that had drawn him far out into the Highlands in his youth. As the account of his trek twenty years before through the aftermath of the Moray Floods suggested, exposure to wild places and

---

[1] NLS MS 9394, fols 7, 66.

wild weather had always held a deep attraction for him. Certainly, now it was his only solace in dealing with the acute agitation he experienced. He later revealed to his second wife the intensity of his reaction. Occasionally with a companion but usually not, he 'took walks in all weathers, sometimes walking all night as well as all day'. As the weeks passed,

> he rose and lay down with the feeling that his heart was broken. He of course shunned all society, and never again recovered any real zest for it. He sometimes thought of imitating his grandfather under like circumstances with a difference – he thought of flying, not to London, but to the backwoods of America, or some place [sic] where he should never see a white face, and becoming a 'wild man', a savage – a personage of whom he always believed himself to share many of the characteristics. Only consideration for his little girls deterred him from such a course.

After months, and possibly years of mourning, it was on one of his solitary expeditions into wilderness that he began to recover after a cathartic moment in stormy weather in the Border hills. He told Cosmo Innes, his closest friend at the time,

> [of] one particular walk taken alone to the waterfall called the Grey Mare's Tail. The whole excursion was performed in pitiless rain and wind, which gave the waterfall every advantage, and it was while battling with the elements in climbing the hill to view it that [he] felt the first return of his natural elasticity of spirit.[2]

Burton used a very particular term – such that Kate recalled it quite specifically years later – to describe his self-image on this flight from his distraught emotional state after Isabella's death. She quoted her husband using the term 'wild man' and then parenthetically added the word 'savage'. However, it seems unlikely that Burton felt an identification with the kind of murderous savagery he associated with the barbarians who threatened the imperial hill stations or those who inhabited the urban squalor of industrialised London or Paris. For one steeped, as Burton was, in the literature of the seventeenth and eighteenth centuries, the wild man would have conjured up ideas of a more equivocal, even admirable primitive, the noble savage associated with the original, innocent, precontractual state of Nature most recently articulated by Jean-Jacques Rousseau, Eliza Burton's favourite philosopher. Although it has been argued that Rousseau's conception was more complex than often previously assumed, he has nevertheless been credited with having

---

[2] Katherine Burton, 'Memoir', pp. l–li.

brought the rather bloodless and benign eighteenth-century notions of the primitive figure up to date and in time for more romantic sensibilities by reimbuing him with 'emotions'.[3]

There is in fact a good deal of an early romantic sensibility, relatable to such notions, in Burton's life and writings despite all of his mid-Victorian credo of self-help, control of the passions, pragmatism and his sardonic asides about fashionable Highlandism. It can be detected in those effusive poems and fictional tales of his teenage years; then in his responses to the beauty and sublimity of nature recorded in the journal of his Highland tour; and it may have been maintained in John Wilson's class by the professor's stirring literary exemplars. It is present in his response to Isabella's romantic poetry, and seems to emerge again in this incarnation of the wild man, when the idyll of his few years with her was lost. He retained a deep attraction to the conception of the figure, alone and lost in Nature, which he later expressed very fully in the pages of his book describing solitary roaming in *The Cairngorm Mountains* (1864) and in his *Blackwood's* articles on wanderings in the Alps. In these he expressed frustration at the kinds of human actions or interference that acted to constrain the solitary wanderer's unfettered access to wilderness.

The Cairngorm book, which was written in the same period as he was working on his *History*, was driven partly by a desire to celebrate and offer his readers the opportunity to explore a true wilderness, explicitly contrasting this experience with the genteel, guided tourism that obtained in the areas around the Trossachs so associated with Scott's works. By the time of his writing in the 1860s this had reached epic proportions, but he had detected with distaste the early signs as he passed through the area in 1829. In the following decades he retained an instinctive aversion to the constraints involved when the individual wanderer was subjected to the 'guided tour' through nature. In the Alps he was frustrated that in order to experience the ice fields and the glaciers, it was near-suicidal to eschew employing a guide. Despite this he was almost traumatised at the idea. This emerges in a revealing association he makes in recalling a dream, or rather nightmare, experienced while on one of his Alpine explorations.

In the midst of a series of expansive 'scenes and adventures', Burton recalled being 'afflicted with an oppressive dream' of an experience

---

[3] Geoffrey Simcox, 'The Wild Man's Return: The Enclosed Vision of Rousseau's Discourses', in *The Wild Man Within: An Image in Western Thought from the Renaissance to Romanticism*, eds Edward Dudley and Maximillian E. Novak (Pittsburgh: University of Pittsburgh Press, 1972), 223–47 (p. 227).

in boyhood. Although he quite frequently shared with his family recollections of his schooldays, this disturbing memory had previously remained suppressed. But now, apparently out of the blue, his sleeping self 'fixed itself down on a dreary period of school discipline and recalled its most oppressive features all too vividly'. It happened almost literally out of the blue, since the previous day had been filled by images of the Jungfrau spreading 'her vast robe of snow before the sun', and of the great Staubbach cataract glittering in its setting rays, falling on 'the green meadows of Lauterbrunnen'. He could not understand why such a day had brought, not the undisturbed repose he had enjoyed on previous nights as he wandered the Bernese *Oberland*, but 'visions' of a period in his schooldays 'endured under a hard, irritable pedagogue, who made his own life and the lives of all who came about him miserable' (Burton had indeed been subjected by one schoolmaster to beatings so severe that they drew blood). At the time he managed to put the unpleasant associations behind him, for the next day he was off climbing up to 'the lone inn on the Wegernalp' and subsequent exploration of the Grindelwald glacier.

However, by the time he came to reflect on 'a dream which was not a dream', he had worked out what had triggered *der Albtraume*.[4] For the first time in his wandering whether in the Scottish Highlands or in the Alps, he had required to put himself 'under the jurisdiction and authority of a guide'. He knew rationally that this made sense given the next day's objectives, but a fundamental sensibility was affronted by 'the suffering of spirit endured through some three days of the detested bondage of guidehood'. These reflections form the preamble to his book on the Cairngorms, which had been written, he reiterated, to urge the reader to 'shake himself free' of any such 'detested bondage' and 'independently step out' beyond any such constraints. Guidebooks defining where to go, what to see and what to believe meant it was 'not alone in submission to the iron rule of the professional guide that this degrading phenomenon is developed'. Those who meekly accepted such limitations were accepting 'a system of voluntary slavery'. In his book, he announced, he would champion a liberating approach contrasting his favourite area, a wild

---

[4] Burton's allusion is to Byron's nightmarish poem 'Darkness':

'I had a dream which was not all a dream.
The bright sun was extinguish'd, and the stars
Did wander darkling in the eternal space[.]' Page, ed., *Byron: Poetical Works*, p. 95.

Scotland free to be enjoyed without constraint, with the landscape once sacred to Scott's novels but now in 'bondage'.[5]

The book is indeed full of descriptions and celebrations of solitary wandering in wild places, the Cairngorm range often compared to Alpine settings and in the terms of a Burkeian aesthetic of the Sublime. In Glen Lui, 'the extreme loneliness of the scene fills the mind with a sense of awe', though also of a beauty that recalls for him one of Wordsworth's poems, and later a quote from *Ossian*. In his account of traversing Ben Macdui, he recalled another kind of wild man, the 'Fahn', traditionally to be glimpsed in the mountain mists clutching his pine tree as a staff: no 'phantom of the burial-vault or the deserted cloister' could compare with such 'spirits of the air haunting this howling wilderness'. James Hogg, Burton recalled, had asserted in poetry and prose that he knew a man who had seen it. Pressing on to Loch Avon, Burton again refers to Hogg with whom he had a standing feud concerning the length of the Loch. 'His recollections were taken from that brilliant assemblage of choice spirits on its brink recorded in the early "Blackwoods".' Although 'James' had maintained his position in their final discussion, Burton thought his view was more 'a sort of gauge of the Shepherd's spirits'. If at times accompanied by phantoms and terrors, he associated wanderings alone and certainly untrammelled by 'guides' or 'guidebooks' with free minds, free spirits. He was surprised once to hear Jeffrey recall a ramble about Loch Katrine before its 'touristification', but it was not 'natural' to associate tales 'of such free life' with the old Whigs. He felt a much more powerful association of sojourns in untamed landscapes with the likes of Hogg, or John Wilson and Thomas De Quincey: 'I have often heard Professor Wilson revel with a sort of wild delight on his roving days', while 'De Quincey's wanderings were of an astounding kind, with a dash of the supernatural about them'.[6]

Yet the wild man and the quieter, solitary *persona* – less troubled, but still most comfortable finding solace in a communing with wilderness – oscillated throughout Burton's life with the Janus-image of the savage, a figure whose origins lay in the alternative conception of early human life as developed in the previous century. While the wild man and wilderness could represent an opportunity of fleeing from tragedy and in less traumatic circumstances a liberation from oppressive constraints, Burton

---

[5] John Hill Burton, *The Cairngorm Mountains* (Edinburgh: Blackwood, 1864), pp. 1–5.
[6] Ibid., pp. 28, 50, 94, 96–7.

had an equally intense awareness of man as savage. In his socio-political thinking he was keenly aware of the threats posed by the savage, partly those on the Empire's frontiers, but especially by the 'city savages' who most immediately represented the potential irruption of the barbarian's untrammelled passions into civilised life. Unlike most of the eighteenth-century Scottish *philosophes*, he had a distinct anxiety that advancing civilisation could be thrown into reverse, in conditions of either urban squalor or colonial chaos.[7]

Burton retained a fascination with this encounter of the savage and the civilised: the juxtaposition of the two states was increasingly evident as the Empire encroached further on spheres viewed as primitive, a contrast that seemed at its most stark and intriguing as for many Victorians in the white man's incursion into the Dark Continent. The issues came into particular focus in the late summer of 1863 just before Burton published *The Cairngorm Mountains*, when one of the great African explorers took up temporary residence at the Burton family home, Craig House. John Hanning Speke had spent several years on expeditions that penetrated deep into central Africa in pursuit of the sources of the Nile. Once it became known that Speke had kept a detailed diary of his most recent adventures, there was intense competition to publish the account, and John and William Blackwood secured the publication rights. The trouble, as they soon discovered, was that Speke, 'verbose and discursive, with a cigar in his hand', couldn't write. John Blackwood turned to Burton, who agreed to revise the material into a readable narrative. The book was a great success, though fate had in store for Speke the kind of ironic doom sometimes reserved for those who venture all in fearless explor-atory adventure: three years later, while cleaning his gun after a pleasant afternoon's game shoot in Wiltshire, the weapon went off, killing him instantly.

What is of immediate interest is the way in which Burton recast the book. Speke, and initially the Blackwoods, had in mind a publication in the great tradition of Victorian scientific discovery and reportage. A rather different approach emerged when Burton met Speke; soon after-wards, John Blackwood reported to his nephew that 'B(urton) thinks it will be the most complete characteristic picture of savage life that ever was'. Under his influence, the original scientific purpose shifted towards 'a narrative portraying the triumph of Speke over nature and inferior races',

---

[7] John Hill Burton, *Political and Social Economy: [. . .]* (Edinburgh: Chambers, 1849), pp. 21–2, 312–13.

and subsequently his perception of what should be the central theme – 'the explicit portrayal of savage life, and the implicit triumph of Speke over it' – became predominant. Speke's own Introduction to the book had originally been 'an invitation to the reader to view the African people in light of an almost Rousseauian view of the "Noble Savage" existing in a state of nature once common to all humankind'; but Burton's revision presented 'a naked, dark Africa disconnected from and untouched by European impulses and civilization'.[8]

The conception of the savage handed down by the historical sociologists, primitive inhabitant of the first 'stage' of human existence and prey to unchecked passions, thus continued to be a source of fear but also fascination for Burton. In this he was not alone: as the nineteenth century advanced, the Victorian imagination viewed primitive peoples with a 'mixture of fascination and loathing '. In times of emotional stress and trauma, and more generally when he could throw off the constraints of civilisation's oppressive guards and 'guides' and escape into wilderness, Burton revealed as much of a romantic identification with Rousseau's natural primitive as at other times a Victorian frisson of fear contemplating the atavistic barbarian. Through much of his life there remained a continuing interplay and ambivalence concerning the wild man and the savage.[9]

THREATS AT HOME AND ABROAD

In the early 1850s, through the dark months and years after Isabella's death, it was Cosmo Innes who most often accompanied the distraught writer on his escapes into wilderness. He had known Innes for some years, probably since their involvement in the founding of the Spalding Club established in 1839 to publish historical works related to Aberdeenshire, but it was from this period that their relationship deepened. Innes had by now, despite his episcopalian background, become thoroughly embedded in the establishment of Whig Edinburgh: admitted to the Bannatyne Club in Scott's day, he was Sheriff of Moray from 1840 until 1852 when he resigned to succeed Thomas Thomson as Principal Clerk of the Court of

---

[8] David Finkelstein, *The House of Blackwood: Author–Publisher Relations in the Victorian Era* (University Park: Pennsylvania State University Press, 2002), pp. 53, 59–66.

[9] Hayden White, 'The Forms of Wildness: Archaeology of an Idea', in *Wildman Within*, eds Edward Dudley and Maximilian E. Novak, 3–38 (p. 34).

Session. He had also been Professor of Civil (from 1862 Constitutional) History at the University of Edinburgh since 1846. As Burton slowly came to terms with his loss, the long weekend sojourns with Innes 'generally ended by his accepting the proffered invitation to dinner' on their return. Burton was usually the only guest around this family table. His attention was increasingly drawn to Innes's eldest daughter. As his spirits recovered, it was Burton who did most of the talking, drawing on 'a wonderful stock of lively anecdotes and jokes'. His affections were kindled, he told her later, by her 'irresistible bursts of laughter' at his stories. Katherine became his second wife on 3 August 1855.[10]

In one sense at least after the mid-century, events brought Burton a greater degree of security. In the spring of 1854, the post of secretary to the Scottish Prisons Board became vacant. Henry Cockburn dropped a line to Burton drawing attention to the opportunity, but adding that he would not trouble with a recommendation to 'the Advocate' since his views on Burton's suitability for preferment were well known. Cockburn saved himself some effort and was correct in his anticipation that Burton's turn had come. However, in the wider world new threats were emerging. The sense of socio-political insecurity reflected in Burton's writings and correspondence in the 1840s had largely been concerned with the danger of domestic social upheaval and the urgent need to ameliorate the effects of rapid urbanisation and industrialisation. In the same year as his appointment to the Prisons Board, he reiterated warnings of the dangers posed by 'artificial' systems in political economy that sought to defy the 'natural laws'. These concerns were articulated in the entry on 'Communism' that he contributed to the eighth edition of the *Encyclopaedia Britannica*, the article also issued as a separate publication. Although the potential of such ideas to incite social unrest within Britain had partially receded, Burton still perceived that close at hand through much of Europe 'a communistic spirit of the most dangerous kind still smoulders, ready, when an occasion offers itself, to burst forth in a consuming flame'.[11]

A similarly latent and unpredictable threat even closer to home centred on the outbreaks of infectious disease, which the failure to effect public health reforms rendered a constant danger. A severe outbreak of cholera had swept the nation in 1848–9 accompanied by high rates of mortality, not least in Edinburgh. Shortly thereafter, Burton entered

---

[10] Marsden, *Cosmo Innes*, pp. 25–6; Katherine Burton, 'Memoir', p. liv.
[11] NLS MS 9395 fol. 162; John Hill Burton, *Communism, From the Eighth Edition of the Encyclopedia Britannica* (Edinburgh: Neill & Company, 1854), p. 45.

the lists, in the *Edinburgh Review*, in support of a number of public health reports produced by Chadwick and the General Board of Health. He warned the upper and middle classes that they could not quarantine themselves 'by mere walls and lanes, and remain safe'. The cholera had spread in such a way that 'once introduced within the limits of a city community, none were wealthy or moral or wise enough to be safe from its stroke'. The failure of the governing elites to follow the Board's advice threatened all and reflected attitudes that were a danger to the social order itself.[12]

Such social insecurities remained ever present, if in abeyance beyond the mid-century, but for much of the 1850s the additional threat of foreign war and even invasion became more prominent, and both Burton and his second wife were caught up in responding to the periodically fevered national mood. It was Kate who made by far the more adventurous and dangerous contribution: soon after the outbreak of the Crimean War in 1854 and a few months before her marriage, she journeyed in difficult conditions to join Florence Nightingale in her effort to improve conditions at the British hospital at Scutari. She must have arrived just as, in addition to an existing cholera outbreak, the first mass casualties arrived from the early battles at Inkerman and the Alma. In the later 1850s Burton faced no comparable challenges when he joined the Advocates Company of the Volunteer Rifle Militia, set up throughout the country in response to a perceived threat of invasion from France. No rifles were fired in anger but Burton was recalled as a 'zealous' member of the Company offering a field attached to his home on Lauriston Place as the venue for the faculty's soldiery to carry out their drill. Not long returned from the ferocity of the Crimean conflict, quite what Kate Burton thought as she looked out on the rather ageing, and in some cases no doubt portly, faculty members on manoeuvres has not come down to posterity.[13]

However, the numbers who responded to the call for volunteers attested to the widespread sense of alarm that persisted to the end of the decade and beyond. And the threat from France had not been the only cause for anxiety originating beyond the seas. Shortly before, the Indian Mutiny had

---

[12] [John Hill Burton], 'Sanitary Reform', *ER* 91 (1849–50), 210–28 (pp. 213–14, 216, 227–8).

[13] NLS MS 9983, fols 43–4; Trevor Royle, *Crimea: The Great Crimean War 1854–1856* (London: Little, Brown, 1999), pp. 249, 252–5; J. M. Grierson, *Records of the Scottish Volunteer Force* (Edinburgh and London: Blackwood, 1909), pp. 1–3; William Stephen, *History of the Queen's Rifle Volunteer Brigade* (Edinburgh: Blackwood, 1881), p. 169.

threatened the jewel in the Empire's crown. That conflict, together with the Crimean War, had highlighted the poor conditions, from food to sanitary arrangements, available to the ordinary soldier. Burton reinforced the need for change in a *Blackwood's* article publicising the Report of the Commission appointed to examine army sanitary conditions. His language in the piece attested more generally to the sense of threat that had gripped the nation 'as one deadly emergency arose after another', and the subsequent sense of relief: after passing through 'the hottest of fiery ordeals [. . .] the nation is safe, and we ourselves are safe'.[14]

But it had been an uncertain outcome. Over nearly twenty years, Burton had been alert to a spectrum of internal and external threats to British civility and progress. Through much of the 1840s he had attacked a socio-political system unable to shake itself free of protectionist economic theories while millions starved. He consistently railed against the sectarian divisions that had obstructed the development of a national education system, and warned that without this and other social reforms, society would again be exposed to the revolutionary chaos that had erupted abroad. There was fertile ground for the reception of 'artificial' and 'communist' ideas and demagoguery among the mass of 'city savages' as well as the thousands displaced into the new coal and iron fields. In the other area of change that might alleviate the conditions favourable to 'barbarism' – reform of public health – arrangements had stalled: his friend Chadwick, the great leader in 'sanitary science', had been pensioned off in 1854 with the abolition of the first Board of Health, and the imperial parliament itself had just been engulfed in the kind of severe fog or 'miasma' that both Chadwick and Burton believed had caused the mass outbreaks of cholera and other infectious disease over the previous decades. On the frontiers of the Empire, while on the one hand the 'New Zealanders', who had been cannibals 'just the other day', seemed to be civilising at a scarcely credible rate and challenging white superiority, the Indian 'race', which was supposed to be 'docile' when faced with a bit of British pomp and circumstance, had come perilously close in 1857 to reclaiming their country from its Empress.[15]

---

[14] [John Hill Burton], 'The Soldier and the Surgeon', *BM* 84 (1858), 1–24 (p. 3).
[15] For his ironical comments on the 'miasma' that descended on Westminster in 1859, and his encomium for Chadwick 'cast down', see [John Hill Burton], 'Mephitis and the Antidote', *BM* 85 (1859), 222–39 (pp. 222–3, 232–5); for the rapidly civilising indigenous New Zealanders – 'clever barbarians', so cause for reflection – see [John Hill Burton], 'The New Zealanders', *BM* 70 (1851), 414–30 (pp. 421–2, 430); for the supposedly 'docile' peoples of India, see Burton, *Emigrant's Manual*, p. 18.

In his final articles related to political economy, in 1858, Burton put a brave face on it all, insisting that 'our late terrible trials' had shown no signs of moral decay in the imperial project. Yet he made the observation having been prompted to reflect on the reasons why the empires of Rome and Spain had come to dust. He had observed in various ways over the years that history suggested that a linear march to progress and civilisation could not be guaranteed, and now he reiterated that, depending on the conditions, the danger of regression was ever there even for Saxons: he reflected on the ex-convicts and escapees, who, in Tasmania, had formed bands of 'bushrangers', and regressed to 'all kinds of horrible vices', including cannibalism; and on the reported behaviour of civilised Britons 'of rank and respectability' toward the 'aborigines' of Australasia, which recalled 'the picturesque horrors of Hernan Cortes and Pizarro '. It is unsurprising that almost the last of his contributions on political economy should incorporate such reflections on the lessons of history. Through the 1850s, Burton's social *locus* – the places in which he lived, as well as the relationships most important to him – were progressively bound up with history, and specifically with Scottish history. This increased as the years wore on, though the signs were there as the decade dawned.[16]

HISTORIC RETREATS

On Friday, 21 June 1850, T. B. Macaulay rose at an early hour, and together with 'H and Baba', his sister Hannah and her daughter Margaret, made haste to Euston Station to catch the train for Edinburgh. The full route was scarcely five years old and locomotive technology such that the noise as they 'whirled along' precluded much conversation. Macaulay read *Don Quixote* again – 'always delightful'. It was ten at night before the train pulled into Waverley but since it was midsummer's day it would still have been light when they reached their accommodation and found supper waiting, together with a note and offer of assistance from John Hill Burton.[17]

The decade ahead marked a gradual shift in the focus of Burton's life and literary endeavour from the proselytising, campaigning outputs of his pen on behalf of reform toward productions on Scottish historical subject

---

[16] [John Hill Burton], 'Our Convicts – Past and Present', *BM* 83 (1858), 291–310 (p. 293); *Emigrant's Manual*, Preliminary Dissertation, p. 91, 'Australia', p. 121.
[17] William Thomas, ed., *The Journals of Thomas Babington Macaulay*, 5 vols (London: Pickering & Chatto, 2008), II, pp. 260–2.

matter. Burton thought Macaulay the greatest living British historian, and their correspondence continued as Macaulay laboured on further volumes of the *History of England*. It shows Macaulay highly appreciative of the information and interpretations that Burton had provided on various issues, including the significance of 'the commercial relations between England and Scotland after the Restoration'. As Burton commenced work on the initial volumes of his own *History*, the two men continued to exchange draft material, and it is recognised that Burton 'had given Macaulay much help' in the Scottish parts of the *History of England*. However, closer to home, two other men would become much more influential in his historical endeavours. One was Cosmo Innes, both as an individual, and as the leading figure in a nexus of historical scholars and neo-antiquarians who were transforming the source material available on Scottish history. The second was the publisher, John Blackwood, who would provide consistent support and encouragement over many years in bringing a comprehensive national history to fruition.[18]

Following his second marriage in 1855, Burton abandoned the New Town and set up home with Kate in Lauriston Place, just behind Keir Street where he had first lived on arriving in the city and close to the Old Town walls and Heriot's Hospital. They seem to have spent six largely happy years there from the summer of 1855 until early 1861 in a semi-rural environment with views north to the Castle and the Old Town and south over open land, occupied largely by rabbits, to the Burgh Muir where the Scottish armies had mustered of old. Kate believed that it was from the time of their marriage that Burton decided to write a much more extensive *History of Scotland* than that covered by his 1853 volumes. By 1860, the city was expanding to the southwest, consuming the open fields between the Burtons' home and Morningside. Burton sought refuge deeper in the countryside to the south. He had remembered a childhood enthusiasm of his second wife for a romantic but dilapidated mansion that stood on Easter Craiglockhart Hill commanding extensive views across the city and down the Forth to the sea. Craig House had a long history, probably originating as a medieval defensive tower, and was subsequently associated with many romantic legends relating to Queen Mary, James VI and other historical figures. With his knowledge of Scottish architectural history, Burton would have recognised its features, though undistinguished, as reflecting the Scots baronial style. In this conducive and

---

[18] NLS MS 9407 fols 173–97; NLS MS 9983 fols 25–35, 39; Thomas, ed., *Journals*, III, p. 303, footnote 2 to entry for Tuesday, 2 November 1852.

atmospheric setting Burton, displaying 'increasing unsociability', would become absorbed in historical research and writing.[19]

It would be wrong to suggest that in the previous decades, though subordinated to his concern with contemporary reform, he had ever lost his early fascination with the Scottish past. He maintained some historical writing and research during the 1830s mainly through short review articles for *Tait's* and the *Westminster Review*. And as the 1840s progressed he was able to increase his profile in historical work in editing texts for the established book clubs, whose cultural significance he referred to as comparable to the eighteenth-century notion of the 'republic of letters'. Early in the decade, in conjunction with David Laing, he edited a collection of Jacobite documents for the Abbotsford, followed in 1849 by an edition of the *Darien Papers* for the Bannatyne itself. Between these in 1847 came a double biography of Duncan Forbes of Culloden and Simon Fraser, Lord Lovat, to a degree also an editorial task utilising a range of newly discovered manuscript documents. The Book Club editions kept him in touch with the revolution in records scholarship first associated with members of the clubs like Thomas Thomson and Laing and carried further more recently by Joseph Robertson and Cosmo Innes, who had been trained in records scholarship by Thomson.[20]

Innes acted as something of a bridge between the earlier, exclusive book clubs of Scott's time and the broader-based effort at recovering and publishing Scottish historical material, which gathered pace from the mid-century. He had supported Joseph Robertson in the foundation already mentioned of the Spalding Club in 1839. The Spalding heralded 'a new breed of historical societies', whose participants and publications were not limited to a few dozen of the elite. The Spalding's membership had some overlap with the Bannatyne but, of greater significance for the decades ahead, it attracted a younger generation of 'fast-rising antiquaries and historians', including, besides Robertson, Burton himself, John Stuart, George Grub and William Forbes Skene. Most of those named were also members of the Spottiswood Society, active in the 1840s in

---

[19] Katherine Burton, 'Memoir', pp. liv–lviii; Charles J. Smith, *Historic South Edinburgh*, 2 vols (Edinburgh: Charles Skilton, 1979), II, pp. 284–91.
[20] Burton, *Book-Hunter*, pp. 277, 284; John Hill Burton and David Laing, eds, *Jacobite correspondence [. . .]* (Edinburgh: Abbotsford Club, 1840); John Hill Burton, ed., *The Darien Papers [. . .]* (Edinburgh: Bannatyne Club, 1849); John Hill Burton, *Lives of Simon Lord Lovat, and Duncan Forbes of Culloden: From Original Sources* (London: Chapman and Hall, 1847).

the publication of Scottish episcopalian material, and were later founder members in 1867 of the most productive of the societies that embraced a much broader membership, the Scottish Burgh Records Society (SBRS). The SBRS issued fifteen burgh source editions between 1868 and 1880, stimulating through the 1870s 'an unprecedented boom in the publication of sources relating to Scotland's towns'.[21]

As the character of the societies changed, the emphasis was placed on issuing publications less for bibliophile appreciation of their scarcity and beauty than as models of accuracy and authenticity. This did not however herald a return to a 'dry-as-dust' treatment of the past but rather the opportunity to appreciate the past on its own terms. There were increasing instances of productions that incorporated facsimiles of both original printed documents and manuscripts. This trend reached a peak in the three-volume *National Manuscripts of Scotland* (1867–72), which reproduced extracts from 300 primary documents to trace the history of Scotland through eight centuries. It was edited by Robertson and Innes and commissioned by Register House using the advanced process of photozincography, so securing a visual impact previously unattainable. The immediacy of the experience 'could suggest to the reader that the sources were speaking for themselves', and were not only repositories of facts but 'the products of past lives'. The aim was 'to help the reader forge a connection with a past which [. . .] had a direct causal relationship with the present via the totem of historical progress. Sources were a bridge through time[.]' The title of the work 'strongly implies that its purpose was to present a collective past that would appeal to all Scots'.[22]

This engagement with the meaningfulness and 'materiality' of these sources 'as artefacts as well as texts' was accompanied in the third quarter of the century by a growing appreciation of the nation's archaeological antiquities and what might be described as their narrative potential and relation to written history. Just as the book clubs were expanding their cultural reach by opening up membership and access to their publications, the Scottish Society of Antiquaries (SSA) was also passing through a process of renewal. For Burton personally, the Society may have provided the same kind of structured and sheltered social environment characteristic of the Advocates Library and the book clubs, as he gradually abandoned efforts to make the journey from Craig House to attend other forms of social gathering in the city. It appears to have been

---

[21] Marsden, *Cosmo Innes*, pp. 29–30, 32–3, 93–5, 121.
[22] Ibid., Chapter 7, pp. 205–38, particularly pp. 208, 221, 238.

only from the mid-to-late 1850s that he became more involved: he was elected a Fellow in 1858, was on the ruling Council in 1862–3 and subsequently acted as Librarian from 1863 to 1866.[23]

It was in this period that friends of Burton such as Innes, Robertson, John Stuart and J. Y. Simpson were driving on with a determination not only to reinvent antiquarianism as 'archaeology', a strictly empirical science, but also in effect to 'nationalise' prehistory. The aspirations had been articulated early in the 1850s by another close friend of Burton, Daniel Wilson, then Secretary of the Society of Antiquaries in his opening address to its anniversary meeting in November 1851. Wilson urged that the government must provide proper recognition of the Society's efforts and the funding to develop 'a National Archaeological Museum for Scotland'. The Society had formally transferred its collections to the government in an effort to attract state support, but Wilson drew attention to how niggardly had been the response – approval of the free use of some 'rooms' in the Royal Institution – in comparison to the levels of funding allocated to other institutions, both within Britain and in relation to 'Continental Museums'. Wilson clearly located the issue in terms of growing concern across a range of issues, regarding 'justice to Scotland'.[24]

In other nations, he observed, there had been 'a keen spirit of nationality and patriotic sympathy', but among Scottish politicians and landed elites there appeared to be 'a decay in the old generous spirit of nationality', leaving unaided the Society's researches into 'the primitive antiquities and history of our country'. The Society's aim, Wilson reminded his audience, was to advance '[a]rchaeological science, to promote popular education, and to excite a national interest in the preservation of the monuments of early art and ancient civilization'. It was quite wrong to consider that 'our national antiquities are inferior in interest or value

---

[23] [Anon], *General Index and Index of Illustrations to the Proceedings of the Society of Antiquaries of Scotland, Vols I–XXIV* (Edinburgh: SSA/Neill, 1892), pp. vi–vii, xiii.

[24] The drive from the mid-century to establish national museums in the Scottish capital has recently been associated with the (now rather elastic) term 'unionist-nationalism': L. Andersson Burnett and A. G. Newby, 'Unionist Nationalism and the National Museum of Scotland, c. 1847–1866', in P. Aronsson and M. Hillström, eds., *Making National Museums: Setting the Frames* (Linköping University Electronic Press: 2007), pp. 83–94. However, the SSA's focus was on the recovery of the early national past in emulation of continental European, especially north European, nations in a discourse, discussed further below, centred increasingly on Scottish 'nationality'. See pp. 207–10.

to those of any other country in Europe'. On the contrary, recent scholarship had indicated that Scotland offered 'one of the richest, though least explored fields' for revealing early historical development. Rapidly increasing numbers of visitors to the Society's collection were 'striking evidence of the great change which has taken place in late years in the estimation of Antiquarian pursuits'.[25]

Burton had previously evinced an equivocal attitude to 'antiquarian pursuits', though the fact was that his own early interests in Scottish folklore, traditional ballads and ancient remains reflected an antiquarian turn of mind. Later, his apparently lightweight though highly successful publication *The Book-Hunter* (1862) can be interpreted as coming to terms with the issue in response to the advances in antiquarian endeavour that had been occurring through the mid-century, as well as the rising public interest alluded to by Wilson. Characteristically, it was based on a series of articles in *Blackwood's Magazine* in 1860–1, then frequently reissued in book form by Blackwood to the end of the 1880s. As the work proceeds, it comes to reflect a fundamental shift in perception of the new science and the potential value of the source materials being made available: recent records scholars had 'raised archaeology out of that quackish repute which it had long to endure under the name of antiquarianism', and commenced an approach based on 'practically grasping historical facts and conditions'. It seems likely that not only for Burton, but for many in the wider Scottish reading public, the success of *The Book-Hunter* represented a recognition of the potential of the new source materials as well as an affectionate valediction for approaches to Scottish antiquities whose time had gone.[26]

The Scottish scholars Burton specifically lauded in *The Book-Hunter* were Thomas Thomson and David Laing, but naturally also his friends Joseph Robertson and Cosmo Innes. It was only late in life that Innes used his extensive knowledge of the new sources to publish two relatively limited works of narrative history. The first, *Scotland in the Middle Ages*, was largely a transcription of his lectures at the university, while his subsequent *Sketches of Early Scotch History and Social Progress* incorporated

---

[25] Daniel Wilson, 'Anniversary Address', in *Proceedings of the Society of Antiquaries of Scotland: Sessions MDCCCL–MDCCCLIV* I (Edinburgh: Neill, 1855), 2–7 (pp. 2–6). The issue of lack of support for Scottish 'Antiquities' including the creation of national museums was included in the 'Scottish Rights' agitation which developed from the following year: [Anon] *Address to the People of Scotland and Statement of Grievances* (Edinburgh: Johnstone and Hunter, 1853), pp. 17–20.

[26] Burton, *Book-Hunter*, pp. 3, 48–50, 260, 278–9.

material from the introductory prefaces to his source editions. Many of those editions, produced for the Bannatyne, Spalding and Maitland Clubs, concerned ecclesiastical records from the twelfth to the sixteenth centuries, and a number of others drew on materials from the 'charter rooms' of great landed families. However, Innes also aspired to use the emerging documentary evidence to present a complete national picture, replacing what he regarded as the inadequate Old and New Statistical Accounts. He therefore orchestrated the publication of the multi-volume *Origines Parochiales Scotiae* (1851–5), which 'detailed the antiquities of Scotland's parishes with a marked emphasis on the pre-Reformation period'. Despite this emphasis in *Origines Parochiales Scotiae*, Innes's work on the university records, and the five volumes of family history that he published between 1848 and 1864, also made available a wealth of original material from the sixteenth to eighteenth centuries.[27]

There had been a further major achievement for Innes and one that would be influential on Burton's later historical narrative in finally bringing to publication in 1844 the long-delayed first volume of *The Acts of the Parliaments of Scotland* (*APS*). Innes's mentor in records scholarship, Thomas Thomson, had earlier published ten volumes of *APS*, but following Treasury criticism for financial mismanagement had been removed from office. Innes would have been particularly pleased to see at last the publication of Volume I, since it covered the period 1124–1423 and had been conceived as 'illustrating the origins of Scotland's constitution and independence'. Although he had a traditional historiographic view of comparative decline under the Stuarts, Innes's work reflected a highly positive view, and one that certainly conveyed to his son-in-law the progress the nation had made in these medieval centuries.[28]

Besides Cosmo Innes, as time went on the most frequent visitor willing to trudge out from the city to visit Burton in his baronial fastness on the edge of Craiglockhart Hill was John Blackwood. Blackwood had

---

[27] Cosmo Innes, *Scotland in the Middle Ages: [. . .]* (Edinburgh: Edmonston and Douglas, 1860); Cosmo Innes, *Sketches of Early Scotch History and Social Progress: Church Organization, The University, Home Life* (Edinburgh: Edmonston and Douglas, 1861); Marsden, *Cosmo Innes*, pp. 49–50, 115, 179; Cosmo Innes, ed., *Origines Parochiales Scotiae: [. . .]*, 3 vols (Edinburgh: Lizars, 1851–5).

[28] Cosmo Innes, ed., *The Acts of the Parliament of Scotland, I,* AD M.C.XXIV– AD M.CCCC.XXIII (London: House of Commons, 1844); Thomas Thomson, ed., *The Acts of the Parliaments of Scotland II–XI* (London: House of Commons, 1814–24).

been guiding the fortunes of *Blackwood's Magazine* since 1845, and on the death of his brother Robert in 1852 had assumed leadership of one of the most powerful publishing houses in the country and indeed the Empire. Their association and growing friendship developed through the 1850s and despite political differences continued for many decades. Blackwood's daughter Mary had happy childhood memories of the Blackwoods' family Sundays, including frequent visits to Craig House when the two men would become lost in talk, 'and the short winter afternoons would begin to close in' before Blackwood collected himself and set off back to town. It is certain that the 'talk' would often have centred on one or other of the many contributions on Scottish history that Burton made to Blackwood's publications from the late 1840s until the main body of the *History of Scotland* appeared in 1867–70. Over this period, besides successful books, Burton published 20 substantial articles in *Blackwood's Magazine*, almost all addressing some aspect of Scottish history.[29]

In the preface to the second edition of his main *History* (1873), Burton acknowledged the central role that Blackwood had played in supporting the endeavour and urging him on to produce 'a complete History, beginning with the earliest identification of each of the scattered districts that, one by one coming together, made up the kingdom of Scotland'. Blackwood, he believed, had realised better than he had himself that the extensive research that had gone into discreet articles and collections presented the opportunity for a more ambitious and comprehensive account. Far from expressing commercial concern at the 'waxing bulk' of the work, Blackwood 'was always ready to bid me be of good cheer, and to assure me that the matter was not unworthy of the many pages it threatened to fill'. It has recently been shown that, as had previously been true for novels and works of science, at this juncture 'the agency of the publisher' became important 'in the making of history books'. British publishing houses were often seeking books that could be marketed to the general reading public: they were not aimed primarily at students or at scholars in the limited number of academic posts pursuing an 'austere professionalization'. Across Britain, like Burton, 'many of the writers whose history books were published in this period were not university-based academics but men and women of letters'. Publishers sought writers who had a reputation for

---

[29] Finkelstein, *House of Blackwood*, pp. 10–11; Mrs Gerald Porter, *Annals of a Publishing House: John Blackwood* (Edinburgh and London: William Blackwood, 1898), pp. 170–1.

knowledge and research, but could also appeal to readers who 'continued to relish a strong retelling of the old stories'. The influence of publishers in this regard extended to national histories: Blackwood's role with Burton seems comparable to Alexander MacMillan's engagement with Edward Freeman and J. R. Green a little later in London.[30]

The increasing number of articles and books Burton published with John Blackwood examined subject matter that would later be incorporated in his *History* and be recognised by readers and reviewers alike as collectively helping to build new perceptions of the Scottish past. The following section considers the range of this subject matter. Its themes included the achievements of Scottish architecture; the singular canon of vernacular balladry and song; the new and validated work on early history and 'historical antiquities' that threw light on the early church and 'the dark ages'; a new respect for characteristic institutions of the Scottish medieval world, including legal and constitutional structures and the universities; and finally a rediscovery of the almost unique longevity and influence on both domestic and European history of the Franco-Scottish Alliance. In these ways the stage was set for the reconception and public recognition of Prehistoric Scotland, Roman Scotland and Medieval Scotland, besides an appreciation of the nation's international significance in the history of early modern Europe.

'A MASS OF FRESH MATERIAL FOR ITS RECONSTRUCTION'

It appears to have been a recommendation from W. E. Aytoun to Robert Blackwood that led to Burton's direct involvement in a culturally influential publishing venture in the late 1840s and early 1850s. Its purpose was to recover and make more widely available evidence surviving from the Scottish past that was longer lasting than most written sources and was, almost literally, written in tablets of stone. Throughout Burton's correspondence in these years there appear regular short letters from 'R. W. Billings' enclosing picturesque sketches of Melrose Abbey, Huntly Castle, Elgin Chapter House and many similar subjects. The book clubs

---

[30] Burton, *HOS* (1873), I, pp. vi–viii; see also NLS MS 4230, fols 93–4; Burton wrote to Blackwood of his satisfaction when the first volumes appeared in 1867, but was conscious 'that all would not have availed if I had not been so well supported at No. 45' – John Blackwood's office at 45 George Street: NLS MS 4218, fols 181–2; Leslie Howsam, *Past into Print: The Publishing of History in Britain 1850–1950* (London: British Library, 2009), pp. 5–8, 26–7.

had brought a new focus and emphasis on the recovery of the past in terms of text – publication of original and authentic early books and manuscript documents. The extension of this effort to what could be captured of the images available in the physical survivals of the past was perhaps inevitable given the increasing focus on the pictorial and indeed the photographic in the second quarter of the century.[31]

Robert William Billings was sending the sketches to Burton as part of their collaboration in the multi-volume *Baronial and Ecclesiastical Antiquities of Scotland* (1845–52), a highly ambitious project aiming to illustrate the range of medieval and early modern architectural styles in the nation's past.[32] The anticipated cost was so great that a formal financial partnership was formed including Billings and the Blackwood brothers though the publishers provided the main contribution. Burton does not seem to have been involved in the partnership, but did become 'the fourth member of the team' when asked to contribute the historical 'letterpress' to accompany the engravings produced from Billings's drawings and sketches. There was no doubt about Billings's artistic ability, and he engaged first-rate engravers who used high-quality steel, not copper plates. The result was a triumph and was supported by a lengthy subscription list that included many Scottish landowners and especially many of the Scottish urban and professional elites, prominent among them Burton's Whig mentors Lord Murray and Andrew Rutherfurd, the current Lord Advocate. It was reprinted in 1855, then in 1901, an edition introduced with an enthusiastic appreciation by Sir Rowand Anderson, the leader in Scottish architecture at that time, and was widely used by architects who knew it simply as 'Billings'. It was recently reissued in two volumes with a new Introduction, from which the above summary is taken, by Ian Gow, Chief Curator of the National Trust. In Gow's estimation the original publication,

> presented a survey of Scotland's stock of architectural monuments that, for the first time, brought home to the Scots that this was a sufficiently distinctive national asset to celebrate and take pride in, while these same plates were to inspire her contemporary architects to evolve one of the earliest attempts to forge a national style of European significance.[33]

---

[31] NLS MS 9393, fols 31–2, 38–9; NLS MS 9394, fols 166, 194, 220.

[32] Robert William Billings, *The Baronial and Ecclesiastical Antiquities of Scotland*, 4 vols (Edinburgh: Blackwood, 1845–2).

[33] Ian Gow, 'Introduction', in *The Baronial and Ecclesiastical Antiquities of Scotland: Illustrated by Robert William Billings, Architect*, 2 vols (Edinburgh: Birlinn, 2008), I, vii–xxvii (pp. vii, xviii–xix).

This echoes the way Burton reviewed the project at the time. The early castellated buildings, before the fourteenth century, he observed, had reflected a 'community in manners and national spirit'. Even among the subsequent period of 'grim old keeps', it was becoming clear that the exteriors displayed some surprising attention to ornamentation, and from the sixteenth century there occurred the 'magical' development of great houses with 'rich and airy outlines': this was partly a consequence of French influence, but it was 'by no means a servile adoption. It was greatly varied and adapted to circumstances by the Scottish artists, who have really had the merit of creating out of it a national style.' Assessing previous efforts, Burton concluded that Scotland's architectural antiquities 'had received less justice than those of any other civilised country', but when Billings's work was done 'we shall be able to boast that no other nation possesses so complete, and at the same time effective and artistically pleasing, a record of its notable antiquities'.[34]

Billings was no soulless copyist: his original drawings were all 'executed in brilliant watercolour', and Gow observed that as 'a child of the Picturesque' he had a sure eye for the most attractive presentation of the buildings: there was '(p)icturesque bravura aplenty in the published plates'.[35] However, besides being picturesque, the drawings were strictly accurate, reflecting a commitment to reproduce authentic copies of the buildings and their exterior and interior decorative embellishments. The endeavour had much in common with the aims of the Book Club editors – and even more with the publishing efforts of records scholars like Innes and Robertson – to present to the Scottish reading public, copies (including in some cases facsimiles) that were reproduced as nearly as possible to the originals. Here the reproductions were not written records but images of survivals hewn in stone.

The 'Billings' publication set the tone in the ensuing decades for others to celebrate the vibrancy and national distinctiveness of Scottish architecture in the centuries before the Union as well as its significance to national history. In the 1880s MacGibbon and Ross extended the reclamation of the tradition with greater emphasis on 'domestic' structures, which they introduced as representing 'a most complete and unexplored' repository reflecting 'the growth of our national life and manners'. It was therefore important to relate the effort to written sources. They concluded that the native tradition was at least as strong as elsewhere: it was clear

---

[34] [John Hill Burton], 'Baronial and Ecclesiastical Antiquities of Scotland', *BM* 68 (1850), 217–28 (pp. 225–6, 228).

[35] Gow, 'Introduction', in Billings, *Baronial Antiquities*, p. xxvi.

that Scotland, like every other country in Europe during the period from the thirteenth to the sixteenth century, possessed a Castellated or Domestic Architecture of its own, and that even in the seventeenth century, when almost everywhere else the Renaissance style reigned supreme, the native style still flourished.

Previous inattention to conservation of the edifices arose 'from their bearing on the architectural and national history of Scotland not being sufficiently understood and appreciated'. Greater efforts at their preservation must be welcome 'to every one interested in our national history'.[36]

Given his extensive involvement in the Blackwoods' venture, it is not surprising that Burton was knowledgeable on the history of Scottish architecture; but he was also anxious that, besides the enjoyment of Billing's picturesque record in itself, there was a need to more completely 'extract the archaeological riches of which it is a treasury'. It is not difficult to see that he would have perceived this as analogous to what the historian could expect to fashion from the retrieved and objectively presented texts of the records scholars or from the accurately researched physical artefacts reconceived and presented by the new archaeologists. As time went on, he retained the conviction that the 'most enduring testimony to the social habits of early times is architecture'; and he would ensure that the subject was given its proper place in the history of Scotland, if couched within his own Whig-Teutonist interpretation of that 'enduring testimony'.[37]

A number of Burton's *Blackwood's* articles conveyed his growing realisation that the country's prehistory and early history now required to be treated more seriously. This emerges for instance in his reviews of *The Archaeology and Prehistoric Annals of Scotland* (1851) by Daniel Wilson, and of the second edition of Robert Stuart's *Caledonia Romana* (1852). What had changed – as he would later expound at greater length in *The Book-Hunter* – was the methodology and reputation of 'antiquarian' endeavour. The antiquary 'or the archaeologist, as he now calls himself', was no longer the 'fusty custodier' of a random collection of 'auld nick-nackets' (an allusion to Scott's *Antiquary*), but one able to fashion new historical constructs: 'He is now the scientific analyser of the wrecks which time has left, erecting out of his researches, by rigid induction,

---

[36] 'Preface', in David MacGibbon and Thomas Ross, *The Castellated and Domestic Architecture of Scotland from the Twelfth to the Eighteenth Century*, 5 vols (Edinburgh: David Douglas, 1887–92), I, pp. v–viii.

[37] [John Hill Burton], 'France and Scotland', *NBR* 24 (1856), 289–324 (p. 320); Burton, *HOS* (1873), III, pp. 427–36; VII, pp. 103–10.

so much of the history of the past, as his materials will afford.' Burton drew attention to Daniel Wilson's conclusion that many finely wrought, 'prehistoric' objects were 'indigenous' and not Roman as previously believed. The precious metal survivals indicated a level of civilisation much greater than had been assumed, most impressive perhaps the many gold objects found 'especially in Scotland' but also the striking items worked in other metals and stone. He urged that if there were a more systematic arrangement for bringing the 'Scottish archaeological vestiges' together, 'a magnificent national museum would soon exist, capable of teaching more of the history of the dumb past than a record commission': its potential display even of stone artefacts would surpass the 'markedly inferior' collection established by the Danish archaeologists in Copenhagen some years before.[38]

Burton was clearly aware of the arguments in favour of a national museum which, as already described, Wilson was making through his role as Secretary of the SSA. In that address, it is noticeable that Wilson associated closely the activities of the archaeologist and the historian. It was of interest to both disciplines that a scientifically organised national museum be established – what he termed a museum of 'Historical Antiquities' – not only for the study of the objects themselves but in order to reveal 'the primitive antiquities and history of our country' and to understand the nation's 'primitive history and national manners'. A similar message was conveyed by Charles, Lord Neaves, in his opening address as chairman at the Society's annual meeting on St Andrew's Day, 1858. Neaves had been Solicitor General for Scotland in Lord Derby's conservative administration earlier in the decade and was now a judge of the Court of Session. In his address – almost certainly heard by Burton since he was at that point elected a Fellow – Neaves sought to emphasise the study of antiquities as important in being 'a help to history, as to those periods which exhibit historical records', and as 'a substitute for history as to those earlier periods of which no written memorials remain'. With the promise of expanded premises for the Society and its antiquities, he foresaw (correctly) a new era attracting

---

[38] Daniel Wilson, *The Archaeology and Prehistoric Annals of Scotland* (Edinburgh: Sutherland and Knox, 1851); Robert Stuart, *Caledonia Romana: A Descriptive Account of the Roman Antiquities of Scotland*, 2nd edn, revised by David Thomson (Edinburgh: Sutherland and Knox, 1852); [John Hill Burton], 'The Romans in Scotland', *BM* 74 (1853), 557–68 (p. 565); [John Hill Burton], 'Vestiges of the Ancient Inhabitants of Scotland', *BM* 69 (1851), 660–72 (pp. 660–2, 666–7).

many new artefacts to the national collection where, by classifying and arranging 'they would serve to illustrate the national history'. Burton would later make good use of the evidence produced by 'scientific archaeology' and ensure in his *History of Scotland* that the nation's early past, its 'primitive history and national manners', was suitably incorporated.[39]

A number of the other, more specific themes that were the subjects of Burton's articles for John Blackwood and later fed into his *History* centred on publications by the 'Book Club men'. One of the aspects of early history that most fascinated Burton, and again one related to physical survivals and arresting imagery, centred on what he regarded as the country's almost uniquely rich heritage of 'sculptured stones'. It was, he considered, to the great credit of the Spalding Club and the zeal of its secretary, John Stuart, that this repository of the nation's past had been rescued from the wild speculations of unreconstructed antiquarianism: 'the true spirit of historical inquiry can only rest on such accurate, unimpassioned, untheory-begotten representations' as were conveyed in Stuart's own comprehensive work *Sculptured Stones of Scotland* (1856–67). In his 1857 review of the first volume, Burton was particularly enthusiastic that the publication incorporated one hundred monuments that had been 'fac-similed with marvellous accuracy'. He had certainly himself visited many of the stones in Aberdeenshire and the east of Scotland. Despite his usual Teutonism, his respect for the evidence and anticipation of the light that further attention to such remains would provide led him to urge that more attention be given to the survivals in the Celtic west and southwest. He was concerned also that the remains of the 'Scottish Church' at Iona should be protected from the 'iron heels of well-shod tourists': great men were buried there beneath carved stones, which revealed 'vestiges of ancient Scottish art'.[40]

Later, in *The Book-Hunter*, Burton reiterated his admiration for what Stuart had achieved, and commended the Spalding for having 'deviated from the printing of letterpress [. . .] into pictorial art'. His fascination for these physical survivals, as conveyed to the world in high-quality

---

[39] Charles Neaves, 'Opening Address', in *Proceedings of the Society of Antiquaries of Scotland*, III (Edinburgh: Neill, 1862), 152–8 (pp. 152–3, 158); A. H. Millar, revised by Robert Shiels, 'Neaves, Charles, Lord Neaves', in *ODNB*, accessed 6 March 2021; Burton, *HOS* (1873), I, pp. 77–131.

[40] John Stuart, *Sculptured Stones of Scotland*, 2 vols (Aberdeen: Spalding Club, 1856–67); [John Hill Burton], 'The Sculptured Stones of Scotland', *BM* 81 (1857), 602–11 (pp. 602, 607); Burton, *HOS* (1873), I, pp. 132–67.

facsimile, echoes his enthusiasm for the accurately depicted architectural antiquities contained in 'Billings', also achieved through technological advances in image reproduction a 'steely finesse' excelling the work based on traditional copper plates. This susceptibility clearly accorded with the increasing use and appreciation of facsimiled text and manuscripts in other book club publications and in *National Manuscripts of Scotland*.[41] It was a sensibility that may appear at first sight to be a rather incompatible mix of the empirical/materialist and the romantic: the 'materiality' of surviving antiquities was ever more carefully conserved, accurately authenticated and depicted, yet there was a desire to let the past appear and so be experienced 'for itself'. However, this may be considered ultimately resolvable in that its purpose was to appreciate the otherness of the past through the original remains left behind as immediately and authentically as possible.[42]

A further feature given attention in Burton's later *History* – the characteristic traditions of the Scottish universities – was likewise anticipated in articles he contributed to *Blackwood's* on 'Student Life in Scotland'. These related to the publication of Glasgow and Aberdeen university records issued by the Maitland and Spalding Clubs and edited he noted 'with that peculiar archaeological strictness which has been applied to this class of documents, through the special skill of Mr Cosmo Innes' with aid in the Maitland volume 'from his ablest coadjutor in Scottish archaeology, Mr Joseph Robertson'. There was for Burton 'something to our eyes extremely interesting' in the manner in which the Scottish universities had preserved through much political and social change 'characteristics of the university system, as it existed in all its grandeur of design in the middle ages'. The collection of 'remarkable papers' contained in the Club publications represented a rediscovery – 'opens up and presents, in valuable and full light' – the universities' particular historical trajectory as founded in 'the great system of the European universities'. This explained the retention of a Scottish cultural Latinity until the end of the seventeenth century, such that George Buchanan could emerge as the 'most illustrious writer in the Roman tongue' since the classical age. It also helped to explain the divergence from the English universities

---

[41] Innes Cosmo, ed., *Facsimiles of the national manuscripts of Scotland [. . .]*, 3 vols (Southampton: Ordnance Survey Office, 1867–72).

[42] Burton, *Book-Hunter*, pp. 377–9, 371; Gow, 'Introduction', in Billings, *Baronial Antiquities*, pp. ix–x.

which had failed to retain anything of the 'broad liberal basis' of the continental tradition still traceable in Scotland.[43]

The efforts of the records scholars played a significant part in revising previous historiographic judgements on the medieval world generally and on the perception of medieval Scotland. In his review of the university records publications, Burton recognised that in the thirteenth to fifteenth centuries the church had promoted learning with 'zealous energy', allowing a 'remarkable' and 'admirable' constitutional independence to the universities. This had created an international 'freemasonry of intellect' and a cosmopolitanism that the nineteenth century could not match, but should regard 'with a respectful awe'. A number of the ideas in these articles would resurface in his later *History*. They echoed his perception of the medieval world in his article on Billings: those picturesque architectural depictions provided 'a register of what has been achieved in the great medieval art throughout Scotland'. This openness to the merits of the pre-Reformation world has been partly attributed to the Episcopalianism that both Innes and Burton shared with various other leading scholars of the period. However, while recognising this, Richard Marsden also traced changing attitudes and much greater attention to Scotland's medieval heritage among prominent Presbyterian writers on ecclesiastical history from the mid-nineteenth century: this did not accord, Marsden observed, with the notion that 'Enlightenment obsession with societal progress' was still alienating the Scots from their past.[44]

Burton was highly attuned to the implications and promise that the productions of the new records scholars held out for narrative history. He particularly commended Innes as the scholar 'who found and taught the secret of extracting from ecclesiastical chartularies, and other early records, the light they throw upon the social condition of their times'.[45]

---

[43] Cosmo Innes, ed., *Munimenta Alme Universitatis Glasguensis: Records of the University of Glasgow From Its Foundation Till 1727*, 4 vols (Glasgow: Maitland Club, 1854); Cosmo Innes, ed., *Fasti Aberdonenses: Selections from the Records of the University and King's College of Aberdeen 1494–1854* (Aberdeen: Spalding Club, 1854); [John Hill Burton], 'Student Life in Scotland', *BM* 76 (1854), 135–50 and 422–35 (pp. 135–6).

[44] [Burton], 'Student Life', pp. 138–9; Burton, *HOS* (1873), III, pp. 402–-7, 415–17; [Burton], 'Baronial and Ecclesiastical Antiquities', p. 222; Marsden, *Cosmo Innes*, pp. 115–26.

[45] [Burton], 'Student Life', p. 136; Burton, *Book-Hunter*, pp. 278–9.

This appreciation of the value of such 'extractions' in providing new insights for narrative history meant that in Burton's own later *magnum opus*, several centuries could be incorporated in a much more positive light within the national annals. For Burton (and certainly Innes) this was particularly the case in the three centuries following the millennium. In his second volume, he complemented the narrative of events in this period with chapters that explored the earliest developments in law, the feudal parliament, the rise of the burghs, economic advances and cultural achievement.[46] His conclusion was that the nation was advancing in civilisation at a steady pace in almost all of these fields. For instance, Burton recorded the substantial growth in Scotland's 'trading and municipal power'. The northern burghs began aspiring to the power of the Hanseatic towns of the Baltic, while the strength of the 'burghal parliament' developed among the Royal Burghs in the south had been tenacious enough to survive into the nineteenth century. The nation's complicated trade tariff was itself 'a symptom of wealth and civilisation', while agricultural practice had become 'systematic and under regulation and supervision'. More generally, adopting a methodology of scrutinising gleanings from official records, trade regulations and religious chartularies, Burton proceeded to describe 'many incidental matters that speak of comfort and wealth [. . .] in old Scots life'.[47]

One of the most convincing aspects of this civilisational progress was in the evidence that could be drawn from developments in architecture, for Burton a prime indicator of social development where written records were scarce. The earliest 'fine specimens' of baronial architecture like Bothwell, Kildrummie and Dirleton he thought may have been built by English invaders, though there was no trace of the great Norman fortresses, with their gothic architectural features, that had kept England in subjection. On the other hand, he noted that 'ecclesiastical buildings in that style in Scotland are abundant and magnificent'. The impressive abbeys of Dunfermline, Arbroath, Jedburgh, Kelso and Coldingham were 'great studies for the historical architect'. Burton was quite conscious of the historiographic shift that such evidence suggested. The early medieval centuries should not be viewed according to the subsisting view of the Scottish medieval world as characterised by social chaos and a lack of civilisation:

---

[46] Burton, *HOS* (1873), II, chapters XVI and XVII.
[47] Burton, *HOS* (1873), II, pp. 88–92, 105–10.

> These noble buildings could not have been raised in a country where there did not exist riches. It will not harmonise with the proverbial way of dealing with the subsequent condition of the country to say it, but yet I cannot but believe that Scotland was a wealthy country for that day.[48]

The historiographic revision is underscored in quoting Cosmo Innes's observation that the fine architecture of religious houses like Kelso was proof of the skill and taste of the builders 'at a period which the confidence of modern times has proclaimed dark and degraded'. Indeed, it is clear from Burton's citations that many of these positive assessments of progress in Scotland in the early medieval centuries owed a great deal to the records scholarship and writings of Innes.[49]

The impact of recent efforts in records scholarship was not limited to these elements of socio-economic and cultural development. As we have seen, besides his many editions of chartularies and family records, Innes had succeeded in completing Thomas Thomson's work and finally publishing the missing first volume of the *APS*, covering the period 1124–1423. The approach both men had followed in arranging the surviving material, as well as Innes's emphasis on the development of Scottish statute law rather than on the parliament as a representative body, permitted a different historical perspective to the one reflected in the devalorising dismissals of eighteenth-century historians and jurists:

> [t]he nation did indeed have its own legal and even constitutional history. The APS trumpeted that history by rendering obscure and distasteful sources orderly and palatable, and by extending the evidentially sound origins of Scottish law and thereby Scottish society back to the twelfth century.[50]

Burton maintained that Scottish 'statute law' only began to develop properly from the early fifteenth century when James I returned from England having observed English practice. Nevertheless, in his account of the period from 1000–1290, he does trace the origins of the Scottish feudal parliament from the later thirteenth century, as well as forms of early law like the Code of the Burgher Corporations, citing Innes's preface to Volume I of the *APS*. Innes himself tended to view the period after the Wars of Scottish Independence (1296–1357) as one in which the nation's progress stalled and Scottish history saw a declension into feudal conflict and ecclesiastical corruption leading to the Reformation.

---

[48] Ibid., pp. 99–102, 105.
[49] Ibid., pp. 87, footnote 1; p. 96, footnote 1; p. 97, footnote 1; p. 105 footnote 1; p. 107, footnote 4; p. 109, footnote 1; p. 110, footnotes 1 and 2.
[50] Marsden, *Cosmo Innes*, p. 85.

Burton was much influenced by Innes and certainly shared the 'Teutonist' thinking that, at least partly, lay behind such judgements. For Burton, Scotland would not have the opportunity for comparable social progress until the long conflict with England ended in 1707.[51]

In practice, Burton's *History* went on to present a much more nuanced and differentiated picture. He certainly did maintain that during the long conflict with England, for much of the period from 1350 to the Reformation there was little evidence of 'material progress' in wealth-creating fields like trade and manufacturing; and in architecture only Melrose Abbey could compare with the earlier great religious foundations.[52] Yet his account also valorised prominent aspects of institutional and cultural achievement in the later medieval centuries, including the nation's constitutional development and its commitment to education and scholarship.

In a largely sympathetic account of the development of the Estates and of Scottish legal principles, he again drew on the *APS* and related records publications. It was unhistorical, he observed, to make invidious comparisons on the basis of 'modern English constitutional notions' and so infer 'that the Estates of Scotland were not a properly constitutional parliament'. The later medieval Estates had maintained a close control on the royal prerogative, and although its 'permanent committees', particularly the Lords of the Articles, had later been 'sometimes invaded or perverted', they were for long a reasonable attempt to secure the benefits of separate parliamentary chambers. The Estates had also striven against royal attempts to monopolise justice, and periodically asserted an appellate power over the judgments of the king's justiciars through the Lords Auditors 'holding delegated power from the Estates as the supreme court of Parliament'. The elements of Burton's account relating to the Estates' standing committees clearly rely on other source editions associated with the *APS*, which Thomas Thomson had managed to publish in 1839, the *Acta Auditorum* and *Acta Dominorum Consilii*.[53]

Burton paid particular attention to the democratic spirit of the Scottish system in its adoption of civil law, 'a flexible system [. . .] easily adaptable to the desires of a free people', which the English were forced to draw on

---

[51] Burton, *HOS* (1873), II, p. 60, footnote 1; p. 65, footnote 1; pp. 80–1, footnote 1; p. 111.

[52] Ibid., III, pp. 430, 438–40.

[53] Ibid., III, pp. 386–99, including footnotes at pp. 390–4; Thomas Thomson, ed., *The Acts of the Lords Auditors of Causes and Complaints: [. . .]* and *The Acts of the Lords of Council in Civil Causes [. . .]* (London: House of Commons, 1839).

'for relief from the strange vagaries and utter injustices committed by the chaotic common law when let loose with absolute power'. The Scottish 'adaptation' had kept to the fore 'the broad principle that all are equal in the eye of the law':

> There is no precedent for privilege of peerage, for forest law, or for game law, to be found there; hence it suited Scotland, where the spirit of community did not readily adapt itself to the prerogatives of class, which the Normans had established in England. There are but scant vestiges of this spirit in the old customs of Scotland [. . .]. Cultivated lands and crops, whoever owned them, were protected by the exaction of damages or recompense from any one doing damage to them. We have seen how certain French visitors were alike amazed and indignant when they found such claims asserted by very peasants.[54]

Perhaps prompted by his early radicalism, Burton reiterated this early commitment to legal principles and arrangements (much noted by later reviewers) that sought to protect the weak: it was not 'in the spirit of the constitution' to establish the legal exemptions and privileges that were introduced in England and 'have it in their nature to set class against class'. In Burton's presentation of the later medieval period, this bound people and nation together in an almost organic and unique fashion:

> the best testimony to the character of the national institutions is to be found in the tenacity of the people in holding to their 'auld laws and lovable customs'. [. . .] As yet we have come across no contest of class against class. It would be difficult to trace the history of any other part of Europe, through the same centuries, without finding this sort of testimony to the dissatisfaction of the people with the institutions within which they lived. [. . .] Whether or not the Scots were, as some have held, subjected to a hard feudalism, their condition seems to have been congenial to them. High and low, they fought together, and were of one mind[.][55]

At the same time Burton's account underscored the efforts at this time – as in 'almost all the periods of the history of Scotland' – to high levels of literacy and scholarship. This was true of school education but further attested in the foundation of three universities in the course of the fifteenth century. This helped to explain why universities throughout Europe later 'swarmed with learned Scotsmen'. As he had previously done in his *Blackwood's* review of the Maitland and Spalding Club volumes discussed above, Burton observed that this needed

---

[54] Burton, *HOS* (1873), III, p. 396.
[55] Ibid., pp. 398–9.

to be understood in terms of the Scottish universities' close association with 'the great confederation of literary republics' represented by the medieval continental universities: these Scottish seats of learning were regarded by the church as 'the same in rank' as the foundations in Paris or Bologna, and as far as possible endowed with the same 'wealth and grandeur'. This provided Scots scholars with 'privileges of citizenship and community over Europe, the breadth and fullness of which it is difficult now to realise'.[56]

This attention to the European dimension in scholarship anticipates how Burton's account of the later medieval and early modern centuries would come to incorporate further positive perspectives on the national past centring on the international significance of Scottish history and culture. It is appropriate before leaving the influence of the book clubs and the new records scholarship to trace the origins of this broader perspective and positioning of the nation in history, since it had much to do with Burton's response to the research efforts of foreign, particularly French, scholars whose labours were not only appreciated but also published by the clubs. Between 1856 and 1863, years in which he became fully committed to the composition of a national history, Burton published seven substantial articles, all but one in *Blackwood's*, that addressed a variety of aspects of the participation of Scotland and the Scots in broader European history.[57]

Three of the articles were based on notices of works by the French scholars Alexandre Teulet and Francisque Michel. Both men first visited Scotland in the late 1830s and established close relations with David Laing, long-time secretary of the elite Bannatyne, one of the clubs that supported the publication of their work. Michel in particular maintained regular contact with Laing over the ensuing decades and sought to keep in touch with many other leading records and book club figures including Thomas Thomson, David Irving and W. B. D. Turnbull, secretary of the Abbotsford Club, which also supported publications by both Frenchmen. Michel revived these contacts during visits to Edinburgh in the mid-to-late 1850s and formed new relationships with the younger

---

[56] Ibid., pp. 399–407.
[57] [John Hill Burton], 'France and Scotland', *NBR* 24 (1856), 289–324; 'The Scot Abroad: The Man of Letters' *BM* 79 (1856), 439–55; 'The Scot Abroad: The Man of Council', *BM* 80 (1856), 91–103; 'The Scot Abroad: The Man of Art' *BM* 80 (1856), 548–63; 'The French on Queen Mary', *BM* 86 (1859), 516–36; 'The Scot in France', *BM* 92 (1862), 543–70; 'The Frank in Scotland', *BM* 93 (1863), 330–54.

generation of Scottish researchers including Burton's friends J. T. Gibson-Craig, Cosmo Innes and Joseph Robertson. In the intervening decades Michel had not been slacking, and these later visits were soon followed by the publication in 1862 of his monumental two-volume compendium of source documents *Les Écossais en France, Les Français en Écosse*. Michel had hoped that the Bannatyne would support the publication, but in the event, it was published in London.[58]

Teulet had been more fortunate, and through the previous decade the Bannatyne had brought out his three-volume compilation *Papiers d'État* [. . .] (1851–60), also exhaustive but dealing specifically with the sixteenth century. Burton's review of the first two of these volumes appeared in the *North British Review* in February 1856. He began by regretting that while modern scholarship had destroyed the 'simple, ancient nationality' of Scotland founded on myth and legend there had been no attempt at a reconstruction to show how 'the realm of the Bruces and Stewarts' had managed to fashion 'a separate nationality out of chaos'. Burton was, then, focusing on the period from the early fourteenth to the seventeenth century, when for Innes decline had set in and when for others, too, Scottish history represented the story of an obscure state ravaged by feudal strife and religious discord, and largely peripheral to mainstream European history. However, the range of sources uncovered and presented by the 'French antiquaries' helped to ensure that he would later convey a richer, more positive sense of the role of Scotland and the Scots, one located much more centrally within the history of early modern Europe. This is anticipated early in his consideration of Teulet's volumes, which for Burton stimulated a sense of Scotland's significance on the international stage: history tended to focus on the individual development of states and their conflicts with each other but here was an international alliance that might be accounted 'one of the most exciting and pleasing chapters in the history of modern Europe'. The long friendship of Scotland and France was of 'signal interest for its historical peculiarities', and had been highly influential in the development of European states.[59]

---

[58] Claudine I. Wilson, 'Francisque Michel and His Scottish Friends', *The Modern Language Review* 30 (1935), 26–35; [Jean Baptiste Alexandre Théodore Teulet], ed., *Inventaire chronologique des documents relatifs à l'histoire d'Écosse* [. . .] (Edinburgh: Abbotsford Club, 1839); Francisque Michel, ed., *Le Roman des Aventures de Fregus* [. . .] (Edinburgh: Abbotsford Club, 1841); Francisque-Michel, *Les Écossais en France, Les Français en Écosse* (London: Trübner, 1862).
[59] [Jean Baptiste Alexandre Théodore Teulet], *Papiers d'État*, [. . .], 3 vols (Edinburgh: Bannatyne Club, 1851–60); Burton, 'France and Scotland', pp. 289–90.

This was a perspective that Burton clearly found striking and new. It seems likely that he took his cue for a revisionist view of the international significance of Scotland's history from Teulet's own observations. Burton expressed great admiration for Teulet's skills in the new scientific antiquarianism, but he also commended the French scholar for a broader historical understanding, demonstrated in the way he had organised which presented the mass of material and as Burton observed was also evident in his preface. There, Teulet had emphasised that the reliance on original documents, avoiding history based on 'inexact or prejudiced narratives', was particularly required in the sixteenth century, during which Europe had been swept by political and religious passions and 'marked by one of the greatest movements of the human mind'. But he also went on to emphasise that this portentous age was one in which Scotland had acted a 'most important part in the history of Europe'. Teulet would later reiterate the point in the introductory 'Advertisement' to his third and final volume, which extended the international reach to incorporate new and original source material relating to Scotland from the Spanish archives. This should allow narrative historians, Teulet observed, to pursue a fresh approach to the policy of Philip II, 'one of the most powerful princes in Christendom [. . .] in regard to a Queen and State (Scotland) at that time of no little weight in the affairs of Europe'.[60]

Burton was clearly aware of Teulet's third Bannatyne volume when he contributed a further article to *Blackwood's* in November 1859 on various books that had been published by French scholars on Queen Mary. Here he expressed a conviction that the material that was emerging would 'change the aspect of the history of the period in the hands of whoever may next write it': modern records scholarship, he continued, was often permitting a better understanding of the past the further it receded, and correcting 'intermediate historians'. Burton was coming to the conviction that to properly understand 'the wondrous events of this period in Scotland, we must look at them not merely at home but from the centre of European politics': in that context Scottish history in the period became 'far less of a shambles' than when viewed in isolation. Indeed, he continued, the French scholars had made plain 'the very close connection between the fate of the Queen of Scots and the marvellous events which in her day reconstructed the map of Europe'. It had been an epoch of revolutions and the rise and fall of empires, and 'all this mighty drama went on with this young queen of a small northern

[60] Teulet, *Papiers d'État*, I, pp. ii, iv; II, p. ii.

country, almost as much the centre and pivot of the whole as the heroine of a romance is the centre of all its versatile and marvellous combinations'. As this passage anticipates, Burton would not exclude an aura of romance and high drama from his account of Mary and her times. However, this was balanced by a sense of the centrality of the nation's role in one of the great epochs of change across Europe. By setting the history of Scotland in a broader context, 'it becomes at once obvious how much for Europe and the future rested on her destinies'.[61]

Soon after his 1856 review of Teulet's *Papiers d'État*, Burton published three of the articles referred to above, each with the prefix 'The Scot Abroad': the first focused on the achievements of men of literary renown, the second on those who had risen to high position in European states and armies and the third on contributors to art. The period they covered extended from the Wars of Independence to the eighteenth century. There is a good deal of 'nationality' in the articles. Although he accepted that the visual artists were concentrated on the later centuries, on broader culture his account celebrated achievements stretching from the dominance of Duns Scotus on a level with Aquinas in fifteenth-century thought to the leading role of Buchanan in sixteenth-century Latinity and to the Scots professors and medical men who had distinguished themselves in continental universities through much of the period. Burton waxed lyrical on 'the profusion of intellectual wealth which Scotland has cast abroad'. The second of these articles, on 'The Man of Council', had some overlap with Teulet's sixteenth century French material but extended across a broader timescale from those who led Scottish diplomatic and commercial initiatives in the Hanse, Holland and France from the early fourteenth century, up to the leading military and political roles filled by Scots in sixteenth- to eighteenth-century Sweden, Russia and France: if such reliance on foreigners raised questions about the patriotism of the rulers they served, it should nevertheless be 'a just object of pride' that so many Scots had achieved such high offices.[62]

Some years later, in 1862–3, Burton reviewed Michel's two volumes for *Blackwood's*. He recognised how much greater was the achievement of the French scholar who had 'ploughed up the field' of source materials where Burton's own earlier articles had merely 'turned a sod or two'. Michel's scope extended from the time of Charlemagne to the age of Scott. Burton was typically sarcastic on the supposed early contact with

---

[61] Burton, 'The French on Queen Mary', pp. 518, 521.
[62] Burton, 'Man of Letters, p. 455; Burton, 'Man of Council', p. 94.

the Carolingian emperor, but Michel's new materials reinforced his sense of the international significance of Scotland's role in Europe, particularly through the alliance with France: from the time of the Hundred Years War, the two countries had become 'united together by ties so strong, both in romantic interest and political importance, to the destinies of Europe, [. . .].' Later he repeated that in the centuries after the Wars of Independence, the Scottish-French alliance would impact substantially on 'the destinies of the European nations'.[63]

Burton drew partly on Teulet but particularly on Michel in his highly successful *The Scot Abroad* (2 vols, 1864), which partly recycled his review articles and elaborated on Scottish achievements within the European world from early medieval times to the eighteenth century, particularly when opportunities were limited at home. Burton's main *History* commenced publication just three years later, so that *The Scot Abroad*, periodically reissued when the *History* itself was republished, in effect constituted a companion work. It dealt extensively with the 'Ancient League' with France, from political and military aspects to legal and ethnological survivals reflecting the long history of the alliance. However, the work included a range of other Scottish cultural involvements and achievements across the continent over the centuries, supplementing Burton's effort in the main *History* to incorporate subject matter beyond the political and constitutional narrative, as well as to underscore Scotland's European significance. There is proper acknowledgement in *The Scot Abroad* of his debts to both French writers including the manner in which Teulet had arranged his material so as to 'bring out momentous historical truths in their due series'. Burton was quite conscious of the potential impact of such efforts on the presentation of Scottish history:

> In the hands of the first historian who has the fortune to make ample use of them, these documents will disperse the secluded and parochial atmosphere that hangs about the history of Scotland, and show how the fate of Europe in general turned upon the pivot of the destinies of our country.[64]

The first historian to make use of them would be John Hill Burton, and in his national *History* it was now Teulet's material in particular on which Burton drew to emphasise Scotland's continuing international significance

---

[63] Burton, 'Scot in France', pp. 544, 546.
[64] John Hill Burton, *The Scot Abroad*, 2 vols (Edinburgh: Blackwood, 1864), I, p. 235. On broader cultural history, see Vol. I, ch. V, pp. 236–328; and Vol. II, ch. I, 'The Scholar and the Author', pp. 1–130, and ch. IV 'The Artist', pp. 309–69. *The Scot Abroad* was reissued in 1881, 1898 and 1900.

in political history after the Hundred Years War and throughout the sixteenth century. Even after Flodden, his account emphasised that France 'expressed great anxiety to keep up the ancient league', citing the new sources as demonstrating Scotland's active role in the interplay of broader European politics including French ambitions of 'competing with Charles V for the empire'. Burton was enabled to illustrate the nation's continuing interaction with France at the highest level, for instance in highlighting the potential impact of James V's marriage options on 'the destinies of Europe', ending with his admission to the French royal family. Later, Burton drew substantially on Teulet's diplomatic source material, as well as the recent work on Mary and Catherine de Medici by his compatriot Pierre-Adolphe Chéruel, to tie in many of the events in Scotland around Mary's reign to European-wide diplomatic, dynastic and religious movements.[65]

This allowed Burton, for instance, to elaborate on the interactions of the two sides at Carberry Hill – the confrontation in June 1567 between an alliance of Scottish Protestant 'Lords of the Congretation' and the forces of Queen Mary, which ultimately led to her exile – as a kind of international diplomatic negotiation. Previous historians like William Robertson and P. F. Tytler were aware that the French ambassador, Le Croc, was 'in the field' but gave him only a brief mention and the whole engagement little more. Burton devotes four or five pages to what he presents as the 'Conference at Carberry', highlighting Le Croc's intervention as driven by concern for the impact on international relations.[66] A sense of Scotland's significance and participation in a Europe-wide dynastic and religious struggle could be evidenced from both the general correspondence that had been uncovered on the machinations of Catherine de Medici and more in-depth material such as the memoir of her emissary Castelnau de Mauvissière, sent north from his mission to England in 1565 in response to Mary's demands for aid from France. Burton was always keen on new evidence that shone 'light' on previously obscure machineries in history and was particularly enthused by Castelnau's lengthy record, which having 'only recently become known, throws a powerful light on the inner workings of the political mechanism'.[67]

---

[65] Burton, *HOS* (1873), III, pp. 86, 93–4, 131–2, 163–6; IV, pp 90–100; A. Chéruel, *Marie Stuart et Catherine de Médicis: Étude Historique sur les Relations de la France et de l'Écosse dans la Seconde Moitié du XVIe Siècle* (Paris: Hachette, 1858).

[66] Robertson, *History of Scotland*, II, pp. 83–4; Tytler, *History*, III, p. 255; Burton, *HOS* (1873), IV, pp. 241–6.

[67] Burton, *HOS* (1873), IV, pp. 127–9, and footnote, p. 129.

For Burton, most portentously, the materials revealed, or brought into clear relief, a series of events that began with a shift in French policy towards Scotland around the time of Mary's first marriage to Francis II in 1558. In its imperial ambitions and continental rivalries, France seemed to be viewing the country less as the ally of old and more as a province to be ruled and even annexed. This was not lost on the Protestant 'Lords of the Congregation' and was one of the 'great external political events' that embedded the Scottish Reformation and led to rapprochement with England. However, this historic outcome was never inevitable and Burton's account goes on to highlight Mary's active role in seeking to orchestrate intervention from the Catholic powers on behalf of the old religion and her own traduced royalty. Teulet had turned up more reliable and extensive evidence of Mary's power and European-wide significance, from details of her great wealth as dowager Queen of France to the extent of her secret communications with continental contacts.[68]

Burton was highly appreciative of the work of the French scholars in revealing so much additional evidence relating to Scottish history, and he was positive about the revelations: 'we are sure of coming out well in all inquiries into our national history and connections'; their work had 'not stripped a leaf from the national laurels', and rather 'revealed their real freshness and brightness'. And he would make good use of them as he had predicted, 'to disperse the secluded and parochial atmosphere that hangs about the history of Scotland'. However, when this new material first appeared in the 1850s and early 1860s, Burton lamented that few would follow the French scholars into the 'dreary wastes and rugged wildernesses' of their researches (an outcome made more certain by the fact that their great source compilations were almost entirely in French – which, however, he himself seems to have read fluently). Similarly, Burton and his close friends were well aware that the issue applied as much to the great accumulation of domestic source material that had been amassed in the first half of the century. All certainly shared a romantic interest in many of the new materials in and for themselves as fascinating reflections of bygone times. But at the end of the day, that is what they might remain. Only a scattering of scholars and collectors would benefit from the great effort that had been made.[69]

And a great effort had been made, utilising structures comparable to those that facilitated the composition of national histories in much

---

[68] Ibid., III, pp. 292–8; IV, pp. 96–7, 265–6, 388–9, 413.
[69] Burton, 'Frank in Scotland', p. 350.

of Europe. Elsewhere national historical associations had promoted the publication of historical journals. This was not required in an Edinburgh that was the home of major periodicals carrying many articles on history, and increasingly, as Burton's contributions to *Blackwood's* attested, on Scottish history. In addition, the accumulating publications of the book clubs had made available a repository of the historical source editions that were typically 'of vital importance in fostering national history across Europe. [. . .] in many places the origins of publishing medieval sources lie in the early nineteenth century.'[70] This was certainly true in Scotland, the effort extending well beyond the medieval sources. However, as Innes ruefully observed in the introduction to his 1861 *Sketches*, 'the reading public' were largely unaware of the interpretative prefaces he had contributed to so many source editions: the Book Club publications, he observed, were never intended to be 'popular', and even amongst the 'small proportion of the public' who received them 'the large quartos sleep undisturbed on the library shelf'. In his review of the university records published by the Maitland and Spalding Clubs, Burton echoed Innes's observations on such productions. They were not books to be enjoyed 'at the winter fireside': apart from the prefaces, neither they nor the many ecclesiastical 'chartularies' that Innes himself had so carefully edited 'profess to be readable books' and had 'all the substantive dryness of records'. Yet 'imbedded within them' lay the materials from which general social history could be fashioned.[71]

As Burton recalled in the preface to his greatest work, he had watched through these decades as there accumulated 'heaping over every existing history of Scotland a mass of fresh material for its reconstruction'. At an earlier stage, Joseph Robertson had seen the significance of the new, objective and empirical research into records and remains as ultimately a preparation for a new and better narrative history. By 1860 the sources were available to pursue such an endeavour. Burton always thought Robertson's knowledge of the subject made him the obvious choice for the job, but he never obliged. Innes's two books of historical *Sketches* were just that, valuable but fragmentary essays focused on a number of specific, largely medieval themes. It was Burton himself, evidently with

---

[70] Stephan Berger with Christoph Conrad, *The Past as History: National Identity and Historical Consciousness in Modern Europe* (Basingstoke: Palgrave Macmillan, 2015), pp. 168–70.
[71] Burton, 'Student Life', p. 136.

some regular reassurance from John Blackwood of a Sunday afternoon, who would supply 'the national want'.[72]

The great, half-century-long effort by the book clubs, the records scholars and the enterprising publishers had indeed made available a deep repository of new material on which to found a reworking of the nation's past. In some specific instances, the new sources would of themselves determine how the traditional narrative would change or be augmented – the very availability in a reasonably ordered and printed form of early medieval constitutional sources, for instance, or the new perspectives facilitated by evidence drawn out of the French and Spanish archives. Yet this alone is insufficient to explain the success of Burton's greatest work as a national history. Taking a more comprehensive perspective, the following four chapters analyse the eight-volume *History* as a whole in terms of four major themes, which are in each case related to the historian's engagement across a remarkably heterogenous range of experience and influences within the social and cultural world of his time, through which he conveyed the new material in ways recognisable to and admired by a readership which shared that world.

---

[72] Burton, *HOS* (1873), I, p. vii; D. J. Withrington, 'Aberdeen Antiquaries: The Founding of the Spalding Club in 1839', *Aberdeen University Review* 44 (1971), 42–55, p. 47.

4

Utilitarian History

'A SCEPTICAL AND FAITHLESS INQUIRER'

IN CERTAIN SECTIONS OF his *History*, Burton adopts a noticeably more sober, sceptical and didactic tone than in others. His scepticism, expressed in relation to the use of sources by previous Scottish historians and antiquarians, as well as to historiographic 'partiality' and to 'conjectural' approaches, is complemented in periodic, confident endorsements of empiricism and inductive reasoning. At the same time, he is critical of works in which he believes such thinking has overreached itself and begun to rear up an 'artificial' or mechanistic historical positivism. In what – for one steeped in radical and reformist movements through the middle decades of the nineteenth century – might be viewed as a predictable reflex, where he endeavours to have history teach by example, his touchstone is the triumph of the 'practical' course of action presented as the obverse of the abstruse and speculative.

These tendencies run in veins throughout the *History*, though his scepticism perhaps appears most explicitly and extensively in his first two volumes: Volume I covers the period from Agricola's Invasion in AD 80 until the Treaty of Falaise in 1174 and Volume II carries on to the death of James II at the siege of Roxburgh in 1460. This is understandable, since in these centuries lay the greatest challenges in deciphering and deconstructing source material and providing what Burton considered appropriate evidential underpinning for his narrative. He issues regular reminders to his readers of the unreliability of many of the traditional sources – from the 'fabulous' historians of the medieval/early modern period to the obsessive antiquarians of the eighteenth and early nineteenth centuries – and the need to base any historical claims on empirical foundation. The sources he regarded as 'fabulous' included earlier medieval works like the metrical *Orygynale Cronikil of Scotland* by the fourteenth-century poet Andrew Wynton and the fifteenth-century *Scotichronicon* compiled by Walter Bower and John of Fordun, as well as later contributions claiming to trace the nation's complete history, such as the *Scotorum historia* (1527) of Hector Boece and George Buchanan's *Rerum Scoticarum historia* (1582). Burton made a point of reminding his readers that these had been written in partial terms to serve contemporary medieval or early modern royal masters, and had uncritically accepted 'fables' of Scotland's origins in the distant past to legitimate the nation's claim to an existence that was in reality often under threat.[1]

There is some scathing commentary in his first volume on the obsessiveness of recent antiquarian writers indulging, on minimal evidence, their exotic theories on sculptured stone symbols or the nature of Druidism. In another instance the 'unintelligible pedantry' of the antiquarians and their controversies on the origin and nature of the Pictish language attracts his ire:

> Scott saw its ludicrous proportions; and it is likely that posterity will remember the Pictish question in the discussion between Monkbarns and Sir Arthur Wardour after the volumes of Whitaker, Goodall, Pinkerton, Chalmers, Ritson, and Grant have been long entombed in their proper shelves.

In little more than a sentence, almost every significant historical-antiquarian writer on such subjects over the previous hundred years is swept up and buried in the cob-webbed depths of the library. Figures like John Pinkerton, George Chalmers and Joseph Ritson had indeed engaged in bitter controversies over the nation's roots on the supposed linguistic evidence of the Celtic or gothic origins of the Pictish people.[2] However, Burton was anxious to emphasise that a sceptical view of such antiquarian obsessions was in no way a criticism of 'the science of etymology'. The problem lay in the failure to search out suitable empirical underpinning: 'The lesson it teaches is not to ask of a science what it cannot give. Etymology can only profitably accompany a substructure of facts, which it harmonises and adorns', otherwise, 'it runs wild, and is lost in abstraction.' His own position, he makes clear, will be that of a 'sceptical and faithless inquirer', interested only in subject matter that 'does not yield an immediate harvest to the bold guesser, but must be extracted by toilsome inductive criticism'.[3]

---

[1] Burton, *HOS* (1873), I, p. 122, footnote 1; p. 356, footnote 3; III, pp. 413–17.
[2] Ferguson, *Identity of the Scottish Nation*, pp. 250–80.
[3] Burton, *HOS* (1873), I, pp. 146–50, 195, 210–11.

In his discussion of contemporary thinking on the 'Unrecorded Ages'– prehistory – he considered it reasonable that there had been a broad division into the stone, bronze and iron periods because this had been arrived at 'by a method thoroughly philosophical, according to old rules, in as far as the first process has been an extensive analysis of phenomena, and the next an induction from the results of the analysis'. However, a more in-depth understanding of these epochs and the rationale of their sequence had not yet been achieved and should not be the subject of speculation. In this passage, Burton actually goes on to summarise briefly what a 'conjectural history' attempt at this might look like – 'Let us set out in the method of the moralists and political philosophers of the last century' – only to dismiss it as historiographic old hat: '[t]he northern archaeologists, however, knew that the day for such vague systems was over, and they had conceived a more ambitious project'. Seeking to understand early institutions by conjecture and analogy would no longer do: 'the philosophical method of adjusting these things from what is deemed knowledge of human nature, and the habits of barbarous and primitive communities, is not so satisfactory as it used to be.'[4]

He clearly admired the Scandinavian scholars – 'the northern archaeologists' – who were in close touch with Burton's friends in the Scottish Society of Antiquaries and had been advancing a more critical approach to prehistoric remains and laying the foundations of a new prehistoric taxonomy. He appears to have visited the most advanced national institution, the Museum of Antiquities in Copenhagen, and was certainly knowledgeable about its collections. What he admired in their work was its reliance on empirical analysis of 'the relics themselves', the artefacts and associated survivals, as the foundation of their thinking. Even in relation to these efforts however his scepticism urged caution: at least so far, the evidence was 'too narrow for conclusions so grand'.[5]

Burton's sceptical attitude regarding previous interpretations of the Scottish past continues into his second volume, which incorporates a lengthy revisionist presentation of what he considered Edward I's policy towards Scotland and much of the first half of Volume II gives an impression of the historian in didactic mode. Even compared to

---

[4] Ibid., I, pp. 125, 353–4.
[5] Marinell Ash, '"A Fine Genial Hearty Band": David Laing, Daniel Wilson and Scottish Archaeology', in *The Scottish Antiquarian Tradition: Essays to mark the bicentenary of the Society of Antiquaries of Scotland and its Museum, 1780–1980*, ed. A. S. Bell (Edinburgh: John Donald, 1981), pp. 86–113 (pp. 101–2); Burton, HOS (1873) I, pp. 130–1 and footnote 1, p. 131.

Volume I and certainly to later parts of the *History*, there is much less room for incident, stories and colourful description. The didacticism partly founds on racially based assumptions and explanations as to how Scottish history should be perceived in the period, particularly the Teutonist ideas with which Burton is often associated. In his assessment the reign of Malcolm III (1058–93) and his wife Margaret, a scion of the exiled English Saxon royal line, was a 'turning point' at which a previously Celtic court became predominantly Saxon 'with a dash of Norman to adorn it'. And he presents Scottish social, political and legal structures of the next two centuries as 'in spirit the same as the English', essentially because of their shared Anglo-Saxon heritage.[6]

Allied to his insistence that history should be founded on credible facts and inductive reasoning, and that it should abjure conjectural or abstract thinking, his approach to events themselves reflects a concomitant admiration for practical thought and actions. Where periodically he is most obviously in didactic mode and has history 'teaching by example', there is both critique of speculative thinking and conversely illustration of the value of the practical. For this reason, he would have viewed the 'dash of Norman' that he discerned appearing at Malcolm's court as no bad thing: for Burton, the irruption of the Normans into Britain would have a lasting impact on Scottish history as well as English because 'the Norman brought the spirit and practice of organisation. He had learned it in a great school. He came last from the country which was the representative of Latin civilisation, and of the imperial organisation.' It was a legacy evidenced in 'those minute practical inquiries [. . .] in the wonderful record of Doomsday'. These notions inform his reappraisal of the greatest of the Norman rulers, Edward I. Far from his established characterisation as the 'Hammer of the Scots', his real ambition was just to be 'an organiser and reformer'. This was

> the real source of his severities. He saw before him the splendid vision of the British Isles under one scheme of strong orderly central government, blessing all classes of the community; and his fury when thwarted [. . .] drove him to cruelty.

It was the natural frustration of 'a thoroughly practical man'.[7]

The valorisation of practicality recurs as the *History* proceeds, particularly in its treatment of political history. Although, as we shall see,

---

[6] Burton, *HOS* (1873), II, pp. 57–8, 95–6, 104–5.
[7] Ibid., I, pp. 351–3; II, pp. 159, 221–4.

in many passages Burton's narrative reveals a fascination with elements of the Scottish past that are 'curious' or 'picturesque' and previously hidden in the sources, in the political sphere he is dismissive of events that had no 'practical conclusion' or outcome. For instance, in the convoluted machinations that characterised the period of the regents who successively ruled Scotland after Queen Mary's downfall in 1567, it was 'unnecessary to burden history' with matters that 'came to no practical issue'. Those who achieved some measure of success, like Regent Morton, did so as 'bold, crafty, practical in design, speedy in action'; in contrast, the head of the rival and doomed house of Hamilton is presented as characterised 'by his inability to steer through practical life that great wealth and influence with which fortune had endowed him'. Burton assessed the contribution of other potentially capable figures of the time, such as the ambitious courtier, Maitland of Lethington, or the humanist and constitutional writer George Buchanan in similar terms: too many of Lethington's abilities 'were rather rhetorical than practical', and though Buchanan's writings aspired to be 'practical works', in reality his oratorical 'flight' was 'too high and classical to give instruction on the practical working of the constitution of his country'.[8]

Later, in his fifth volume, Burton addressed the moves to take forward an incorporating Union after James VI's accession to the British crown in 1603. As always, he is sensitive to his audience, and aware that a 'full statement of the details of such a process is not always popular with readers '. However, certain 'political features' are worth attention, and in examining these his touchstone is again the 'practical'. Just as occurred a century later, as soon as commissioners were appointed on either side, the English became anxious about allowing the Scots participation in their foreign trade. Although this effort at union was unsuccessful, Burton commented that it did provide a 'practical service' to those involved later, in the sense of identifying and exploring the potential difficulties. It provided a lesson from history, a 'practical anticipation' of what not to do, which Burton illustrated through examining Francis Bacon's speech in support of the measure and comparing his ideas with later experience. Bacon's 'lofty and pensive eloquence' and 'contempt for paltry difficulties' had failed to provide 'any practical grasp' of what might be achieved and how to go about it. The opportunity was lost, too much high-flown oratory and vision again getting in the way. In the same vein, Burton commended in the following reign the 'practical utility' of the way the

---

[8] Ibid., V, pp. 97–9, 131–2, 139–40, 160, 165.

parliamentary Estates had been reorganised in 1639–40 after the abolition of episcopacy (again citing precedent in imperial Roman practice).[9]

There are recognisable elements of this discourse in Burton's account of the incorporating union during the Cromwellian Commonwealth of the 1640s. He pays particular attention to a comprehensive report produced for the new government on Scottish trade and shipping by one Thomas Tucker. Burton uses this document, quite appropriately, not only for its valuable historical content, but also as 'an interesting example of this spirit of the immediately practical, of which the Protectorate Government was full'. He expresses great admiration for a range of that administration's 'acts of material utility', indeed its anticipation of 'modern utility', in efforts to abolish feudal practices. Conversely, there may have been 'a theoretical discontent' at the situation and a desire among the Scottish populace to restore the king, but it 'had little active vitality, and perhaps it was in human nature, that the material prosperity of the people soothed such political irritation as came of mere abstract principles'.[10]

Burton had covered the period from 1689 to 1748 in his earlier two-volume *History of Scotland*, published in 1853. He used much of this material to complete his later eight-volume work, but it had become much longer than originally anticipated and he rewrote and compressed parts of the earlier version. So it is in the second volume of the 1853 publication that he delivered on his stated intention to provide an account of the Union process in much greater detail than had appeared before. In Burton's presentation, it could only have been secured through the peculiar abilities of 'the British people' to pursue a constitutionalist negotiation and bring it to a successful practical conclusion: 'continental nations' that were used to military or dynastic means of forming unions or empires would have regarded the proposed effort through negotiated agreement as 'utterly insane, as indeed it would have been, if laid before two nations less endowed with practical sense and business habits'. The

---

[9] Burton, *HOS* (1873), V, pp. 401, 408–9; VI, p. 283.

[10] Ibid., VII, pp. 55–7, 62. Burton's evidence was drawn from a source edition published by the Bannatyne Club, one of the many instances in which his volumes are indebted to the retrieval, over the previous half-century, of records bearing on Scottish history. It had been 'presented' to the Club by Burton's most enthusiastic mentor among the old Whigs, John Archibald Murray: *Report by Thomas Tucker upon the Settlement of the Revenues of Excise and Customs in Scotland, AD MDCLVI* (Edinburgh: Bannatyne Club, 1824).

joint meeting of commissioners had 'no known precedent in the annals of the world' – but 'the British people are unrivalled in the capacity of adjusting the views of collective bodies, presenting them in systematic order, and drawing from them clear, practical results'. The Scots' claim to equal trading privileges appeared the great stumbling block. The English might see this as a sacrifice, but in Burton's perception the real danger was to their practical cast of mind: since the consequences of the threat to their trade were uncertain, the issue 'became more theoretical and visionary in their eyes'. However, the problem was one 'founded, not on reality, but on artificial opinions, and it insensibly disappeared as it was practically handled'.[11]

For Burton it is typically the 'theoretical and visionary' that is contrasted with the practical, and can overwhelm it even if, as in the following instance, those who were visionary had a claim to respect. In his account of the later years of the Scottish Revolution parliament at the turn of the eighteenth century, Burton describes how, besides the older generation of politicians driven by 'expediency and party spirit', a younger 'patriotic' or 'national' party developed whose members 'said what they thought' and had the making of 'practical strugglers against political iniquity'. The opportunity was open to them, for 'they were placed in practical positions – they had votes in parliament, and they could make speeches there – a novel privilege, in which they indulged to excess'. The trouble was that '[t]heir principles were naturally vague and impracticable' – here in fact a particularly parlous combination of the 'visionary' and the 'theoretical', since they were distilled from 'a mixture of medieval chivalry and old speculative republicanism'. Inevitably then, though their patriotism had earned them the respect of posterity, they failed to 'bless their country with much of the practical fruit of beneficent legislation'. For Burton this was all perfectly personified in the head of the party, Andrew Fletcher of Saltoun, all of whose projects 'had a tendency to Utopianism; and it was the force of his general character, rather than the practicability of his suggestions, that made him a leader'. So, though he and his party had a significant influence on events, because they had no consistent 'practical objects', it was never decisive.[12]

It is noticeable that Burton often adopts this discourse when he is dealing with potential or actual Anglo-Scottish union: whether the aspirations of Edward I; the failed effort in 1603; the Cromwellian union; Fletcher

[11] Burton, *HOS* (1853), I, pp. 397–403.
[12] Ibid., I, pp. 258–63.

and the Patriots' federal ideas in 1703; or the actual Treaty of Union in 1707. The ultimate achievement was the triumph of the practical and the patient working through (not contempt for) 'paltry difficulties' – the setting aside of the visionary. Time and again it had been close, even for brief periods accomplished. But only in 1707 did it fully come to pass, and it was still under threat for some time afterwards. For this strand in Burton's cast of mind, the treaty had not come about through Godolphin's gold (he absolved the Scots politicians of the charge of bribery), nor the triumph of far-seeing statesmanship, nor even an inevitable recoalescing of Saxons; but rather the last in a series of unheroic, dogged efforts across the centuries to secure a desirable political utility through the actions of practical men.

THE AGE OF THE PRACTICAL

To understand the formative influences that shaped these veins of scepticism, empiricism and practicalism in the *History*, it is necessary to attend to Burton's early commitment, sustained through the 1830s and 1840s, to utilitarian ideas, and in particular his exposure to a steady shift in the endeavour of prominent utilitarians from merely editing specific Bentham texts or offering further theoretical exegesis on them, toward the implementation of social change in practice. In doing so, it is appropriate to recognise the significant role he played in advancing the reputation of major figures like Jeremy Bentham and David Hume as the great modern exponents of utilitarian thinking in a variety of ways that consciously aimed at a broader dissemination of their ideas to a wider reading public.

Arriving in Edinburgh in 1830 with his ideas and beliefs just in process of formation, he had been swept up in the enthusiasm for change. For many middle-class reformers who wished to see more root-and-branch social change, Bentham's ideas seemed to offer a more radical prescription than the limited reform envisaged by the Whigs. As we have seen, in the following years Burton was frequently in the company, or in regular correspondence, with Benthamites like Bowring and Edwin Chadwick as well as Weir and Tait in Scotland. His most substantial literary effort in these years centred directly on Bentham's *œuvre*, the collected *Works*, which John Bowring had been charged with producing. The edition with Tait as publisher came out in eleven volumes between 1838 and 1843, nominally under Bowring's 'superintendence'. However, Burton's editorial role was substantial, so that for over five years, already a supporter and familiar with Bentham in print, he read it all again with the addition of voluminous manuscript material. From the autumn of 1837, Burton was in regular correspondence with leading Benthamites like John Stuart

Mill, Richard Doane and Southwood Smith, as well as Chadwick, in relation to the project.[13]

This was partly because these individuals had been associated with specific Bentham works that had previously appeared as single publications and needed to be revisited and brought into relation with the new material being incorporated. From various observations in their letters, it seems clear that these figures, all of whom had been *protégés* and supporters of Bentham and had known him well, soon developed a confidence that Burton (who had never met him) could be entrusted with orchestrating the legacy of 'the Prophet'. Mill was appreciative of Burton's approach: in the autumn of 1838, he responded on an issue related to his original Introduction to Bentham's *Rational of Evidence*, advising that he had not considered the matter recently, so that 'once more I leave the matter to your discretion'. The same confidence is shown by Southwood Smith, who had taken responsibility for preparing the first volume of the *Christomathea*: since he had been unable to resolve a number of 'difficulties & doubts', he advised that he was also sending Bentham's original manuscript 'that we may have the advantage of your eye & mind to go over the doubtful passages'.[14]

Burton went further in his efforts to make Bentham's ideas accessible to a wide readership. In 1843, as the final volume of Bentham's *Works* appeared, he authored two related publications whose purpose was to 'mediate' between the reading public and the eleven weighty volumes issued by Tait. In the Introduction to his *Benthamiana*, he acknowledged that Bentham had come to be viewed as 'an unreadable author', but stated that he intended to introduce passages illustrating the 'rhetorical flourishes' that could also be found in Bentham's writings, though he was explicit in his intention to intersperse more difficult passages that would provide a fuller understanding of Bentham's thought. In his belt-and-braces effort to convey 'an outline of the Utilitarian Philosopher's system' to the public at large, Burton appended to the work an abridged version of the second publication he composed in the same year, *Introduction to the Study of the Works of Jeremy Bentham*.[15]

---

[13] Jeremy Bentham, *The Works of Jeremy Bentham [. . .]*, 11 vols (Edinburgh: William Tait, 1838–43); NLS MS 9391, fols 186–9, 204, 210; NLS MS 9392, fols 3–6, 38–9.

[14] NLS MS 9391, fols 196–7, 209; NLS MS 9392, fol. 7; Doane showed a similar confidence, NLS MS 9392, fol. 63.

[15] John Hill Burton, ed., *Benthamiana, or, Select Extracts from the Works of Jeremy Bentham [. . .]* (Edinburgh: William Tait, 1843), pp. viii–ix, xi, 347–405.

In the prefacing 'Advertisement' to the *Introduction*, one of the first points made was to emphasise the 'practicality' of Bentham's ideas, and this remained a recurrent theme: for instance, in demonstrating that Bentham's views of proper conduct in private and public life constituted a 'practical ethics'; or that his elucidation of the concept of 'Evidence' was such as to provide a legislature with 'the means of creating and applying to practical use a store of facts, covering the whole field of human action, and forming an experimental foundation' for the regulation of society. Bentham had approached his 'chief object', the improvement of government, as a 'practical philosopher', and in considering existing systems his aim was to mould 'established institutions and opinions to the best practical results'. Although Burton emphasised that Bentham's philosophy was best understood in terms of 'its reference to practice' and 'the extent to which it is acted upon', he did give some attention to its theoretical underpinning including the central 'greatest-happiness principle'. He noted that there had been 'references' to such a utilitarian principle in Aristotle, Beccaria and Priestley; but he was firmer in asserting that Bentham 'found the theory of utility to a certain extent promulgated by Hume'.[16]

Shortly after the final Bentham volumes were published, Burton began work on his most ambitious endeavour to date, the *Life and Correspondence of David Hume* (1846), also published by Tait. Burton was fortunate in that he was able to use and partly incorporate an archive of previously unpublished letters and other material that had been lodged with the Royal Society of Edinburgh on the death of the philosopher's nephew, Baron Hume. The work was positively reviewed, partly because Burton was perceived as maintaining a balanced handling of potentially contentious issues. At various points, Burton's exegesis on Hume's work suggests how it may have influenced his own approach to history. For instance, despite Hume's historiographic reputation as an apologist for the Stuarts, Burton admired the 'wonderful impartiality' to be found in his political *Essays*. Even if Hume did have a general partiality for monarchy, it was, 'a partiality of a calm utilitarian character, which would not be inconsistent with an equally great esteem for a well-ordered republic'. As we shall see, impartiality was one of the most admired attributes of

---

[16] John Hill Burton, *Introduction to the Study of the Works of Jeremy Bentham, by John Hill Burton, Advocate, One of the Editors of the Collected Edition* (Edinburgh: William Tait, 1843). See pp. 3–4 and footnote; pp. 43, 47. On the other thinkers, pp. 17–19.

Burton's own *History*. He also commended Hume as having been the first to give proper attention to the history of 'the people', their 'manners, and general social condition', an approach in which Burton would later be seen to have broken new ground in his Scottish history.[17]

Burton's commentary on Hume confirms that it helped to consolidate his own historical scepticism, as well as his conviction that whatever historical truths and conclusions could be drawn must depend for their credibility on solid empirical evidence. Both were required, and for Burton, Hume's central mistake in the *History of England* was a result of his scepticism being led astray, due to insufficient facts:

> Unquestionably the doubting or inquiring spirit is a valuable quality in a historian; for the narratives of human affairs are full of falsehoods, which it is the philosophical historian's function to discard. But the sifting will not be satisfactory, if the materials subjected to it have not been largely and laboriously collected; and the charge against Hume is that he applied it to imperfect data.

It was our 'enlarged knowledge of the matters to be subjected to sceptical analysis', which had now produced 'the right conclusion'.[18]

But perhaps the most consistent theme in Burton's commentary on Hume is his presentation of the philosopher as the originator of modern utilitarianism. Though he celebrated 'the boldness and greatness' of the metaphysical undertaking represented by the *Treatise*, Burton appeared particularly concerned to refocus the attention of his mid-nineteenth century audience on Hume's ethics. A much later scholar, seeking to revise the 'customary' estimation of Hume as an epistemologist, pointed out that Hume thought of himself 'primarily as a moralist', and that though this was demonstrable in his works, it was also confirmed by his life and letters as 'an outstanding biographical fact'. Burton may be said to have used the 'Life and Letters' format to begin to shift the perception of Hume and his work in a similar direction.[19]

---

[17] John Hill Burton, *Life and Correspondence of David Hume: [. . .]*, 2 vols (Edinburgh: William Tait, 1846), I, pp. 136–40; II, pp. 129–30; [William Empson], 'Life and Correspondence of David Hume', *ER* 85 (1847), 1–72 (pp. 4, 72); [William C. Lake], 'Life and Correspondence of David Hume', *Q Rev* 78 (1846), 75–113 (pp. 76–7, 113); [James Moncrieff], 'Life and Correspondence of David Hume', *NBR* 7 (1847), 539–60 (pp. 539–40).
[18] Burton, *Life of Hume*, II, pp. 67–8.
[19] T. E. Jessop, 'Some Misunderstandings of Hume', in *Hume*, ed. V. C. Chappell (London: Macmillan, 1966), 35–52 (p. 37).

And for Burton, Hume's ethics were from an early stage centred on the principles of utility. This was 'only indistinctly shadowed' in the third book of the *Treatise*, but in Burton's perception the letters Hume wrote at the time, including those to Francis Hutcheson, revealed 'the fundamental principles of his system' and 'how far he saw into the depths of the utilitarian system;', proving 'that it was more completely formed in his mind than it appeared in his book'. However, in Hume's later writings and particularly in the *Enquiry concerning the Principles of Morals*, he had laid out the 'full development, so far as it was made by (him), of the utilitarian system'. For Burton, the leading principle throughout the *Enquiry* was 'that its tendency to be useful to mankind at large, is the proper criterion of the propriety of any action, or the justness of any ethical opinion'. He took note of the critique of Hume by James Balfour of Pilrig, that men had shown an 'unhesitating adoption and practice' of great virtue without any awareness of the utilitarian principle. However, Burton observed, Balfour's point was merely an indication that Hume had needed to 'enlarge the scope' of his investigations, as would be clarified by 'a supporter of the utilitarian system, as it has been more fully developed in later days': Bentham would begin to examine 'how far the theory has been practically adopted by mankind at large'.[20]

Similarly, Burton observed that Hume had left himself open to the charge of 'expediency' because he 'estimated actions according as they accomplished what appeared at the moment to be good or evil, without any regard to their ultimate consequences'. But the position was retrieved through Bentham's development of the argument: Hume 'certainly left for Bentham the task of making a material addition to the utilitarian theory, by applying to it the secondary effects of actions. [. . .] [A] good measure must not be carried through the legislature by corrupt means', because the example set may later 'produce more bad measures than good, by lowering the tone of political morality'. Nevertheless, Hume had laid the foundations for utilitarian thinking extending from ethical principles to political action: for Burton, Hume's essays on 'The Original Contract' and 'Passive Obedience' were 'but a farther adaptation to politics of those utilitarian theories which Hume had previously applied both to private morals and to government'.[21]

---

[20] Burton, *Life of Hume*, I, pp. 111–12, 344–6.
[21] Ibid., I, pp. 290–1, 349.

The availability of the unpublished Hume material was a real opportunity for Burton. At the same time a publication incorporating all aspects of his life and work in the febrile atmosphere three years after the Disruption had its risks. In 1843, the Established Church of Scotland had split in two after a decade of religious controversy, and David Hume had long been regarded by many Scots Christians as a champion of religious infidelity. Despite this, Burton was willing to promote a sympathetic account of the man and a well-rounded account of his works because he perceived there the foundations of a utilitarian social code:

> [I]n Ethics he was the first to make an Utilitarian morality assume the aspect of a theoretical system, which it was the task of a great successor, aided by subordinate labourers, to apply to the practical operations of mankind, and to spread widely over the earth.

Hume's theoretical coherence was important, but it was his 'great successor' – Bentham – who would follow up and ask 'how far the theory has been practically adopted by mankind at large', and adapt it 'to apply to the practical operations of mankind'.[22]

There was substantial critical coverage of Burton's *Hume* and general praise for his presentation and exegesis on the previously unpublished material as throwing new light on the philosopher's character and intentions. The work cemented his literary reputation, although the more establishment journals were not responsive to his effort to locate Hume at least in part as a precursor to Bentham. Unsurprisingly the *Westminster Review* was more attuned to the associations Burton had promoted, its reviewer welcoming

> the epitomiser of Bentham in his new character of the biographer of Hume. The transition was not unnatural. In the complexion of their minds, as well as in the general features of their philosophies, Bentham and Hume present many points of coincidence; and he who had shown a true appreciation of the intellectual products of the one had given the guarantee of his aptitude to do justice to the mental and moral qualities of the other.[23]

This estimation of Burton has been echoed in recent times. The respected scholar of utilitarianism J. H. Burns acknowledged Burton's 'decisively important' contribution to the dissemination of Bentham's ideas and his *Hume* as 'the first major work of the kind, and [...] a

---

[22] Burton, *Life of Hume*, II, p. 519.
[23] [R. N.], 'Life and Correspondence of David Hume', *W Rev* 46 (1846–7), 144–74 (p. 145).

moment of some importance in the development of Hume studies': in view of 'Hume's central significance for the Scottish Enlightenment as a whole', Burns continued,

> this may suggest that we should see John Hill Burton as an important figure in the conservation and dissemination of the Benthamic texts, but also as one channel whereby the work of perhaps the greatest philosopher of the eighteenth century was transmitted to the Victorian age.[24]

Indeed Burton's role in substantiating for mid-nineteenth-century Scotland the nature and achievements of what became known as the Scottish Enlightenment deserves recognition: in addition to the two-volume *Life of Hume* (1846), he published shortly afterwards the philosopher's international correspondence, *Letters of Eminent Persons addressed to David Hume* (1849), and a decade later the first, much admired and reprinted edition of Alexander Carlyle's *Autobiography* (1860). Certainly, the reviews of his *Life of Hume* welcomed it as presenting not only the man but 'his Times', the opportunity to celebrate 'the Augustan age of Scotland': the work provided a more comprehensive sense of the period, 'a clear and unobstructed view of the Scottish Philosophy and French Encyclopaedism of the last century, revolving in a system of which David Hume is the sun and centre'.[25]

Yet in the perception of some of Burton's radical friends, Hume, and even Bentham, were still to a large extent only theorists. A drive to apply a radical pragmatism to the social and economic problems of the age infused the thinking of leading figures in the growing Victorian central state in the 1830s and 1840s. Burton came to know many of them well, both directly and through correspondence on various reform initiatives and legislative proposals. As Edwin Chadwick struggled to finalise the 'Sanitary Report', Burton was in regular, almost monthly contact through much of 1841 and 1842 on both the Scottish aspects of the document and on the preparations for framing new 'pauper' legislation for both England and Scotland. Burton must have felt this was the real thing: many of the

---

[24] J. H. Burns, 'Bentham and the Scots', *Journal of Bentham Studies* 7 (2004), 1–12 (pp. 2, 5).

[25] J. H. Burton, *Letters of Eminent Persons addressed to David Hume* (Edinburgh: Blackwood, 1849); John Hill Burton, ed., *The Autobiography of Dr. Alexander Carlyle of Inveresk 1722–1805, with a new introduction by Richard B. Sher* (Bristol: Thoemmes, 1990); [Anon], 'Burton's Life of David Hume', *Tait's* 13 n.s. (1846), 137–45, 205–15 (p. 137); [R. N.], 'Life of Hume', *W Rev* 46 (1846–7), 144–74 (p. 144); [Lake], 'Life of Hume', *Q Rev* (1846), pp. 93–5.

Benthamites he had known were writers and publishers, dismissed by the opponents of change as the 'Philosophic Radicals', steeped in abstruse Benthamite texts. Chadwick, supported by W. E. Hickson, the new editor of the *Westminster*, saw the danger in this over-identification with theory, and both shared their views forcibly with Burton.

Addressing the issue of 'pauper management' in a letter to Burton in January 1841, Chadwick specifically contrasted his own poor law proposals with Bentham's writings, which contained 'important principles' but which he rejected as impractical:

> I have had great prejudice to contend with, as being a Benthamite & a theorist & I would suggest that it would be safer to base the questions as to the Scotch poor laws on the necessities of the labouring classes rather than to any referrence [*sic*] to Mr Bentham[']s views.

Similarly, Hickson told Burton that he wished to refocus the *Westminster* on 'practical questions of administrative reform'. In a subsequent letter, discussing two articles on Bentham that Burton had proposed to send him in early 1842, Hickson extended his scepticism of theory even to 'the Prophet' himself:

> The analysis should have a practical bearing upon the most important topics of the day. I am myself, (& I believe the Public are with me) profoundly indifferent to all abstruse speculations which have no practical bearing upon the every day [*sic*] questions of human interest. I care little for the discussion of where Bentham was right or where wrong what I want to know is where the most useful remarks are to be found on administration or other reforms for which we are now struggling.[26]

Burton reflected such convictions in the books he published around the mid-century on aspects of political economy. The first of these, *Political and Social Economy: Its Practical Application*, appeared in 1849 and was followed in 1852 by a further version of the book aimed at younger students, *Political Economy for Use in Schools and Private Education*. In between, he published *The Emigrant's Manual* (1851). In these contributions, he made some obeisance to recognised theorists like Adam Smith and more recently J. R. McCulloch and John Stuart Mill.[27] However, in general the works accord with the trend in Burton's reformist thinking in the previous two decades: their purpose is to be practically useful

---

[26] NLS MS 9406, fols 97–8; NLS MS 9392, fols 25, 91.
[27] His most frequent reference is to John Stuart Mill: see Burton, *Political and Social Economy*, pp. 41–2, 69–70, 191–2, 194.

in bringing about social change. As the full titles imply, these contributions reflected the view that traditional political economy needed to give greater consideration to its social implications and its 'practical application'. Burton lamented that the usual treatment of the subject presented only 'cold formulas and abstract laws' instead of the kind of guidance that might inform 'a rule of life, with reference to evils that may be practically avoided, and good that may be rationally anticipated'. The simplified 1852 version is 'for use' in public and private education. The work on emigration is a 'manual', largely a compendium of useful facts on colonial destinations, specifically addressing 'Emigration in Its Practical Application to Individuals and Communities'.[28]

It must all have been reinforced by the opportunity that he was afforded to observe, through regular correspondence with Chadwick, the efforts to forge the foundations of 'welfare'. Ultimately that dogged pursuit of local information, gathering of facts, reliance on statistical comparisons and relegation of theory, even Bentham's theory, did pay off. The 'Sanitary Report' was the greatest of the nineteenth-century 'blue books', and seemed to promise a raft of social and public health improvements (in the drive for which Burton himself would play a significant role). Burton learned the lesson that critical turning points and social progress sometimes depended on the dogged determination of practical men engaged in unadorned practical endeavour, and it was a lesson that, as a historian, he would not forget.

A little over a decade later, appointed secretary to the Scottish Prison Board, Burton himself joined the Victorian state that was seeking to tackle mid-century social ills through improved 'administration or other reforms'. He held the position throughout the years he researched and wrote the *History*. Burton was convinced that such practical experience of the machineries of government or of legal process had benefit and application in the writing of history, particularly where facts were scarce. A more cautious, sceptical perspective could be expected, where 'one has felt the practical difficulty of the question, whether a certain piece of business should originate with the Treasury or the Board of Trade, or whether some question can be decided in the Court of Chancery, or must go to a common-law court'. The general point of the value to the historian of having practical 'business' experience was one his second wife

---

[28] Burton, 'Introductory Notice', *Political and Social Economy*; John Hill Burton, *The Emigrant's Manual: [. . .]* (Edinburgh: Chambers, 1851); [John Hill Burton], *Political Economy, for Use in Schools [. . .]*, eds W. and R. Chambers (Edinburgh: Chambers, 1852).

recalled him repeating frequently, and it helps to explain why he was periodically so alert to the influence, or potential influence, of political practicality in history.²⁹

Such pragmatism was a feature of Victorian Britain as a whole, and clearly informed the efforts of Burton's friends among the English reformers. It would however have had particular resonance among many of Burton's Scottish readers. In this period two common notions of Scottish character have been identified in celebratory speeches and in literary accounts of Scottish life. On the one hand was the figure of 'the metaphysical Scot', a *figura* drawing on Scotland's perceived profile in the world of learning, particularly philosophy. On the other, and a self-image likely to have been adopted by much greater numbers, stood 'the stereotype of the enterprising, practical, thrifty, hard-headed Scot'. Perhaps the most comprehensive contemporary expression of such values was contained in the works of the Scottish writer Samuel Smiles. Smiles had a Scottish upbringing and university education, and subsequently like Burton was much influenced by utilitarian principles as advocated by the likes of Chadwick. For Smiles, men should be judged above all 'not by precepts but by practice'.³⁰

Smiles's best-known book, *Self-Help, with Illustrations of Character and Conduct* (1859), is full of exhortations to attend to 'the practical' in human endeavour. This he commended through biographical analysis of social and cultural leaders, many of them Scottish, whose practical approach to education and life had brought about progress in history often, though not exclusively, through the inventions and arts of the industrial age. Burton's summation of the careers of great historians like Gibbon, Hume, Robertson and Macaulay as evidencing the benefit of their being 'men of business' and of a practical turn of mind, is highly reminiscent of Smiles's biographical analysis of 'men of genius'

---

²⁹ Burton, HOS (1873), I, pp. 371–2, footnote 1; Katherine Burton, 'Memoir', pp. liv–lv. In his *Life*, Burton had quoted Hume making a similar point on the value of developing suitably sceptical historical judgement, practical experience of life and business: see Burton, *Life of Hume*, I, pp. 277–8.

³⁰ Robert Anderson and Stuart Wallace, 'The Universities and National Identity in the Long Nineteenth Century c. 1830–1914', in *The Edinburgh History of Education in Scotland*, eds Robert Anderson, Mark Freeman, Lindsay Paterson (Edinburgh: Edinburgh University Press, 2015), 265–85 (pp. 266–7, 272); Asa Briggs, *Victorian People: A Reassessment of Persons and Themes, 1851–67* (Chicago: University of Chicago Press, 1972), pp. 116–19, 125–8, 138.

as invariably also 'men of business' and practical application. Smiles's book appeared just as Burton began work on his *History*, and was an immediate success, selling 20,000 copies in a year, and over a quarter of a million by 1905. The periodic recognition and admiration in Burton's *History* for regimes and leaders whose focus was on political and social utility, and who facilitated historical progress based on practical thinking and action, would have resonated with many of his Scottish readers in the closing decades of the nineteenth century.[31]

---

[31] Samuel Smiles, *Self-Help, With Illustrations of Character and Conduct* (London: Murray, 1859); see for instance 6, 28–32, 41–2, 122–3, 290–1, 326–9, 378–80 and on 'men of genius', particularly 263–72; Burton, HOS (1873), I, p. 372, footnote.

5

Romantic History

THE AUTHOR AND HIS READERS

IN MANY PASSAGES OF his full *History of Scotland*, Burton's narrative reflects quite different, even contrasting characteristics when compared to the sceptical and practicalist perspectives described in the last chapter. These have much in common with elements of the romantic literature that had swept all before it earlier in the century and had strongly influenced other cultural forms including painting and the theatre.

In recent times, scholars have identified one of those elements as a recurring 'performative' tendency in writers of the period, authorship becoming 'a site of negotiation between writers and readers'. The most prominent example is perhaps the 'the Author of Waverley', only one of the crowd of *personae* through which Scott interacted with his readership; but it is also found in the work of other literary figures such as John Galt, another favourite author of Burton from his early days. Both Scott and Galt exemplified the habit of a demonstrative (if in their case often disguised) authorial engagement with their readers that is noticeably a feature of Burton's narrative. Galt's fiction was often mediated through 'performative' devices in which his writing 'calls attention to itself as narrative construct', and in which the writer's 'presence as author and storyteller can be clearly felt'.[1]

---

[1] Caroline McCracken-Flesher, 'Walter Scott's Romanticism: A Theory of Performance', in *The Edinburgh Companion to Scottish Romanticism*, ed. Murray Pittock (Edinburgh: Edinburgh University Press, 2011), pp. 139–49 (pp. 143–4, 149); Jerome McGann, 'Walter Scott's Romantic Postmodernity', in *Scotland and the Borders of Romanticism*, eds Leith Davis, Ian Duncan and Janet Sorensen (Cambridge: Cambridge University Press, 2004), pp. 113–29

Burton's regular authorial presence in the *History* sometimes takes the form of asides, often knowing or ironic, that bridge across from his historical subject matter to reflect on or refer to his audience's contemporary experience.[2] More frequently this habit presents as a dialogue – or 'negotiation' – between the author (sometimes 'Author'), and his readers in which he appears like a speaker before an audience or the accused before a jury – 'the author pleads' or 'the author may be charged with the offence' or 'in answer [. . .] the author has to say' – to excuse or justify too much 'discursiveness', 'tedious minuteness' or 'dreary' source material interrupting the story. In his initial volumes, he is quite dismissive of the more prosaic elements in the early sources: he uses them extensively where they provide material that might engage and stimulate his readers' attention, but not where their descriptions go on 'with a minuteness that becomes tiresome' – that is, his audience can be assured that he is not a self-obsessed antiquarian of the previous century. For instance, after David II's capture at Neville's Cross in 1346, 'there is a wearisome succession of treaties' on the matter and he will touch only briefly on 'the tedious negotiations for his ransom'.[3]

In the *History*, 'incidents' and stories are important partly because they provide colour, adventure and opportunities to provide pictorial imagery and illustration but also because they provide 'relief' from what he considers 'dreary' sections of his narrative. In recounting the circumstances of James III's minority, his language reflects this attentiveness to keeping his audience engaged: a rebellion by the Lord of the Isles is given particular attention because it 'has a curious history' involving 'an astounding document' on possible feudal homage to the English king; soon followed by diversions on the tales of 'an insane archbishop' and a French ambassador 'whose personal history in interesting'. This contrasts with a demonstrative distancing from source documents which are 'tediously elaborated with feudal technicalities' or just not 'interesting'. These concerns recur as the *History* proceeds. Having spent some time on

---

(pp. 118–19); Angela Esterhammer, 'John Galt's Fictional and Performative Worlds', in *Scottish Romanticism*, ed. Pittock, 166–77 (pp. 167–9).
[2] See for instance Burton, *HOS* (1873), I, p. 54, footnote 2; p. 63, footnote 1, p. 267, footnote 1, p. 371, footnote 1; II, p. 98, footnote 1; III, p. 432, footnote 1; IV, pp. 358–60 and 360 footnote 1; VII, p. 467, footnote 1.
[3] Burton, *HOS* (1873), I, p. 37, footnote 1; p. 329, footnote 1; pp. 332–3, 336; II, p. 155, footnote; IV, p. 360, footnote 1, 398, footnote 1; V, p. 385 footnote 1; VI, p. 118; VII, p. 77, footnote 1.

military engagements during the Regency of the Earl of Arran in the mid-sixteenth century, Burton seems to assure his readers that relief is at hand and he will 'turn aside from this weary conflict with England'[.] And during the Earl of Morton's Regency in the 1570s, he is almost apologetic that he must give some space to 'a dry and profitless story' of the ineffective diplomatic efforts of the English ambassador, Bowes. Later he can relieve his narrative of the struggles between episcopacy and presbytery under James VI with a series of disputes between the king and the more zealous ministers which to an extent 'are quaint and picturesque'. However, just as he seeks to provide relief from 'the monotonous flow of diplomatic correspondence' concerning Mary's demise, so in these debates 'there is a uniformity [. . .] that becomes tiresome'. He is, though, keen to ensure that 'enough has been given to reveal the character of the scene'.[4]

As he moves on to the 'statecraft' and official correspondence surrounding the Union of the Crowns, Burton announces that he will give it short shrift since it 'does not make lively reading for the present day'. It is at first more surprising – given his attention elsewhere to the picturesque – to learn that for similar reasons he will avoid giving much attention to descriptions of the kind of overblown feasts and pageants that accompanied James's progress south and were a common feature of both the Elizabethan and Jacobean courts: 'there is a tiresomeness in reading the history of the successive culinary efforts [. . .]. The accounts of the pageantry and mimicry at these receptions make dreary reading[.]' Less surprisingly he finds, in practice, a reason to a give a fairly extensive account of the revelries: 'the only excuse' being that comparing those of Elizabeth with those of James helped illuminate the king's self-indulgent character. But such incidentals only became interesting when combined with fateful incidents by a master narrator:

> Scott's account of the revelries at Kenilworth may be taken by the general reader as a good type of that kind of entertainment. Though it is as precise as the dull memorials of the Court chroniclers, it is read with interest, because all its elaborate escapades are worked into a story of deeply pathetic and tragic incidents.[5]

It was important for Burton that he was, like Scott, 'read with interest'. He sought to maintain an authorial engagement with 'the general reader', and was anxious where possible to present events 'worked into a story'.

---

[4] Ibid., III, pp. 2–4, 17–20, 249; V, pp. 172, 279–80, 309.
[5] Ibid., V, pp. 356, 363–4.

'ELEMENTS OF OLD ROMANCE'

Even in his first volume covering the period to 1174, once through his summation of what can be gleaned from classical historians and a critical outline of antiquarian claims relating to the post-Roman period, we are periodically into a world of the romantic both in Burton's manner of recounting heroic tales and in his referencing these to the romantic literature of his own era. Rather typically, while dismissing the Arthurian and related romances as medieval creations, he provides a fairly extensive account of all those knights, magicians and dragons, noting that Scott held the 'great romance of Sir Tristrem' to be the work of 'the Scottish Merlin, Thomas of Ercildoune'. However, it is 'the Ossianic literature' to which he gives particular attention, locating its origins in Celtic tales of the hero-kings, to which Macpherson,

> the great literary artist brought a knowledge of the Arthurian romances and the Norse Sagas, with a study of the Homeric literature [. . .]. Above all, he brought to his work the true power of a great poet [. . .] who drew inspiration from the scenes in which his heroes were to act, – stormy seas, precipices, cataracts, gloomy forests, and huge mountains, all frequented by misty clouds or swept by hollow winds.

Proceeding to provide an account 'of the brilliant romances that record the chivalry at the courts of the two phantom monarchs, Arthur and Fingal', he explains he has done so because they arose from the condition of Scotland after the Empire's collapse and helped shape Scotland's later development: the 'sources' even of the heroic fables must be scrutinised for elements of truth, so '(w)e cannot well detach all this matter from Scots history'.[6]

In his second volume covering the later twelfth century up to 1460, Burton's cautiously empirical and revisionist approach to Edward I's dealings with Scotland begins to transform into something much more 'literary' and dramatic, infused with a sense of the fateful consequences surrounding significant figures and incidents, often conveyed as 'stories' or episodes. The shift in approach is announced in characteristically dramatic terms as Robert Bruce abandons the English court in 1306 and is quickly 'located' in the realms of romance in a long footnote recounting the manner of Bruce's parents' meeting as an encounter of courtly love. Conversely, from wise statesman, Edward becomes the villain of a medieval *chanson*, imprisoning the heroically presented Countess of

---

[6] Burton, *HOS* (1873), I, pp. 170–4, and 174, footnote 1; pp. 178–9 and footnotes.

Buchan, so no longer 'the chivalrous knight, who had wept over the loss of his loved Eleanor'. There follows a series of the adventures of Bruce and his companions while evading capture in which history and 'romance' intermingle: his oft-expressed disdain for 'fabulous' history appears suppressed, allowing tales to be told on the rather thin premise that 'we possess a clear and picturesque narrative of the whole' and 'the story was believed in Scotland at the time'. Rather defensively, Burton observes that John Barbour, whose epic poem *The Bruis* he draws on, had no 'luxuriant imagination' and wrote just thirty years later, so his work was no 'Arthurian romance'. Despite having indulged in another tale of the Aberdeen citizenry expelling an English garrison, he footnotes a recent examination of it 'bringing home the whole story to Hector Boece's inventive genius'.[7]

In Burton's fourth volume, much of it devoted to 'Queen Mary' and events associated with her, a distinct discourse of the theatrical and of fateful drama becomes evident. This is considered in more detail in Chapter 7. Prominent as it is, however, it does not preclude presentation of Mary's story as a romantic adventure. Recounting her voyage to Scotland in August 1561, Burton quotes then paraphrases the effusive style of the most 'vivid' source to convey her passionate regret at leaving France. Such passages consistently undermine his own more sober assessments suggesting that, at heart, Mary is a product of the intrigue-ridden French court. And he waxes lyrical on how, at this stage at least the Scots were drawn to this queen, who presented herself in scenes full of colour and romance:

> The old warlike and chivalrous feeling of the people found more to stir it in this delicate woman than in many a hero. She had often shown her beautiful face under the helmet, mounted on her charger at the head of her troops. In more peaceful days, the peasantry of the borders and the Highlands were familiar with the airy form sweeping past on a milk-white steed, at the stag-hunt or the hawking, followed by all the chivalry of her court.[8]

Contemplating her marriage to Henry Stewart, Lord Darnley in 1565, Mary found herself in conflict with Regent Murray and the other Protestant lords. In Burton's description of Mary and Darnley as they ride south from Perth to avoid Murray and his supporters, he may be said

---

[7] Ibid., II, pp. 233–4 and 234, footnote 1; pp. 243, 250–4 and 254, footnote 1; p. 256, footnote 3.
[8] Burton, *HOS* (1873), IV, pp. 19, 53, 70.

to milk the tropes of Scott's fleeing lovers, while at the same time again setting aside his scepticism on sources:

> Murray himself held Lochleven Castle, on the line of their journey; the Earl of Argyle was to descend with a force from his fortress of Castle Campbell, on the brow of the Ochils; and the Duke of Chatelherault had made his preparations at Kinneil, near to the ferry where the betrothed lovers would cross the Forth[.]

Betrothed lovers, ferry crossings and ambushes from the hills. Burton cannot resist the tale, though at the end of it he admits that of supporting evidence 'there is scarcely a vestige'. He then fashions a dramatic conclusion to the following chapter, conveyed in novelesque terms, as the pair commence another breathless flight, this time from Edinburgh after Rizzio's murder.[9]

Mary's encounters with James Hepburn, Earl of Bothwell are presented in similar terms. Following his trial and acquittal for Darnley's murder, Bothwell forced Mary to go with him to his 'grim fortress' of Dunbar. Despite the lack of any real evidence, Burton allows the reader's imagination to dwell on the dastardly possibilities: 'A young and lovely princess taken captive and immured in the fortress of a profligate and unscrupulous baron, is one of the most approved elements of old romance, giving room for the imagination to revel in all horrors and tyrannies.' Burton's alternative explanations for Mary's fateful commitment to Bothwell are also rooted in 'old romance': she may simply have been overwhelmed by a hopeless passion; or the incidents revealing her despair could simply attest

> that the unhappy woman was the mere helpless victim of fraud and force – a sort of realisation of the old stories about giants and enchanters, or of the romances with the tyrant lord who, gifted with powers almost as preternatural, seizes and imprisons the doomed princess.[10]

During Mary's reign, through the regencies that governed Scotland in her son's minority (1567–79) and into the reign of James VI, a pattern recurs that recalls his handling of a number of the events as already described: he gives particular attention to subjects that are susceptible of presentation as a mystery story or adventure story; incorporates warnings as to the credibility of evidence for them; but proceeds to tell the

---

[9] Ibid., IV, pp. 120–21, 155. The final sentence of the next chapter also reads like a fictional 'cliffhanger' following the night-time explosion that assassinated Darnley, p. 192.

[10] Ibid., IV, pp. 217, 247.

tale, accompanied by allusions to romantic or vernacular literature. An example is his handling of Mary's incarceration at Lochleven in 1567. This was high nineteenth-century romantic territory with tourists flocking to the location, and Burton initially seeks to de-romanticise the venue as just a 'narrow square tower of Scotland'. It was not 'a sort of shrine', as it is treated by the thousands who now visit, for whom 'the half highland lake and the green ruin on the island have their charms as a piece of landscape'. Yet he cannot leave it there. A few pages later, he again asserts that in terms of 'authentic history', what happened during the captivity is 'almost an entire blank, although the rumours of the day, and the traditions invented and believed in later times, have thickly peopled it with incidents'. Characteristically he then recounts a variety of the tales, including Mary's final escape, at its centre one of those feisty, lower-class minor characters so beloved of romantic fiction. Burton links this man, Willy Douglas, to letters written later by Mary on his behalf when she thought him in danger, which 'will recall some incidents in the "Abbot" and show what suggested them to Scott'. This type of allusive linkage, not uncommon in Burton, functions to create a rather porous boundary between history and literature, a kind of mirror image of Scott's own habits in this regard. Scott had built substantially on Douglas's historical 'part' to create the character of Roland Graeme in *The Abbot*, prompting one modern critic to observe how Scott had taken 'great liberties in depicting those characters who loiter on the fringes of history, and who perform the link between historical and fictional events in his novels'.[11]

There are similar features in Burton's treatment of the story of the 'fiendish' abuse of the wife of James Hamilton of Bothwellhaugh, who assassinated Regent Murray in February 1569: '[A] story converting this well-planned murder into a frantic act of retribution for certain deeds of fiendish cruelty has found its way into ordinary history, though it bears on its face the palpable characteristics of romance.' For all that, he tells the tale with various embellishments, which include linking the 'strangely fabricated story' to 'one of the noblest of modern ballads – Scott's 'Cadyow Castle' – as well as to related material in the Scots ballad collection edited

---

[11] Burton, *HOS* (1873), IV, pp. 358–60; pp. 366–7, footnote 2. In a footnote he actually acknowledges that 'the author' can be accused of 'the offence which he denounces' in dwelling on the Lochleven scenario, and a rather lengthy defence follows (p. 360, footnote 1); Christopher Johnson, 'Historical Note', in Walter Scott, *The Abbot*, ed. Christopher Johnson (Edinburgh: Edinburgh University Press, 2000), 463–8 (p. 468).

by Burton's friend James Maidment.[12] The outbreak of virtual civil war in 1570–1 provided the opportunity for Burton to recount further tales of doubtful provenance that should really have fallen below his own standards of research but cannot be resisted, particularly where some old-ballad colour can be drawn in. He described how, in the course of the struggle, the leader of the Gordons burned the Castle of Towie, whose lady, 'tortured between the duty of feudal hatred and the appeals of her smothering children', had refused its surrender. Burton's observation that 'one of the finest among the touching and beautiful pieces in the popular ballads of the Scots people' had been inspired by the scene 'supposed to have passed' in the burning house is sufficient excuse to reproduce the entire ballad in a footnote.[13]

So, in his volumes dealing with the early centuries and up to the early modern period, Burton gives much greater attention to 'the elements of old romance' than might be expected from his accompanying scepticism regarding the truth of many of the adventure stories and picturesque scenes. Some of this will continue, but towards the end of his fourth volume, he signals a change: with Mary's flight into England, the tales of her 'personal adventures' must give way to a narrative based on 'materials more like a lawsuit, than a romance with a wandering princess as its heroine'. He is referring here to the 'State Papers', official records and correspondence of the Elizabethan state, which may not convey romance of that kind, but 'are full of matter bearing on the facts and spirit of the history of the time, and on the character and conduct of those who acted in it'.[14]

The rationale for nevertheless giving attention to these new sources is elaborated in one of those discursive authorial engagements with his reader-audience: some might hold a view that 'pure history [. . .] ought always to be the statement of the historian who is presumed to be perfectly impartial', after he has weighed and analysed the evidence; however, '[I]n answer to such a view, the author has to say' that to avoid a history 'so overlaid with theories, conjectures, and angry controversy', it

---

[12] Burton, *HOS* (1873), V, pp. 12–15 and p. 12, footnote 1; Walter Scott, 'Cadyow Castle', in *The Poetical Works of Walter Scott*, ed. J. Logie Robertson, MA (London: Henry Frowde, 1894), pp. 667–70, 689; James Maidment, *Scotish [sic] Ballads and Songs: Historical and Traditionary*, 2 vols (Edinburgh: Paterson, 1868), II, pp. 39–48, 330–1.

[13] Burton, *HOS* (1873), V, pp. 69–70 and p. 70, footnote 1. The ballad is known as 'Captain Ker' or 'Edom o' Gordon', though Burton gives no title here.

[14] Burton, *HOS* (1873), IV, p. 395

was best to rely on primary documents, with the historian simply ordering them as coherently as possible. This method should rely on 'quoting the words of the documents themselves, when it happens, as it often does, that the sense cannot be trusted into other words without the risk of being perverted'. These observations anticipate what, in the following three sections, are proposed as further central characteristics of Burton's historiography and as illustrating those aspects of his work that reflect not only romantic content, but identifiably romantic methodology: an emphasis on attending to the *actual words* and language of the sources; and a search, partly achieved through such attention, for the 'spirit of the history of the time'.[15]

THE PAST SPEAKS

Burton frequently commends attention to the actual wording of the sources as conveying the sheer particularity and difference of the past. Froissart could be trusted since he had spoken directly with the French knights who were at the Battle of Otterburn: '[t]he (English), on coming within two bowshots of them, were received after a manner so strange that it must be told in the words of the great chronicler himself[.]' Similarly, however far-fetched to nineteenth-century ears, the tales of prophetic warning to James IV before Flodden in 1513 should be heard, on and in their own terms: '[t]he spirit of such a story is best understood in the words in which it is chronicled[.]'[16] Yet as noted above, he also welcomed arriving at a point early in the sixteenth century when the comparatively voluminous sources in the State Papers became available. Not only were the papers extensive, but since they were almost never written for publication the words their authors set down could largely be taken at face value. The spirit of the time could be discovered here as readily as in a story of romance with a princess at its heart. Indeed, the characteristics of the past could not be more starkly exposed than in the private, intentionally secret correspondence involving the masters of intrigue at the heart of the Henrician and Elizabethan state machines. Through such sources the past was able, almost literally, to speak for itself. The first of these figures is Cardinal Wolsey, whose 'indubitable' and 'emphatic language' illuminates the conditions in Scotland during the conflict with England in the early 1520s. Burton delights in Wolsey's contest in subtle

---

[15] Ibid., IV, p. 398, footnote 1.
[16] Ibid., II, p. 367; III, p. 74, footnote 1.

statecraft with Archbishop Beaton, chancellor of Scotland, which allows him to recount 'one of the most curious little stories of subtle and treacherous diplomacy on record', an attempt to lure Beaton to the border and kidnap him. Burton tells the tale, but must underscore it by reproducing the original source: 'Wolsey's explanation cannot be told so distinctly as in his own words[.]'[17]

On various occasions, Burton introduces such passages from original sources with the observation that not only would his own version distract from the immediacy of what was being revealed, but that something authentic would be 'spoiled'. In late 1523, with a Scots army on the border, English spies were keeping the English general Lord Dacre informed, and Burton draws on his reports to Wolsey for a 'picture' of what was going on: 'Dacre, writing to Wolsey on the 27th of December, reports, on the telling of one of these "espials", a scene that explains itself, and would be spoiled were it to be told in other words.' Burton recognised that the increasing availability of original source documents through the efforts of the book clubs and the early- to mid-century records scholars was helping to expunge the danger of historians 'spoiling' history through conjecture. The 'revelations of the social condition and character of the times', which Burton drew from accounts of the Jacobean bishops, were extracted from the volume *Original Letters relating to the Ecclesiastical Affairs of Scotland*, published by the Bannatyne Club in 1851. In the final tale, Burton introduces Adam Bellenden, Bishop of Dunblane, 'rejoicing in a gleam of good fortune; but it is only a gleam, with shadows behind it. His story would be spoilt in any telling but his own[.]'[18]

In the following reign, Burton found Charles I's 'secret instructions' to the Marquis of Hamilton, his Commissioner in Scotland, particularly fascinating as revealing both the underlying policy as well as the 'superficial acts to be done'. Charles's own words must be heard: the 'instructions reveal everything, and would be spoilt by explanation or comment'. In the same way, on the other side of the divide, since Robert Baillie was actually with the Scottish covenanting army on its march to the border in 1639, he should be heard directly: '[t]he account of the material condition of the host would be spoilt if given in any other than Baillie's own words.'[19]

Earlier, it was for similar reasons that Burton celebrated his arrival at the point when he has available John Knox's *History of the Reformation in Scotland* as a source:

---

[17] Ibid., III, pp. 98, 105–6 and footnote 2, p. 105; pp. 113–14.
[18] Ibid., III, pp. 179–80, 108; V, pp. 453-61; [Anon], *Original Letters relating to the Ecclesiastical Affairs of Scotland* (Edinburgh: Bannatyne Club, 1851).
[19] Ibid., VI, pp. 200, 262.

> There is certainly in the English language no other parallel to it in the clearness, vigour, and picturesqueness with which it renders the history of a stirring period. Whoever would see and feel the history of the Reformation in Scotland – and in England too, for that matter – must needs read and study it.

Partisan it surely was, but if his readers wished to 'see and feel' the character of those times, even 'the living spirit of partisanship', they must view them through the actual words of this leading figure in 'the broad clear light of that wonderful book'.[20] Burton returns to the point when he presents the first of many encounters between Mary and Knox: they had often been described, but Knox's *History* 'is the source of all the others, and to that we must go back as the sole authority for the scene. It is extremely picturesque and lifelike', and seemed to do 'honest justice' to both parties. It is worth reiterating that capturing and presenting what Burton describes as picturesque was an important part of the purpose. A reliance and respect for original sources and authenticated records should not be confused with the efforts of Dr Dryasdust. Many of the most romantic and picturesque scenes that Burton incorporates in his account of Mary's reign rely on and reproduce the accounts of participants, or contemporary historians like Knox or Buchanan, which 'cannot be better told' than in their own words – for instance the account by Lord Ruthven of his involvement in Rizzio's murder; or the popular reaction and suspicions after Darnley's murder; or the contemporary description of Mary's escape from Lochleven.[21]

At the same time, Burton's 'picturesque' did not refer only to colourful romantic tales or descriptions of striking and curious scenes but extended to arresting, even tragic events which, if unpleasant, would command attention and were illustrative – painted a picture – of the times. For instance, in the mid-sixteenth century, though moving on from the medieval chroniclers' chivalric picturesque scenes, he draws on the 'vehement colouring' of John Knox's own *History* to recount the arrest and death of the Protestant martyr George Wishart in the same terms. And in portraying the ageing Knox himself, Burton could not pass over 'that exquisite little sketch' by a contemporary observer

> of the old decrepit man, in his dress of marten fur, creeping, with the aid of his zealous secretary, along the street, and helped into the pulpit, 'where he behovet to lean at his first entry; but ere he had done with his sermon he was so active and vigorous that he was like to ding the pulpit in blads and fly out of it'.

---

[20] Ibid., III, p. 339.
[21] Burton, *HOS* (1873), IV, pp. 28, 149, 153; p. 197, footnote 1; pp. 365–6.

Burton's response to an eyewitness account of the execution in 1573 of Kirkcaldy of Grange, one of the last Scottish lords to stay loyal to Mary Stuart, provides a further example of his alertness to how the difference of past times could be illustrated best through such contemporary testimony. He was clearly intrigued by the story of a prophecy attributed to Grange's erstwhile friend John Knox that the soldier could still expect salvation, which would be signalled when, on the gibbet, his head would finally turn towards the sun. Burton, seemingly quite conscious of the historiographic shift, follows on by drawing a distinction between how 'a philosopher' might interpret such an account, as contrasted with the perspective required to sense and appreciate the subsisting conditions or 'nature' of the past: 'to feel and know the nature of the times, it is well to have such stories as they are originally told'. The original sources, as he had previously observed, 'leave nothing for conjecture'. In general, there was no longer an option for historians. Comprehending the past required attending directly to its own words through which 'it cannot be better told'.[22]

LANGUAGE AND HISTORY

But if the past speaks, what language does it use? Once the historian begins to valorise and incorporate passages from sources contemporaneous with the times whose particular 'spirit' or 'characteristics' they are asserted to reveal, the traditional linguistic uniformity of the history text is broken. Voices other than the author's become more prominent. Like other eighteenth- and nineteenth-century historians, Burton, of course, wrote largely in his version of standard English. His style was criticised by one or two contemporary reviewers as 'uneven' due to his periodic use of rather idiomatic terms, but most seem to have found him 'fresh', 'clear' and 'vigorous'. Amongst the other languages of Scotland, Burton had little knowledge of Gaelic, a deficiency that he would not have considered in any way problematic. It was a standard shibboleth of his Teutonism that the Gaels had fallen backward in civilisation, the languages of the Highlands and Lowlands reflecting their racial diversity and division; and that Lowland Scots had proved impervious to any absorption of Gaelic words or influence – an assumption later shown to be quite wrong. By contrast, the Scots language itself figures prominently in various phases of the *History*. This was largely new in narrative history, and cannot be

---

[22] Ibid., III, p. 256, footnote 3; V, pp. 52, 128–9.

separated from the increasing emphasis on founding history on original sources which, from the medieval period through to the seventeenth century at least, inevitably involved documents in varieties of the Scots tongue. There had been some of this before – Tytler had appended source documents 'printed for the first time', some of which were in Scots, at the end of his volumes, and occasionally included vernacular in his main text, though usually with footnoted translations.[23]

Burton does not have a great deal more Scots in his own main text. However, his quotations from Scots sources are at times extensive and are incorporated as footnotes on the relevant pages as the original text or as examples and illustrations. They are clearly designed to be read in conjunction with and to support the main text – part of that self-conscious dialogue of the author and his readers. In some passages they provide evidential 'foundations', and occupy at least half of the page. The reproduced material is in fairly broad medieval and early modern Scots without translation. There are few opportunities for this in Burton's early volumes, where his scepticism concerning the 'fabulous' histories has been so evident, though he does reproduce a number of passages from medieval Scots chronicles.[24]

However, his most extensive use of Scots-language sources relates to the later fifteenth and the sixteenth centuries. Although other works in the vernacular are used, many passages are drawn from *The Historie and Cronicles of Scotland* written in the mid-sixteenth century by Robert Lindsay of Pitscottie. These excerpts are often not just extended citations or random insertions but have a purpose of 'picturesque' illustration, partly in the sense of presenting a more arresting image but invariably also as helping to demonstrate the particular 'curious' manners and beliefs of different periods or events.[25] Pitscottie's *Historie* was first published in 1728 and republished in Edinburgh by Constable in 1814. It was originally conceived as a continuation from the death of James I in 1437 of John Bellenden's Scots version of the Latin history

---

[23] Ferguson, *Identity of the Scottish Nation*, pp. 287, 219; see Tytler, *History*, II, pp. 126, 130, 348–9 and footnotes, but these passages are unusual. Some documents in Scots appear as appended sources, though most are in English: for example, Ibid., II, pp. 387–94, 399–402; III, pp. 365–423.

[24] Burton, *HOS* (1873), I, p. 13, p. 442, footnote 1; II, p. 339, footnote 1; p. 344, footnote 1; p. 371, footnote 1.

[25] Ibid., III, p. 20, footnote 1; p. 25, footnote 2; pp. 27–8 and p. 28, footnote 1; pp. 35–7 and p. 35, footnote 1; pp. 67–70 and p. 67, footnote 1; p. 70, footnote 2; pp. 74–5 and footnote; pp. 81–2, p. 330, footnote 2.

of Scotland by Hector Boece. Pitscottie's account was much admired by Walter Scott 'for his language, anecdotes, and knack of presenting a scene – and as a relief from contemporary dry-as-dust writing, especially John Pinkerton's *History of Scotland* (1797)'. Burton would have been well aware of Scott's admiration since he knew Scott's poetry and prose intimately; excerpts from Pitscottie appear in *Tales of a Grandfather*, in various Waverley novels and in Scott's published Notes to his epic poem *Marmion*.[26] Burton's own deployment of passages from original sources in the early modern vernacular functions to reinforce the romantic interest in the tone and tenor of past times. This is also reflected a little later in his periodic use of George Buchanan's Scots writings, not least his 'picturesque accounts' of events around Darnley's murder. For Burton, the work of the great humanist served to convey 'a very distinct impression of the power of the old Scots tongue, and its capacity to stand alongside of the language of Rome, preserving the same grand historic step'.[27]

The reproduction of Scots-language sources continued as Burton addressed the increasing importance of ecclesiastical controversies in James IV's reign. Appropriately, here he began to rely on John Knox's *History*, again citing passages that were just about understandable to a native Scots speaker in the nineteenth century, though perhaps challenging to others.[28] However, Burton returned to Pitscottie when addressing the growing rivalry with England in the early sixteenth century as a prosperous Scotland developed its naval power and mutual accusations of piracy led to conflict on the high seas. His account of the sea battles between Scots and English squadrons involving the 'great sea-captain' Sir Andrew Wood are supported by lengthy footnote passages from Pitscottie's *Historie* beginning with the 'picturesque account' of achievements in Scots naval construction and continuing with the 'expressive' description of the naval engagements themselves. Scots has only a periodic appearance, as Burton proceeds with a lengthy narrative on the diplomatic, political and military history of James V's minority and the wars involving Henry VIII.

---

[26] [J. G. Dalyell], ed., *The Cronicles of Scotland, by Robert Lindsay of Pitscottie [. . .]*, 2 vols (Edinburgh: Constable, 1814) (originally entitled *Historie and Cronicles of Scotland: From the Slauchter of King James the First to the Ane thousande five hundreith thrie scoir fyftein zeir*, ed. AE J. G. Mackay, 3 vols (Edinburgh: Blackwood, 1899–1911)); W. W. Scott, 'Lindsay, Robert, of Pitscottie', *ODNB*, accessed 10 March 2021.

[27] Burton, *HOS* (1873), IV, p. 197, footnote 1; pp. 275–7, footnote 1.

[28] Burton, *HOS* (1873), III, p. 42, footnote 1; p. 43, footnote 1.

Here, his reliance is chiefly on sources like the State Paper Office documents and ambassadorial correspondence. However, the language does maintain a presence where he links political and ecclesiastical issues to literary productions. A brief allusion in official correspondence prompts the quotation of excerpts from Sir David Lindsay's 'celebrated satire of "The Three Estates"'; as well as a 'highly coloured illustration' of clerical abuses, and a satirical version by an early sixteenth-century poet of the curious practice of ecclesiastical 'cursing'.[29]

Burton closed his third volume with a general survey of social, institutional and cultural history from the wars of independence to the Reformation, including the vernacular epic histories and the works of the late medieval and Renaissance poets: the conflict with England meant that the epics of Barbour, Wynton and Blind Harry were animated by 'the deepest feelings of national hatred' for those beyond the Tweed, but this led at times to 'composition which has the dignity and power of the heroic' and so the 'peculiar character and influence of this special literature commend it to the historian'. A general history was not the place to go into detail, but typically he did provide a 'picturesque' and thus 'characteristic' sample. The passage is drawn from *The Complaynt of Scotland* (1548), written under pressure of Henry VIII's 'cruel wars'. Although he notes that the document had a practical political purpose, what he most wants to share is the way in which the writer

> takes up his position with much picturesqueness:– '. . . Beside the foot of ane little mountain, there ran ane fresh river as clear as beryl, whar I beheld the pretty fish wantonly stertland with their red vermyl finns, and their skails like the bright silver[.]'

Given his relatively frequent citations from sources in Scots, it may seem surprising that further instances are not provided at this point. Rather, and in accord with his general approach, he considered that 'a fair test of the character of the language' would have emerged naturally from the sources themselves in the passages he had previously presented.[30] In Volume IV, Burton interrupts his narrative at the point when Mary is forced to abdicate in favour of her son, to devote a chapter to church organisation and discipline as the Scottish Reformation was consolidated in the 1560s. Here he takes the opportunity to explore the development of Scots-language

---

[29] Ibid., III, p. 67, footnote 1; pp. 69–70, footnote 2; p. 307, footnote 1; pp. 322–4 and footnotes; p. 330, footnote 1; pp. 333–6 and footnotes.
[30] Ibid., III, pp. 413, 417; p. 418, footnote 3; p. 423, footnote 2.

songs for the new kirk, and though he expresses some doubt as to the effectiveness of their mimicking the profane ballads, he is concerned to provide examples of such verse and explore further aspects of the vernacular ecclesiastical music tradition.[31]

A number of Burton's citations suggest that his inclusion of Scots-language sources and illustrations drawn from vernacular literature was stimulated and facilitated by the availability of publications on traditional Scots ballads and poetry whose appearance seems to have intensified in the decade or so from the late 1850s. Prominent among them were volumes compiled by men he had known well since his days in the Advocates Library. At various points Burton cites James Maidment's *Scotish [sic] Ballads and Songs* (1859), David Irving's *History of Scotish [sic] Poetry* (1861) and David Laing's *Compendious Edition of Psalms and Spiritual Songs commonly known as the Gude and Godlie Ballads* (1868), as well as Laing's earlier *Select Remains of the Ancient Popular Poetry of Scotland* (1822). Burton was also familiar with W. E. Aytoun's *The Ballads of Scotland* (2 vols, 1858), which he reviewed very positively in *Blackwood's Magazine*. On the late medieval and Renaissance poets, Burton referred his readers to recent specialist works including Laing's scholarly editions of Dunbar (1834) and Henryson (1865) and anticipated edition of Sir David Lindsay (1871).[32]

As Burton moves on in Volumes IV and V to his coverage of the later sixteenth and the seventeenth centuries, another 'tongue' becomes periodically prominent. This has been called the 'second language of Scotland' by David Murison in an essay written some decades ago. He used the phrase in the context of an analysis of Scott's *Heart of Midlothian*, and specifically of the utterances of its heroine, Jeannie Deans: she used Scots when expressing love of her sister but changed register as the profligate Staunton

> presses her to forswear herself: 'He has given us a law [. . .] for the lamp of our path; if we stray from it we err against knowledge. I may not do evil, even that good may come of it [. . .]'. This is the second language of Scotland, the heritage of the sixteenth century, of the English Bible and Calvinist theology.

---

[31] Ibid., IV, pp. 350–2 and footnotes.
[32] David Laing, ed., *A Compendious Edition of Psalms and Spiritual Songs* (Edinburgh: Paterson, 1868); and *Select Remains of the Ancient Popular Poetry of Scotland* (Edinburgh: Laing, 1822); David Irving, *The History of Scotish [sic] Poetry [. . .]*, ed. John Aitken Carlyle, MD (Edinburgh: Edmonston and Douglas, 1861); Maidment's *Scotish [sic] Ballads and Songs* are cited above; Burton, *HOS* (1873), III, p. 322, footnote 1; p. 419, footnote 1; IV, p. 352, footnote 1; V, p. 14, footnote.

Murison noted the contrast that Scott had drawn between Jeannie's sister Effie returning from her illicit tryst singing the Scots ballad 'The Elfin Knight', and her father's diatribe against dancing, 'couched as Scott himself admits, in the language of a Cameronian tract of 1728'. The Cameronians were amongst the purest of the covenanted Presbyterians and strict adherents to the fundamental doctrines of the Scottish Reformation. Burton quotes in full the 'expressive enunciation' of the originating document of that ecclesiastical revolution, the 'First Covenant', drawn up in 1557:

> We, perceiving how Satan, in his members, the Anti-christs of our time, cruelly doth rage, seeking to overthrow and to destroy the evangel of Christ and His Congregation, ought, according to our bounden duty, to strive in our Master's cause even unto the death, being certain of the victory in Him[.][33]

In his passages on ecclesiastical history, Burton was able and willing to make extensive use of sources that his readership could confidently view as being as authentic as possible. As was the case for some of his Scots-language sources, Burton's attention to this 'second language of Scotland' was facilitated by the availability of iconic source texts freshly recovered and published through the middle decades of the century by leading book clubs, and edited to contemporary standards by respected records scholars. He was able to draw its tone and tenor from the narratives and direct speech episodes made available in these recent editions of, for example, Knox's *History of Scotland* (within his *Works*, 1846–64), Robert Baillie's *Letters and Journals* (1841–2), David Calderwood's *History of the Kirk* (1842–9) and John Row's *History of the Kirk* (1842). The original authors had lived through, and often participated in, the events they described. This did not mean they should always be taken at face value but for Burton, if they were listened to critically, they provided voices as direct and authentic as could be found.[34]

---

[33] David Murison, 'The Two Languages in Scott', in *Scott's Mind and Art*, ed. A. N. Jeffares (Edinburgh: Oliver and Boyd, 1969), 206–29 (pp. 223–4); Burton, *HOS* (1873) III, quoted, p. 345.

[34] John Knox, *The Works of John Knox*, ed. David Laing, 6 vols (Edinburgh: Bannatyne Club, 1846–64); Robert Baillie, *The Letters and Journals of Robert Baillie, A.M. [. . .]*, ed. David Laing, 3 vols (Edinburgh: Bannatyne Club/R. Ogle, 1841–2); David Calderwood, *The History of the Kirk of Scotland*, ed. the Reverend Thomas Thomson, 8 vols (Edinburgh: Wodrow Society, 1842–9); John Row, *The History of the Kirk of Scotland [. . .]* (Edinburgh: Wodrow Society, 1842).

However, it is clear that Burton had also read deeply in the relatively obscure texts of the most persecuted Presbyterians and periodically his text incorporates the expression of the transcendental religious enthusiasm he found there. Some of this could be found in Robert Wodrow, whose writings fascinated Burton as calling up the 'spirit' of a different age. Wodrow's *History* had also been relatively recently republished with scholarly attention and a more accessible format, and his name was adopted by the Book Club responsible for a number of the works referred to above. In addition, Burton drew even more directly upon the testimonies of the persecuted to be found in obscure collections, long out of print but perhaps discovered in his 'book-hunting', and in one case given to him by a friend, the Reverend Charles Roger, who led one of the surviving Seceder churches and so could be counted 'one of the professed representatives of the old Covenanters'.[35]

This linguistic register rather drops out of sight in much of the rest of Volume IV amidst the dramas and conspiracies of the remainder of Mary's reign, but it reappears in his fifth volume, which covers the period from the Earl of Murray's Regency (1567–70) until 1625, first of all in the last flourishes from Knox's *History* – including his debates with Kirkcaldy of Grange and his admonitions of Mary, 'revelling in his own wonderful gifts of denunciatory eloquence'. However, he goes on to recognise this rhetoric in Knox's successors, who had their successes 'in Knox's own style'. One of these was Andrew Melville, who led the triumphant assertion of the legal and liturgical forms of Presbyterianism in the late 1590s, incorporating 'much of that peculiar rhetoric of which we have seen some specimens'. Burton was ever conscious of over-burdening his readers, and he acknowledged that too much of this could become 'tiresome'; however, as first encountered, it conveyed 'a sense of the novel and the picturesque'.[36]

As he proceeds, Burton draws attention to a distinct though related discourse. This is particularly associated with the periodic outpourings of fervour and renewal that characterised religious 'revivals'. The first of these had occurred in the disturbed political and religious conditions around the 'Raid of Ruthven' (1582), when James VI was temporarily

---

[35] Robert Wodrow, *The History of the Sufferings of the Church of Scotland [. . .]*, ed. the Reverend Robert Burns, 4 vols (Glasgow: Blackie, 1829–35); Burton drew the immediate testimony of participants from, for instance, the collection *Faithful Contendings displayed; [. . .]* (Glasgow: John Bryce, 1780); his friend Charles Roger had provided a copy of *A Collection of the Dying Testimonies of some Holy and Pious Christians [. . .]* (Kilmarnock: Calderwood, 1806).

[36] Burton, HOS (1873), V, pp. 50–2, 300, 307–9.

held hostage by the Earl of Gowrie. The Presbyterian ministers maintained pressure on the court by seeking subscription to a publicly shared statement of beliefs drawn up in the document sometimes known as the 'Second Confession of Faith', part of which is introduced by Burton: 'the object was to lift up a testimony against the enemy. That this testimony was lifted up with power and terseness, the following passage will perhaps satisfy the reader[.]' The language of the subsequent popular 'revival' was different – an enunciation of overwhelming religious conviction and emotional transport. Burton drew attention to this 'peculiar rhetoric', providing a lengthy passage illustrating its distinctiveness.[37]

From the 1630s and the start of the struggles with the later Stuart kings, it was the renewal of the old Covenant that was for Burton the 'master-stroke of policy', at least partly because it gave them 'all the advantage of its denunciatory rhetoric [. . .] – they were but repeating in the hour of their own difficulty and peril what the nation had uttered in a previous time of peril'. Referring to his own account of the original Covenant, Burton reminded his readers of 'how fiercely and potently the denunciatory clauses of this document had been drawn'; and proceeded to associate this directly with the 'Supplicants' articulation in 1638 of their ecclesiastic and political demands 'announced [. . .] with a distinct candour'. To properly understand the events that followed, 'it is as well that, before going further, we take the impression of their distinct utterance'.[38] Burton continued consistently as the *History* proceeded to incorporate evocations of this 'distinct utterance', some associated with the public sphere though others with the inner workings of the head and heart. In his coverage of the Killing Times, he allowed it to speak for itself at possibly its most extreme and intense in the writings of Robert Hamilton a leader of the 1679–80 Insurrection. Hamilton is quoted in quasi-biblical terms as justifying killing men at the Battle of Drumclog (1679) where the covenanters had a short-lived triumph. However, in a long footnote Burton also lets him speak in a different strain: 'this hard fierce man had his tendernesses, and they seem to have been peculiarly rich and overflowing'.[39]

Though Burton rather played down the significance of the repression in the southwest as among the causes of the 1689 Revolution that overthrew the Stuart royal line, he again gave recognition to the distinctive

---

[37] Ibid., V, pp. 206–10, 300–2.
[38] Burton, *HOS* (1873), VI, pp. 183, 191–2, 232, 272–3.
[39] Ibid., VII, pp. 227–8 and 228, footnote 1.

discourse contained in the accounts of the 'sufferers and sympathisers' of those who had been persecuted. This is partly illustrated through an extensive listing of the title pages of the literature of the covenanters, collectively representing a particular enunciation of the martyrology of Scotland. However, Burton observed, 'the reader' should turn especially to Wodrow's *History* to appreciate 'the spirit and literature of the period [. . .]. There were many in his own day, and there still are some, to whom the matter of his discourse can never be tedious.'[40] Following his account of the military history of the Revolution, Burton ends his seventh volume with some fifty pages on ecclesiastical issues from 1689 to the end of the century. In terms of the present discussion, it is notable that it is the singularity of the discourse of the 'enthusiasts' with which he ends the chapter and the volume, and which he recognises as perhaps the most memorable religious feature of the time. It might be judged 'far less pleasing' than 'fairer' intellectual productions, but it illustrated the distinctive expression of the covenanters' religious conviction in 'declamations against the tyranny to which they were subjected'. It manifested

> a terse, strong, effective style, turned to the purpose of rapid and powerful declamation. These documents are rarely matched in earnestness and strength. The words are sonorous and abundant, yet never too many to enfeeble the stern fierceness of the writer's thoughts. There is a luxuriance of imagery – frequently Scriptural – but it is always apt and expressive; and however coarse or irreverent it may be, it is never allowed to degenerate into feebleness or incoherence [41]

Burton could be equivocal about the 'second language', particularly in relation to its 'denunciatory' strand. Critical comments occur periodically: the enthused rhetoric could become indigestible. At other times there is a knowing, satiric tone in his descriptions and paraphrasing of this discourse. However, just as in his deployment of Scots-language sources, he recognised that if he was to properly convey what was 'characteristic', 'curious', 'picturesque' and 'distinctive' about Scottish history – in this case in relation to the historical articulations of its predominantly Presbyterian faith – he required to let the nation's second language speak for itself. So he weaved it into the *History*, both in the main text and in footnotes with no little empathy for its intense cadences. Its forms varied from the 'denunciatory eloquence' of Knox and the Reformation preachers to the 'sonorous and abundant' words of the covenanter documents 'rarely matched in

---

[40] Ibid., VII, pp. 274–6 and footnotes; p. 279.
[41] Ibid., VII, pp. 467–8 and 467, footnote 1.

earnestness and strength', and to the quiet, near-mystical, inner transports of the saints. It is not constantly present but it is given – sometimes with a wry smile – appropriate prominence in those places where the historian's godly Scots contemporaries would have expected it to be.

THE SPIRIT OF THE TIMES

Burton, then, takes frequent opportunity to incorporate in the *History* the actual words of the characters and the documents that inform his narrative. The reason for doing so is to gain a full appreciation, emotional, spiritual, intellectual and even pictorial, of the past – 'to see and feel the spirit' of the Reformation, or elsewhere 'to feel and know the nature of the times'. The author is present, but often it is to say 'listen to these other voices'. Too arrogant or insensitive an interruption by the historian carries the danger that the reader's understanding of the difference of those times will be distorted, will be 'spoiled'.

Burton consistently sought to leaven the main political narrative with incidents that are arresting, 'curious' and 'picturesque', partly to retain the interest of his readers but also because their unfamiliar or unexpected characteristics revealed and reflected the prevailing historical 'conditions'. In this respect, the Picturesque shifts beyond its literary-aesthetic associations to signify and facilitate a new historiographic perspective and appreciation of the past. More than once, he juxtaposed this empathetic approach to former times with the judgement of 'philosophical historians', reflecting only the morality of their own age. The contrast was apt: 'philosophical historians', by which he meant most of his predecessors, were interested to trace the great stadial shifts from barbarism to civilisation, and in history teaching moral improvement by example. Burton is not entirely divorced from that background. More prominent, however, is a curiosity and sensitivity about 'the conditions' or 'the characteristics' or 'the spirit' of past times, and an awareness of the duty to respect them. The key was in attention to and careful interpretation of original sources, which could provide the necessary insights and avoid historical errors.

Burton exemplified this in describing the charges of abuse that had been levelled at the clergy of the old church in the decades before the Reformation. Many of these criticisms might have been justified but he exempted the practice of churchmen, particularly bishops, taking 'concubines' and fathering offspring. Some writers who, 'at a later period, interpreted the history of the times' thought that when they traced an eminent figure as the son of 'a Popish clergyman' they had identified 'an origin more infamous than ordinary illegitimacy'. In fact, at the period in question the practice was perfectly respectable since it was sanctioned by widespread official recognition. Previous historical confusion had resulted from a disjunction 'between the spirit of the age and the spirit of the writer dealing with it'. It is notable that he provided supporting evidence drawn from Innes's *Sketches*, and went on to emphasise that the only way to avoid such errors was 'by familiar acquaintance with contemporary documents'. The acceptance and recognition of the bishops' illegitimate offspring 'was expressly and definitely set forth in public documents and the title-deeds of estates'.[42]

The need to understand and accept the past in and on its own terms is made explicit in other instances, particularly where Burton thinks his contemporary readers might find it difficult to comprehend the reasons or motivations driving what seem to be an unexpected or inexplicable turn of events. In 1650, before the disastrous battle of Dunbar, General David Leslie's tactics of holding the high ground along the Forth and cutting off Cromwell's supply routes would probably have succeeded in forcing a retreat south as the English general himself recognised. Burton noted that there had been historical controversy over the claim that Leslie was forced to relinquish his advantage at the insistence of Presbyterian zealots who wished to destroy Cromwell's army of 'sectaries'. That a decision which led to the conquest of Scotland could have been forced on Leslie in this way might seem hardly credible, but Burton is clear: '[t]o one conversant with the spirit of the times nothing seems more natural than this. Cromwell being mercifully delivered into their hands, it was fitting that they should stretch forth their hands and accept of the gift.'[43]

A further example can be found in Burton's view of the 'long controversy' concerning the 'Wigton Martyrs'. These two women had been condemned in 1685 for their refusal to take the 'abjuration oath', which required subjects to swear allegiance to the Crown and renounce the Covenant. The traditional account indicated that they been unjustly condemned and put to death in a particularly cruel fashion by drowning. However, there had been challenges to the credibility of the whole story, asserting that the women had received a trial 'in proper form'. But for Burton this was precisely 'the real significance' of the event – illustrating, for his contemporary readers, a fearful time that nevertheless needed to

---

[42] Burton, *HOS* (1873), III, pp. 309–11 and 310, footnote 1.
[43] Ibid., VII, pp. 23–4.

be understood on its own terms. The jury may have been properly constituted, but it consisted of men who were

> prepared to wreak their vengeance on their hated enemies as far as the law would permit them. The affair was thus a memorable example of the prevailing spirit of the times. It was not so much that the Government with its own hand acted the executioner, as that it let loose the spirit of hatred and tyranny in the districts where it grew out of local conflict.[44]

Indeed, many of Burton's textual and authorial themes and habits accord with the intention, periodically made explicit, to capture and present the 'conditions' or 'spirit' of past ages. He was concerned to present Scotland's history in ways that would engage his audience of readers, and present the nation's past to them in ways that respected, and gained respect from, its foundations in original and authentic sources. Modern appreciation of the spirit of times past would be 'spoiled' unless they were appreciated in and on their own terms, as expressed and recorded by those who lived through them.

THE ROOTS OF ROMANCE

Burton's attitude to Walter Scott was, to an extent, equivocal. Associated politically with anti-Tory positions throughout his adult life, Burton could be jocular if not sarcastic about Scott's Tory-antiquarian enthusiasms. Yet, as he was working on his own *History of Scotland*, he was quite explicit in his appreciation of how Scott's work had conveyed new insights into many aspects of the nation's past, overtaking traditional efforts: 'Scott's fictions contain fuller revelations on many features in the career of his own country than the histories of the gravest and dreariest of her investigators.'[45] And like almost any member of the reading public in the first half of the nineteenth century, he was deeply versed in Scott's novels and poetry. References to them peppered his articles and books throughout his life, but the earliest evidence comes from his surviving literary juvenilia, probably designed to be shared with his young contemporaries in the Blackwoodian Society of Writers in Aberdeen.

A variety of short stories and effusive poems adopt many of the standard literary devices of early nineteenth-century romantic literature. Tales commence in picturesque and desolate ruins that foretell a landed family's downfall or introduce the story of a crusading Scottish

---

[44] Ibid., VII, pp. 253–5.
[45] Burton, *Book-Hunter*, pp. 270–4; Burton, *Scot Abroad*, II, p. 133.

knight. Parted lovers are bound by a 'Talisman', or exchange lockets of hair. Some heroes die tragically despite finding a 'token', a locket that can explain the mystery of their birth; those who triumph return to the ancestral hall where awaits a lost lover or an 'old, Grey haired Bard' with a harp and a 'Minstrel's Song'. There is a good deal of patriotism running through these early productions, partly centred on Wallace but – rather surprisingly given Burton's later views – a tear is also shed for the fate of the Jacobites. The stories are interspersed with reflective efforts on 'the Study of Nature'.[46]

In what appears to be the latest essay written in the late 1820s, he addressed the relation of fiction and history. Scottish vernacular traditions were particularly rich and had inspired 'many of our most beautiful & interesting Novels'. Fiction, and Scott in particular, is at the forefront of his mind as a major inspiration and as capturing the romance of Scottish history so far:

> in Scotland, we have our own dear superstitions of Bogles, Brownies, & Water Kelpies. If we look into the Novels by the Author of Waverley, which are certainly the best of the day, we will find in these evidently vulgar Superstitions, an interest & a fascination which can scarcely be accounted for otherwise, than by the wild and boundless field, which the Author has to go upon. It is one striking feature of Romance, that it is chiefly confined to such Countries, as are wild, mountainous, & inaccessible.– Thus England is not a romantic Country[.]

However, for this nascent historian, fiction was ultimately not enough – 'to make a Tale truly interesting' it should be extracted from the repository of remarkable occurrences and beliefs to be found in 'the dark Stream' of history.[47]

Scott was not the only teller of fictional tales that were influential in Burton's early adult years. As noted above, later allusions suggest that he was particularly keen on the novels of John Galt. In some of his best-known novels, Galt reflects the social change impacting on the late eighteenth-century small-town bourgeoisie and local gentry in novels with an episodic, anecdotal structure imbued with self-satire and ironical commentary on how historical change impacts his characters and narrators. This incorporated a new perspective on former times. The historian of Gudetown – thrice elected *The Provost* – found himself, on the death of his old adversary Bailie McLucre, reflecting on how

---

[46] NLS MS 9428, fols 6–7, 16, 59, 142, 143–5, 160–1.
[47] NLS MS 9429 fols 36–8.

the passing years had altered attitudes as to how far municipal bailies could be seen to profit from their involvement in public works. If he had seemed to treat lightly 'doings that are now denominated corruptions', it was simply to record 'that such things were' rather than commend or condemn them:

> Indeed, in their notations, I have endeavoured, in a manner, to be governed by the spirit of the times in which the transactions happened; for I have lived long enough to remark, that if we judge of past events by present motives, and do not try to enter into the spirit of the age when they took place, and see them with the eyes with which they were really seen, we shall conceit many things to be of a bad and wicked character that were not thought so harshly of by those who witnessed them, nor even by those who, perhaps, suffered from them.

The Provost concluded that he had no right to subject the past, even 'that method of administration in which the like of Bailie McLucre was engendered', to ethical yardsticks of the present: '[t]he spirit of their own age was upon them, as of ours is upon us'.[48] A degree of respect and understanding were due to past times, and even some lassitude allowed in judgements on the actions of men living under different conditions and trials. Literature scholars emphasise the satire and degree of self-delusion in Provost Pawkie's view of changing times, though as one writer has put it, the perceptive reader of Galt's book in any age might be drawn to the conclusion that 'to judge one age by another's standards is an error'.[49]

For Burton, the potential and the validation for a translation of some of the characteristics of fiction into historical narrative can perhaps be traced most directly to the influence of Walter Scott on Patrick Fraser Tytler, and to Burton's subsequent appreciation of Tytler's achievement. As already described, Scott had urged Tytler to produce a national history that could be made 'popular' by incorporating in the narrative 'romantic anecdotes illustrative of the manners of his countrymen'. Scott welcomed Tytler's initial volumes in a review in the *Quarterly Review* for their 'beauty of language' and 'graphically descriptive' passages, a number of which he reproduced: Scotland had found a historian whose narrative was sufficiently animated by tales of a 'romantic character', and who had 'no time for the vulgar opinion that the flattest and dullest mode of detailing events most reflects the truth'. It is highly probable

---

[48] Burton, *Scot Abroad*, I, p. 327; NLS MS 4403, fol. 83; John Galt, *The Provost* (Edinburgh: Foulis, 1913), pp. 173–4.
[49] Duncan, *Scott's Shadow*, pp. 232–5.

that Burton read this review. A number of the reviews of Tytler's subsequent volumes that appeared in *Tait's Magazine* were contributed by Burton himself, and one alludes directly to Scott's approbation in the *Quarterly Review*.[50]

At least in the limited period he covered, Tytler did indeed seek to elicit from his readers a new empathy with the past, 'the spirit of the age' of the late medieval world, and did so partly through imaginative writing bound up with pictorial description calling up the Picturesque. Burton's reviews demonstrate that he admired much of what Tytler had done – the dogged search for new and original sources, which, however, should be used with imagination and narrative verve to seek to reclaim and to treat with respect the 'character' or 'spirit' of other times. Notably Burton also began to sound a critical, even valedictory note in regard to respected eighteenth-century Scottish historians. Just as Tytler himself had questioned the efforts of Hailes, Burton moved towards a critique of the likes of Hume and Robertson: neither had penetrated into the 'fountainhead' of original documents and conveyed what was discovered with such authorial verve. Compared to these predecessors, Tytler's *History* had been delivered with 'more graphic force, a closer appeal to fact, and a firmer reliance on the naked truth of character and circumstance'. In Tytler's work, 'the style, or rather the spirit, of modern History' had become as vivid and arresting as fiction: '[I]f the novelists have, of late, invaded the province of the Historians, the latter have, on the other hand, learned something of dramatic effect from the pages of Historical Romance.'[51]

If Burton was enthusiastic about Patrick Fraser Tytler as a historian of Scotland, like many others (though certainly not all) he considered T. B. Macaulay to be the greatest historian of his time. Burton would come to know Macaulay well, and by the mid-century they were exchanging draft material. However, there is good evidence that Burton's assumptions on history-writing were challenged and directly influenced at an

---

[50] See above, p. x [ch 1, p. 10]; [Walter Scott], 'Tytler's History of Scotland', *Q Rev* 41 (1829), 328–59 (pp. 337–9, 349, 358); [John Hill Burton], 'Tytler's History of Scotland. – Vol. VI', *Tait's* 4 n.s. (1837), 769–80 (p. 769).

[51] See for instance, Tytler, *History*, I, pp. 183, 311, 325; [John Hill Burton], 'Tytler's History of Scotland' (Vol. VII), *Tait's* 7 n.s. (1840), 613–28 (p. 613); [John Hill Burton], 'Tytler's History of Scotland' (Vol. VIII), *Tait's* 9 n.s. (1842), 314–28 (p. 328); [John Hill Burton], 'Tytler's History of Scotland' (Vol. IX), *Tait's* 11 n.s. (1844), 85–94 and 156–63 (p. 85).

earlier stage by Macaulay's 1828 *Edinburgh Review* article on the subject. In that essay, Macaulay had argued that the writing of history should seek to balance 'Reason' and 'Imagination': it was not of course acceptable to invent material to supplement known facts, however the 'perfect historian must possess an imagination sufficiently powerful to make his narrative affecting and picturesque'. Too many modern historians had erred on the side of reason, partly seduced (as even Hume was) by their desire to present events from a particular perspective. History was disappearing amidst the controversialist positions adopted by the authors:

> they miserably neglect the art of narration, the art of interesting the affections, and presenting pictures to the imagination [. . .]. The most characteristic and interesting circumstances are omitted or softened down, because [. . .] they are too trivial for the majesty of history.

If, instead of accounts of high politicking, Clarendon had been 'the Boswell of the Long Parliament', he could have made his cavaliers and roundheads 'talk in their own style', or could have 'reported some of the ribaldry of Rupert's pages, and some of the cant of Harrison and Fleetwood'.[52]

Macaulay went on to argue that 'the perfect historian' was one in whom 'the character and spirit of an age is exhibited in miniature'. This meant that, besides the great events and figures, he should also consider

> no anecdote, no peculiarity of manner, no familiar saying, as too insignificant for his notice [. . .] Men will not merely be described, but will be made intimately known to us. The changes of manners will be indicated [. . .] by appropriate images presented in every line.

Manifestly responding to Scott, whose fiction had 'used those fragments of truth which historians have scornfully thrown behind them', he urged that amongst the battles and political changes, the historian should 'intersperse the details which are the charm of historical romances'.[53]

There is much in this analysis and advice that resonates with the aspects of Burton's later *History* highlighted in the previous sections. From Burton's surviving manuscript material, it is possible to trace directly the article's immediate impact on him. When he first read it, Burton was engaged in drafting a two-part essay that was very probably intended to be read to his contemporaries in Aberdeen's Society of Writers. The subject was 'On

---

[52] [Thomas Babington Macaulay], 'History', *ER* 47 (1828), 331–67 (pp. 331–2, 361–2).
[53] Ibid., pp. 364–5.

Imagination as connected with Civil History', and the thrust of the essay was clearly to confirm the superiority of 'philosophical history' as distinct from antiquarianism and historical romance. However, it is obvious that Macaulay's essay, which he had read in the midst of his composition, threw him off course. Just as he is formalising his first 'Canon of Historical Credence' – that no 'individualization or colouring of facts is to be made by the Historian' – he introduces a quote from a 'singular review' that had just appeared with an apparently contradictory message:

> A truly great Historian would reclaim those materials which the Novelist has appropriated. The History of the Government, and the History of the People would be exhibited in that mode in which alone they can be exhibited justly – in inseparable conjunction and intermixture. We should not then have to look for the Wars & votes of the Puritans in Clarendon, and for their phraseology in Old Mortality; for one half of King James in Hume, and for the other half in the fortunes [sic] of Nigel.

Though not immediately convinced, in the midst of his confident assertion of the 'canons of historical credence', he seemed to hesitate: '[h]ow is the phraseology of the days of Old Mortality to be introduced in History?' It is clear that part of Burton's intention had been precisely to emphasise the distinction between history and the omnipresent historical novel, and at this stage he struggled with the notion that everyday conversations 'should be snatched from the hands of the Novelists, to be committed to the Historians of the age'. Yet doubts had appeared in his response to Macaulay's article: perhaps there was room for 'modern Historians' to attend to the 'Anecdotes of other times', articulated in voices 'from the highest to the lowest', even in the phraseology of *Old Mortality*, just as the novelists could do. And perhaps history was concerned not only to find precedents and exemplification, but also to portray the nation's past in its own terms and for itself. After all, 'we are blessed with authors now living who have thus illustrated our National Manners as indellibly [sic], as if they had been engraved on the Brazen Tablets of History.'[54]

Macaulay's essay was in accord with a related cultural trend when he urged that historians should aspire to 'exhibit' the character of past ages 'by appropriate images presented in every line'. In the course of the 1820s, as we have seen, Scott's literary depictions of the nation's past

---

[54] NLS MS 9430, fols 1–38, particularly fols 9–10 and 32; [Macaulay], 'History', p. 365.

encouraged and validated the trend among the growing community of Scottish artists to choose many historical subjects drawn from his works. Burton was attuned to the trend from an early stage – his articles for the *Aberdeen Magazine* in 1831–2 incorporated critical reviews of some of the earliest major exhibitions at the Royal Institution. However, the trickle of historical-genre paintings became a flood through the 1830s and 1840s. Burton had many exemplars on which to call for the depiction of 'graphic events', 'finished portraits' and iconic settings, which commentators later noted running through his *History*.[55]

These influences contributed to and reinforced the deeply imbued sensibility of the Picturesque, which can be traced in the record of his thoughts committed to the private diary of his highland tour in 1829. In that journal there were already indications of how such sensibility could extend beyond the aesthetic appreciation of poetry and painting to the appreciation of a range of survivals of the past as illustrations and signifiers of the difference of former times. Later, the effort to capture and 'exhibit' in history 'the spirit of the times' or 'spirit of the age', the phrases used by Galt, Tytler and the young Macaulay to express a more empathetic approach to history, became a prominent feature in Burton's work. As described above, there were different ways to realise the intention. Picturesque and curious stories and encounters were included as illustrative of the period, even though the evidence they 'happened' might be at best thin. Incidental details and low-born figures are included to embellish the scenes of great events. Images are conjured for the reader through references to contemporary literature and painting, allusions which, he knows, he and the reader share. Attention is devoted to the surviving physical antiquities of the past as illustrations of the character of their times. Sometimes he steps forward himself to draw attention, rather didactically, to some occurrence as demonstrating the 'spirit of the times'. However, among the most powerful ways of conveying such understanding, and one frequently resorted to, was to let the sources speak in their 'own words'.

This impulse had also been central in driving the ambitious effort in records scholarship and the publication of Scottish historical source material, which had been gathering pace since the 1820s and has already been discussed. Burton was intimately involved in several of these cultural

---

[55] John Morrison, *Painting the Nation: Identity and Nationalism in Scottish Painting, 1800–1920* (Edinburgh: Edinburgh University Press, 2003), pp. 111–17; Macmillan, *Scottish Art*, pp. 182, 187; see pp. 182, 187, 222–5.

endeavours, and with the two men who took over leadership of the 'revolution' in records scholarship in the mid-century, Joseph Robertson and Cosmo Innes. It has been convincingly argued that Innes managed, as it were, to bring antiquarianism up to date: he saw antiquarian researches as able to demonstrate progress and to achieve a 'rapprochement' with Enlightenment values, but in ways that 'actually built on the new romantic interest in Scottish history'. Notions of progress were central to his antiquarian work, and he strove to imbue it with a 'more theorised interpretation of source materials'. At the same time, he was developing an approach to serious historical inquiry in which 'his portrayals of the past were simultaneously imbued with a strong romantic sensibility'.[56] Walter Scott stood at an early stage in this transition, as Burton acknowledged in passages of *The Book-Hunter*. Burton was aware of the close association between antiquarianism and romantic fiction, and made a point of noting that it was a Borders antiquary 'who first suggested to Scott the idea of improving the Jacobite insurrections, and, in fact, writing Waverley'. Within a few pages of each other, he gives descriptions of the aims of Scott and Innes, which are not dissimilar. While Scott's time was past, the cumulative labours of the records scholars created conditions that were 'pregnant' with the potential for future historical effort.[57]

This was antiquarianism worthy of respect, since it was founded on the careful preservation and publication of the rediscovered documents. The book club editors could offer personal views in the prefaces and perhaps footnotes, but the original documents were respectfully and carefully reproduced. It was 'a principle of honour throughout the clubs that the purity of the text shall not be tampered with; and so, whether dark or light, faint or strong, it is a true impression of the times'. The texts provided a kind of direct access point facilitating a new understanding and appreciation of past times. Critics might say that the long obscurity of the reproduced works was due to the fact that they had been bad or second-rate books in the first place. However, those 'who love these recovered relics of ancestral literature' would respond:

> In the first place, and apart from their purely literary merits, they are records of the intellect and manners of their age. Whoever desires to be really acquainted with the condition of a nation at any particular time [. . .] will not attain his object by merely reading the most approved histories of the period. He must endeavour to live back into the times, and to do this most effectually

---

[56] Marsden, *Cosmo Innes*, pp. 45, 61, 114.
[57] Burton, *Book-Hunter*, pp. 270–1, 276–9.

he had better saturate himself to the utmost with its fugitive literature, reading every scrap he may lay hand on until he can find no more.

Some might claim, he continued, that 'what is recalled out of the past loses the freshness and the fitness to surrounding conditions which gave it pungency and emphasis in its own day'. In fact for Burton, it was 'precisely' its difference with 'our method of thought and our form of language' that it is so valuable: '[I]t breaks in with a new light upon the intellect of the day, and its conventional forms and colours.'[58]

Burton worked into his *History* many of the characteristics that his Scottish readers would have anticipated from the presentation of the Scottish past in the works of Scott and in the literature and art that his *œuvre* inspired. Yet these were incorporated in a form shorn of the doubts that many hard-headed Scots Victorians may have had about relying on fictional romance for their view of the past. A fundamental shift had occurred through the intervening revolution in the availability and perception of source materials. This shift may partly have superseded romantic literature, but it reflected and incorporated the characteristics of romantic history. As he had observed before, the book club publications did not claim to be 'readable books'. However, they presented an opportunity for a retelling of the past in a new narrative. That narrative was required to reflect a rediscovered interest in and respect for the Scottish past grounded in original documents and on 'the purity of the text' through which it could be clearly viewed in all its variety. For Burton, as far as serving the interests of history was concerned, Scott the Book Club Man had performed at least as great a service as the Author of Waverley.

---

[58] Burton, *Book-Hunter*, pp. 292–4.

6

Gothic History

WEIRD STORIES

IN THE FIRST VOLUME of his *History*, in the midst of passages that reflect his fascination with Norse mythology and in which he recounts various tales of the Sagas, Burton turned aside for a moment to consider the origins of the Norse term 'wyrd' or in Scots, 'weird'. He initially associates it with the Nornir, the Norse equivalent of the Fates of classical mythology and notes its double meaning as denoting both one of those figures but also 'fate' in the general sense. In Scotland, he went on, it had long been used in these ways but also alluded to the wider range of meanings that would be obvious to anyone consulting the Scots Dictionary of his old colleague from the Advocates Library John Jamieson, and 'reading the quotations from Scots literature in prose and verse' associated with the term. Burton had clearly done so and might have added that readers carrying on through his *History* would find in many passages that range of meanings exemplified. Some of this certainly derived from that fascination for the strange or 'curious' that might be expected of one with lifelong if often cautious and sceptical antiquarian enthusiasms. A little later, he enthused that what remained of a prehistoric structure at Torwood in Stirlingshire 'is wonderful and as mysterious as it is wonderful'; and digressed on the 'mysteries' of the great repository of prehistoric standing stones in Scotland. But an attention to the uncanny and unexplained recurs as his volumes roll on through the centuries, a characteristic that extends beyond the merely curious to a preoccupation with the grotesque, supernatural and even demonic.[1]

---

[1] Burton, *HOS* (1873) I, pp. 97–8, 139–44, 227–8 and 228, footnote 1.

In proceeding to describe the struggle between 'heathendom' and advancing Christian influences after the fall of Rome, Burton lingered on material drawn from Pictish, Celtic-Christian and Norse mythology with their associated terrors. At an early point he is unable to resist recounting the tale of how 'with horrible distinctness' St Jerome as a child in Gaul had seen the Scots 'eating human flesh; [. . .] they cut off the buttocks of the herdsmen, or the breasts of women, and eat them as special luxuries'. Subsequently the Norse *Eddas* cannot be passed over in summary – 'an abridgement of them would be dry and useless' – so he recounts over ten pages of stories from the northern legends. Similarly, he dwells on the 'dark histories' of the later sagas: a passage from *The Death-Song of Lodbroc* deserves to be reproduced 'as a climax or paroxysm of the turbulent and bloody spirit of Saga literature'. A little later in Volume I the first signs appear of his periodic habit of literally 'underwriting' the narrative with lengthy footnotes – often incorporating passages in Scots – that actually tell the stories about which his main text expresses scepticism. For instance, he summarises the 'picturesque story' of the revenge killing in the late tenth century of an early King Kenneth by Finella, the wife of a 'Maarmor', or earl. But he cites below the more 'highly theatrical shape' provided by medieval chroniclers like Boece, Wynton and Fordun, adding that the 'picturesque district between Fettercairn and the sea is alive with traditions of Finella and her witcheries'.[2]

Proceeding to the reign of Macbeda (1039–56), the opportunity could hardly be passed over to continue the theme of 'witcheries' and supernatural intervention in juxtaposing the historical and Shakespearean versions of 'Macbeth'. However, he offers a generalisation, which reveals something of the mindset that gave prominence to these themes in his *History*. Much, he observes, in Shakespeare's play was anachronistic, but not all:

> Some things in the tragedy of Macbeth are powerfully characteristic to those accustomed to the spirit of past Scots life and history. Take, for instance, the weird sisters, so grand a contrast to the vulgar grovelling parochial witch of England, and so accurately in keeping with what we know, from criminal trials and otherwise, of the wilder crews frequenting such witchland as Scotland and the Harz can afford.

Before finishing with him, Burton reflects on why such *diablerie* came to be associated with Macbeth, prompting a citation of the lines from the

---

[2] Ibid., I, pp. 204, 219–33, 322–5; p. 339, footnote 1; Fettercairn is a small village in Burton's native Aberdeenshire.

Scots chronicler Andrew Wynton suggesting that the king had been the product of a tryst between his mother and the Devil appearing as a man. The diversion ends with a link to the literature of his own time, noting that Walter Scott, 'finding this wild legend unappropriated, brought it, with his usual sagacity, into the Lady of the Lake'. As his narrative moves on to the point at which he can use the Anglo-Saxon Chronicle, though complaining of its 'dry unimpassioned distinctness', he is again drawn to passages where there is a *frisson* of horror.[3]

Burton's penchant for macabre tales resurfaces in his treatment of particular events during the reigns of the early Stuarts. The first of these centres on the murder of James I in 1437 and this is considered in more detail in the following section. In his preamble to the demise, some decades later, of James IV at the Battle of Flodden (1513) Burton gives particular attention to the strange, otherworldly tales and premonitions in traditional accounts: 'Stories were afterwards remembered of portents and prophesies – stories which perhaps took their colour from the gloomy events which they professed to have foreshadowed.' A 'visionary seer' appeared to the king who, having warned him to desist and 'abjure the counsel of women, vanished into the world of spirits, whence he had come'. This is one of the occasions in which he fully reproduces his source in the Scots narrative of Lindsay of Pitscottie since 'the spirit of such a story is best understood in the words in which it is chronicled'. Burton goes on to provide in the main text an English language account of a further prophecy supposedly announced by a mysterious herald summoning the Scots gentry to appear before his master 'in the other world', all of those named later discovered to have fallen in the battle. As before, the same passage is then cited and reproduced from Pitscottie.[4]

The mysteries of the Gowrie Conspiracy, the ill-conceived attempt by the Earl of Gowrie and his brother to kidnap James VI and avenge their father's death, had already attracted perhaps disproportionate attention from previous historians including P. F. Tytler and William Robertson. It has been suggested that even for the sober and sceptical Robertson, the affair functioned as 'the opaque, imaginative centre' of

---

[3] Burton, *HOS* (1873) I, pp. 343, footnote 1, p. 348, footnote 1; pp. 432–4; Walter Scott, 'The Lady of the Lake', Canto Third, v, in *Poetical Works*, ed. J. Logie Robertson, pp. 230–1.

[4] Ibid., III, pp. 74–5 and footnotes.

his *History*.⁵ However, as critics would later observe, Burton accorded it more extensive coverage than any of his predecessors. Although he made good use of the evidence discovered later – the original letters of one of the conspirators, Robert Logan of Restalrig – Burton's narrative retained a sense of the mysterious and 'opaque' character of the affair. While Robertson and Tytler had alluded only briefly to its supernatural associations, Burton's account dwelt on them: for many, 'some mysterious vestiges of magic or sorcery added their dread influence to the strange tragedy. The Ruthven family had an evil reputation as dealers with the black arts.' The 'horror thus conjured up' was founded on rumours of dealings 'in sorcery, necromancy, witchcraft, and magic', and it was rumoured that when James returned to safety across the Forth, 'there was ebbing and flowing three times at that tide; and that the water betwixt Leith and Burntisland was blackish'. Loath to leave 'the mysteries or enigmas of this strange affair', Burton went on to draw extensively on Logan's eerily conspiratorial letters.⁶

These passages incorporate a further instance of Burton's tendency to allusive commentary, calling up for his readers associations bearing contemporary cultural resonance. The letters made 'repeated reference to Logan's stronghold of Fast Castle, on a rock near the southern entrance to the Firth of Forth': the conspirators and their victim were to come, he quoted Logan, 'to my house of Fast Castle by the sea'. Burton observed that the 'grim stronghold, so well-known from Scott's *Bride of Lammermoor*, was signally well adapted for such an enterprise [. . .] it belongs to a coast terrible to the mariner'. The history of the Gowrie Conspiracy did indeed have a 'pervasive influence' on Scott's novel, perhaps the pre-eminent example of his combining Scottish history and 'Gothic fiction'. As Burton indicates, it was widely believed that Fast Castle was the model for the dismal tower Wolf's Crag, which was all that ill fortune had left the novel's hero and which Scott portrayed as 'a symbol of unvaried and monotonous melancholy, not unmingled with horror'. Besides such literary associations, many of Burton's Scottish readers would have been familiar with the paintings of Fast Castle by Scott's friend John Thomson, who painted it several times, the most famous being *Fast Castle from*

---

⁵ D. J. Womersley, 'The Historical Writings of William Robertson', *Journal of the History of Ideas* 47 (1986), 497–506 (p. 502).
⁶ Tytler, *History*, IV, pp. 276–97; Robertson, *History of Scotland*, III, pp. 48–68; Burton, *HOS* (1873), V, pp. 316–52.

Below, which depicted the fortress on precipitous cliffs above a raging sea in terms of the terrifying sublime.[7]

As Burton's narrative moves further into the seventeenth century his penchant for weird tales shifts towards those imbued with elements of terror. He is periodically explicit in addressing the horrors of civil warfare, including accounts of slaughter and rapine suffered by towns like Aberdeen and Dundee, as well as Newry in Ireland. For instance, he draws on eyewitness accounts of how, during Montrose's campaign of 1644–5, after routing the covenanter army before Aberdeen the soldiery, 'seeing a man well clad, would first tyr [strip] him and save the clothes unspoiled, then kill the man', proceeding to detail this local chronicler's account of the indiscriminate slaughter that followed in the town. Six years later, the Cromwellian general Monk stormed Dundee, two days after the royalist defeat at Worcester. The slaughter here, noted Burton, 'has attracted a mysterious and horrible interest'. Not untypically, although he goes on to question the veracity of the horror stories, he reproduces various of the claimed atrocities, always alert for an arresting image: local tradition held 'that the carnage did not cease till the third day, when a child was seen in a lane called the Thester Row sucking its murdered mother'.[8]

In an aside, Burton reveals something of his thoughts while composing these accounts, and exemplifies his habit of conveying striking events in pictorial terms or with pictorial references. He notes that during the Thirty Years War towns that – like Dundee in this instance – held out against a besieging army could be 'handed over to the license of the soldiers, who slaughtered and pillaged, as we may see in Callot's etchings'. Here he refers to the series of etchings by French engraver Jacques Callot, *Les Grandes Misères de la Guerre*, which depicted the gruesome carnage inflicted on defeated communities during the Thirty Years War. The referencing of that conflict is further attested where Burton draws on

---

[7] Burton, *HOS* (1873), V, pp. 348–51; J. H. Alexander, 'Historical Note', in Walter Scott, *The Bride of Lammermoor*, ed. J. H. Alexander (Edinburgh: Edinburgh University Press, 1995), 333–8 (pp. 335, 338); Catherine Jones, 'History and Historiography', in *The Edinburgh Companion to Sir Walter Scott*, ed. Fiona Robertson (Edinburgh: Edinburgh University Press, 2012), pp. 59–69 (p. 68); Scott, *Bride of Lammermoor*, p. 59; for Thomson's paintings, including *Fast Castle from below*, see https://www.nationalgalleries.org/search/artist/rev-john-thomson, accessed 26 May 2021.

[8] Burton, *HOS* (1873), VI, pp. 341–2, 368; VII, pp. 41–2, and 42, footnote 1.

the eyewitness testimony of Sir James Turner to illustrate the barbarity of the slaughter around Newry and elsewhere in Ireland; and incidentally also provides further indication of how easily he fell into a literary mindset attuned to the work of Walter Scott. Burton's description of Turner as 'a soldier of fortune' and '*ritter* of the Thirty Years War' irresistibly recalls *Rittmeister* Dugald Dalgetty and Scott's *Legend of the Wars of Montrose*. Burton cites the edition of Turner's *Memoirs*, which had been published by the Bannatyne in 1829, but they had also earlier been identified by Scott in his Introduction to the novel as providing one of the chief models for the returning Scottish mercenary.[9]

Although Burton actually downplays the significance of the 'cruel inflictions' of the Killing Times as causes of the 1689 Revolution, he nevertheless incorporates the tales of innocents faced with merciless cruelty and murder in some detail. For the fate of the covenanter martyr, John Brown of Priesthill, he draws particularly on Patrick Walker and Robert Wodrow as sources since each embellished the tale with 'his own impressive and picturesque incidents'. Burton reinforced the horror of the scene by drawing on the eyewitness account left by John Graham of Claverhouse who, when his soldiers hesitated, slaughtered Brown before his family. In the separate case of the Wigton Martyrs, he hints at 'a doubt of the truth of the whole story'. Still, taking a cue from their reported fate, he grasps the opportunity to explore the full range of judicial killing available at the time.[10]

For Burton, of the period from the Restoration in 1660, 'we have hardly any better picture' than the tales of the persecuted, and he ends with the deaths of a number of those imprisoned in dark, overcrowded vaults in Dunottar Castle, their commemorative monument, he notes, figuring at an early stage in Scott's *Old Mortality*. The custodian of the ruins would later select for visitors 'that one among the many vaulted apartments which had the best attributes of picturesque horror. Of

---

[9] For interpretation of Callot's work and images of the etchings, see Katie Hornstein, 'Just Violence: Jacques Callot's Grandes Misères et Malheurs de la Guerre', *Bulletin: The University of Michigan Museums of Art and Archaeology* 16 (2005), at http://hdl.handle.net/2027/spo.0054307.0016.102, accessed 25 May 2021; Burton, *HOS* (1873), VI, p. 342 and *Scot Abroad*, II, pp. 133–4; James Turner, *Memoirs of his own Life and Times* (Edinburgh: Bannatyne Club, 1829); Walter Scott, 'Introduction to a Legend of the Wars of Montrose', in *Introductions and Notes from The Magnum Opus:[. . .]*, eds J. H. Alexander et al. (Edinburgh: Edinburgh University Press, 2012), 354–66 (pp. 357–61).

[10] Burton, *HOS* (1873), VII, pp. 251, 253–4.

certain narrow clefts in the wall he assured his audience that the hands of the victims were fastened into them with pegs.'[11]

DEMONS IN HISTORY

In a number of episodes of the *History*, the roles of leading figures are portrayed in diabolic terms: their culpability for dark deeds has an otherworldly dimension.

The first such instance centres on the events leading to the murder of James I in 1437. The plot is introduced in terms of the melodramatic preamble and denouement of a crime novel or play. Burton then reveals 'the real chief worker of the coming tragedy' – not the two likely suspects who were potential claimants to the crown, 'but Sir Robert Graham, who had no such claim'. As often in these passages, Burton maximises the sense of the mysterious at work: 'Portents and dreams and prophesies were rife [. . .].' Also characteristic is his effort to provide a 'picture' of the *finale* with some visual flair and drama:

> It was on the evening of the 20th of February [. . .] the king, disrobed, and wrapped in what would now be called a dressing-gown, lingered before the fire of the reception-room, chatting with the queen and her ladies, when ominous sounds were heard. Three hundred of the wild Highlanders were breaking their way into the monastery [. . .]. The party within looked to the fastening of the doors, and found that they had been tampered with by treacherous hands within. The next glance was to the windows, but these were too well secured to permit escape.

As the action reaches a climax, the language becomes highly wrought:

> The murderers rushed like a tempest through the buildings, and, not finding their victim, were fain to believe that he had escaped [. . .] however [. . .] [I]t was short work to tear open the flooring, and then their victim stood before them.

In his treatment of the subsequent events, Burton lingers long and in detail on the descriptions – 'all too horribly distinct' – of the torture and death of James's murderers. In addition, he makes a particular point of presenting Sir Robert Graham, the leader of the conspirators, in diabolic terms as the 'demon hero of the tragedy', the account dwelling on his 'strange peculiarities of character'.[12]

---

[11] Ibid., VII, pp. 274, 278–9 and 278, footnote 3.
[12] Burton, *HOS* (1873) II, pp. 405, 407–9, 412–13.

However, Sir Robert Graham is not the last dark character to be presented in 'demonic' terms in the *History*. In his passages leading to the introduction of James Hepburn, the Earl of Bothwell, Burton mined the available sources to draw on rich veins of supernatural material. In advance of the murder of Henry, Lord Darnley – a crime widely believed to have been orchestrated by Bothwell – Burton incorporated in footnotes supporting the main text the scene-setting that he found in the Scots vernacular version of George Buchanan's *Detectio*. Buchanan had presented the house to which Mary's consort was led to his doom as a place conjuring mysteries and terrors. Burton maintained this atmosphere in his own narrative, this time drawing on a passage from Lindsay of Pitscottie, which again is reproduced in the citation. From the first Bothwell is identified as a personification of evil, and in an account that sustains a sense of his almost supernatural rise to power and control over Mary, Burton presents Bothwell as 'that mysterious demon of our history'. This kind of association extends to the Earl's activities once banished from the realm: all of Europe learned 'that the active demon of the great tragedy commanded a fleet of pirate vessels, and had become the scourge and terror of the traders in the North Sea'. It was a fitting end, given his 'evil repute in his high office of Admiral of Scotland'. Burton ends on Bothwell by recounting the 'story of the confession', supposedly made on his deathbed, to the effect that the influence he gained over Mary was attributable 'to the science of the sorcerer or magician, in which he had been an ardent student and accomplished adept'. Despite suggesting that the 'story' was quite improbable, Burton evidently cannot resist this final supernatural gloss on the character of the 'mysterious demon'.[13]

Towards the end of the seventeenth century, there appears another of those figures whom Burton presents as exerting 'demonic' influence on significant events. This was Robert Ferguson, sometimes known as 'Ferguson the Plotter' for his suspected involvement in various intrigues in this period in support of different sides at different times. He is introduced first in relation to involvement in the Ryehouse Plot of 1683, an alleged conspiracy to overthrow Charles II and prevent his brother James succeeding to the throne. Burton avails himself of a contemporary description to present a suitably devilish portrait of one who makes his appearances fitfully, a shadowy, wraith-like presence. Ferguson next

---

[13] Ibid., IV, pp. 186 footnote 1; p. 197, footnote 1; pp. 224, 227, 247, 464, 470–3 and p. 471, footnotes 1 and 2.

surfaces in 1689–90 amidst the convoluted conspiracy known as the Montgomery Plot, an attempt by disappointed and disaffected Scottish lords to re-establish the Stuarts: it was discovered and collapsed, apparently through the leaders' treachery to each other. In the midst of their allies in London, Ferguson had appeared 'fugitively and indistinctly'. It hardly seemed credible that he had so quickly switched sides: however, in Burton's perception he was one of the 'historical characters' for whom it was unwise 'to apply ordinary rules of credibility; and if we take the word of Annandale, he was the master-demon of this plot, as he had been of the conspiracies on the other side'.[14]

Something of the sensibility behind Burton's presentation of particular episodes in history as subject to such mysterious, dark figures influencing and at times causing and controlling events may be gleaned from an article he wrote specifically devoted to 'Ferguson the Plotter', published in *Blackwood's Magazine* in 1852. In his introductory remarks Burton observed that those used to dealing with street mobs testified to 'mysterious figures' recurringly spotted as apparently 'the presiding demons of the scene', yet never found among those brought to book:

> [a] misty consciousness that such beings had played a powerful part in the evil drama remained; but of their individuality as human beings walking the earth and capable of being apprehended by the detective force [. . .] there was no distinct trace.

For Burton, this resonated with 'an impression vividly created by some names which are found crossing the page of history. In times of terror, and excitement, and crime, they are sure to be prominent and conspicuous' – but then they are gone, and in 'the seizures, imprisonments, trials, banishments, mutilations, hangings, beheadings, disembowellings, and quarterings, they have no more share than disembodied spirits'.[15]

DARK PACTS AND DOUBLES

To return for a moment to Mary and Bothwell, Burton's depiction of James Hepburn, as the 'mysterious demon of our history', colours his presentation of the doom of Mary Stuart and the nature of their relationship. Under the 'absoluteness of the mastership' of this diabolical character, Mary could be seen as traduced by something like supernatural power. She had entered a compact not just of the corporeal but one

---

[14] Burton, *HOS* (1873), VII, pp. 246, 348.
[15] [John Hill Burton], 'Ferguson the Plotter', *BM* 71 (1852), 703–19 (p. 703).

that required 'giving herself over, body and soul to one [. . .] of his sensual and tyrannical nature'. This is how Burton presents the controversial 'casket letters', seen as central to determining Mary's complicity in Darnley's murder, whose authenticity was still hotly debated in Burton's time. In these love letters her 'passionate vehemence [. . .] expresses the unconditional surrender of the writer's heart, its utter hopeless captivity, its owner's abject resignation to the will and humour of the victor'. Consequently, the ability to make any moral choice of her own concerning the murder has been lost: 'she would not do it for her own particular revenge, she does the bidding of the spirit that has mastered hers'. And Burton again emphasises that her sacrifice is not only of this world: '[h]er life, her fair fame, her infant child, her immortal soul – all will be thrown at his feet.'[16]

In the period that witnessed the fateful encounters of Bothwell and Mary, Burton appears intrigued with and repeatedly returns to the relationship between two other prominent figures. William Kirkcaldy of Grange was one of the Scots Lords who rose against Mary and Bothwell in the critical year of 1567 and was quickly appointed to the command of Edinburgh Castle. Although his military leadership was largely responsible for the defeat of Mary's forces at Langside (1568), he remained equivocal in his attitude to the Queen and changed sides after coming under the influence of William Maitland of Lethington, whom he released from confinement in the Castle in 1569. Both were executed in 1573, having sought to hold the fortress as Mary's last champions. In Burton's earliest references to the two men, they are presented as fundamentally different in character. Grange is typically described as honourable, even 'the flower of chivalry'. Lethington is portrayed as an amoral and manipulative trickster: his world was that of 'the craft and wisdom of Machiavelli'.[17]

Burton's presentation of the relationship between the two men runs through a series of episodes in which the chivalrous and heroic character of Grange is slowly darkened and corrupted, though 'his fall came not from treachery of nature'. As events come to leave them hopelessly isolated in the Castle, Burton's allusions reveal that he conceived the two men as increasingly locked in a Faustian relation. Grange's corruption was an inevitable consequence of a fatal pact: 'for men who follow such desperate courses, it is ever the bargain with fate, that they know what it

---

[16] Burton, *HOS* (1873), IV, pp. 224, 247, 258, 261–2.
[17] Burton, *HOS* (1873), III, pp. 343–6; IV, pp. 310–12; V, pp. 28, 54.

has in store for them'. And although he outlines other possible reasons – Mary's 'siren' influence, a radical change of heart – the impression from Burton's final allusions is that 'Lethington's subtle logic mastered his judgment': just before his execution, it 'appears that Grange grew pious and penitent, and laid much store by an expression of Knox, implying that there was yet salvation for him, but none for the Mephistopheles who had led him astray'.[18]

In the following century, for Burton, there was a certain 'grandeur' to the great ecclesiastical conflict that led to the civil wars of the 1630s and 1640s, even in Archbishop Laud's 'wild dream' of episcopal uniformity. By contrast, in the period after the Restoration in 1660 leading on to the Killing Times, episcopal oppression 'from its commander, Archbishop Sharp, down to the humblest curate [. . .] was material and self-seeking'. Yet Burton's extensive coverage of Sharp's character, political duplicities and fate – over forty pages in two sustained sections – has as much to do with the spirit world as the material: besides 'material fear' the people had 'a suspicious horror of him, as one who had made a compact with the spirit of evil'. There is indeed something distinctly of the literary-gothic, and particularly the Scottish literary-gothic, about Burton's presentation of Sharp almost as a delusive 'divided self': we hear his self-justifying inner thoughts as he seeks excuses for his presentation of one *persona* to the covenanters as their representative at court and another to the court itself as he manoeuvres to have himself made Archbishop of St Andrews. The account of this double dealing is the prelude to his slaughter on Magus Muir in May 1679 as a betrayer of the Covenant, apparently delivered into the hands of his killers through a course of chance events – though Burton gives prominence to the assassins' belief that it was all supernaturally providential.[19]

There is first a lengthy account of the perfidy of Sharp to the covenanting cause, formed almost entirely of quotations from the archbishop's own letters from London, Burton weaving these together to produce 'a self-drawn picture of duplicity', which builds for nearly fifteen pages. Much of a later chapter is devoted to the circumstances surrounding Sharp's death and its aftermath. Burton precedes this account with a tale that actually does present Sharp as a *doppelgänger*, exactly in the terms in which nineteenth-century Edinburgh would have understood

---

[18] Ibid., V, pp. 115, 126, 128. Elsewhere in the *History*, Burton indicates familiarity with 'the Mephistopheles of Goethe': I, p. 226.
[19] Ibid., VII, pp. 129–46, 197–221.

the term, one able to appear in two places at once as a result of 'spiritual' and probably diabolic assistance. Burton himself draws attention to the fact that Robert Wodrow, who recorded the story, did not venture even at the turn of the eighteenth century to include such superstition in his published *History* but put it in a 'private note-book' that was only later printed (for the Maitland Club in 1842–3) as his *Analecta*. Nevertheless, he proceeded to recount a similar story, also drawn from the *Analecta*, suggesting that Sharp was communing with 'the muckle black devil'. In a further preamble to the Sharp murder, Burton recounts a related mystery concerning an earlier attempt on Sharp's life in 1668 by an Edinburgh shopkeeper and covenanting sympathiser named James Mitchell, in which the long-winded legalese of the *State Trials* account that Burton drew on is spiced up with a kind of breathless crime-novel delivery.[20]

Finally, Burton elaborates on the successful assassination and events around it. The conspirators, mainly Fife 'peasants', had originally simply wished to teach a lesson to a local oppressive sheriff-substitute, William Carmichael. What drove them to commit the crime is not clear at this stage: Burton accepts that at the start they did not set out to kill either Carmichael or Sharp but were open to interpret, as God's will and guidance, any opportunities that came their way. The sequence of events is told very much as a defined story. A sense of the group psychology and progress of the assassins is conveyed early on by handing over the narrative to a kind of collective-subject or consciousness, allowing Burton to convey the intensity and improve the fluency of the material available in his sources. His narrative of the murder concludes with an extensive account – which maintains a sense of the mysterious and providential – of the murderers' flight, continuing to use their direct testimony to convey the sense of a dream-like progress across the country, mysteriously 'protected by a higher power' through a series of miraculous escapes and incidents. At one point they are actually entertained as Cavalier troopers, so that in the end, to a predestined deliverance, 'the Lord wonderfully carried them through [. . .]'.[21]

---

[20] Burton, *HOS* (1873), VII, pp. 198–207; Robert Wodrow, *Analecta: or, Materials for a History of Remarkable Providences [. . .]*, 3 vols (Glasgow: Maitland Club, 1842–3). Burton's research notes on the *Analecta* survive and include the entry, 'Archp [sic] Sharp a double [sic] ganger': NLS MS 9426, fol. 44; 'The Trial of James Mitchell [. . .]', in *A Complete Collection of State Trials [. . .]*, compiled by T. B. Howell, 34 vols (London: Longman, 1816–28), VI, pp. 1207–61.

[21] Burton, *HOS* (1873), VII, pp. 207–21.

At the same time, different aspects of the otherworldly had been given prominence. The attackers riddle his coach with bullets but Sharp is not killed:

[t]he Evil one was notoriously known to have the power of contracting with the lost souls he dealt with for exemption from the leaden bullet; but his power did not extend to 'the edge of the sword', sanctified of old as the avenger of wickedness.

And later, when the archbishop's tobacco box is opened, a bee flies out and is identified as his 'familiar'. Burton explains that the 'creature was an agent or ambassador from the prince of the powers of darkness ever at hand'; and adds, '[h]ence the German legend of the bottle-imp – a creature lying lethargic when the world is behaving well, but showing animation and activity when any mischief likely to promote its master's interest is brewing'.[22]

It is appropriate here, in tracing Burton's attention to tales of malevolent supernatural influence, to return for a moment to Robert Ferguson 'the Plotter', since the *Blackwood's* article referred to earlier reveals that Ferguson too was a figure he associated with a dark pact. Burton had clearly read what he terms a 'master-sketch' of Ferguson by Walter Scott. This is contained in explanatory notes to the poem *Absalom and Achitophel* in Scott's edition of Dryden's *Works*. Scott refers to Ferguson's 'dark and bloody intrigues' and his 'mystic correspondence' in coordinating the Monmouth conspiracy, yet another 'Plot', this time aimed at the overthrow of James II in 1685. However, if he took something of a dark and mystic cue from Scott's account, Burton develops much further the otherworldly associations of how, in the Ryehouse plotting, the Earl of Shaftesbury ('Achitophel') and Ferguson were bound together using the same Faustian trope he had earlier conjured to summarise the relation of Lethington and Grange. One, Shaftesbury, was a 'despotic spirit', ever overcoming conscience; the other, Ferguson, a coarser but 'active instrument, who ministered to Achitophel's restless wishes, as the servile demon of the diabolical tales ministers to the capricious will of him who has bought superhuman services for the price of his soul's welfare'. He has no doubt, anticipating the description in his later *History*, that Ferguson 'was the presiding genius and the exciting demon of the Ryehouse Plot [. . .][,] the secret agent of the darkest intrigues of the violent men who demanded blood'. In the article, such language recurs: Ferguson 'was the suggesting

---

[22] Ibid., VII, pp. 211–16.

and controlling spirit of this diabolical enterprise', and mysteriously disappears when the game is up, 'under the protection of his spell'.[23]

Ideally cast in his character and his actions to be the last of these 'master-demons' of the *History*, Simon Fraser, Lord Lovat intrigues his way through Burton's final volume, covering the period to 1748. He too is a plotter, amorally switching sides in a lifelong search for power and preferment; presenting one face to the established powers while acting an entirely opposite part in Jacobite plans. He even has a potential 'other' in Duncan Forbes of Culloden, and Burton had written a 'double' biography of the two men published in 1847 contrasting Lovat's duplicity and darkness of character with Forbes's upright but suggestible personality. It comes as something of a surprise that there is nothing of the supernatural or Faustian in the passages that describe Lovat's duplicities and his dealings with Forbes. Rather, they are presented as personifications of 'distinct periods in the history of civilisation', one of which is passing away: Lovat was 'a type of the old reign of fraud and force, rendered the more conspicuous by protruding into an era of transition [. . .].' He could never have suborned Forbes, whose character presaged the world of 'the moral and social reformer', on the cusp of modernity.[24] Things had changed.

The change is presaged in Burton's rather enthusiastic signposting for his readers of sources in which they can find fuller accounts of Scottish early modern supernatural beliefs. It is notable that these are works chiefly published or republished in the three or four decades before he was writing, including editions produced for the book clubs or written by close friends like Robert Chambers and Kirkpatrick Sharpe. He is particularly sorry to lose the contributions of Robert Wodrow, whose *History of the Sufferings of the Church of Scotland* he had used extensively, partly because it had preserved 'rare works' and 'manuscript sources'. Wodrow's *History*, written in the early eighteenth century when he was the minister at Eastwood, near Glasgow, had been composed partly in defence of the covenanters but it continued to be valuable in view of his 'dogged reliance on the primary sources'. However, for Burton, 'he left behind him, though unconsciously, something still more interesting to the curious' – this was the *Analecta*. There was nothing Burton liked better than a source that had been intended

---

[23] Walter Scott, 'Explanatory Notes', in *The Works of John Dryden*, ed. Walter Scott, 18 vols (London: Miller, 1808), IX, pp. 363–8; Burton, 'Ferguson the Plotter', pp. 708, 710–11.

[24] Burton, *Lives of Lovat and Forbes*, pp. vi–vii.

'to conceal from a prying world' the beliefs of a writer who had sufficient doubts to exclude tales and 'private experiences' from his published work but reveal them in full in the secret narrative of a credulous man of his time, 'a believer in nearly all the current superstitions of his age'.[25]

But Wodrow, too, stood at a transition:

> [t]he interesting and curious phenomenon of the supernatural period, ramifying, as it were, into the subsequent age of serenity and indifference, is seen in the writings of Wodrow, and especially in that confidential note-book which is the repository of his secret and fugitive thoughts.

What the minister of Eastwood had committed to paper in the *Analecta* concerning miraculous occurrences and supernatural interventions – believed by his acquaintances and half-believed by a scholar like himself – had extended the age of 'significant marvels' and 'legends'. Some of these Burton had already used and he incorporated a series of others in a lengthy valedictory note on Wodrow: his 'tremulous dubiety is indeed indicative of the fading away, in the new generation, of the bold supernatural traditions which he inherited from the old'. It is manifest that Burton thought the effort rather admirable and certainly valuable, as capturing all those 'interesting and curious phenomena' of the last supernatural age: even if Wodrow often did not know 'what to make of it', he 'tells the tale as it was told to him'.[26]

Burton's disappointment is almost palpable. He had entered the age of 'indifference' to the miraculous and uncanny. There would be no more weird stories to tell.

DARK IMAGINATIONS

Burton exhibits a number of recurring elements in his perception of Scottish history in the passages analysed above. He is certainly drawn to the curious and bizarre, best revealed in those often vernacular sources with their strange tales. This extends at times to a morbid, almost voyeuristic attention to rather horrific and murderous scenes. Overlaying both is a residual fascination with superstitions and supernatural interventions still credited (as he might have said) by the vulgar and not long abandoned by the educated. Finally, there appears a recurrent theme of virtue seduced and overthrown and society suborned by evil figures

---

[25] Burton, *HOS* (1873) VII, p. 116, footnote 1; p. 277, footnote; L. A. Yeoman, 'Wodrow, Robert', in *ODNB*, accessed 14 March 2021.
[26] Burton, *HOS* (1873) VIII, p. 381, footnote 1.

who exert their baleful influence while remaining in one way or another undetected. The influences that shaped such preoccupations can be traced throughout his adult life, and would be sustained through various social settings and relationships, some of which appear unexpected in post-Enlightenment Edinburgh. However, contributory experiences were present from early in his life.

The area 'between Fettercairn and the sea', which he described as so full of the tales of Finella and her 'witcheries', Burton had traversed on many occasions in the long treks he made each summer from his home into the Cairngorm mountains. He was also deeply versed in both the original balladry of Aberdeenshire, probably the most extensive repository of its kind as existed anywhere in Scotland, with all its elements of *diablerie*; as well as in the Scottish literary publications of the early nineteenth century from the works of the 'Wizard of the North' to the 'terror fiction' of various *Blackwood's* writers. This influence of the otherworldly in both his local experiences and in the broader literary culture of the time is reflected in Burton's *juvenilia*. His poems incorporate a recurrent strain of the darker themes in folk culture, and his teenage notebooks already demonstrate an interest in the demonic in other lands. In his wanderings, Burton would often have come across the 'mysterious' prehistoric structures and the sculptured stones with their arresting imagery. His 1851 *Blackwood's* article, centred on Daniel Wilson's book on Scotland's prehistory, combined commendation of the cool inductive approach of the new archaeology with a sensitivity to the mysteriousness and the imaginative impact of the depictions on the stones. The impression on the beholder was such as to cause 'disturbed sleep': they are 'like nightmares [. . .] writhing snakes, intertwined and knotted [. . .]; crocodiles with heads at either end of the body; horribly contorted grinning apes'. He would later provide a detailed and animated description of the stones in the *History*, particularly commenting on the 'versatility of form and motion in them, much of it horribly grotesque', and their association with local supernatural legend.[27]

Soon after he arrived in Edinburgh, Burton was in correspondence with Joseph Robertson on the subject of superstitions and witchcraft, Robertson recommending a range of works on 'fairy legends' in different cultures, including an essay in Scott's *Border Minstrelsy* (final version, 1830) and other material in *Marmion*. Notably, given Burton's

---

[27] NLS MSS 9429, fols 25–7; NLS MS 9428, fol. 145; [Burton], 'Vestiges' (1851), p. 670; *HOS* (1873) I, pp. 142–4.

use of it on similar issues much later in the *History*, Robertson advised him to consult John Jamieson's *Scots Dictionary* (1808–25) for the background to Scottish superstitions. Burton's article on 'Witchcraft in Scotland' for *Tait's* in 1836 illustrates his wide reading on the subject, including Walter Scott's *Letters on Demonology* (1830). For the *Westminster* Burton had also reviewed the recently published *Criminal Trials* (1833) by Robert Pitcairn, whose 'stories' illustrating the social significance of popular superstitions and the admissibility in former times of supernatural evidence within legal process intrigued him as they had Scott.[28] As noted above, Burton alludes at various points to Scott's 'appropriation' of elements from the Scottish annals with associations of horror or the supernatural in poetical works or novels like his 'most porous Gothic story', the *Bride of Lammermoor*. The readers of the *History* would have been attuned to such cues: Scott's fictions in poetry and prose 'were central to developing and popularising an identifiably Scottish Gothic'.[29]

Among the other Scottish novelists prominent earlier in the century, Burton particularly admired the works of John Galt. Galt had sought to capitalise on the market for the three-volume novel, publishing several in the early 1820s including *The Spaewife* (1823). The novel centred on those events leading to James I's demise, which Burton recounts in terms of such horror and the demonic influence of Sir Robert Graham. These events are known in unusual detail on the basis of a near-contemporary record and in his citation of this early source in his *History*, Burton noted that it had been printed on three occasions, most recently by Galt, 'as a historical illustration of his novel of The Spaewife'.[30]

The novel has some claim to be the most otherworldly of Galt's books. However, the contemporary source document that both Galt and Burton drew on is actually rather equivocal about Sir Robert 'Grame'.

---

[28] NLS MS 9402, fol. 24; [John Hill Burton], 'Witchcraft in Scotland', *Tait's* 3 n.s. (1836), 17–26 (pp. 17–20 and footnotes); Walter Scott, *Letters on Demonology and Witchcraft* (London: John Murray, 1830), p. 10; Robert Pitcairn, *Criminal Trials in Scotland [. . .]*, 3 vols (Edinburgh: Bannatyne Club, 1833); [John Hill Burton], 'Pitcairn's Criminal Trials in Scotland', *W Rev* 19 (1833), pp. 332–60.

[29] Fiona Robertson, 'Gothic Scott', in *Scottish Gothic: An Edinburgh Companion*, eds Carol Margaret Davison and Monica Germanà (Edinburgh: Edinburgh University Press, 2017), 102–14 (pp. 104, 110–11).

[30] Burton, *HOS* (1873), II, p. 409, footnote 1.

It does allude to him as 'that odyus and false traitour' as he participates in the attack on James. However, the author has already given a good deal of support to Graham's self-justification for rebellion as resistance to tyranny as well as revenge for the execution of his relations. There is absolutely nothing of the 'demonic'. But in the novel Graham is diabolically possessed and portrayed as a master of diabolic temptation: the Earl of Athol, initially shocked at the proposed assassination, is 'overpowered by the demon who so openly tempted him'. Once they are at Perth, Graham, in beggarly clothing from his wanderings, reveals himself to The Earl and Lord James in 'a dreadful voice', and Atholl responds as before: 'Avaunt! fiend! demon! Tempt me no more!' and reproves Stuart 'that you will not help me from the fangs of this fiend?' It is the 'Graeme' (yet another spelling) of *The Spaewife*, rather than the 'Grame' of his historical source who shares the otherworldly characteristics of Burton's 'demon hero of the tragedy'.[31]

However, attuned as he was in private life and literary tastes to supernatural and traditional lore, the young lawyer who arrived in Edinburgh in 1830 was determined to succeed in a modernising, Whig-dominated public world of the law. He was soon a *protégé* of figures like Sir William Hamilton and various among the Whig grandees, men not normally associated with the 'weird' and otherworldly. It might have been expected that such a reformer and radical would soon leave behind the *glaumerie* of the muirland witches and the Rhymer asleep under the hill. Hamilton in particular might seem to be the personification, the pre-eminent inheritor, of the late Scottish Enlightenment. Strongly influenced by Dugald Stewart and engaged through the 1830s in a re-examination of Thomas Reid's philosophy, he was surely fully immersed in the rational philosophical discourse of his great eighteenth-century predecessors. And yet '(b)eneath the calm classical surface of early nineteenth-century Edinburgh lay elements of the fantastic and mystical'.[32]

This was true to a surprising extent, not only of various figures in the circle of acquaintance around Hamilton which Burton joined in the early 1830s, but of the great man himself. Hamilton's efforts to save and update Common Sense philosophy went hand in hand with an exploration of a range of psycho-medical theories that laid claim to 'scientific'

---

[31] John Galt, *The Spaewife; A Tale of the Scottish Chronicles*, 3 vols (Edinburgh: Oliver & Boyd, 1823), III, Appendix No. 10, pp. 289, 303–4, 311; I, p. 292; II, pp. 185, 315–17.

[32] David and Francina Irwin, *Scottish Painters at Home and Abroad: 1700–1900* (London: Faber, 1975), p. 262.

veracity, as well as an openness towards and inquiry into supernatural and spiritualist phenomena. Burton recalled later that Hamilton's 'comprehensive method of enquiry brought him deep into the literature of witchcraft, sorcery, necromancy, alchemy, astrology, and all the old superstitious sciences'. Hamilton's favourite tome was apparently a work by Christopher Irvine, a seventeenth-century Scottish writer whose magical/alchemic ideas Hamilton used to illustrate his conviction that the contemporary theorising and exploration of unseen forces was not new.[33]

Among the regular visitors to his soirées, besides philosophy and history, there were interests and debates on a range of issues that stretched from the possible unconscious powers of the mind over the physical world, as claimed in 'mesmerism' (hypnosis) or 'animal magnetism', to the publications on witchcraft and demonology emerging as part of the German romantic movement. Hamilton's closest friends in this circle were two 'literary advocates', John Colquhoun and George Moir. Colquhoun was a sheriff-depute, a judicial law officer, but his great enthusiasm was as a proponent of 'animal magnetism', the theory that the body contained an invisible force or 'magnetic fluid' that could act on others in a way analogous to magnetic force. He was particularly intrigued by cases involving claims of clairvoyance. Moir was deeply interested in witchcraft, magic and the 'grotesque horrors' of 'daemonology'. As already noticed, he had written of the Scottish past as particularly rich in illustrations of the occult: for Moir, this extended from the tales of medieval wizards like Thomas of Ercildoune to those supernatural forces at work before Flodden, both of which would be accorded attention in Burton's *History*. Burton was certainly closely associated with Hamilton and the circle that included Colquhoun and Moir through the 1830s and into the mid-century; and reviewing Hamilton's biography in 1870, he recalled quite distinctly the obsession with the 'marvellous physical and psychological phenomena so rife twenty-five years ago'.[34]

In addition, from the 1830s into the mid-1850s, he came to socialise with a number of other figures who were also fascinated with evidence

---

[33] [Burton], 'Veitch's Memoir of Hamilton', pp. 200, 205. Christopher Irvine, *Medicina Magnetica: or, The rare and wonderful Art of Curing by Sympathy: [. . .]* (Edinburgh, n.p., 1656); see Allen G. Debus, *Chemistry and Medical Debate: Van Helmont to Boerhaave* (Canton: Watson, 2001), pp. 111–12.

[34] Veitch, *Memoir of Hamilton*, pp. 144–5; Alan Gauld, 'Colquhoun, John Campbell', ODNB, accessed 4 December 2019; Brian Hillyard, 'Moir, George', ODNB, accessed 4 December 2019; see above pp. 24–5 and Moir, 'Demonology', pp. 25–46; [Burton], 'Veitch's Memoir of Hamilton', p. 209.

of the dark side of human nature and with the supernatural world. Familiarity with the individuals themselves and with their literary works meant further exposure to the speculation concerning the relation of the spiritual and material worlds and fascination with stories of the macabre and occult that characterised aspects of Edinburgh culture through the middle decades of the century. Thomas De Quincey could be charming and eloquent in company, but those in the Edinburgh literary world who knew him well also experienced the emotive, otherworldly outbursts of a highly charged imagination and often tortured mind. The younger James Hogg recalled that De Quincey would suddenly emit, 'on the spur of the moment, wailing passages of almost unearthly beauty and pathos, unsurpassed by anything in the 'Suspiria'. Years later, Hogg could still recall the impact of 'the weird power of these strange glimpses of his inner life', De Quincey's voice seeming 'to lift me, by some magic, far away from the dimly lit room to behold scenes which no Dante has ever described'. Burton must often have experienced these unsettling outbursts. For a recent biographer of De Quincey, they were fundamental reflections of a psyche that sought victimhood as a means of heightening emotional intensity: 'Playing the victim enabled De Quincey to indulge his passion for the sublime', conceiving himself as 'the central figure in a Gothic drama of flight and pursuit [. . .]. And if he was not actually being pursued, his imagination conjured demons.'[35]

Reference has already been made to the dinner that Burton and J. R. Findlay attended at De Quincey's cottage near Lasswade in 1852. In the midst of the repast, De Quincey suddenly switched from discussing history and the classics to the possibility of identifying 'all the marks of Antichrist'. That evening other dark topics were in the air, not least murder: as Burton and Findlay left to return to Edinburgh there were 'some jokes about the possibility of our being attacked and garrotted'. Talk of murder would not have shocked Burton. He certainly knew his Scott and Galt, but he had little or no interest in subsequent mainstream developments in the Victorian novel, his wife recalling that he 'disliked almost equally the philosophical novel, and the domestic or social novel'. Rather he developed an enthusiasm for the increasingly popular crime fiction of the 1850s and 1860s. Kate recalled that when a novel was

---

[35] James Hogg, 'Days and Nights with Thomas De Quincey', in *De Quincey* collected by Hogg, 169–205 (pp. 171, 175); Findlay, 'Personal Recollections', pp. 142–3; Robert Morrison, *The English Opium-Eater: A Biography of Thomas De Quincey* (London: Weidenfeld and Nicolson, 2009), p. 276.

recommended to him, his response was to enquire whether there was 'plenty of murder in it'.[36]

It seems inconceivable that Burton would not have read De Quincey on murder. His first essay on the subject, *On Murder Considered as One of the Fine Arts*, was published in *Blackwood's Magazine* in 1828, just at the time when Burton recalled it being avidly devoured by his group of aspiring *litterateurs* in Aberdeen. De Quincey returned to the subject, again in *Blackwood's*, in November 1839 after Burton was first introduced and began to socialise with him; and later again in 1854 with a *Postscript* that examined a series of early nineteenth-century murders by a man named John Williams, particularly the way in which the killer had sought 'to intensify the sense of panic, terror, and defencelessness' of the victims. In this and his other works on the theme, he was helping prepare the ground for an entire literary genre, delineating the 'key features of the detective novel'. It might be added that the opportunity was provided by the openness of *Blackwood's* to a literature of violence and 'terror fiction'.[37]

De Quincey's writings on murder, and particularly the *Postscript*, incorporated elements that went beyond mere sublunary motivations and passions and called up notions of the fiendish and diabolic. In the course of the essay De Quincey does discuss the murderer's motives for the killings, including simple theft as well as the public rumour of a possible love-rivalry with his victim. Yet his language points to a presumption of less worldly drives. Williams is 'one born of hell'; a 'hell-kite, that knew not what mercy meant'; he is not a man, but 'that dreadful being' or 'the diabolic man, clothed in mystery'. De Quincey was fascinated and intrigued by how 'the one demon' had terrorised the entire country yet had managed to avoid capture and to murder again, mounting a 'resurrection on some stage of horror'. Although Williams was eventually caught, De Quincey's account played up the almost providential escapes and the mysterious progress Wilson was able to achieve to sustain his reign of terror. In De Quincey's portrayal of this demonic figure, 'clothed in mystery', there seems much that is characteristic and prescient of those

---

[36] Findlay, 'Personal Recollections', p. 133; Katherine Burton, 'Memoir', pp. xlii–xliii.
[37] Robert Morrison, ed., *Thomas De Quincey on Murder* (Oxford: Oxford University Press, 2009), pp. xx–xxi, xxiv); Robert Morrison and Chris Baldrick, eds, *Tales of Terror from Blackwood's Magazine* (Oxford: Oxford University Press, 1995), pp. xiii–xviii.

'presiding demons of the scene', who for Burton flitted through history ever present 'in times of terror, and excitement, and crime', yet mysteriously disappearing until the next outrage, defying detection.[38]

In the course of the 'many pleasant evenings' De Quincey spent at Catherine Crowe's house in Darnaway Street, it is scarcely conceivable that the talk would not have turned often to murder. Not only had De Quincey returned to the subject with gusto in the 1839 and 1854 essays, but Crowe was building an increasingly successful reputation as a writer of fiction pulsating with rich veins of homicide. De Quincey admired Crowe's work in terms that clearly anticipate some of the leading characteristics of crime fiction. Besides murder, Crowe's interest in the supernatural had been growing since the mid-1840s. In 1845 she translated Justinus Kerner's *Die Seherin von Prevorst* as *The Seeress of Prevorst*, an account of the visions of a 'somnambulist clairvoyant' that had earlier interested Sir William Hamilton. Kerner, a friend of Goethe and a practising physician seems to have come to believe that these experiences of a local forester's daughter were a manifestation of the seamless relation between the physical and spirit worlds posited in the theory of 'animal magnetism'.[39]

After the *Seeress*, Crowe produced *The Night Side of Nature* (1848), also influenced by German writers. Here she argued against those who regarded supernatural phenomena such as 'prophetic dreams, presentiments, second-sight, and apparitions' as 'mere subjective illusions'. Much of the work however consists of tales of the supernatural: chapters are devoted to accounts of 'Wraiths', 'Haunted Houses', 'Apparitions' and the like. Crowe's chapter on 'Doppelgangers, or Doubles' reflects her knowledge and evident admiration for notions of 'a kind of magnetic phenomena', which had been theorised by 'the physiologists and psychologists of Germany'. One of those was Kerner and this was the thinking behind his explanation for *Die Seherin* – and the theory championed by John Colquhoun, Hamilton's close friend. The extent to which, in

---

[38] Thomas De Quincey, 'A Postscript to "On Murder Considered as One of the Fine Arts"', in Morrison, ed., *De Quincey on Murder* (Oxford: Oxford University Press, 2009), 95–141 (pp. 104, 107–10, 120, 130, footnote 4).
[39] Alexander H. Japp, 'Thomas De Quincey: His Friends and Associates', in Hogg, ed., *De Quincey*, 1–70 (p. 55); Joanne Wilkes, 'Crowe, Catherine', in *ODNB*, accessed 20 October 2020; Findlay, 'Personal Recollections', in Hogg, ed., *De Quincey*, p. 153; Catherine Crowe, *The Seeress of Prevorst [. . .]* (London: Moore, 1845); Veitch, *Memoir of Hamilton*, pp. 144–5.

his later writings including the *History*, Burton was intrigued by and attuned to the supra-natural beliefs to be found in the likes of Robert Wodrow's *Analecta* becomes less surprising given the subjects of conversation to which he was regularly exposed in Hamilton's literary circle or over an evening with Catherine Crowe, Thomas De Quincey and Charles Kirkpatrick Sharpe.[40]

Much in the life of Sharpe speaks to a fascination with the occult and with traditional superstitions, particularly those to be found in the annals of the sixteenth and seventeenth centuries concerning which he was very knowledgeable. At an earlier stage, in 1818, he had published what is still regarded as a valuable history of witchcraft in Scotland in his Introduction to the *Memorialls* [sic] of the seventeenth-century clergyman, Robert Law. In the previous year he edited and published James Kirkton's *The Secret and True History of the Church of Scotland* (1678). Burton's extensive treatment of Archbishop Sharp in the *History* owes much to the influence of Kirkpatrick Sharpe, particularly Sharpe's edition of Kirkton's *Secret History* and the appended narrative of James Russel, one of the assassins.[41] It might be added that it was Sharpe's editorial exegesis on the Kirkton *History* that allowed Burton to heighten the supernatural nuances in recounting the Archbishop's murder. He was able to incorporate the 'bottle imp' devilry because Sharpe had reinstated the tale of the escaping bee as a diabolic 'familiar', which Wodrow had excluded from his published material. And neither the State Trials account nor Wodrow mentions the power, referred to in Burton's account, that diabolic spells could render the devil's own invulnerable to gunfire but not to 'the edge of the sword'. However, in his commentary on the Archbishop's murder in the main Kirkton *History*, Sharpe had cited the folk beliefs that witches' spells could provide 'gun-shot invulnerability'.[42]

---

[40] Catherine Crowe, *The Night-Side of Nature; Or, Ghosts and Ghost Seers*, 2 vols (London: Newby, 1848), I, pp. 21–3, 266–7.

[41] Robert Law, *Memorialls [sic]; or, The Memorable Things that fell out within this Island of Brittain [sic] from 1638 to 1684*, ed. Charles Kirkpatrick Sharpe (Edinburgh: Constable, 1818); James Kirkton, *The Secret and True History of the Church of Scotland [. . .]*, ed. Charles Kirkpatrick Sharpe (Edinburgh: Ballantyne, 1817); Burton indicates (*HOS* (1873), VII, p. 216, footnote 1) that besides this edition of Kirkton, his sources were the State Trials account and Wodrow's *History*.

[42] Kirkton, *Secret History*, pp. 419–21, footnote; and p. 85, footnote; Burton, *HOS* (1873), VII, p. 216, footnote 1.

In his account of the Sharp murder, Burton moulds the source material and the presentation of the protagonists into narratives of which Thomas De Quincey would have been proud. He is not content with an objective authorial account: the reader must be presented with the perspective of the murderers (as with that of the earlier would-be murderer, James Mitchell), and be brought to understand what was in their minds, just as De Quincey had taken his readers into that of John Williams. Burton repeatedly seeks to excuse a degree of looseness in the use of sources in order to get at the motivation of the murderers. Their supposed remarks made in the course of the deed 'may be not accurately reported', but he records them because they conveyed 'the spirit by which they felt themselves driven to the deed'. Whereas in 1817 Sharpe had taken a superior position as a modern, tolerant (episcopalian) editor mocking and denouncing the actions of the 'fanatics', Burton allows them to speak for themselves, to share the narrative and to provide his readers with the progress of a horrifying crime told from their own point of view. Burton, also an episcopalian, was no more sympathetic to any vindication of the crime than Sharpe. But in his use of the available sources, he argues once again that, rather than 'precise accuracy', it was 'of far more importance to bring out the spirit at work in those concerned'.[43]

Thomas De Quincey is not the only literary figure whose work is called to mind by Burton's presentation of the Sharp murder. Burton uses the source material in the *Secret History* to reconstruct the narrative of the assassination and its aftermath in a form reminiscent of the elements of providential progress and expressions of millenarian, predestined certainty created around Balfour of Burley and his associates in Scott's version of the events in *Old Mortality*; and even the providential, 'justified' mentality that overcomes the doubts of Robert Wringhim as he pursues his murderous intentions in James Hogg's *Confessions*. Indeed, Sharpe's edition of Kirkton's *Secret History* has been seen as influential on the narrative structure of Hogg's *Confessions*.[44] In his account in the *History*, Burton elaborates on the heightened religiosity that drove the murderers; their sense of justification for sins committed under God's grace and vengeance; and their mysterious and implicitly predestined

---

[43] Burton, *HOS* (1873) VII, pp. 214, 216.
[44] Walter Scott, *The Tale of Old Mortality*, ed. Douglas Mack (Edinburgh: Edinburgh University Press, 1993), pp. 36, 42, 174–5, 180–2, 262–4; James Hogg, *The Private Memoirs and Confessions of a Justified Sinner*, ed. David Groves (Edinburgh: Canongate, 2008), pp. 136–7, 148–51; Groves' 'Introduction' to *Private Memoirs*, xv–xxix (pp. xxiv–xxv).

journey of escape. Given his familiarity with pertinent works of Scott and Galt and his acquaintance with James Hogg (and perhaps also his later influence on Robert Louis Stevenson), it is unsurprising to find in Burton's account of these and other events the characteristics of what has recently been delineated as 'Calvinist and Covenanter Gothic'. He could certainly be quite explicit in relating what he perceived as the 'weird' vein in the Scottish past as evidenced in the dark elements in folklore, to a susceptibility to the kind of Manichean view of good and evil that led to the witchcraft persecutions and in turn to the kind of self-justified sinning that could have (and, he implies, in the Killing Times of covenanter persecution, would have) murderous consequences.[45]

By the 1830s and 1840s, Kirkpatrick Sharpe was probably best known in Edinburgh and well beyond for his art and antiquarian collection. It seems clear that on numerous occasions, particularly through the 1840s up to Sharpe's death in 1851, Burton was one of a select band who had access to it. While the subject matter of his paintings was extremely varied it is unsurprising, given Sharpe's predilections, to find well-represented works that conveyed images of the horrors of war and martyrdom and depictions of the grotesque. In the *History*, Burton associated descriptions of outrages in the British civil wars with comparable horrors in the same period in Europe and specifically their depiction in the 'Miseries of War' series by the French artist Jacques Callot. Besides his depictions of mass killings and ravaged towns in the Thirty Years War, Callot's work included engravings of physically deformed vagrants, and he contributed to the genre of paintings of demonic possession often in the context of exorcism rituals. In the Kirkpatrick Sharpe sales catalogues there are several lots of such works by Callot, one of them specifically listed as 'Callot's Miseries of War', so it is likely that it was in Sharpe's company that Burton came to associate these historical events with Callot's explicit imagery of murderous atrocity.[46]

Closer to home, perhaps the darkest imagination amongst the rapidly expanding group of Scottish painters in the first half of the nineteenth century was that of David Scott. Burton's first acquaintance with Scott's

---

[45] Alison Milbank, 'Calvinist and Covenanter Gothic', in *Scottish Gothic*, eds Davison and Germanà, pp. 89–101; Burton, HOS (1873), VII, pp. 113–18.
[46] [Anon], *Catalogue of the highly interesting and valuable Collection [. . .] of the late Charles Kirkpatrick Sharpe [. . .]* (Edinburgh: Constable, 1851), pp. v–vi, 47; Allardyce, ed., *Letters from and to Charles Kirkpatrick Sharpe, Esq.*, II, p. 573; Jane Kromm, *The Art of Frenzy: Public Madness in the Visual Culture of Europe, 1500–1850* (London: Continuum, 2002), pp. 50, 71.

paintings was almost certainly in 1831 and 1832 when he reviewed exhibitions at the Scottish Academy of Painting, Sculpture and Architecture, precursor of the Royal Scottish Academy, for the *Aberdeen Magazine*. Although he criticised Scott's work from a rather conservative perspective because he failed to 'adhere to nature', he was clearly struck by Scott's arresting imagery. Though faced with some hundreds of works, in both years Scott was among the painters he singled out for comment: the pictures were

> undoubtedly evidence of a strong original genius. 'Remorse' represents a murderer chained to his victim, and about to turn his sword against his own breast [. . .]; the satanic expression in the face of the murderer is strongly delineated, and the livid colour of the bleeding victim is fine.

In the following years, Burton came to know Scott and his work well, probably through their mutual friendship with William Spalding. Burton had great respect for Spalding and it is likely he would have been influenced by his friend's hopes that Scott was the great master he had hoped to see emerge in Scotland. Burton later acknowledged Scott's 'grand conceptions', as well as Spalding's disappointment that, in his view, the painter had a tendency of lapsing into the 'grotesque' in his most ambitious paintings.[47]

There is certainly no doubt of the arresting nature of Scott's imagery, perhaps especially his 'scenes of death and psychological turmoil'. There were also prominent strains of the mystical and magical in his work, which can be related to that fascination with early modern mystic/scientific speculation already traced in the Hamilton circle: Scott's 'strange, emblematic illustrations' for a book on popular astronomy

> propose a metaphoric communion between art and science that suggests the seventeenth-century world-view of the likes of such magus figures as Athanasius Kircher. Perhaps here Scott is being genuinely original in his response to the spiritual crisis of post-Enlightenment Scotland.[48]

His work was original and unsettling, often infused with a dark and morbid tone. Many of his greatest paintings, like *The Traitor's Gate* and

---

[47] [John Hill Burton], 'Sayings and Doings in the Modern Athens: No. 1', *Aber M* 1 (1831), 167–71 (p. 169); 'Sayings and Doings in the Modern Athens: No. 2', *Aber M* 2 (1832), 98–104; Burton, 'Life of Spalding', pp. xv–xvi.

[48] See the assessment of Scott, especially his 'Philoctetes Left on the Isle of Lemnos [. . .]', by Eric Dugdale: 'Philoctetes', in *Brill's Companion to the Reception of Sophocles*, eds Rosanna Lauriola and Kyriakos N. Demetriou (Leiden: Brill, 2017), 77–147 (p. 114); Macmillan, *Scottish Art*, p. 207.

The Spirit of the Storm, convey a dark and portentous atmosphere centred on a 'heroic struggle with fate'; while in his biblical pictures, 'grand as they are, tragedy and terror are accentuated at the expense of other and more spiritual qualities'. Scott's 'draughtsmanship' has been criticised but to an early, more sympathetic critic, it seemed rather 'as if he, like the Gothic sculptors, had felt that exaggeration expressed his ideas better than normal'.[49]

It comes as no surprise that Thomas De Quincey responded to Scott and his work. The two met relatively late in Scott's life, but certainly dined together with Ralph Waldo Emerson when he visited Edinburgh in early 1848. At their first encounter, De Quincey had found Scott rather dull but then visited his studio 'where he was transfixed by Scott's picture of "The Resurrection on the Day of the Crucifixion"'. De Quincey quickly detected a sympathetic spirit: 'now I have been an hour with him among the tombs, I find him quick with thought and the most interesting of men'. Burton would have been able to view many of Scott's paintings at the annual exhibitions of the Royal Scottish Academy where, despite the controversies, he did exhibit throughout the 1830s and 1840s. Again, however, he would have been able to dwell at greater leisure on the painter's work during perambulations with Kirkpatrick Sharpe around Sharpe's private collection, where they could contemplate many of his works.[50]

Here was a further source of exposure to a cultural vein running through Edinburgh society in the decades leading up to the composition of Burton's Scottish history. It was characterised in Scott's case by imagery of psychological anguish, of the magical and the 'grotesque'. However, it extended more generally in Burton's acquaintance and experience to a fascination with the interface of the material and spiritual worlds; to what was bizarre and alien in the superstitions and atrocities of past times; and to contemporary fictional and non-fictional stories of murderous crime and horror. Burton's exposure to such tendencies from the

---

[49] James L. Caw, *Scottish Painting Past and Present, 1620–1908* (Edinburgh: Jack, 1908), pp. 122–3, 125–8; images of Scott's works can be viewed at https://www.nationalgalleries.org/search/artist/david-scott, accessed 26 April 2021.

[50] Morrison, *English Opium-Eater*, p. 356; Charles Baile de Laperrière, ed., *The Royal Scottish Academy Exhibitors 1826–1990 [. . .]*, 4 vols (Calne: Hilmarton Manor Press, 1991), IV, pp. 127–9; [Anon], *Catalogue of the Extensive and Valuable Library [. . .] and a portion of the Cabinet of Pictures of the late Charles Kirkpatrick Sharpe* (Edinburgh: Constable, 1852), p. 52.

1830s to the mid-1850s was particularly concentrated around (though not exclusive to) his relations with the Hamilton circle, as well as with De Quincey, Crowe, Sharpe and David Scott. These experiences accumulated over earlier formative influences in folk culture and balladry, which incorporated many similar themes and characteristics. For the historian they combined to shape a thought-world – one shared by many of his readers – that was attuned to the periodic appearance in the Scottish past of events and figures whose presence called up and should be expressed in a variety of the tropes of the gothic imagination.

7

History as Theatre

THE PICTURESQUE STAGE

THE LANGUAGE AND METAPHORS of the stage, its scenes and its tragedies, are recurring motifs in Burton's narrative. They are not constantly present but they are periodically so prominent as to merit attention and analysis. Even in passages where theatrical language is not being used in a sustained way, Burton does seem to reach naturally for such forms of expression.[1] The occasional use of such metaphoric language would hardly merit comment. However, more consistent recourse to theatrical concepts can be traced in his visualisation of events as a sequence of scenes and dramas played out on 'the historical stage'; in the presentation of historical process in the terms of classical tragedy; and in the use of figurative language that references the physical reality and structures of the contemporary theatre in his time.

This section addresses the first of these themes: the history-stage is at times conceived as a kind of viewing frame in which picturesque or dramatic historical events are captured or through which they pass in sequence. In describing the joint Scots–French invasion of England in 1327, Burton is pleased that he can draw on that 'master of narrative and description' Froissart, who 'at once brings on the stage the Scots troops with vivid distinctness in all the peculiarities in which they differed from the heavy chivalry of the day'. James IV's mistresses

> are seen in succession passing in splendour before an admiring people. At the beginning of his reign, while he is yet a boy, his mistress, Lady Margaret Drummond, comes on the stage conspicuous in her grandeur, to become still more conspicuous in her fate[.][2]

---

[1] For instance, Burton, *HOS* (1873), I, pp. 158, 170; VI, 303.
[2] Ibid., II, p. 298; III, pp. 80–1.

The history of the Regencies in the third quarter of the sixteenth century is presented as an unfolding series of dramas, in which the characters of the Regents themselves, as well as other leading figures, struggle to keep their feet 'in the shiftings of the tragic drama'. Soon after the Raid of Ruthven in 1582, the young James VI is removed from the Gowries' control in 'the next scene of the shifting drama'. Indeed, Burton's summation of the rest of James's reign in Scotland is of a fateful narrative of shifting scenes – 'a stage where rapid changes followed each other and violent passions took their swing'.[3] These 'shiftings' of the drama require the stage to be periodically cleared for further scenes. In 1567, the show trial to exculpate Bothwell is the 'first performance on the stage thus cleared for the movements of the great actors', after which events 'followed each other rapidly, and thickened to a conclusion'. Two years later, under Regent Murray, the story and significance of the French page Nicholas Hubert, executed for his role in Darnley's murder, is but 'a small item of the last great State tragedy ere the stage is cleared for another'.[4]

All of Mary Stuart's direct conversations with Knox in the early 1560s are presented as dramatic dialogues, their characters emerging from the exchanges. Burton's emphasis on allowing the past to be heard in its 'own words', which should not be 'spoiled' by 'abridgement', has been discussed in Chapter 5. In the passages where the *History* is conveyed in this theatrical discourse, he can take advantage of the opportunity to use direct speech with those engaging in dialogues given the 'lines' they actually spoke, as far as possible drawn from first-hand accounts. Burton commends Knox's own account of his first exchange with Mary because it is 'extremely picturesque and lifelike', and when they come to debate the issue of resistance to princes, 'the very words [. . .] are necessary to express its import'.[5]

The story of Mary and Bothwell is conceived in classically tragic terms and is considered fully below. In advance comes the entrance of an apparently minor character: '[I]t is at this juncture that another remarkable actor in the tragic events to come appears on stage – David Rizzio, the Italian.' Central to Burton's fourth chapter on Mary is a lengthy account of the story and demise of Rizzio. Although in 1565 Bothwell was already coming to the fore, 'another actor in the great tragedy was to precede him. The Italian was daily becoming more offensive[.]' The

---

[3] Ibid., V, 28, 197, 407.
[4] Ibid., IV, pp. 208, 215; V, p. 9.
[5] See p. 124; Burton, *HOS* (1873), IV, pp. 28–30, 61–3, 73–4.

narrative of the plot and murder is borne along through one 'little scene' after another. Much attention is paid to visual imagery in conveying these episodes, a careful scene-setting. Rizzio had become used to 'decorating his person extravagantly'; even just before his death, 'he was clothed in "a nightgown of damask, furred, with a satin doublet and hose of russet velvet"'. Lord Ruthven, 'the chief actor in the affair' of the Italian's murder, is given his own 'little scene', which of course 'must be told in his own words'. Similarly, in the following reign, Burton presents extensive direct quotations from James VI's dialogues with a recalcitrant Presbyterian clergy unwilling to proclaim the 'official' account of the Gowrie affair, since the exchanges conveyed 'a scene such as any abridgement would despoil of its picturesqueness'.[6]

Other passages of the *History* are comparatively still and silent, but it is a dramatic stillness. At the very start of his fourth volume Burton presents, in a kind of 'freeze-frame', the group of international *dramatis personae* on whom Queen Mary's fate as well as the outcome of the Scottish Reformation will depend. One by one they are introduced as characters. These figures are not actually interacting at this juncture – they are pictured as poised, ready for the action to begin. Burton's imagination seems periodically drawn to such silent, arrested images. In his previous volume, he had captured David Beaton, the future Cardinal, in terms that recall these vignettes: '[I]n the midst of the noisy and ferocious troubles of the times, there is something sublime in this subtle spirit standing apart shrouded in silent mystery.' Similarly, in the course of one of the dramatic dialogues with Knox, Burton highlights a long moment in which Mary is transfixed at the revolutionary implications of Knox's harangue: '[t]he narrator here tells us that "at these words the queen stood, as it were, amazed more than a quarter of an hour".' The fall of the Earl of Morton in 1581 is depicted as a set-piece 'scene' of confrontation before the king and Council that might explode into bloodshed at any point, with subsequent elements also almost arrested in time: the image of Morton, once seized, is of passion immobilised, trapped 'like a ferocious wild beast in the toils'. Cast as a kind of audience, the Presbyterian onlookers – despite Morton's support for the new church – also do not move: they 'stood idly by as the tragedy was acted'.[7]

---

[6] Ibid., IV pp. 111, 140–55; quotations from pp. 145, 149; Burton, *HOS* (1873), V, pp. 339–44.

[7] Ibid., III, p. 113; IV, pp. 1–5, 30; V, pp. 177–9.

Later, fateful events in the religious struggles of the seventeenth century are captured as though almost literally in a picture frame. Most portentous of all was the signing of the Solemn League and Covenant in Edinburgh: the covenanters act out this national drama in a setting and backdrop that Burton recognised to have become iconic in recent Scottish art:

> The stage on which this scene was enacted was the Greyfriars' Churchyard. The selection showed a sound taste for the picturesque [. . .]. The old Gothic church of the Friary was then existing; and landscape-art in Edinburgh has by repeated efforts established the opinion, that from that spot we have the grandest view of the precipices of the castle and the national fortress crowning them.

On this occasion it was such worldly glories 'which the actors on the scene were so vehemently repudiating'. Later, Burton draws attention to the striking setting of Glasgow Cathedral – 'conditions of time-honoured ecclesiastical magnificence' – for the famous and fateful General Assembly held within the Cathedral in November 1638. He again underscores the irony of how the scene of 'pompous ceremonial', which he describes in some detail, contrasted with the intentions of the clergy who were present: 'A second time that community which abjured all pomp and all attempt to draw influence from external conditions, was fortunate in a fitting stage for the enactment of a grand drama.'[8]

TRAGIC DRAMAS

Burton's narratives of a number of major historical events are hedged around with the terms of theatrical tragedy. On some occasions, the accounts are announced by an 'opening scene' on which, as it were, the curtain goes up.

In the case of the Wars of independence, this is slightly delayed: the death of Edward I's wife Eleanor was 'a domestic calamity befalling the chief actor; it is of moment, for it appears to have postponed the opening of the drama'. Still, open it does, particularly when William Wallace 'steps upon the stage'; though since nothing is known of his previous

---

[8] Burton, *HOS* (1873), VI, pp. 186, 222.

roles, almost like any travelling player or jobbing thespian, 'he comes to do his part like any actor who may just have figured in any other character, tragic or comic'. His part is of course gloriously tragic, but soon after the curtain descends on Wallace in 1306, Robert Bruce abandons the English court and 'it was clear that a new act in the drama of the Scots conquest had opened'. In a further instance later in the *History*, Burton describes how in 1571 the revelations of the 'Rudolphi affair' – a plot to assassinate Elizabeth I and replace her with Mary Stuart – brought England centre stage in the impending struggle with the Catholic League: 'the revelations made that country the chosen theatre of the performance. When the projects so plotted in secrecy came suddenly into action in Paris, this was naturally set down as the opening scene of the great tragedy[.]'[9]

Burton's attention to the 'gothic' aspects of the Gowrie Conspiracy have been explored in the last chapter, but his account of the event also exemplifies his presentation of history as theatre. As elsewhere, he is careful to set out for his readers the settings through which they will require to follow the sequence of scenes. He mines the testimonies from the subsequent investigation not only to set out the roles of the main characters but also, rather typically, to draw on minor cast members to provide detail and colour. The main action is then introduced in dramatic style, with the picture of the king being throttled at a tower window, after which Burton switches the perspective and 'joins' his readers, as the audience, to view those rescuing the king: 'We must now follow the other actors in the tragedy to the turret chamber', and from the official narrative he draws 'a minute account of the scene acted'. He can therefore provide a detailed and rather exciting account of the violent struggles in and around the turret, which thus 'made a very distinct story'. When at last 'Sir John Ramsay gave the Earl of Gowrie ane dead stroke', there ended 'the great act of the tragedy'.[10]

However, the elements of classical tragedy are most evident in Burton's account of the progress of Mary Stuart. Her first choice of husband in Scotland, Henry Stewart, Lord Darnley, is presented as a character entirely subject to his passions appearing in more than one scenario in tragi-comedic terms. Following his final such appearance, Burton has the contemporary audience (and his readers) turn to focus on a new and fateful figure: 'The eyes of onlookers now came to be

---

[9] Burton, *HOS* (1873), II, pp. 115,179, 233; V, p. 110.
[10] Burton, *HOS* (1873), V, pp. 318–19, 320–6, 352.

fixed on Bothwell as one whose destinies seemed to be linked to those of the queen[.]' The leading players are presented as responding to an immanent, fateful orchestration: once aware that Darnley's enemies are plotting his murder, Mary begins to behave 'completely in harmony with the part acted by these performers in the tragedy'. And following the assassination, Mary is presented as the 'wretched victim' of her own passions. The narrative is couched in terms of the irresistible fatality of classical tragedy, the participants subject to hidden and powerful forces:

> The tone of the history of Scotland now takes a peculiar turn. Events on the surface contradict the tenor of the influences below; and the plot hurries on, like that of a romance or a drama, to be reversed when the unseen powers find their opportunity and reveal themselves. [. . .] [A] new light sprang up in men's minds when they saw the mighty reward at which the chief actor aimed.

In the rush of events, mortal agency is helpless to resist these fateful forces and can only 'let the evil destinies that ruled the land have their swing'.[11]

A little later, Burton begins his examination of the 'casket letters', the authenticity of which was still a hotly contested issue at the time of his writing and a central issue in determining whether Mary had been complicit in Darnley's murder. It was just the kind of issue on which Burton liked to parade his objectivity, and he rather ostentatiously critiques the bias of previous vindicators or accusers of the Queen. However, since from 1567, 'the ruling power in Scotland' had taken a public stand on their validity, it became 'the historian's proper duty to deal with what was known to, and consequently influenced, the actors at large on the political stage'. He makes a point of highlighting Mary's fear that Bothwell would betray her just as 'Jason' had done in the Medea, 'the terrible creation of Euripides'. On this issue, as on many others, Burton's allusions suggest he was writing with a sensibility of a close relation between history and literature. The letters are conceived as offering an instance, a kind of template from history, for writers of fictional tragedy.[12]

Even after Bothwell has been banished and Mary herself has fled over the border, her fate is to continue an 'incarnate peril', constantly threatening 'some fresh astounding change in the eventful drama of

---

[11] Ibid., IV, pp. 159, 161–2, 183, 207–8.
[12] Ibid., IV, pp. 253–4, 253 footnote 1, pp. 259, 272.

which she was the heroine'. With her final move to Fotheringhay, there opens 'the scene of the concluding tragedy of her tragic career'. In general, Burton clearly doubts Mary's innocence of many of the charges against her, but he seems less concerned with the long controversies of whether she was right or wrong, than capturing the denouement in the terms of classical drama:

> [A] beautiful queen, a captive and a victim to a cruel rival, was the cynosure of all chivalry, for whom there would be endless conspiracies [. . .]. That she should die seemed the hard doom of fate, as in some Greek tragedy when a sacrifice must be made to appease the angry gods and save a people from ruin.

At this point it is Elizabeth's part and character that prompt Burton to an association with another of the 'masters of tragic genius'. The English queen had implied in correspondence with courtiers that Mary's summary dispatch would not displease her. Burton is led to quote passages from Shakespeare's *King John* on the subject of royal complicity in murder. In the end, Burton observes, each queen 'acted her part' very differently, though with little to be admired in the way Elizabeth 'concluded the scene'. The honourable refusal of Mary's immediate jailers to murder her was the '(o)ne ray of goodness in the whole dark scene, but it is one that does not brighten up the chief actress'.[13]

BEHIND THE CURTAIN

Burton displays a consistent fascination with the secret machinations, and 'deep' or hidden factors that may be driving events 'on the surface' of history. As already described, he delighted in the availability of Charles I's 'secret instructions' to his Commissioner in Scotland because they revealed the gulf between the king's true intentions and the 'superficial acts to be done'. In the previous century, he was equally pleased to have available the revelatory correspondence of Wolsey in the early sixteenth century; as well as, in the ensuing decades, that of the English diplomatic officials sent to Scotland – Sadler, Throckmorton and Randolph – whose 'garrulous vivacity' he contrasts with the approach of Maitland of Lethington who, frustratingly, 'commits no unnecessary secrets to paper' and so reveals nothing 'of the tendency of the times'.[14]

---

[13] Burton, *HOS* (1873), V, pp. 251, 256–8, and 258, footnote 1.
[14] Ibid., VI, p. 200; V, p. 130.

It is not therefore surprising to find Burton particularly frustrated at the opacity around the relationship that developed between Mary Stuart, once in exile in England, and the Duke of Norfolk. The motives of 'the principal actors in it or their abettors' are obscured by 'secret movements', which confuse the 'perplexed spectator'. Nevertheless, despite the efforts to isolate her, Mary 'continued able to touch such wires as could stir or shake the States of Europe'. The 'perplexed spectator' was of course the historian (and his reader). However, it was possible for the 'hidden movements' to be revealed. There was nothing Burton liked better than sharing a dramatic, enlightening revelation from records of the Machiavellian spymasters of the Elizabethan state machine: part of the mystery of the matchmaking between Norfolk and Mary was that Bishop Leslie, Mary's loyal 'ambassador' in England, was plotting with Norfolk for a Spanish invasion – but 'an accident opened up the whole plot to Cecil, as with the rising of the curtain in a play'.[15]

Burton incorporated in the *History* descriptions of various pageants and 'mummeries' associated with the early modern royal courts, events with an obvious performative character. It may however be revealing that in the midst of these passages, he launches into a lengthy comparison of such pageants with nineteenth-century pantomime, which he (incorrectly) considers as derived from them. The Jacobean efforts, he considered, would be tedious for a modern theatrical audience since pantomime now depended on 'machinery'. For the audience,

> all in front is bright fairyland [. . .]. But the adult spectator knows that in the dingy and dirty recesses behind, there is an organisation of ugly machinery – windlasses, ropes, pulleys, and levers – with which mechanics of the most unideal kind are hard at work, raising or sinking heavy weights; while complicated arrangements are worked by anxious attendants, to prevent the fairy beings who have disappeared into thin air on the bright side, from being dashed to pieces on the dark.

All of this was quite manifest in the early seventeenth century, when 'severance between the spectacle and the mechanism was impossible', so that there was now more 'real pageantry' in an evening at Drury Lane.[16]

Burton presents at least one radical change of circumstances explicitly in terms of those sudden, arresting 'revolutions' in the narrative that

---

[15] Ibid., IV, p. 436; V, pp. 244, 105.
[16] Burton, *HOS* (1873), IV, pp. 24–7, footnote 3; pp. 24, 191; V, pp. 362–3. Modern pantomime is derived from the Italian *Commedia dell'arte*: Bill Findlay, ed., *History of Scottish Theatre* (Edinburgh: Polygon, 1998), pp. 180–1.

were characteristic of pantomime. After the Restoration, the machinations of Archbishop James Sharp in London to re-establish episcopacy came to fruition during the session of the Scottish Estates in 1661:

> The plot is now completed. Sharp had announced the prospect of a proclamation, assuring his friends of the preservation 'of the established worship, discipline, and government' of their Church [. . .] Suddenly, as in one of the revolutions of a pantomime, the whole apparatus of the Presbyterian polity is swept from the stage, and Prelacy stands in its place as the established 'discipline and government'.[17]

Burton's observations on the crudely exposed trickery of the Jacobean pageants do not reflect his usual appreciation of the different characteristics of former times. However, they may provide some insight into his cast of mind when at times he deploys the language of stagecraft for statecraft: the activity on the stage involves more than the presence and declamations of the leading players. 'Apparatus', 'mechanisms' or 'machinery' is activated, often 'behind the scenes', or before 'the curtain rises', which if 'glimpsed' may determine and explain the events superficially presenting to history. Another sudden transformation of events three decades earlier is thus presented in similar terms to Sharp's ecclesiastical 'pantomime revolution'. In this case, it concerns Charles I's decision in 1638 to 'surrender' to the demands of the Scottish covenanters, shortly after sending secret instructions (which Burton had just quoted) to his Commissioner Lauderdale, with the opposite determination:

> And now there comes a new act in the drama, as we see it in the face of the external history of the times. It is all a surprise, as if the curtain rose on novelties brought to perfection in secret behind the scenes – unless indeed the passages just quoted be held to afford a glimpse of the inner mechanism.[18]

Throughout the previous year, 1637, increasing popular unrest had been directed at Archbishop Laud's efforts to impose a new Prayer Book on Scotland. Burton commented that such a crisis, though initiated only 'by a paltry rabble', was nevertheless 'often the occasion that brings men of gravity and responsibility forward on the political stage. The machinery of government is set in motion, and they have to choose what part they will take[.]' Indeed, similar conceptions and language characterise Burton's summary of his entire account of the events leading to the adoption of the National Covenant of 1638, through which Scotland would have its greatest influence on seventeenth-century Britain:

---

[17] Burton, *HOS* (1873), VII, p. 145.
[18] Ibid., VI, p. 202.

I have thought it right to indicate with a cautious minuteness, which may be counted tedious, such traces as appeared to reveal whatever inner agency – social, political, or religious – may account for the events occurring up to this point [. . .]. The forces that were to come in conflict may now be considered as embodied against each other, and coming forth in the face of day with all the world a witness of their contest. Hereafter, then, the same minuteness of detail may not be necessary. From the preparations behind the scenes we pass to the front of the historical stage, and see the events of the drama following each other in rapid succession, and with a visible chain of connection needing little explanation.

Some decades later at another critical moment, this time in the rapids of the 'Glorious Revolution', Burton describes how numbers of Scots appeared in London in 1689. Some were supporters of King James, hoping to find opportunities 'at the centre of all the critical movements of the juncture'; however, they found themselves in the minority and 'disappeared from the active stage'.[19]

These instances suggest a notion of the stage, not only as a frame for picturesque and dramatic imagery and interaction, but as a setting with a dimension of depth. From its recesses, events may bring men of responsibility 'forward on the political stage'; statesmen can displace opportunists to occupy 'the active stage'; the performance is made visible to all as 'we pass to the front of the historical stage'. This clarity does however require the historian's 'cautious minuteness' in examining the 'preparations behind the scenes'. In the course of his Regency, Arran temporarily lost custody of the young James VI after the Raid of Ruthven; contemporary correspondence, Burton observed, is full of rumours of conspiracies internal and external, but these are only 'the crowd of chimeras, with their phantom actors, through which the searcher after realities in these diplomatic mazes must wander'.[20]

In summary, at certain times, Burton's allusions to the history-stage conceive it as a kind of frame within which to display particularly 'picturesque' images and the succession of arresting and colourful scenes. He adopts a darker conception governing the 'great State tragedies', in which the leading figures are fatefully driven by their passions and subject to latent external forces that 'will have their swing'. Yet this sense of predetermined destiny is balanced by a notion that there are equally hidden, but mortal, machineries that operate behind the 'shifting scene' of

---

[19] Burton, HOS (1873), VI, pp. 159–60, 174–5; VII, p. 284.
[20] Ibid., V, p. 192.

surface history that it is possible to recover and display. Besides the actors at the front of the stage, there is an 'apparatus' or 'machinery', which at critical junctures may be activated in 'secret movements' behind the superficial appearance, or by the pulling of 'hidden levers' and 'wires', to control or defy the intentions of the leading players. For Burton, it is an important part of the historian's task to detect the evidence of that shifting machinery and 'reveal whatever inner agency' is at work.

SOURCES OF THE PERFORMATIVE

It has already been noticed that a recurring vein of authorial presence or 'performance' can be traced in Burton's volumes. He appears much more attentive and aware of engagement with his 'audience' of readers than most previous Scottish historians, and anxious that their interest should be sustained.[21]

There is no evidence as to whether Burton attended the theatre as a youth in Aberdeen, though there were theatres in the town at the time. Certainly, one of his first acts after coming to Edinburgh late in 1830 was to visit the theatre, and in an early article for the *Aberdeen Magazine* in 1832 he included an account of a dinner, with Robert Burns's son as guest of honour, at the Edinburgh Shakspearian [sic] Club, 'a society consisting of gentlemen of the stage, their patrons, and acquaintances, and all true lovers of the drama'. It would not be surprising if Burton's friend William Spalding had also been present, or at least had soon joined this club on his arrival in Edinburgh. At the time he must have been at work on his well-received first publication on the attribution to Shakespeare of the play *The Two Noble Kinsmen* (1833). As Burton recalled later, in the ensuing years as he advanced his academic career, Spalding contributed a periodic 'brilliant paper' on theatre to the *Edinburgh Review*.[22] These articles would have familiarised Burton with the language and concepts used in the contemporary appreciation and criticism of theatrical drama.

There are certainly echoes of Spalding's ideas in Burton's presentation of events in his later *History*, including those 'shifting scenes'. To maintain dramatic effect, Spalding emphasised how Shakespeare had been alive to the need for a succession of connected scenes: the five great tragedies impress by 'the variety of characters, all true and vivid, yet all

---

[21] See above, pp. 115–16.
[22] Maver, 'Leisure and Culture', pp. 377, 412; NLS MS 9402, fol. 12; [Burton], 'Sayings and Doings', *Aber M* 2 (1832), p. 100. On Spalding, see above, pp. 32–3.

unlike, who figure in the shifting scene; (and) the variety of grouping with which these characters successively appear'. The subject matter of impassioned love in *Romeo and Juliet* is reflected 'in its action, at once rapid, crowded and self-dependent [. . .] [the scenes] fleet onwards in quick succession, and each new scene is the consequence of the former'. Unsurprisingly, given his great interest in art, Spalding was sensitive to the pictorial or painterly in Shakespeare, while he also viewed the playwright's great achievement as reclaiming 'the fatalism of Attic tragedy'. Spalding was sceptical about the earlier centuries of Scottish history as suitable material for lofty and serious drama, but he did consider the reigns of James V and VI (including subjects like the Gowrie Conspiracy) as suitable for dramatic treatment. Burton may have retained something of his old friend's views on this, since his own presentation of history as theatre is concentrated in, though not confined to, the mid- to-late sixteenth century.[23]

The period from around 1820 to the middle of the century saw a significant expansion in the number and nature of theatrical performances in Scotland. There was a positive explosion of new plays based on Scottish history, largely as mediated through Walter Scott's novels. These dramas were adapted not by their author but a range of others, often actors or actor-managers. However, in effect, Scott did write for the theatre: adaptations could be virtually 'lifted directly from the novel', since his 'dialogue was fresh and lively, bringing his characters, particularly the Scottish ones, immediately to life'. Until at least the mid-century this constituted a new 'National Drama' whose core repertoire included *Guy Mannering*, *Rob Roy*, *The Heart of Midlothian*, *The Abbot* and *The Bride of Lammermoor*, together with *The Fortunes of Nigel*. It is not certain whether Burton, in his early outing in Edinburgh, attended the Theatre Royal or the Caledonian, but in the 1830 season the former included versions of *Guy Mannering*, *The Bride of Lammermoor* and *The Fortunes of Nigel*.[24]

The settings of these plays made the commissioning of new and picturesque stage scenery an important element in the promotion of plays to the public. This became a valuable source of income for leading

---

[23] [William Spalding], 'Recent Shakespearian Literature', *ER* 71 (1840), 446–93 (pp.484, 485–6, 478–9, 492); [William Spalding], 'White's Scottish Historical Dramas', *ER* 84 (1846), 223–36 (pp. 225–6).

[24] Bell, 'The Nineteenth Century', p. 142; H. Philip Bolton, *Scott Dramatized* (London: Mansell, 1992), pp. 91, 303, 432.

artists like David Roberts and Alexander Nasmyth and a significant factor in the subsequent development of Scottish romantic landscape painting. All of this increased the importance and attention given to the supporting apparatus around and on the stage. Burton's periodic references to historical figures coming to the front of the stage, or into the 'active stage', appear to relate to the physical conditions that characterised most theatres at the time. Actors playing characters with a leading part in particular scenes would necessarily move forward to where the gas lighting was best and out of the gloom at the back of the stage. This was less of an issue in popular theatre, but in the 'legitimate theatres' it was only as lighting improved that the actors made 'a gradual retreat upstage into the midst of increasingly complex scenery'. Equally, those players who were not well illuminated in the gaslight – later, 'in the limelight'– could only be 'glimpsed' in the semi-darkness at the rear of the stage. This helps to explain elements of Burton's historical narrative: when 'the historical stage is occupied by shadows, the mind gets bewildered among them, and we cannot easily see and estimate any morsels of actual truth that may come forward'. To the 'perplexed spectators', players would have appeared, like those figures dimly perceived in the conspiracies around the young James VI, as no more than 'phantom actors' lost among 'a crowd of chimeras'.[25]

As already noticed, in the period that witnessed the rise of the National Drama a sufficient number of Scottish painters turned to events drawn from the nation's own history to constitute a recognisable historical *genre* in art. Many of these compositions depicted dramatic and fateful scenes particularly relating to the later sixteenth and early seventeenth centuries. The work of the leading figure, Sir William Allan, included depictions of various scenes characteristic of theatrical *tableaux* and later presented in dramatic and 'picturesque' detail by Burton, including *The Murder of Archbishop Sharp* (1821); *The Regent Murray Shot by Hamilton of Bothwellhaugh* (1825); and *The Murder of Rizzio* (1833). Allan's main source for the *Sharp* came directly from James Russel's eye-witness account, which Burton also used, appended to Kirkton's *Secret History* as edited by Kirkpatrick Sharpe. Burton's theatrical presentation of the dialogues between Queen Mary and John Knox, emphasising that they were virtually alone in the 'arena' of debate, recalls Allan's *Knox Admonishing Mary Queen of Scots*, in which 'all anecdotal detail

---

[25] Lachlan Goudie, *The Story of Scottish Art* (London: Thames and Hudson, 2020), p. 189; Irwin, *Scottish Painters*, p. 139; Bell, 'Nineteenth Century', pp. 150, 189, 172; Burton, HOS (1873), I, p. 95.

is shorn away and there is nothing to distract attention from the main protagonists'.²⁶

Allan was followed by a number of other 'historical painters' resistant to the domestic genre derived from David Wilkie: they included Allan's pupil, Thomas Duncan; Robert Scott Lauder, who returned to Edinburgh from London in 1852 to take up the Mastership of the Trustees' Academy; and Spalding's friend David Scott. Scott had also painted Rizzio's demise in a typically individual, almost Goyaesque style and, in the period when Burton knew him personally and visited his studio, followed the trend towards depicting fixed and dramatic historical moments, including *Mary Queen of Scots Receiving the Warrant of her Execution* (1840). Scott also produced works related to the Shakespearean dramas so beloved of William Spalding.²⁷ The National Drama and historical-genre painting met in many of Robert Scott Lauder's works of the 1840s and 1850s. As early as 1831, of over 350 paintings in the Scottish Academy exhibition, Scott Lauder's *The Bride of Lammermoor* was one of those particularly admired by Burton. The drama in Scott Lauder's later historical canvases is manifest and has in more recent times been criticised as verging on melodrama:

> if they had been actors in dramatic productions of *The Fair Maid of Perth* (1848 and 1854), *Quentin Durward* (1851), *The Heart of Midlothian* (1842), or *Guy Mannering* (1843 and 1855), to list only those of Scott's works that inspired pictures that Lauder exhibited at the Royal Scottish Academy, they would rightly be accused of over acting.²⁸

Burton would have viewed these and similar works at the annual RSA exhibitions but his access to extensive private collections, particularly that of Kirkpatrick Sharpe, provided opportunities to supplement his knowledge of recent Scottish art with a wider range of dramatic history painting.

---

²⁶ Burton, *HOS* (1873), IV, pp. 28–31, 73–4; Irwin, *Scottish Painters*, pp. 210–11; an engraving of the *Murder of Sharp*, now lost, is in Irwin, *Scottish Painters*, Plate 98; Allan's *Murder of Rizzio* can be viewed at https//www.nationalgalleries.org/search/artist/sir-william-allan; an engraving of Allan's *Knox Admonishing Mary* can be viewed at https//www.nationalgalleries.org/art-and-artists/134942/john-knox-admonishing-mary-queen-of-scots; both accessed 26 May 2021.
²⁷ Caw, *Scottish Painters*, p. 126. David Scott's *Rizzio*, *Caliban and Ariel*, and *Puck Fleeing before the Dawn* can be viewed at https//www.nationalgalleries.org/search/artist/david-scott, accessed 26 May 2021.
²⁸ [Burton], 'Sayings and Doings', *Aber M*, I (1831), p. 169; Macmillan, *Scottish Art*, p. 204.

In the same period, Scottish painters produced a range of works drawing on religious history, including reverential and elegiac scenes of domestic worship or of watchful conventicles in the hills. However, again like Scott Lauder in his biblical paintings, many were 'more interested in the drama [. . .] than in the spiritual significance of the Gospel story', and captured fateful and dramatic scenes from the ecclesiastical struggles of the sixteenth and seventeenth centuries. Episodes whose 'picturesque incidents' and settings Burton conveyed in his *History* as emblematic of Scotland's covenanting past had been depicted in well-known canvases like Thomas Duncan's arresting *Death of John Brown of Priesthill* (1844) and the iconic *Signing of the National Covenant in Greyfriars' Kirkyard* (1821) by William Allan himself. There is no doubt that images such as Allan's were in Burton's mind when he emphasised the 'picturesque' stage setting in Greyfriars' Kirkyard chosen for the signing of the Covenant. Burton described the 'stage' and the 'actors in the scene' and acknowledged a backdrop that had been scene-painted by 'landscape-art in Edinburgh': by this he meant the 'repeated efforts' that had adopted the perspective looking west from Greyfriars and the Grassmarket, thus offering dramatic skies and sunsets, and incorporating 'the grandest view of the precipices of the castle and the national fortress crowning them'. Previously the setting was probably best known from Alexander Nasmyth's *Edinburgh Castle* (1831), and besides Allan's work, was familiar to Burton from James Drummond's depiction of *The Porteous Mob* (1855).[29]

Interspersed periodically among Burton's 'shifting scenes' are episodes that, by contrast, are depicted as fixed in time, though still dramatic: he calls up individual vignettes and broader groups of figures in characterful guise, some with passions arrested and all, at least temporarily, motionless. These are reminiscent of the *tableaux*, which had a long history in performance art and were still a feature in theatrical performance in the first half of the nineteenth century. In the two decades after Burton's arrival in the city in 1830, 'the passion for tableaux in which Wilkie had indulged in Italy in the late 1820s, had spread to Edinburgh'. The theatre

---

[29] Caw, *Scottish Painters*, pp. 115; Duncan's John Brown and Nasmyth's *Edinburgh Castle* are reproduced in Irwin, *Scottish Painters*, plates 58 and 91; Drummond's *Porteous Mob* can be viewed at: https//www.nationalgalleries.org/art-and-artists/4837/porteous-mob, and Allan's *Signing of the Covenant* at https//artuk.org/discover/artworks/the-signing-of-the-national-covenant-in-greyfriars-kirkyard-edinburgh-93072 (both accessed 26 May 2021); Burton, HOS (1873), VII, pp. 251–2; VI, p. 186.

in Aberdeen staged two series of 'Les Tableaux Vivans' in the 1831–2 season drawn from the Waverley novels and Shakespeare. The reviewer in the *Aberdeen Magazine* was appreciative, but his view that the tableaux 'in the Edinburgh Theatre' were better presented confirms that the fashion was already well-established in the capital. The displays involved actors in a fixed but dramatic and 'expressive' pose, with the whole scene theatrically lit. The concept had also passed over into the art of painting in the eighteenth century and Burton was an admirer of the 'intensely theatrical' works of that period, which were well represented in Sharpe's collection. In Edinburgh, the *tableaux* form was given a further lease of life by D. O. Hill (one of several artists Burton recalled as friends) through his work with Robert Adamson between 1843 and 1848, in perfecting the calotype.[30]

Early in that decade, Patrick Fraser Tytler drew his Scottish history to a close. While in his reviews of Tytler Burton welcomed the way in which he had managed to incorporate the romantic and picturesque into history, he was also attuned to how far Tytler's deployment of 'dramatic effect' had contributed. The 'superiority' of Tytler's work was founded on his refusal to take information 'at second hand', giving him the power 'of making the original actors speak for themselves and, in many instances, in spite of themselves'. This achieved a 'freshness' that was new in Scottish history, offering the potential to reinvigorate familiar episodes like the murders of Rizzio and Darnley through 'employing, in many instances, the very language of the actors and contemporary chroniclers of events'.[31]

Burton's appreciation of Tytler in these terms extended to the physicality or apparatus of the stage, anticipating such language in his own later *History*. His allusions stretched the simple metaphor of historical action as theatrical performance almost to breaking point. In the theatre, when the curtain comes down, the action – each act – comes to an end; in the history-theatre, the motivations and machinations of the characters and their influence on events can be shrouded, but they roll on. They can only be properly perceived or uncovered by the kind of historical effort represented by Tytler's deep probing in the manuscript sources: 'the very pith and marrow of authentic history'. In this way, Burton wrote, the 'secret

---

[30] Irwin, *Scottish Painters*, p. 287; [Anon], 'Memorabilia of the Month', *Aber M* 2 (1832), 111–14 (p. 114); [Anon], *Catalogue of Sharpe* (1851), pp. 34–5, 37, 48; Burton, *Scot Abroad*, II, p. 235; NLS MS 9445, fol. 8.

[31] [Burton], 'Tytler's History' (1840), pp. 613, 618, 621.

springs of action are unveiled', permitting his readers to see 'behind the curtain': amidst the real and imagined conspiracies and duplicities that swirled around Mary's long imprisonment in England, not only are we admitted into the surface action, but '[o]f the scenes behind the curtain, connected with the tragedy of Fotheringay, Mr Tytler has given an account replete with dramatic interest'.[32]

These expectations of 'modern history' as providing both a narrative with the immediacy of a dramatic performance, but also insights into the unseen mechanisms driving surface events, recur in Burton's reviews of Tytler's final volumes. In this respect also he drew a contrast with the most prominent eighteenth-century Scottish historians. Neither Hume nor Robertson could be said, like Tytler, to have 'dramatized the great events they recorded, and placed the leading characters of history on the scene before us, surrounded by their natural accessories, and all in action, – each speaking his own words'. Tytler had achieved this by 'ransacking' original papers, 'eavesdropping' on the direct testimony of those involved 'and thus laying bare every throb of their hearts before the spectator'. Such had been considered 'below the dignity of legitimate or classical history; which only dealt in lofty generalities and sweeping results' thus failing to trace 'the great or more minute springs which guided the complex movement'. In contrast to the stately generalisations of Hume and Robertson, in Tytler events could be viewed 'as nearly as possible as they actually appeared to the spectators, or to the actors in the scenes described' – indeed, '(w)e are admitted behind the scenes, to see how passion and interest animate and influence men of all degrees'.[33]

In ways he would take further than Tytler, Burton foresaw how the protagonists' 'own words' could themselves carry dramatic impact; and how the evidence discovered could be shown to reveal the true motives of an individual character or detect the hidden machineries of the mysterious or tragic plot. Burton's own *History* illustrates how this provided opportunities for the historian to engage with his readership and 'share' perspectives in a way akin to the role of the playwright or of the 'performative' fiction writers of the first half of the century. In recent times, scholars have returned to the relation between history-writing and other forms of literary composition including drama and the changing perception across the centuries of how far those other forms

---

[32] [Burton], 'Tytler's History' (1842), p. 316.
[33] [Burton], 'Tytler's History' (1842), p. 328; [Burton], 'Tytler's History' (1844), p. 85.

could be legitimate vehicles for recounting the past.[34] Burton was writing at a juncture when, particularly within emerging academic structures, the leeway allowed in answering the point narrowed. Within decades it had narrowed further, and for 'professional' historical narration a cool, objective norm largely prevailed. At the time Burton believed – and as will become evident many of his reviewers and readers agreed – that he was exemplifying an objective and 'scientific' approach founded on well-evidenced facts. Yet this was not infrequently interwoven with asides and diversions into novelesque romance, folk tales and fables. As described above, he was equally open to drama as a rhetorical mode that could be fashioned in a variety of ways to connect with a readership familiar with the National Drama and the physical reality of the theatre. Indeed, in one of his Tytler reviews, Burton observed that 'Shakespeare taught his countrymen a lesson in the art of writing History, by which few of them have yet profited'.[35]

The growing attention to Shakespeare among leading Romantics had an impact on Scotland, and Burton seems to have been well read in his plays, no doubt partly as a consequence of his friendship with William Spalding. Indeed, Spalding has been identified as playing a foundational role in the modern development of Shakespearean studies while in his Chair at St Andrews. The relation between Scott and Shakespeare in the nineteenth century has begun to be explored both in regard to Scott's view of his predecessor and the perception of their wider cultural roles.[36] However, in the broader context determining Burton's presentation of 'history as theatre', it is impossible to ignore the pervasive influence of Scott even though he wrote so little directly for the theatre. The redecoration of the Glasgow Theatre Royal in 1841 included, in the Lower Circle boxes, scenes from popular Shakespeare plays but across the Second Circle there were both 'Medallions in alto relievo' and 'Vignettes' that depicted 'subjects from the most

---

[34] See for instance Jan Mosch, 'Introduction', in Joachim Kupper, Jan Mosch, Elena Penskaya, *History and Drama: The Pan-European Tradition* (Boston: De Gruyter, 2019), pp. 1–27.

[35] [Burton], 'Tytler's History' (1842), p. 328.

[36] Neil Rhodes, 'Shakespeare at St Andrews: Origins and Growth of a Tradition', in *Launch-Site for English Studies: Three Centuries of Literary Studies at the University of St Andrews*, ed. Robert Crawford (St Andrews: Verse, 1997), 29–47 (pp. 38–41); Lidia Garbin, '"Not fit to tie his brogues": Shakespeare and Scott', in *Shakespeare and Scotland*, eds Willy Maley and Andrew Murphy (Manchester: Manchester University Press, 2004), pp. 141–56.

striking Scenes of the Dramatised Works of Sir Walter Scott'.[37] For decades following his death, the 'afterlives' of Scott and his works conveyed Scottish historical subject matter to the public in dramatic and performative forms: in the engravings sold separately or in illustrated editions, the historical narrative of so many Waverley novels 'was transformed into a canon of dramatic moments'. In the manner of staging *Rob Roy* during the Scott Centenary commemorations in 1871 (just as Burton's final volumes appeared), 'the play itself was not just performed in all its immediacy, but a piece of theatrico-national history was also literally re-enacted'.[38]

It had been Scott, together with J. G. Lockhart, who had urged William Allan to switch from his exotic eastern canvases to Scottish history, initiating a genre that produced so many dramatic depictions of events in the nation's past. It was Scott's *œuvre* that provided the subject matter for the National Drama, presenting the novels and their related historical events in ever more theatrical guise. And it was Scott who had urged Patrick Fraser Tytler to produce 'a right history of Scotland', which had to involve 'bringing to light' all the available sources but would be made popular through the force of its graphic narrative. As a consequence, the cultural world that Burton inhabited in the decades after his arrival in Edinburgh was thoroughly familiar with, even immersed in, the association between history, painting and the theatrical. This shaped the way in which he perceived historical events and the historian's role in presenting them. It also meant that many members of the 'audience' for his own most ambitious historical production were attuned to a way of seeing and narrating history that incorporated, at the appropriate junctures and with recognisable cues, the most dramatic performances in the Scottish past.

---

[37] Bell, 'Nineteenth Century', p. 149.
[38] Ann Rigney, *The Afterlives of Walter Scott: Memory on the Move* (Oxford: Oxford University Press, 2017), pp. 38, 73.

8

On the Pedestal, 1871–81

'THE HISTORIAN OF SCOTLAND'

BURTON AND HIS REPUTATION may have faded from sight over the years but it was considerable in his own time and for decades later. When he passed through London a year after the appearance of his final volumes in 1870, the journal of the Athenaeum, which had elected him a member 'without application or ballot', respectfully reported that Dr Hill Burton was passing through town on his way from the continent, having been gathering materials for 'a revised edition of his well-known "History of Scotland"'. The role of Historiographer Royal for Scotland to which he was appointed when the first volumes of his national history appeared in 1867 should not be dismissed as a meaningless sinecure. Through much of the nineteenth century, after the equivalent English post was abolished in 1837 (and decades before the modernisation of the history chairs at Oxbridge), the post became 'the first public and official recognition of the new method of historical composition and learning', and its incumbents 'were all both researchers and editors on the one hand, and popularizers of history on the other [. . .].'[1]

It has been suggested that Burton's last work on the reign of Queen Anne, published in 1880 just before his death in the following year, showed evidence of 'failing powers'. However, this judgement was not reflected in most contemporary reviews of the work, particularly in Scottish

---

[1] Katherine Burton, 'Memoir', p. lxv; *Athen*, 16 September 1871, p. 371: the report was also carried by Scottish papers, for example, the *Falkirk Herald*, 21 September 1871, p. 7; Denys Hay, 'The Historiographers Royal in England and Scotland', *SHR* 30 (1951), 15–29 (pp. 22–7).

publications, which continued to acknowledge his standing and, in some cases, welcomed his more selective treatment of the period.² Through the 1870s, Henry Reeve at the *Edinburgh Review* had continued to seek articles from Burton on the work of major continental historians like Von Ranke and Francois Guizot. The great French statesman–historian had indicated that he welcomed the prospect, and sent presentation volumes of his *L'Histoire de France* for Burton's use: Reeve thought it a fitting gesture – 'The Historian of France to the Historian of Scotland'.³

Besides having a significant profile with continental scholars, he was well known to the leading English historians of the time. As already described, he knew Macaulay well and later reminded his readers how he had assisted him in the *History of England*. Edward Freeman wrote to him early in 1870 indicating he was awaiting Burton's final volumes before approaching various Scottish historical issues. When J. A. Froude was in Edinburgh, he stayed with their mutual friend John Skelton, and Burton would join them for dinner at Skelton's house in the Hermitage of Braid, a pleasant evening stroll down the edge of Craiglockhart Hill from Craig House.⁴

None of this is surprising in the light of the attention that Burton's historical efforts received.

HISTORY AND THE UNION

The remaining sections of this chapter assess the reception that was accorded to Burton's full *History of Scotland* as it was issued in two tranches in 1867 and 1870, later consolidated into a final, eight-volume

---

² John Hill Burton, DCL, Historiographer-Royal for Scotland, author of 'The History of Scotland', etc., *A History of the Reign of Queen Anne*, 3 vols (Edinburgh: Blackwood, 1880); Michael Fry, 'Burton, John Hill', in *Oxford DNB*, accessed 1 August 2020; *Sc*, 15 January 1880 p. 5; *Aber J*, 22 January 1880, p. 7; [Margaret Oliphant], 'The Reign of Queen Anne', *BM* 127 (1880), pp. 139–62; *Glasg H*, 29 March, 1880; *Pall M G*, 19 February 1880, p. 12; the *Edinburgh Review* critic was the least impressed, though chiefly as assessed by the standards 'of one who for the last thirty years has adorned the foremost rank of scholars and historians'; [J. K. Laughton], 'Burton's Reign of Queen Anne', *ER* 151, 263–81 (p. 281).
³ NLS MS 9409, fols. 210–13, 283–4; Francois Guizot, *L'Histoire de France, depuis les temps les plus reculés jusqu'en 1789 [. . .]*, 5 vols (Paris: Hatchette, 1872–6).
⁴ NLS MS 9398, fols 120–3, 224.

version in 1873. However, the consolidation incorporated material that had been published years earlier in his much more limited *History of Scotland*, issued in two volumes in 1853. It is appropriate to consider the response to this earlier *History* separately, partly because of the fifteen-to-twenty-year gap, but also because the period that the earlier work covered, 1689 to 1748, and Burton's approach to it, clearly resonated with many of his contemporaries in the early 1850s and informed some of the first history-infused articulations of doubt concerning the 1707 Union.

As already suggested, when Burton had come to those junctures in history that offered the potential for an Anglo-Scottish union, he conceived them in terms of a politics of the 'practical', which had come to fruition in 1707. For many scholars in the first half of the nineteenth century, this marked the end of history as far as Scotland was concerned, and the commencement of a gradual social and cultural fusion, the Scottish past thereafter merging into the history of the British Empire. This was largely how Burton himself viewed matters in the early 1850s when he first formed the intention of compiling a narrative history of Scotland. However, perhaps to his surprise, with only a little application he found that 'it was easy to separate and follow the detached thread of events in Scotland'.[5]

There is a good deal in his 1853 volumes to justify Burton's established reputation as a Teutonist historian: at the end of the day, two essentially similar Anglo-Saxon peoples had been provided with the opportunity for a new fusion by eminently 'practical' statesmen. However, other narratives are to be found running through the work which would not have been lost on his Scottish readership. Lengthy portions depict two independent states in a process of intense and heartfelt hostility. This emerges in his handling of the Darien scheme and pre-Union political manoeuvres; in his account of the Scottish grievances over the Union's implementation to 1712; and in his view of the Jacobite Risings as closely related to, if not actually a result of, those national grievances.

Before 1707, Burton characterised England as blatantly and harshly exploiting her position as the dominant partner in the regal Union. London had drawn away the court with adverse economic effects on Edinburgh while Scotland as a whole had come to be treated not as a partner and an independent 'empire', but as a province. Scotland's great national effort at revival through Darien had been subverted through English diplomatic duplicity and arrogant deployment of her commercial supremacy, the London parliament acceding to the greedy

---

[5] Burton, *HOS* (1853), I, pp. vi–vii.

protectionism of the English merchant class. What support there was in Scotland had been for a federal union, 'not an incorporation of the two states into one', and most had denounced the outcome 'when they found in it the extinction of their nationality'. Potentially critical issues, such as the serious concern over the number of seats allocated to Scotland in the Union parliament, had been brushed aside 'with peremptory conclusiveness'. After 1707, little changes and Scottish grievances become focused on the degree to which English actions appeared to ride roughshod over the institutional guarantees that were supposedly enshrined in the treaty. Burton went on to describe the Scots' perception of new fiscal exactions as both unjust and modelled on English practices imposed by insensitive English officials:

> The Englishman's national character is not the best adapted for such delicate operations. [. . .] The subordinate officer [. . .] has no toleration for any other and goes about his duty among strangers as one surrounded by knaves and fools, whose habits and ideas must be treated with disdain.[6]

More broadly, there had been little respect for the separate judicial and legal arrangements; the separate religious tradition had been affronted by the reintroduction of patronage; and soon the post of Secretary of State for Scotland was abolished. Generally, the London legislature seemed engaged in 'the demolition of the national institutions of Scotland'. All this ultimately resulted in the Jacobite Risings, which on various occasions Burton presents – rather unexpectedly – as 'national' reactions to Scotland's unjust treatment.

By early 1853 when Burton's two volumes were published, few Scots with any interest in politics would have failed to recognise this range of Scottish concerns. For a number of years, disquiet about a similar set of issues had been increasingly evident. Conflict over patronage had again come centre stage, and for many, parliamentary indifference had brought about the fragmentation of the national church in 1843. It was considered that Scotland was seriously under-represented in the 'Imperial' parliament, having been allocated in 1832 little more than half the number of MPs its population justified. (On this issue, Burton himself had made the connection to his own time, noting in his account of the

---

[6] Burton, *HOS* (1853): on English perfidy over Darien see I, pp. 292–3, 299–304, 312–22, 327–30; on the Union as an unpopular, incorporating, not federal arrangement, 'a virtual conquest' sweeping away Scottish institutions, see I, pp. 341, 417–18, 514; II, p. 17–26, 36–8, 71–2, 79, 239–45, 278; on the Rebellions' 'national' character, see II, pp. 367, 415–17, 439.

pre-Union wrangling over Scottish representation that it was a matter 'which does not appear yet to be conclusively settled', and referencing contemporary politics.) The concerns raised by the political representatives that Scotland did have were seen to be either ignored or consigned to the margins of parliamentary sessions. At ministerial level, the Lord Advocate had too many roles – and therefore too many demands on his time to attend properly to Scottish political interests and legislation; and the refusal to re-establish a separate Secretary of State meant representation at Cabinet level by Home Secretaries who had little interest in the nation. At the same time, the fiscal and commercial arrangements between the two countries were perceived as draining Scotland through taxation with little in the way of government grants returning to support Scottish industry and public institutions. Men who were deeply involved in mid-century commercial development, including Burton's friends Duncan McLaren and John Blackwood, were increasingly sensitive to the unjust fiscal arrangements.[7]

As early as the mid-1830s, the more radical-leaning Whigs were concerned that political change was falling short of what had been hoped for after 1832. When Lord John Russell became Home Secretary in 1835, he made an attempt to strengthen ministerial attention to Scotland through a post of Undersecretary in the Home Office with special responsibility for Scottish affairs. His friend Fox Maule, MP for Perthshire and also 'of radical outlook', got the job but 'agreed the results of reform had so far been disappointing: "Scotland must have more attention or she will turn restive"'. A further such effort, establishing a post of Scottish junior Lord of the Treasury did not improve matters much: appointed to the role in 1846, William Gibson-Craig had to fight to obtain papers relevant to Scotland. Even Burton's contacts and mentors amongst the senior Whig lawyers, such as Cockburn, Cunninghame, John Archibald Murray and Andrew Rutherfurd, were coming to sense a disjunction and relative incomprehension between the Edinburgh and London political worlds including, from their direct experience as one or other of the senior law officers, the impossibility of the Lord Advocate's position. English attitudes to the assimilation of Scots and English law, which these men were open to, began to be irritating. Henry Cockburn, who had enthusiastically

---

[7] Ibid., I, pp. 417–19 and footnotes; Michael Fry, *Patronage and Principle: A Political History of Scotland* (Aberdeen: Aberdeen University Press, 1991), pp. 56, 70–2; see also p. 50; NLS MS 4004, fol. 234 and Willis Pickard, *The Member for Scotland: A Life of Duncan Maclaren* (Edinburgh: John Donald, 2011), p. 127.

welcomed assimilation of Scottish political and institutional practices to English norms after 1832, adopted a different position in letters to Burton twenty years later: 'It's the duty of a good *Scotsman* always to proclaim, when it can be done truly, the superiority of the law of Scotland to that of England. If we don't keep our own, they will stuff us with theirs.'[8]

In the later 1840s the first hints appeared of such resentments extending to doubt concerning the 1707 constitutional settlement. In early March 1848, the leading article in *Chambers's Edinburgh Journal*, evidently written by William Chambers himself, considered the progress that had been made in different ways by Edinburgh and Glasgow, set in the context of a broad historical survey commencing in early medieval times. In this perspective, Chambers judged that the Union had been 'doubtless beneficial' in bringing 'internal tranquillity', but he went on to emphasise that the achievements of the two cities were not substantively due to the Union but had been 'self-creative'. For Edinburgh in particular, the Union had been a 'ruinous blow' from which in many ways the city was still suffering, while London had 'overgrown itself, pampered with the wealth – we might almost say the plunder – of three kingdoms'. A line needed to be drawn: 'it is worthy of grave enquiry, whether superior advantages might not have been achieved by a federal instead of a legislative union? The belief is daily gaining ground that a federal compact would have been preferable', allowing the Scots to manage their own affairs. This would have been more satisfactory than seeing national 'business' transferred 'to a city four hundred miles off':

> Stupid as this arrangement is now felt to have been, as if to make matters worse, it has been the inexplicable policy of the last twenty years to abstract institutions from Scotland, and carry them to Westminster, where they are intermingled with the local affairs of England. Against this provincialising of Scotland we make a deliberate protest; not so much from its injury to Edinburgh, as the indignity and injustice of the whole proceeding with respect to the nation.

'English functionaries' needed to be made aware that Scotland was 'not a province of England, but a kingdom which, by treaty, is insured a certain distinct and independent character'.[9]

Still, so far, few others had mentioned the Union. The absence of any Scottish historical perspective that focused on the Union, its causes and

---

[8] Fry, *New Race*, pp. 274–5, 278–82; NLS MS 9395, fols 157, 160. Emphasis in original.
[9] [W]illiam [C]hambers, 'The Two Cities', *Chamb J* 9 n.s. (1848), pp. 145–7.

its aftermath, is perhaps unsurprising. Most of the Scottish elites viewed the results of the treaty as ultimately beneficial and there may be a case for saying that, up to this point at least, it was so much assumed to be a good thing as to have become 'uncontentious' and almost invisible.[10] In addition, almost all respected histories conceived of the Scottish annals as having ended, if not in 1603, then at the latest somewhere between 1689 and 1707, after which, despite Risings presented by the predominantly Whig historians as Celtic barbarism, the Scottish and English stories could only be viewed in terms of an increasingly integrated 'Empire'.

However, Burton was quite explicit about his intention to restore the Union to a proper prominence: '[t]he subject in general has not received fair attention from the historians of the age[.]' In the broader context of European history writers had been seduced into giving attention to dramatic 'military unions', but British histories had made similar mistakes: 'The Union has not been fortunate in the attention it has received in historical literature. The prevailing fashion of history-writing made it secondary to the wars in the works relating to England or Britain at large.' His two 1853 volumes he asserted, with some justification, represented the first widely noticed attempt to give a serious and detailed account of the Union and the events surrounding it. Among Scottish writers, Malcolm Laing 'seems to have grown tired of his work, and desirous to wind it up and be quit of it, after passing the Revolution'. The only published works fully devoted to the subject he dismissed as unreadable – Defoe's 'dense quarto' *History of the Union between Scotland and England*, which was uncharacteristically 'dull' and unapproachable; and the production of a Reverend Ebenezer Marshal in 1799, which 'rests in an undisturbed obscurity, from which it deserves never to emerge'. Burton however, in view of the value of the Union process as 'an historical precedent', announced that he would 'give the steps onwards, with the difficulties encountered, in progressive detail'. And 'progressive detail' – not just concerning the immediate Union process but also the related events before and after the treaty – is what he proceeded to provide. Burton was either being disingenuous or was ignorant of the fact that there had been works after Laing's that had covered the period in some detail. These included fairly substantial narratives of the events in the two histories of Scotland published by James Aikman and John Struthers in the late 1820s and cited earlier. However, these had not received extensive public or critical attention, particularly where

---

[10] Kidd, *Unionisms*, pp. 24–7.

it mattered in the great periodicals of the age. Burton's certainly did, and in ways that drew the Union back out of the past and arguably re-established a historical consciousness of the settlement as relevant to contemporary Scotland and its political and social choices.[11]

In the spring of 1852, around a year before Burton's two-volume *History* was published, two brothers, James and John Grant, launched a letter campaign to protest at the range of 'Scottish grievances' concerning which many others had been complaining privately for some years. Their arguments on the fiscal deficits to which Scotland had been subjected were actually well researched and constructed. However, the Grants and some of their friends made the mistake of associating their well-argued letters and articles with a petition to the queen, protesting at errors in the way government buildings were displaying Scottish heraldic 'honours' and insignia. Early in 1853, *The Times* seized on what its editor clearly recognised as an opportunity to direct some ridicule at those orchestrating the much more serious campaign for 'Justice to Scotland'. From January to the autumn of 1853, the Grants' press campaign and the cartoon ripostes of *The Times* and *Punch* took up much of the campaign effort.[12]

However, in the six months from September 1853, no doubt to the relief of many involved, a more dignified focus on Scottish history appeared in a series of lengthy articles on Burton's *History* in three of the major Edinburgh-based periodicals: *Blackwood's Magazine*, the *North British Review* and the *Edinburgh Review*. They were written (anonymously) by established contemporary Scottish writers who, from a range of ideological perspectives, used Burton's publication in ways that, for the first time in a century and a half, recharged Scottish history and the struggle around the Union in particular with contemporary resonance and significance. Two months after the first article appeared, the inaugural meeting of the National Association for the Vindication of Scottish Rights (NAVSR) was held in Edinburgh. That first article, 'Scotland since the Union', appeared in *Blackwood's Magazine* and was written by William Edmonston Aytoun, Professor of Rhetoric and Belles Lettres in the University of Edinburgh and a regular contributor. Aytoun welcomed the volumes as covering 'a period

---

[11] Burton, *HOS* (1853), I, pp. 404–5 and footnote; Daniel De Foe, *The History of the Union between England and Scotland [. . .]* (London: John Stockdale, 1786); Ebenezer Marshal, *A History of the Union of Scotland and England* (Edinburgh: Peter Hill, 1799); see Chapter 1, footnote 32.

[12] NLS NE.20.f.13, 'Newspaper cuttings of articles mainly by James and John Grant', fols 65–103.

of peculiar importance', for which Burton's previous work qualified him well. The review proceeded to a sustained criticism of Burton's treatment of the Highlanders, extending to a challenge to his general 'Teutonist' perspective. This controversy is discussed in more detail below.[13]

Aytoun then moved on to recognise that the 'great event' of the previous century was the Union, which, 'long delayed by mutual jealousy and clashing interests, has elevated Great Britain to the foremost rank among the European states'. From the start though he is distinctly cautious and conditional on the benefits of the eighteenth-century settlement: '(s)o far the changes have wrought well for Scotland'; and the review reflects Burton's own frank portrayal of the hostile relations that led to the treaty. Aytoun willingly grasped at Burton's resetting of the main drivers for the Union as centrally about the Scots' seventeenth-century pursuit of greater trade and commercial prosperity; the 'frantic' English resistance to this; and the culmination in the Darien tragedy. Previous historians had 'given too much prominence to mere party intrigues and ecclesiastical contests'. Aytoun proceeded to utilise this version of the treaty's history – essentially a marriage of commercial convenience between hostile nations – as the foundation on which to examine the contemporary working of the Union. Up to the last minute, the English were averse to any effort at conciliation:

> [a]s in individuals, so in nations, there are always peculiarities which distinguish one from another; and an overweening idea of their own superiority is essentially the English characteristic. A great deal has been and is written in the South about Scottish nationality – it is, in reality, nothing compared to the feelings which are entertained by the Englishman.

Shortly afterwards there is a further indication that more contemporary concerns are informing his approach to the *History*. As the last Scottish parliament assembled in 1703, Aytoun observed, there was a clear 'determination of the country to vindicate its rights'.[14]

While Aytoun every so often recalls himself and refers to 'the great Union' and the 'blending' of the kingdoms together, much of what he says on the subject remains equivocal. 'The experience of well-nigh a century and a half' suggested that the warnings of Fletcher and others about the 'tendency to absorb and centralise' had justification. The reasons

---

[13] [William Edmonston Aytoun], 'Scotland since the Union', *BM* 74 (1853), pp. 263–83; see pp. 228–33.

[14] [Aytoun], 'Scotland since the Union', pp. 267–71.

advanced for a federal union by Fletcher and others 'were not without their weight [. . .] preserving to Scotland the administration of its own affairs': although, in its own time, he thought the incorporating union the right choice, the English now seemed to regard the arrangement as an annexation of Scotland. The tendency even of statesmen to use 'English', not 'British', when referring to flag or army or parliament, is 'altogether inappropriate, unless, indeed, the Treaty of Union is to be considered an absolute dead letter'. Recent suggestions that 'Scottish nationality' was 'a dream without an object is to deny history [. . .]. The Union neither did nor could denationalise us.' Aytoun was keen to deflect the suggestion that the history he was referring to concerned blusterings about Bannockburn and the like rather than the identity represented by the Scottish institutions and practices, which the Union should have guaranteed. Burton's account of the failures after 1707 to implement the Union in a fair and sensitive manner offered Aytoun further parallels to the situation in the mid-nineteenth century, when 'there has been, for some time past, and still is, a tendency to regard Scotland in the light of a subsidiary province, and to deal with her accordingly'. The attempt to dissolve the Union in 1712 was widely supported, because then too, 'the attempt to provincialise Scotland was felt by all classes'.[15]

Aytoun went on to quote Burton's observation that when introducing the post-Union legal and revenue arrangements 'the Englishman showed his least amiable characteristics [. . .] and goes to his duty among strangers, as one surrounded by knaves and fools, whose habits and ideas must be treated with disdain', adding that the 'spirit' of the historian's remarks was 'not altogether inapplicable even now'. In a further link to contemporary politics, Aytoun lamented the abolition of the Scots Secretary of State early in the eighteenth century and the loading of his functions onto the Lord Advocate, an arrangement 'of which the country has had much reason to complain, and which it certainly ought not to tolerate longer'. And just as the 1712 attempt at repeal of the Union was made to a large extent because 'the country was exhausted of money, by the remittance of so great a part of the public taxes [. . .] to London'; so in his own time, 'while exposed to an equal taxation with England, Scotland does not receive the same, or anything like the same, encouragement of her national institutions'. Aytoun ended by developing more generally the connections to the contemporary situation and the claim of 'Justice to Scotland', which had been 'faintly audible for many years', but was now

---

[15] Aytoun, 'Scotland since the Union', pp. 273–6.

sounding 'throughout the land'. The issues he reiterated were 'substantial and specific', and it is clear that the Union Treaty is under serious critique: it had been supposed to equalise fiscal benefits as well as exactions; to maintain the Scottish Church, legal system and universities; and to secure for Scotland 'local courts, local powers, and a local executive'. However, as he proceeds to evidence in the remainder of the article, in many of these intentions and guarantees, 'the spirit of the treaty has not been observed', and its operation suggested that 'the true position of Scotland is that of a province'.[16]

A few months after Aytoun's article, the second major review of Burton's two volumes appeared in the *North British Review*, established in 1844 to reflect the views of the new Free Church of Scotland. The author was David Masson, who would later achieve a greater reputation in the Edinburgh Literature chair than Aytoun, and at this time was professor of English Language and Literature in University College, London. The title of the piece, 'The Union with England and Scottish Nationality', suggests that once again the *History* was functioning to relate a revived historical consciousness of the terms of the 1707 Union with contemporary issues and concerns that were, as Aytoun put it, 'sounding throughout the land'. Indeed, in Masson's case, he was jointly reviewing (and clearly intent on publicising) the 'Address to the People of Scotland, and Statement of Grievances' published by the NAVSR. Masson's article was briefly and selectively quoted in the early study of Scottish nationalism by H. J. Hanham, and interpreted as illustrating the confidence of Freechurchmen in the Union (unaccountably, since much of it seems to suggest just the opposite), and as a 'classic summary of the Unionist case'. Colin Kidd has recently viewed the essay in not dissimilar terms as evidence of the 'much deeper roots' of the Scots' adherence to unionism in the nineteenth century: Masson was simply confirming the strength at this time of the perception of there being 'two Englands' – the notion that a shared 'Gothic' or 'Teutonic' racial origin had eventuated in a natural, historical re-coalescence of the two peoples.[17]

---

[16] Ibid., pp. 274, 277–83.
[17] [David Masson], 'The Union with England and Scottish Nationality', *NBR* 21 (1854), pp. 69–100; H. J. Hanham, *Scottish Nationalism* (London: Faber, 1969), pp. 72–3; Colin Kidd, *Union and Unionisms: Political Thought in Scotland, 1500–2000* (Cambridge: Cambridge University Press, 2008), pp. 151–3, 158–9. Citations of Masson's article sometimes fail to mention that it was a review of a *History of Scotland*, and also of the NAVSR's 'Address', a number of whose resolutions are reproduced by Masson towards the conclusion of the piece.

In fact, like Aytoun, Masson downplayed the significance that Burton placed on the Teutonic-Celtic divide within Scotland: the 'matter of race' was not a particularly important element in 'nationality', and in any case both nations were a mongrel mix of 'Gothic and Celtic parentage'. Much more significant for Masson were the fundamental differences that 'the separate histories of a thousand years' had established between the Scots and English 'in all the solid constituents of nationality – in traditions, laws, customs, institutions, and acquired modes of thinking', not to mention religious traditions. For Masson, much of this still held true despite the aspiration of some of his contemporaries for a 'fusion' or 'merging' into Britishness: 'Even at the present day the Scotchman, so long as he remains in Great Britain, carries about with him the perpetual consciousness, "I am not an Englishman".' Masson tended to disagree with Burton's more sceptical position on whether the Union had been secured through bribery, and was 'almost certain' that there had been an anti-unionist majority among the people. In any case, it was clear the Scottish commissioners and parliament had aimed 'to reduce the union to the *minimum* compatible' with loss of the legislature, and Masson made a point of listing the Scottish institutions in which 'the two countries were to remain separate as before', including one on which the Scots 'put a mark equivalent to a curse upon whosoever should dare to tamper with it. This was the Scottish Church', and any attempt to do so 'would be, *ipso facto*, a dissolution of the Union'.[18]

Earlier, Masson had made particular mention that an incorporating union 'went sorely against the Scottish grain', whereas a 'commercial union' might have been supported. And after acknowledgements of the benefits of the Union particularly to Scotland, he returned to the issue. There was 'still a possible question' as to whether Scotland 'should have parted, as she did, with her separate autonomy': could a federal union not have been as beneficial? 'We do not know if this question has ever been formally put; but we believe it might be put, and that it would accord with a powerful current of Scottish sentiment at the present time.' Clearly by this point, Masson was directly linking the constitutional debates and options being explored before 1707 with emerging opinion in his own time and introducing the possibility that the settlement arrived at then may have been wrong. He thought it surely not possible that any 'sane Scotchman' would propose a repeal of the Union. However, much of his language as he considers the constitutional options is equivocal.

---

[18] [Masson], 'Union with England', pp. 70–3, 79. Emphasis in original.

It was 'no light thing for a man of any nation to admit that that nation can have received benefits from the loss of her power of independent and exclusive self-government'. It was not just sentiment but 'fact and politics' that even now suggested that Lord Belhaven's view of the baleful consequences of the Union for Scotland did 'not seem yet totally destitute of truth and argument'. And 'no thoughtful and observant Scotchman' could disagree that *'Scotland since the Union, has sustained [. . .] the want of efficient government of any sort'*, and had suffered from *'having such government as has been meted out to her conducted too exclusively on English principles, and with reference to English interests'*.[19]

To properly test these assertions, Masson argued that there required to be a review of 'the history of Scotland since the Union', and he proceeded to outline how this might be approached in four phases. On the first of these from the Union to 1748 he was happy to rely on Burton's *History*, on which he clearly draws to outline the violation of Scottish institutions carried on by English statesmen 'bent on treating Scotland as a conquered territory, and on applying English principles to Scottish society with that unbending rigidity and want of tact, which sometimes marks the English mind [. . .].' After outlining a further two phases, he turned to the most recent period, in which he emphasised the failure of the 1832 reforms to achieve the trumpeted 'political emancipation of Scotland': in reality they had led only to a transfer of Scottish administration to the Home Office (a point well made, he noted, 'at a recent meeting in Edinburgh on Scottish Rights'). The nation therefore remained without progressive government and 'in danger of legislation on alien principles by men trained in the school of Anglican circumstances, ignorant of her condition, and contemptuous of her peculiarities'. This was the reality of 'the history of Scotland since the Reform Bill'. Worst of all was the ignorance and inaction that the British legislature and government demonstrated in the face of the 'ten years' controversy' and the Disruption. This had been

> a national controversy which shook Scotland to its foundations [. . .]. All Scotland was agitated and in the throes of a mighty agony. Well, and what was known of this struggle, and thought of this struggle, in that neighbouring country to which Scotland had transferred the *locale* of her legislature? Nothing, literally nothing.

Here was a critical example of 'the adequacy of that system of government to which Scotland is subject, and which must be traced, however

---

[19] Ibid., pp. 77, 83–5. The emphasis here is original.

reluctantly, to that Union of 1707 to which in many respects we owe so much'. If Scotland had been 'in possession of her own autonomy, or of anything equivalent to it, the Disruption would not have happened'; and if it had held the power to repair its social fractures

> [by its own] political ingenuity, which is the highest right of every independent community, would she have suffered that rent to end in a total rupture of the most solid thing in her commonwealth? [. . .] if Scotland had possessed her autonomy [. . .] the Church of Scotland would have been whole at this day.[20]

In July 1854, around the same time as Masson's contribution appeared in the *North British Review*, a third major periodical carried a prominent review article, this time the august *Edinburgh Review*. The writer was James Dennistoun who, as already noticed, was well known to Burton personally partly through their shared interest in art. However, he was also knowledgeable on Scottish history, having edited a number of post-Reformation source publications for leading book clubs.[21] Dennistoun had approached the volumes unsure of the purpose of a history of Scotland covering a period when the nation had supposedly been 'amalgamated' with England but had been impressed by 'a really formidable result'. He proceeded to draw out a number of the ways in which Burton's account reflected different aspects of Scottish 'nationality'.

These extended to the historian's presentation of the Jacobite Risings as a national reaction: the expulsion of the Stuarts 'assumed the complexion of a national insult', and so the Jacobite disaffections are 'properly included in a work describing the latest efforts of Scottish nationality'. Dennistoun also highlighted a different strain of national identity and one of contemporary relevance in Burton's detailed account of the religious conflicts within Presbyterianism including the Secession movement of 1734, which the reviewer considered might provide 'a key to recent events brought about under somewhat similar influences'. Such controversies 'have not only strongly marked the history of Scotland, but given an impress to her national character, that seems unlikely to wear out'. Similarly, he was alert to Burton's presentation of the Darien scheme, providing quotations from the historian's most highly coloured passages portraying Darien as a national and patriotic effort. Finally, he summarised Burton's account of how Scotland had been failed in the attempted, post-Union 'fusion' of the two countries, through both arrogant English attitudes and selfish fiscal policies, and had suffered for its 'departed nationality'.

---

[20] [Masson], 'Union with England', pp. 86, 89–93.
[21] Boase, revised by Lloyd, 'Dennistoun, James'.

All of this prompted Dennistoun to the association with contemporary events also made by Aytoun and Masson:

> How far the Treaty of Union continues to be fairly observed in its spirit, or whether it has been gradually infringed in the letter, are questions again brought freely into discussion. It is alleged that the progress of imperial centralisation, or a niggardly parsimony, has absorbed many Scottish establishments which were reserved at the Union; that the business of that country is consequently neglected [. . .] in Parliament and the government offices, where her laws, institutions, local peculiarities and interests are ill understood and inadequately represented [. . .]: that the amount of public money dispensed [. . .] for charities, education, national defences, and other local or imperial purposes is trifling and inadequate[.]

So Scotland's position had become 'altogether anomalous, deprived of her national institutions and privileges, yet excluded from an equal participation in those of the empire'.[22]

Reviewers in the London-based periodicals, including one in *Fraser's* by the rising English historian James Antony Froude, were generally very positive, commending Burton's impartial, dispassionate and empirical approach while recognising his ability to rise to graphic and spirited description around his accounts of Darien and the Jacobite Risings. From a quite different contemporary perspective to that of the Scottish reviewers, Froude looked back 'from our present point of view' on a Union whose advantages 'had no apparent evils whatsoever to countervail them'. However, he was not alone in taking notice (not infrequently adopting the terminology of the contemporary Scottish Rights agitation) of Burton's presentation of Scottish 'grievances' before and after the Union, which, coupled with English arrogance, had led to disaster at Darien and later to the Risings: the 'injustice' done to Scotland had aroused the 'old spirit of strong independence', and the Act of Security showed that 'Scotland was not to be trifled with, and could not with safety be longer treated as a mere province'.[23]

The prevailing view of the 1850s Scottish Rights movement owes a good deal to the analysis of Graeme Morton, who rather unusually

---

[22] [James Dennistoun], 'Burton's History of Scotland, from 1689 to 1748', *ER* 100 (1854), 461–90 (pp. 462, 466, 473–4, 477–9).

[23] [J. A. Froude], 'History of Scotland, from the Revolution to the Extinction of the Last Jacobite Insurrection', *Fraser's Magazine* 48 (1853), 127–42 (pp. 132–3, 135–9); [Anon], 'The History of Scotland from the Revolution to the Extinction of the Last Jacobite Insurrection', *Ecl R*, n.s. 7 (1854), 129–44 (pp. 134–5, 137).

considered the NAVSR and its significance in some detail. His analysis demonstrated the consistent concern of those holding different political and religious views that the constitutional arrangements established in 1707 were reducing the country to the status of a 'province' and thereby, in a variety of respects, undermining Scottish 'nationality'. He also highlighted the emergence of references among its supporters to the 'violation of existing nationalities' on the continent and the drawing of comparisons with small independent European states. However, in his conclusion he returned to the notion that the central driver could be reduced to 'its pursuit of better administration of Scotland under the terms of the Union'. This was the determining factor in an outlook for which he coined the term 'unionist-nationalism', and although Morton originally limited its prevalence to the 1830–60 period, it is not infrequently used as shorthand for the predominant ideology of the Scottish middle classes through much of the century – this broadening of the concept referencing other recent writers who 'developed the idiom' in the direction of 'imperialist localism' and 'concentric' identities.[24]

The reception that Burton's 1853 *History* received in the articles just described accorded with what, for some years past, appears to have been a fairly broad swathe of opinion within the Scottish middle class that existing political arrangements had failed to deliver 'justice to Scotland'. Up to this point it may be true to say that this disaffection was predominantly characterised by a resistance to administrative centralisation as the British state consolidated in the English capital. Those who reviewed Burton's *History* clearly did allude to dissatisfaction with centralisation. However, the formulation of the issues in the various forceful protestations outlined above, in common with a number of the publications of the NAVSR itself, cannot easily be reduced to a concern with administrative changes. They articulated a broader discourse, associated with a revived historical consciousness and renewed scrutiny of the implications of the 1707 Union, which extended to a concern for lost 'autonomy' and 'independence', a 'departed nationality'; the loss of peculiarly Scottish institutions rooted in history; the consequent threat to 'denationalise'

---

[24] Morton, *Unionist Nationalism*, pp. 135–54; Morrison, *Painting the Nation*, pp. 6–8, 19–20, 185–6; Murray Pittock, *Scottish Nationality* (Basingstoke: Palgrave, 2001), p. 82; Anderson, 'University History Teaching', p. 5. Morton appears to have subsequently accepted the extension: Graeme Morton, 'Scotland is Britain: The Union and Unionist-Nationalism, 1807–1907', *Journal of Irish and Scottish Studies* 1 (2008), pp. 127–41.

a country that had become governed on 'Anglican principles'; the end of the nation's 'commonwealth' and ultimately of 'Scottish nationality'.

Many modern historians tend to question the credibility of the NAVSR, dismissing its significance with epithets of 'eccentric' and 'romantic' and ushering it quickly out of history.[25] Something of this remains in the assessment of the association in I. G. C. Hutchison's recent general history of the period, though it is notable that he also recognised its substantial contribution 'to significant long-term shifts in Scottish attitudes, as the earlier approach of striving to emulate England had been replaced with a search for equity [. . .].'[26] The potential for a different perspective had earlier been indicated by William Ferguson: the NAVSR 'was warmly backed by most of the town councils in Scotland, by several of the county commissions of supply, and by many professional bodies'. There were 'numerous well-attended public meetings', some working class support and successful efforts to enrol industrialists, so that the movement is perhaps in need of more detailed and considered assessment. While this is not a matter for the present study, it is notable that as Ferguson observed, in the arguments advanced by the NAVSR the perception '[t]hat the Union of 1707 had been carried by bribery and that its provisions had been scandalously broken was a common point of departure [. . .]'[27] A reassessment might include the extent to which the ideas and publications that emerged in the mid-century, including the renewed historical awareness of the period surrounding the Union, influenced the development of the Home Rule movement a generation later. In a recent analysis of the publications of the Scottish Home Rule Association (SHRA) in the 1880s and 1890s, Naomi Lloyd-Jones commented that the widespread emphasis on the concept of unionist-nationalism ran 'a risk of occluding the existence and vibrancy of alternative nationalisms'. Drawing on the SHRA's publications, she

---

[25] The tone was set by Hanham, *Scottish Nationalism*, pp. 76–8; see also Hutchison, *Political History*, pp. 91–5; Finlay, *Partnership for Good?*, pp. 17–20; Devine, *Scottish Nation*, p. 287. Alex Tyrrell has traced the origins and continued prevalence of the historiographic assumption of the movement's 'eccentricity': Alex Tyrrell, 'The Earl of Eglinton, Scottish Conservatism, and the National Association for the Vindication of Scottish Rights', *Historical Journal* 53 (2010), 87–107 (pp. 87–9).
[26] I. C. G. Hutchison, *Industry, Reform and Empire: Scotland, 1790–1880*, Vol. 9. New Edinburgh History of Scotland (Edinburgh: Edinburgh University Press, 2020), pp. 162–5.
[27] Ferguson, William, *Scotland 1689 to the Present*. Edinburgh History of Scotland IV (Edinburgh: Oliver & Boyd, 1968), pp. 319–22.

identified 'a counter-discourse to Unionist-nationalism' in which centralisation was one of a number of issues that were presented 'as a national grievance on behalf of the Scottish people':

> Home Rulers alleged that 'the rights and interests of the Scottish nation' had been 'wantonly disregarded and contemptuously treated' by parliament. This had inaugurated a 'process of decay' which, unless arrested through the creation of a separate legislature, would see Scotland 'cease to be a nation'.

This they viewed as merely underscored by the habit of calling Britain 'England', describing imperial affairs as 'English' and referring to Scotland as though it was 'a mere English county'. But the problem was more fundamental. The incorporating Union had allowed the English to ignore 'the national sentiment of Scotland'. They were thereby 'violating' the central tenet of the 1707 Treaty of Union. Although Lloyd-Jones believed that this was a discourse 'which surfaced in the late 1880s', it has much in common with the commentaries on Burton's volumes in 1853–4 and other publications associated with the Scottish Rights movement in the 1850s. This is not surprising given the familiarity of the leaders of the later movement with the publications of prominent NAVSR figures like P. E. Dove, the Reverend James Begg and Aytoun himself, whose review article built around Burton's *History* was reprinted and issued by the SHRA in 1891. The article by Masson discussed above certainly appears to anticipate federalist, 'home rule' thinking, and suggests that it was already part of public debate.[28]

One of the reasons for the disestimation of the NAVSR centres on a perception of its leading figures as, on the one hand, romantic obsessives, and on the other, disappointed men disaffected within their own spheres. The Association's President, the Earl of Eglinton, is often identified primarily with promoting the neo-medieval 'Eglinton Tournament' some fifteen years before. However, a recent reappraisal has provided a different portrait of a serious and capable leading politician.[29] The early pacemaker of the agitation, James Grant, seems an obvious fit for this

---

[28] Naomi Lloyd Jones, 'Liberalism, Scottish Nationalism and the Home Rule Crisis, c. 1886–93', *EHR* 129 (2014), 862–87 (pp. 863, 873–4); Hanham, *Scottish Nationalism*, pp. 83, 87–8; Harry Gow, ed., *Scotland Since the Union: Being a Reprint of an Article in 'Blackwood's Magazine' for September, 1853 By the Late William Edmonston Aytoun* (Perth: Cowan, 1891); [Masson], 'Union with England', pp. 93–9.

[29] For instance, Devine, *Scottish Nation*, p. 287; but see Tyrrell, 'Earl of Eglinton', pp. 89, 92, 94–5.

kind of characterisation of the movement in his *persona* as a successful romantic novelist. But Grant had an early career as a naval officer with a command at Chatham dockyard, and would have been knowledgeable on the issues of naval procurement and harbours investment that formed part of the NAVSR's well-founded fiscal arguments.[30]

Figures prominent in the launch of the movement, such as Duncan McLaren and the Reverend James Begg, have been described as 'disappointed men' in their own spheres. This may have been true temporarily, but both were leading and influential figures who soon returned to take nationally prominent roles, with Begg in particular continuing to articulate public scepticism on the Union. Patrick Edward Dove, who wrote more than one of the Scottish Rights manifestos, was a respected political economist who gave lectures at the Edinburgh Philosophical Institution and was a serious candidate as successor to Sir William Hamilton in the Edinburgh philosophy chair: he thought history central to Scottish nationality, the relation in his case viewed chiefly through the Presbyterian-providential historiography recently traced by James Coleman.[31] Finally, David Masson was commencing a distinguished academic career and would continue to be a supporter of progressive causes, including women's access to universities, as well as the national liberation movements in Europe through which he developed a friendship with Mazzini. As his review in the *North British Review* showed, he too was attuned to the relation of history and national identity, and towards the end of the century was a mentor to Peter Hume Brown.[32]

Recent assessments of the NAVSR published from the late 1980s to the early 2000s tend to include rather ahistorical or anachronistic references to the movement's relation, or lack of it, to 'modern Scottish nationalism'. This often leads on to an emphasis that there were virtually

---

[30] M. G. Watkins, revised by Douglas Brown, 'Grant, James', in *ODNB*, accessed 16 September 2019.

[31] Hutchison, *Political History*, pp. 91–3; Coleman, *Remembering the Past*, pp. 72–3, 98–9; Hanham, *Scottish Nationalism*, p. 81; Anon, revised by John Cunliffe, 'Dove, Patrick Edward', in *ODNB*, accessed 10 October 2019; P. Edward Dove, *Romanism, Rationalism, and Protestantism, Viewed Historically in Relation to National Freedom and National Welfare* (Edinburgh: Shepherd and Elliot, 1855), pp. 60–8.

[32] G. G. Smith, 'Masson, David Mather'; Dauvit Broun, 'A Forgotten Anniversary: Hume Brown's History of Scotland, 1911', in *Writing a Small Nation's Past: Wales in Comparative Perspective, 1850–1950*, eds Neil Evans and Huw Pryce (Farnham: Ashgate, 2013), 267–82 (pp. 271, 275–6).

no arguments advanced for Scottish political independence, for repeal of the Union or for a nationalist movement of the kind then occurring in Europe. These observations are generally true. However, the corollary tends to be an assertion that the chief concerns were about apparently 'trivial grievances' relating to heraldry and the like, or at most administrative centralisation. The effect, for this period too, has been to occlude the extent to which broader issues of national identity and criticism of existing constitutional arrangements were being articulated.[33]

An alternative view might conceive of the admittedly disparate group of leading figures as independent thinkers expressing from different positions a first articulation of ideas breaking through the curtain of assimilationist assumptions that had been shared by many among the Scottish elite, and that relied on the notion of an incorporating Union bringing about a 'fusion' of Scottish and English civil society and institutions. Indeed, Colin Kidd has maintained that the Union was 'so much part of the wallpaper' of Scottish public life that 'there was no credible, sustained or widely supported Scottish critique of the Anglo-Scottish Union', between the mid-eighteenth century and the 1970s. In this perspective, the Union and 'the Anglo-Scottish relationship' had only 'ephemeral salience' during the nineteenth century, the only exceptions worth mentioning being in ecclesiastical debates leading to the Disruption and some attention in the last two decades of the century stimulated by the pressure for Irish Home Rule. In his analysis, Kidd does not mention the NAVSR at this point, but considers it later as ultimately 'a unionist organisation' whose critiques simply 'reflected the dominant and unchallenged unionism of mid-nineteenth-century Scotland'. However, it is difficult to see how the robust criticism of the 1707 settlement described above – from William Chambers' commentary on this 'stupid arrangement' (shared with his 50,000 readers), to the lengthy articles based on Burton's volumes – can accord with the view that the Union was 'invisible' in the mid-nineteenth century save for commentary that 'focussed on the economic and social

---

[33] Hutchison, *Political History*, p. 91; Cameron, *Impaled upon a Thistle*, p. 63; Pickard, *Member for Scotland*, p. 128; Finlay, *Partnership for Good?*, p.19; Kidd, *Unionisms*, pp. 264–5, 270–1. See also Paterson, *Autonomy of Modern Scotland*, pp. 4–9, 46–102: this secondary-source survey was explicitly introduced as 'an intervention in a political debate' (presumably that of the 1990s on constitutional choices), and 'not an academic history', though it has been influential with historians. It underestimates the degree of concern and conviction in the mid-nineteenth century, traceable in primary sources, concerning the assimilation and neglect of Scottish national institutions.

benefits of the Union', and excluded 'any attempts to discuss the nature of the Union'.³⁴

In the later 1840s and in the 1850s, quite 'credible' questions were indeed being raised and shared extensively about 'the nature of the Union' and its consequences.³⁵ In Scotland, this was at least partly because Burton (with absolutely no intention to question the settlement) had, as it were, taken down the 'wallpaper' and subjected it to detailed scrutiny, an examination widely publicised through the periodicals. For the first time in a century and a half, the arguments for and against the Union had been robustly rehearsed in a Scottish history text and context. At the same time, those arguments had been brought into relation with the various strands of contemporary, mid-nineteenth century disquiet concerning the effects of the 1707 settlement and where it was taking Scotland. It is difficult to see how these critiques can be interpreted as further confirmation of the 'banal unionism' of those involved on the grounds that they were not explicitly seeking repeal, merely rejecting the emerging assimilationist consequences of an incorporating union. The 1707 Treaty was an incorporating Union.

In his account of 'unionist-nationalism', Graeme Morton was quite frank that it had been part of his intention to 'rescue' the determinants of national identity from 'the ephemeral world of culture', and relate them principally to socio-political factors. But the cultural materials and constructs that contribute to national identity were at this very time ceasing to be 'ephemeral' because they were being granted permanency (or at least semi-permanency) in the *longue durée* of new and authenticated national histories. National identity was becoming inextricably bound up with history. At no time was this more the case than in the second half of the nineteenth century. Morton's own analysis illustrates that in seeking to articulate and reassert Scottish national identity, the NAVSR did not have available the kind of national historical narrative that became central to the assertion or reassertion of national identity through much of Europe in this period. Morton went on to record how, unable to rely on any kind of coherent narrative of the nation's past, in the commemorative historical pageants of the age of unionist-nationalism, the 'whole

---

³⁴ Kidd, *Unionisms*, pp. 25–7, 268–71.
³⁵ Tyrrell has shown that there were a range of positions in UK-wide public circulation that were resistant to assimilationist policy, though his overall conclusion seems a variant of the perception of the NAVSR as about 'administrative' decentralisation: Tyrrell, 'Earl of Eglinton', pp. 90–1, 107.

spectrum of Scotland's historical lucky-dip was dredged up', reflecting the fragmented and often conflicting discourses that had been the source of so many animosities and competing accounts of the nation's past. Appeals to history, even by union sceptics, relied on calling up a gallimaufry of symbols, legends and icons dragged out of context and held in place by sentiment. As the 1850s drew to a close and for some time thereafter, Scottish national consciousness remained 'dependent upon the lucky-dip of the historical past', disparate elements, episodically 'dredged up' at commemorative events and unceremoniously – or, rather, ceremoniously – stitched together.[36]

Burton published his comprehensive *History of Scotland* in two tranches a decade later.

CRITICAL ACCLAIM

Among those who reviewed and otherwise responded to the publication of Burton's volumes, almost all were highly enthusiastic, not infrequently suggesting that it had a transformative effect on their perception of Scottish history. Such reactions are reflected in the many articles and reviews devoted to the work in daily and weekly newspapers and journals, as the volumes were issued in 1867 and 1870. Equally admiring responses characterise the more extensive review articles that were published in the *Edinburgh Review* (1867 and 1871), *Blackwood's Magazine* (1867 and 1870), *Macmillan's Magazine* (1867), the *London Quarterly Review* (1867/8 and 1871) and the *British Quarterly* (1867 and 1871). Further afield, there were laudatory reviews in the influential French journal *Revue des Deux Mondes* and the New York-based literary journal, *The Nation*. In addition, the British reviews were carried in the American editions of Scottish and English periodicals, and reproduced in other foreign journals.[37]

The identities of most of the (originally anonymous) authors of the periodical articles are now known. To review, in his own magazine, the volumes he had consistently encouraged Burton to complete, the publisher John Blackwood selected the successful writer Margaret Oliphant in 1867 and then the prominent churchman and academic, Principal

---

[36] Morton, *Unionist Nationalism*, pp. 135, 154, 173–4, 198.

[37] For instance, highly positive reviews of the initial four volumes from British periodicals were reprinted in the *Eclectic Magazine* of New York, and the *Friend of India* published in Calcutta; *Ecl M*, 6 n.s. (1867), 453–6; *The Friend of India*, 16 May 1867, p. 585; full citation of all of the reviews listed are given where first referenced below.

John Tulloch in 1870. The *Macmillan's* reviewer, George Burnett, had originally qualified as an advocate but like Burton was more interested in literary and historical pursuits as well as art and music; he was knowledgeable in Scottish history, particularly the medieval centuries. Both of the articles that appeared in the *Edinburgh Review* were from the pen of Henry Hill Lancaster, another advocate, though more of a practising one; however, he too combined legal work with literary endeavours, including regular contributions to the *Edinburgh Review* on Scottish political history. The reviewer in *The Nation* was William Francis Allen, professor at the University of Wisconsin, later considered a pioneer in his approach to teaching history, including the examination of original sources.[38]

Even in Allen's international perspective it was seen as rather extraordinary that, despite being subject to the strictures of modern historical scepticism and critical research, a national history could be written to encompass nearly two millennia:

> It may fairly be pronounced one of the most important and best-executed historical undertakings of our time. The complete history of any country is, in the rapid accumulation of materials and the stringent demands of criticism at the present day, a task which might well daunt the most courageous. And we can bestow no higher praise upon this book – none, that is, which better expresses its literary rank – than to say that neither England nor America possesses any complete history which can compare with this in merit; nor, in the English language, any modern nation of the European Continent, unless it be France.

There was comparable enthusiasm at home. The work was viewed as having restored the extent and antiquity of the national past: after all the efforts at attenuation since the eighteenth century, what had been produced, enthused the *Scotsman* in August 1870, now fully founded on facts and a strict objectivity, was '*the* History of Scotland [. . .] as full and faithful a record of seventeen centuries as is possessed by almost any other country in Europe'.[39] The welcome the work received was based partly on

---

[38] Authors are identified from *The Wellesley Index to Victorian Periodicals: 1824–1900*, ed. Walter E. Houghton, 5 vols (Toronto: University of Toronto Press, 1966): those named above are considered firm attributions. Biographical information is from the relevant named entries in the *ODNB*, accessed 25 November 2020, except for Allen, for whom see https://dbcs.rutgers.edu/all-scholars/8508-allen-william-francis, accessed 24 May 2021.

[39] [William Francis Allen], 'Burton's History of Scotland', *The Nation*, 19 (1874), 41–3 (p. 41); *Sc*, 19 August 1870, p.5. Emphasis in original.

the manner in which had been written – Burton's approach to evidence or avoidance of worn-out controversies for example – but also on the range of subject matter he had included. The remainder of this section will examine in greater detail the characteristics of the *History* that were so admired by contemporaries and attracted such a positive reception.

Impartiality

The first widely celebrated feature was Burton's studied avoidance of the partialities that had stained previous efforts. Admiration for an unbiased and dispassionate approach was widely reflected in the Scottish-based journals and viewed as exorcising or correcting features that were seen to have brought Scottish history and history-writing into disrepute. Burton had dismissed the obsessive partisanship over the language of the Picts or the religion of the Druids that had come to be associated with the controversies of the antiquarians. He had side-stepped the disputes that, even recently, had been raging over Mary Stuart's guilt. And most importantly, the great majority considered that he had avoided sectarian bias in his narratives of religious conflict. For H. H. Lancaster in the *Edinburgh Review*, the *History*'s 'impartiality, amounting almost to indifference', meant that it 'is not too much to say that the best ecclesiastical history of Scotland yet written is to be found in Mr Burton's pages'. Among others, the *Glasgow Herald*, the *Aberdeen Journal* and, unsurprisingly, the churchman John Tulloch in *Blackwood's*, gave particular attention to Burton's handling of ecclesiastical history: the *Herald* welcomed its 'unbiased narrative' as an antidote to H. T. Buckle's account of the Reformation; for the Aberdeen paper, Burton was of the historical school 'which prefers learning, accuracy, and impartiality'; while Tulloch celebrated 'a spirit of indomitable and thorough research, an impartial judicial temper'.[40]

Many of the London-based reviewers agreed. For the *Athenaeum*, it was for his impartiality that Burton's 'merit is most conspicuous', although 'he is not merely always impartial, he is always interesting'. The *Standard* emphasised that, though written about his own country, the work was free from 'all prejudice, prepossession, or partiality'. Even in the fourth volume, which it thought many would hold a favourite, his approach to Queen Mary typified 'the general coolness and impartiality

---

[40] [Henry Hill Lancaster], 'Burton's History of Scotland: Vols V, VI, VII', *ER* 134 (1871), 100–30 (p. 108); *Glasg H*, 6 October 1870, p. 2; *Aber J*, 22 May 1867, p. 6; [John Tulloch], 'Burton's History of Scotland: Concluding Volumes', *BM* 109 (1871), 794–812 (p. 794).

of his judgement'. His French reviewer saw in Burton a *'sage ami du progrès et juge impartial'*, who brought to issues of controversy *'un tour esprit de légiste, un ensemble d'habitude judiciaires'*. The Scottish elites were of course well aware that besides the domestic audience, many of the publications, especially the periodicals, formed a central cultural reference point not only for England and the rest of the Empire but also for Europe and North America. They would have been quite conscious that these valorising assessments were echoing around the 'civilised' world.[41]

Completeness – Extent

The reviewer who contrasted Burton's volumes favourably with Tytler's *History* because the latter was 'incomplete, both at the beginning and the end' echoed many other commentators. The different dimensions of the 'completeness' on which Burton was so widely complimented can be related directly to the great increase in source material recently made available, presenting an opportunity that his convictions on the primacy of empirical evidence and inductive methods had prepared him to grasp. Relevant for the 'beginning' was his knowledge of the initiatives and publications of friends like Daniel Wilson, John Stuart and J. Y. Simpson pursuing new explorations of 'Prehistory' and early archaeology; and further afield, his awareness and admiration of the work of the Scandinavian scholars. For the later periods, he would make extensive use of the labours of Cosmo Innes, Joseph Robertson and the earlier records scholars to incorporate new and widely appreciated social and cultural dimensions in the *History*, as well as exploiting the mass of material unearthed from continental archives by the likes of Teulet and Michel. Burton had himself extended coverage to the mid-eighteenth century in his initial two volumes, published in 1853. The reviewers of those volumes were anxious to see Scottish history brought down to the present day, one making a point that the work should be a history of Scotland, not an account of the nation 'gathered from histories of the British empire'.[42]

---

[41] *Athen*, 3 September 1870, p. 302; *Stand*, 28 August 1867, p. 3 and 21 October 1870, p. 3; *Lloyd's*, 25 September 1870, p. 5; *Lit Rev*, 25 May 1867, p. 381; Louis Étienne, 'Historiens Modernes De L'Écosse: John Hill Burton', *Revue des Deux Mondes*, 71 (1867), 208–33 (pp. 209, 215): Étienne's review also covered works by H. T. Buckle and Francis Palgrave, but as the title suggests the focus is on Burton's histories, including *The Scot Abroad*.

[42] See above pp. 21–2; Burton, *HOS* (1873), I, pp. 112–13, 125–6, 131; [Masson], 'Union with England', pp. 86–93; [Dennistoun], 'Burton's History', pp. 489–90.

Burton was perceived to have traced the nation's roots deep into the first millennium, so that the 'completeness' was partly about the sheer extent of the period encompassed. More than one reviewer commended Burton's scepticism in relation to 'Scottish legend' and dismissal of the 'fabulous' accounts of the line of kings, which supposedly had stretched back to a pre-Christian era. For Henry Lancaster, Burton had recognised that the 'dawn of true history' should begin with the reign of Malcolm Canmore (1057–93), and underscored Burton's observation that a 'nationality distinct from and antagonistic to the English people' did not predate the reign of Alexander III (1249–86). However, Lancaster's perspective is not how most reviewers tended to view Burton's efforts. For many, of the initial four volumes published in 1867, it was actually the first – covering the earlier centuries – that was one of the highlights and of particular interest. Burton was seen to have struck down flimsy myths, but then fashioned a credible description of origins. The writer in *Chambers's Journal* spoke for many:

> [in] the interesting chapters devoted to the Unrecorded Ages, the author sweeps away the old epics, and the fabulous historians who succeeded them, but he replaces them by valuable results of his laborious learning, and speculations as reasonable as they are ingenious.

This demonstrated that the 'national history of Scotland, properly so called', had commenced in the seventh to eighth centuries. For the Blackwood's reviewer, too, it seemed clear that by the ninth century, 'the kingdom of the Scots had rounded into unity and individuality'.[43]

Scottish commentators were aware of the debt Burton owed to the recent effort in the recovery and classification of records. The reviewer in the *Inverness Courier* also considered that many readers would esteem the first volume 'the most valuable of the four'. The writer noted that Burton

---

[43] [Henry Hill Lancaster], 'Burton's History of Scotland', *ER* 126 (1867), 238–68 (p. 250); [Anon], 'Scotland from Agricola's Invasion to 1688', *Chamb J*, Series 4 v.4 (15 June 1867), 393–8 (pp. 394–5); [Margaret Oliphant], 'The History of Scotland', *BM* 101 (1867), 317–7 (pp. 320–1). A version of Scottish history from the Roman era 'to the present time' had in fact been issued in multiple parts in 1852–5 by the English antiquary and historian Thomas Wright, but received little critical attention, partly perhaps because his scholarship had previously been publicly criticised: Thomas Wright, *The History of Scotland; from the Earliest Period to the Present Time*, 3 vols (London: London Printing Company, 1873–4); Michael Welman Thompson, 'Wright, Thomas', in *ODNB*, accessed 1 December 2020.

had been enabled to extend his coverage due to the material that had been made available through the recent efforts centred on Register House, specifically mentioning the contribution made by Joseph Robertson. More generally, the account of the Roman period down to the union of Scots and Picts contains 'striking information, never before incorporated with our general historical works'. The work of previous writers who had ventured into the earlier centuries, like the antiquarians Joseph Ritson and John Pinkerton, had been 'dry and uninviting', while Tytler's *History* had commenced much later.[44]

In welcoming the 1867 volumes, the *Banffshire Journal* also foregrounded the great advances that had been made in the availability of source materials in the twenty-five years since Tytler's *History*: 'A new History of Scotland! Well all we can say is there is quite room for it', given, the writer went on, the availability of new discoveries of manuscript material, research in state and foreign records and studies of physical remains: '[I]n Scotland, in particular, the study of the monuments of our early history has been pursued with an ardour as commendable as it has been successful.' Previous icons like William Robertson, 'wordy and sententious', had incorporated much now known to be fable, and the reviewer reproduced a number of Burton's passages dismissing such material. Other Scottish and London journals drew this contrast with previous histories. The *Dundee Advertiser* noted how Robertson 'passes over the first 800 years in three or four paragraphs', to be followed by later historians; Tytler 'half-apologises', the writer went on, for starting as late as Alexander III despite the great interest attaching to the preceding centuries. One of Burton's 'distinguishing excellencies' was to have 'opened upon hitherto untrodden and comparatively unknown ground'. Yet this was no antiquarian endeavour: he had been able

> [with] great pictorial power [. . .] to grasp the dead yet storied past [. . .] and to make it live, and move, and speak to modern eyes and ears – and this is precisely what Mr Burton has done with the first thousand years of Scottish history.[45]

---

[44] *Inv C*, 7 March 1867, p. 2.

[45] *Banf J*, 5 February 1867, p. 2; *Dund Adv*, 11 February 1867, p. 4; London commentators also presented Burton as superseding William Robertson and Walter Scott: see [Anon], 'Burton's History of Scotland', *LQ* 29 (1867–8), 284–329 (p. 329). The *Aberdeen Journal* reviewer was more defensive of earlier Scottish histories, while recognising they had addressed 'only a portion', where Burton had 'given us a complete History of Scotland'. *Aber J*, 22 May 1867, p. 6, and 27 July 1870, p. 6.

Completeness – Thematic Depth

This newly credible extensiveness of the national past was partly founded on Burton's familiarity with the evidence-based researches of the neo-antiquarians. However, by the 'completeness' that was so widely celebrated, commentators were also referring to what they viewed as a welcome incorporation of a range of social and ethnographic subjects. Burton adopted a particular narrative pattern in the *History*: for each of the three main 'historical' epochs – the early medieval centuries, the period from the Wars of Independence to the Reformation and the centuries thereafter – he incorporated chapters that sought to convey the 'Progress of the Nation' or the 'Condition of the Nation' for the period in question. It was these sections, addressing subjects like architecture, the universities, superstitions, classical Scots poetry and vernacular ballads, law and urban development, that many commentators received with surprise and approbation as conveying the social and cultural condition of the nation in the different periods. At the beginning of one of these sections, Burton indicated, in characteristically theatrical terms, his agreement with those who now considered that 'the history of a country' required to 'reveal the social condition of the people brought forward to act upon its stage'.[46]

It is notable how much of this breadth of subject matter emerged from Burton's involvement, already traced in chapter 3, with what might be termed the 'culture of Blackwood'. John Blackwood had commissioned Burton in one way or another to write on almost all of the themes involved, many recognisable as topics, particular components of the Scottish past, on which there were aspirations in this period for systematic reclamation or compilation. Burton knew so much about Scottish architectural history, partly from his own attraction to romantic ruins but even more from his involvement in the Blackwoods' ambitious and seminal publication of 'Billings'. Subsequently he had written on almost all of the other themes in articles and reviews in *Blackwood's Magazine*. His knowledge of the ballad and song tradition went back to his Aberdeenshire roots, but his review of Aytoun's *Ballads of Scotland*, published of course by Blackwood, recognised and celebrated a comprehensive compilation of

---

[46] *Aber J*, 27 July 1870, p. 6; *Inv C*, 28 July 1870, p. 3; [Anon], 'Scotland from Agricola's Invasion to 1688', *Chamb J*, Series 4 v.7 (1870), 777–82 (p. 782); *Exam*, 16 February 1867, pp. 100–2 and 15 October 1870, pp. 660–1; *Stand*, 21 October 1870, p. 2; [Anon], 'Burton's History of Scotland', *LQ* 35 (1871), 331–62 (pp. 358–60); Burton, *HOS* (1873), VII, p. 77, footnote 1.

all that had been achieved. He had an early and enduring fascination with the 'gothic' and supernatural associations of prehistoric remains, but this was validated and shared publicly in his enthused response to Stuart's *Sculptured Stones* as an unsurpassed investigation, comprehensively illustrated through facsimile reproduction, of a uniquely Scottish tradition. His account, in the *History*, of the Scottish universities as an evolution from medieval European institutions recalls the *Blackwood's Magazine* articles on 'Student Life' that he built around the university records collections edited by Innes and Robertson.

John Blackwood's professional relationship with Burton appears to reflect his approach with other types of author. In his tenure as editor of *Blackwood's Magazine* (1845–79) and head of the firm (1852–79), he further developed a central element of the firm's marketing strategy, which involved linking the serial or regular publication of authors in the periodical with the rights to subsequent productions in book form. Burton's articles, almost exclusively for *Blackwood's* from around 1850, were the building blocks for his major historical contributions. This all seems entirely in accord with David Finkelstein's analysis of the publisher's sustained relations with individual authors, through whom the firm secured 'a distinctive identity for itself within national and international boundaries'. Subsequently, 'authors and readers were [. . .] invited into an invisible Blackwoodian "community" or "ecumene"'.[47] The sustained relationship with Burton seems to exemplify the publishing firm's 'determination to foster unique "communities" of readers and authors at various stages in its history'. This in effect extended Burton's historical and historiographic influence with the introduction to the reading public, from the mid-century on, of the range of subject matter just described, subsequently reinforced by its incorporation in Blackwood publications, particularly *The Scot Abroad* and the *History of Scotland*. The Scottish periodical-reading public, including the reviewers themselves had been prepared for the inclusion of such matter in Scottish history – and to recognise its significance when it appeared – through the regular coverage of such subjects in the *Magazine*.

As we have seen, for a number of the themes described, Burton owed much to the earlier labours of his father-in-law. His attention to the progress made in a range of aspects of medieval Scottish society owed much to Cosmo Innes's groundbreaking researches in medieval source materials. Innes had pointed the way in his limited forays into narrative history, which had substantial sections on the specific historical trajectories of,

[47] Finkelstein, *House of Blackwood*, pp. 16, 95.

for example, the Scottish universities or Scottish architecture, and Scots literature and language. However, the area in which Innes's influence was probably greatest relates to a further aspect of the *History* that was greeted by many commentators as unexpected.[48]

Constitutionality

There is a tone of enthusiastic surprise and discovery, particularly in some of the Scottish reviews, in noticing Burton's treatment of constitutional features in the Scottish past. Margaret Oliphant thought it central to the 'nationality' that she found in the 1867 volumes:

> Another and still more remarkable national feature is brought out with great force in Mr Burton's narrative, and is, indeed, the development and explanation of the singular vigour of nationality which we have just remarked. It is that, in the very heart of feudalism, the little northern kingdom, torn by wars and conflicts, was at heart a constitutional kingdom[.]

In illustrating 'the administration of even-handed justice', Oliphant then reproduced a lengthy excerpt, one also noted by other commentators, of the Estates' actions to curtail the depredations of French knights against the Scottish peasantry under Robert II. Burton had observed that this 'admitted the existence of civil rights in the meanest inhabitants' – citing evidence from Innes's first volume of *APS*. As previously described, in his subsequent passages devoted to the early development of law and constitutional arrangements Burton had elaborated on this egalitarian reflex, the progressive efforts at parliamentary development and the Estates' assertiveness against the royal prerogative, often relying on the efforts of the records scholars.[49]

The writer in the *Revue des Deux Mondes* also drew from Burton's account of '*la nationalité écossaise*' up to the Reformation a sense of Scotland having less tyrannous constitutional characteristics than England:

> 'L'Écosse, par exemple, n'a pas eu de charte des forêts ni de lois sur la chasse; elle ne porte pas cette profonde marque de la tyrannie normande et du joug de l'aristocratie. Sa royauté n'était pas irresponsable, et les parlemens [*sic*] exprimaient leurs doléances sur la conduit des rois aussi bien que sur celles des ministres et officiers de la couronne[.]

---

[48] Innes, *Sketches*, pp. 220–324; Innes, *Scotland in the Middle Ages*, pp. 251–76, 276–320.
[49] [Oliphant], 'History of Scotland', p. 332; see above, pp. 85–7 and Burton, *HOS* (1873), II, pp. 355–6, 373–4.

A number of other commentators perceived the *History* as offering a revisionist presentation that recognised the degree of constitutionalism in the Scottish past. This was seen as corrective of the portrayal by H. T. Buckle of the Scottish medieval centuries as immersed in feudal chaos and conflict. Among the London critics, there was some recognition of the emergence in Burton's pages of the constitutional assertiveness of the Scottish parliament when the nobility became 'turbulent'; and Henry Reeve at the *Edinburgh Review* thought Burton's presentation of 'the constitutional action of the Estates' to be 'especially valuable & of unusual interest'. However, the Scottish journals were most attuned to Burton's 'excellent' account of the Scottish Constitution: he had demonstrated 'the marked superiority which it had over that of most other nations, in the absence of any invidious rights by which class is set up against class'. The main journals in Aberdeen, Dundee and Edinburgh all noted the sense conveyed in the *History* of the Scottish medieval world as progressive in its legal and institutional development, and civic life.[50]

Reviewers also noted evidence of constitutionality in later times. For instance, Burton was seen to have provided an 'impartial summary' of Regent Murray's character, and to have presented his efforts to bring order and support the reformers as a 'policy as thoroughly constitutional as that of the English statesmen who promoted the revolution of 1688'. Commentators also largely accepted Burton's presentation of Scotland's leading role when the religious and political contests of the earlier seventeenth century came to a head. For Lancaster in the *Edinburgh Review*, the General Assembly of 1638 in Glasgow Cathedral had been 'a meeting of hardly less historical moment than the meeting of the Long Parliament itself, but for which, indeed, it may well be doubted if the Long Parliament would ever have met at all'. The *British Quarterly* agreed: although their 'religious zeal' would eventually go too far, in his account of the actions of the Scottish Estates in 1640–1, Burton had demonstrated that Scotland had inaugurated the 'glorious resistance' to Charles I's despotic intentions: 'but for the resolution displayed by the nation [. . .] the constitutional liberties of England might have been suspended for at least a generation.'[51]

---

[50] Étienne, '*Historiens Modernes*', pp. 232–3; *Exam*, 16 February 1867, p. 101; NLS MS 9409, fol. 263; [George Burnett], 'Burton's History of Scotland: Celtic Scotland and Feudal Scotland', *MM* 16 (1867), 97–110 (p. 110); *Aber J*, 22 May 1867, p. 6; *Dund Adv*, 11 February 1867, p. 4; [Anon], 'Scotland from Agricola's Invasion', *Chamb J* (1867), p. 398.

[51] *Exam*, 8 October 1870, p. 644; [Lancaster], 'Burton's History' (1871), p.115; [H. S. Fagan], 'Burton's History of Scotland', *BQ* 53 (1871), 297–326 (pp. 320–2).

It has been argued that the Scottish nineteenth-century literati purveyed to the prevailing elite a negative view of the pre-Union past, particularly in regard to legal and constitutional development, bewailing 'the excessive powers of an overbearing feudal nobility who oppressed the commons', as well as 'the institutional failings of the legal system and of the tightly controlled unicameral parliament'. This was due, the argument runs, to their 'wholesale acceptance [. . .] of the deconstructive criticism initiated during the Scottish Enlightenment', and was so pervasive as to 'vitiate' the impact of the revolution in records scholarship.[52] If this was true of a number of writers earlier in the century, there is much in Burton's *History* and in the responses to it to suggest that attitudes were rapidly changing. It is clear that this had in fact much to do with Burton's use of the work of the records scholars, not least the reissue of the *APS*, including Innes's publication of Volume I and the Preface with which he introduced it.

The Romantic, the Gothic and the Theatrical

A full consideration, from a modern perspective, of Burton's main work as displaying the characteristics of a national history of the Romantic Age is offered in the final section of this chapter. However, contemporary reviewers were already responsive to at least some of those aspects of Burton's work, which it has been argued above reflect romantic culture and the related aesthetic of the Picturesque.

Burton peppers his *History* with stories and images that he himself often associates with the 'elements of old romance', often commends scenes and events as 'picturesque', and periodically conveys what happened in a narrative style that would not be out of place in works of romantic fiction. Contemporary reviewers recognised this. One London critic viewed the 'great work' as brought to a conclusion in 1870 'with as much freshness, vigour, and picturesqueness as marked its opening chapters'. He contrasted it with previous antiquarian efforts: it contained no 'Dryasdust', elements and was 'as easy reading as any of the Scotch novels – as any of the romances of any nationality'. Burton's presentations of prominent characters were 'pre-eminently well-executed. They range from elaborate and vigorous full-length (portraits) down to the minutest sketches.' Both Scottish and London journals were attuned to Burton's successful incorporation of graphic and pictorial elements in his account. For George Burnett,

---

[52] Kidd, *Subverting*, pp. 254–5.

in the four 1867 volumes 'we are presented with a succession of broad, bold, graphic sketches of events', which drew the reader's gaze and held their attention. Others found the later volumes superior 'in warmth of tone and in picturesque effect'. Several commentators admired his 'portraits of characters' like Knox, Lethington, Buchanan, Archbishop Sharp and Montrose, which, as one writer put it, 'stand out boldly and vividly from the canvas'. Others admired the 'picture of real events' he provided, instancing his graphic descriptions of Mary's escape from Lochleven or of the battle of Langside.[53]

Burton had been an active and enthusiastic participant in the burgeoning enthusiasm for the visual arts in the decades after his arrival in Edinburgh. Probably its most prominent feature had been the extensive use of iconic figures and events drawn from Scottish history as subjects for many of the artists, scene painters and those constructing theatrical and photographic *tableaux*. The widespread appreciation of his 'graphic' and picturesque 'sketches' and 'portraits' was in accord with this imagistic conception of the national past and with his own formative experience in so many public exhibitions and private collections of the depiction, the 'painting', of Scottish history. Even H. H. Lancaster in the *Edinburgh Review*, who judged his early volumes not picturesque enough, recognised Burton's celebration of perhaps the most iconic setting in Scottish historical-genre painting: he had risen to 'an unwonted command of the picturesque when he describes the renewal of the Covenant in Greyfriars' Churchyard under the shadow of the castle-rock, or the meeting of the great assembly of 1638 in the Cathedral of Glasgow'. The *Inverness Courier* agreed, reproducing Burton's description of the signing of the Covenant on 'the stage' of Greyfriars with its 'picturesque' backdrop of the 'national fortress'. Other critics appreciated Burton's retailing of 'the picturesque Raid of Ruthven', and reproduced his version of the dark tale of the dastardly treatment of Bothwellhaugh's wife in 1569 as the motive for Regent Murray's assassination – a story, it may be recalled, whose 'palpable characteristics of romance' Burton had dismissed from history only to retail it in full, elaborating on its associations with traditional balladry and Scott's poetry.[54]

---

[53] *Athen*, 3 September 1870, pp. 301–2; [Burnett], 'Celtic Scotland and Feudal Scotland', p. 97; [Anon], 'Scotland from Agricola's Invasion', *Chamb J* (1870), p. 777; *Exam*, 8 October 1870, p. 644; *Stand*, 21 October 1870, p. 2.
[54] See p. 177 and pp. 121–2; Morrison, *Painting the Nation*, pp. 111–17; [Lancaster], 'Burton's History' (1871), p. 115; *Inv C*, 28 July 1870, p. 3; *Exam*, 15 October 1870, p. 660; Burton, HOS (1873) V, pp. 12–15 and p. 12, footnote 1.

Yet it was also judged that he had not gone too far and actually strayed out of history into fiction. A number of commentators criticised recent historical writing that was overly florid and partisan and therefore potentially misleading, one drawing a further comparison with the English historian J. A. Froude, who had reduced history 'to the level of a sensational novel'. For the *Scotsman* in 1870, Burton's final volumes had recounted 'the stories of individual men which make up so much of the history of nations' without 'the appearance of art', so 'we are sure we are seeing men and things pass before us, not as we might choose to imagine or an author to paint, but as they really existed and looked'. Those who perceived him as showing restraint in avoiding the too-effusively romantic often saw this as positive: in comparison with the likes of Froude and P. F. Tytler, Burton had achieved an appropriate balance between imaginative, 'graphic' description and cool impartiality. The novelist Margaret Oliphant, in *Blackwood's*, somewhat ruefully acknowledged that it was now necessary for credible history to 'turn aside sternly from the embroideries of romance': this was forgivable in order to reveal 'the larger story of national progress'.[55]

Nevertheless, commentators also appreciated his attention to those elements of terror and the occult, which Burton himself conceived as a recurrent theme in the Scottish annals. One presented the final volumes as more or less a substitute for a dark gothic romance. It was 'far more inspiring and interesting than nine novels out of ten of the present time': Burton had conveyed a Scottish history full of gloomy atmosphere and flights, abductions and murders, making it ideal for those 'who can enjoy an historical romance'. Others dwelt on the detailed attention that Burton devoted to the 'still mysterious story of the Gowrie Conspiracy' and his 'considerable pains to elucidate this mysterious affair', which he had pursued into its dark recesses further than any predecessor.[56]

However, no part of the *History* was more characteristic of Burton's fascination with the supernatural features of past events than the forty pages he devoted to the circumstances culminating in the murder of Archbishop Sharp in 1679. Sharp's assassination was the subject of much debate and controversy in nineteenth-century Scotland. However,

---

[55] *Sc*, 19 August 1870, p. 5; *Sat Rev*, 23 (6 April 1867), p. 436; [Fagan], 'Burton's History', pp. 299, 326; *Aber J*, 22 May 1867, p. 6; *Inv C*, 7 March 1867, p. 2; *Banf J*, 5 February 1867, p. 2; *Stand*, 21 October 1870, p. 2; [Oliphant], 'History of Scotland', pp. 317, 321.

[56] *Lloyd's*, 25 September 1870, p. 5; *Exam*, 15 October 1870, p. 660.

as outlined in Chapter 6, Burton's lengthy treatment was couched in terms that had a quite distinct, supernatural aura, with numinous features recurring throughout his detailed preamble, the narrative of the murder and the apparently providential escape of his killers. Many of the Scottish publications gave particular prominence and coverage to Burton's account of Sharp's assassination. On 4 July 1870, the *Glasgow Herald* carried the entire account of the murder (some ten pages of Volume VII) in advance of its full review, and several others did likewise or reproduced anecdotes from the tale, as well as highlighting Burton's handling of the equally dark story of the Wigton Martyrs, which had been the subject of recent controversy.[57]

A number of reviewers also admired Burton's dramaturgical portrayal of events and individuals. Certainly for some, his calm impartiality, though admirable, tended to limit his theatricality: the *Examiner* thought he presented no 'spotless' heroes or heroines, and could not judge his history 'a dramatic history', as could be said of Macaulay's – though the reviewer concluded with Burton's presentation of Mary's death as 'the hard doom of fate, as in some Greek tragedy, when a sacrifice must be made to appease the angry gods'. However, others were attuned to his portrayal of events and individuals as trapped in fateful narratives. The *Saturday Review* thought that this was a prominent characteristic in favourably contrasting Burton's approach to Mary's reign with that of J. A. Froude. Besides his greater knowledge of Scottish history as a whole, Burton was superior in his dramatic narrative – Froude's account, 'is picturesque and all that, but Mr Burton's is tragic; we read it with something like the interest with which we read the Agamemnon or the Oedipus'. Another also drew a contrast with Froude's effusiveness: it was a relief to 'turn to these calm and impartial records, and gather for ourselves a truthful picture of real events; of actors in the great and tragical drama, such as we feel to be true portraits, undistorted by exaggeration, or by any leaven of prejudice.' It is worth observing here that the critics were treating Burton's work as entirely comparable to that of leading historical writers of the day like Macaulay and Froude.[58]

---

[57] *Glasg H*, 4 July 1870, p. 7; *Falk H*, 7 July 1870, p. 6; *Inv C*, 28 July 1870, p. 3; *Sc*, 19 August 1870, p. 5; [Anon], 'Scotland from Agricola's Invasion', *Chamb J* (1870), p. 782; cf. Burton, *HOS* (1873), VII, pp. 207–16. On the general interest in Sharp's fate, see Coleman, *Remembering the Past*, pp. 22–3.

[58] *Sat Rev* 23 (6 April 1867), p. 436; *Stand*, 21 October 1870, p. 2; *Exam*, 8 October 1870, pp. 644–5.

Critics recognised his periodic presentation of the 'historical drama' in terms of the trope, discussed in the previous chapter, of 'the shifting scenes'. The *Chambers's Journal* reviewer was attuned to Burton's allusions to Scottish history as a stage, filling and emptying with characters as events roll on, punctuated by closing scenes: when Mary is first deposed, 'the figure of Murray occupies a foremost position upon the crowded stage, and his character becomes a study of importance'; subsequently, the deaths of Murray, Knox and other leaders leave Morton 'a free arena to act his own part in'; and later '[n]o more curious figure moves across the crowded stage of this strange history than that of Lord Ruthven'. The reviewer reproduced Burton's pathos-laden portrayal of one of Burton's 'last scenes', the death of the Earl of Lennox and commended his approach to 'the tragic termination of the cruel drama' of Mary's life. In *Blackwood's Magazine*, Margaret Oliphant had recognised Burton's presentation of the 'tragedy' of Mary's story as a 'stirring drama' on which 'the curtain rises' when she returns from France. In his final volumes, too, his presentation was described as having 'placed the events of the drama of which he has followed the chequered scenes, in their true light and significance'; and in assessing his account of 'the great drama' of the early 1640s, *The Times* was prompted to refer to his description of 'the shifting scenes' of the civil war.[59]

Whig, Saxon and Celt

Current views of Burton and the significance of his *History* for Scotland in the nineteenth century are not of course all wrong. As already indicated, the volumes contain clearly identifiable assumptions and propositions that accord with Whig historiography, with the addition of his Teutonist ideas. Some of those who reviewed or otherwise responded to the *History* give prominence to such assumptions. Among the Scottish publications, this was perhaps most in evidence in the *Scotsman*'s review, not of the full *History*, but of the initial two-volume work of 1853. Later, the *Edinburgh Review* and *The Times* tended to acknowledge these perspectives. The *Times* reviews reflected the contemporary focus of much English historiography on political and constitutional development. Consequently, although there was recognition that Burton's work on the

---

[59] [Anon], 'Scotland from Agricola's Invasion', *Chamb J* (1870), pp. 777, 779–80, 782; [Oliphant], 'History of Scotland', p. 334; [Fagan], 'Burton's History', pp. 299, 306; *Times*, 17 November 1870, p. 4.

early centuries represented 'a new chapter upon this subject', the final volumes in 1870 were particularly welcomed as the period most attractive to the general reader and 'political student' – and as the period when the Scots' support for Protestantism 'opened a way for the influence of England to penetrate into the life of the nation'. In reviewing the earlier volumes, *The Times* accepted and summarised Burton's presentation of Celtic civilisation as giving way to increasing numbers of teutonic types crossing the border, resulting in something of a 'revolution' in the twelfth to thirteenth centuries in the racial character of the nation (though the reviewer noted that in trying to 'trace its steps [. . .] he almost admits a failure').[60]

However, even among the prominent London journals these ideas were not always given such attention, and sometimes seriously questioned. The *British Quarterly Review* did not allude to Burton's Teutonism. However, the reviewer in the *London Quarterly Review* did, and found it all rather problematic. Burton was 'unfair and inconsistent' when answering the first major question arising from his pioneering work in Volume I – 'Who are modern Scots, and when did this nationality of theirs first acquire something like consistence?' Having 'exalted' the Celtic *Scoti* and admitted they must have absorbed communities of Picts, Saxons and Britons, he had then given 'a backhanded blow', asserting that the new kingdom called Scotland was largely Saxon. The writer also questioned Burton's suggestion that this explained the Highland–Lowland hostilities in the following centuries, noting that there had been many comparable conflicts in other European nations as they developed. The 'blindness to material advantages' that characterised the nation as it developed – the Scottish intellect, the stubborn faith – 'we hold to be more Celtic than Saxon'.[61]

Reviewers in the Scottish publications did not dwell much on Burton's Teutonist ideas, and those who did tended, like the *London Quarterly Review*, to cast doubts on the credibility of Burton's reasoning around the twelfth/thirteenth century revolution. In *Blackwood's Magazine*, Margaret Oliphant conveyed, not unreasonably from Burton's own account, a picture of a gradually coalescing, multi-racial people forming over the previous centuries. In her perception, it had already reached 'a high stage of

---

[60] *Sc*, 14 May 1853, p. 3; [Lancaster], 'Burton's History' (1867), pp. 240–52; *Times*, 22 April 1867, p. 9, 24 April 1867, p. 6, 15 November 1870, p. 4, 17 November 1870 p. 4.
[61] [Fagan], 'Burton's History', pp. 297–326; [Anon], 'Burton's History', *LQ*, pp. 290, 292–3.

national development', which could not have relied much on Saxon blood when, under the threat of external conquest, it produced Wallace: 'No such figure ever appeared among the Saxon masses, upon whom their Norman conquerors trampled as men trample the grapes in the wine-press'.[62]

There is no doubt that, in the course of the *History*, Burton makes some effort to fashion Teutonic ancestral origins for most of the people who lived south of the highland line, but also for those at an early stage occupying the eastern slopes of the Highlands and the north-eastern littoral where the Pictish kingdom subsequently emerged. The *Macmillan's Magazine* reviewer, George Burnett, was knowledgeable in the field and cast doubt on this thinking: recent linguistic and anthropological studies seemed to show the Picts to be of 'more or less Celtic nationality'. For Burnett, the evidence and probability was that the language and culture of all of Scotland north of the Forth and Clyde had been Gaelic; the notion that there had been 'a lost Teutonic tongue' in the north, which had entirely disappeared by the twelfth century, seemed 'incredible', and left Burton in the territory of 'the far-famed discussion between the Laird of Monkbarns and Sir Arthur Wardour'. Burton's racially pure Saxon-origin myth would not pass muster – Burnett believed that physiological evidence indicated 'the preponderance of Celtic blood across Scotland'. He accepted that the Gaels who retreated beyond the highland line 'fell into the rear of civilization', but was clear that Gaelic culture and influence was relatively strong into the twelfth century and beyond. In his perception, even the Scoto-Norman knights at Bannockburn would have come of mongrel stock: 'The mixed Teuton and Celtic blood of the Normans had produced a happy union of the perseverance and deliberation of the one race with the acuteness and vivacity of the other[.]' It seemed to Burnett that the tendency of 'even our best writers' to edit out the Celtic component in the formation of medieval Scotland was a case of contemporary issues getting in the way of historical judgement, perhaps to be traced to 'the reaction from the fashionable Highland mania of the last generation'.[63]

Essentially on the same line as Burnett, the lawyer and historian William Burns saw no credibility in Burton's pulling a fully fledged Saxon Scotland out of the hat by the reign of Alexander III (1249–86). In his *War of Scottish Independence*, published the year after Burton's 1873 edition, he questioned the logic. Burton appeared to accept the existence of a well-established 'united Celtic nation' up to the reign of

---

[62] [Oliphant], 'History of Scotland', p. 326.
[63] Burton, *HOS* (1873), I, pp. 200–1; [Burnett], 'Celtic Scotland and Feudal Scotland', pp. 99, 101–2.

Malcolm Canmore, who died in 1093. However, just a century and a half later, by the coronation of Alexander III, he presented a picture of an almost entirely Saxon nation, 'nourished', Burton had claimed, 'on independence and national pride', and with a long history. How had this come about? 'Are we seriously to understand that the *nation* so described consisted of the remnants of the Anglo-Danish population of the Lothians, supplemented by the captives and fugitives who crossed the border after the Norman Conquest?'

Among the other Scottish reviews, *Chambers's Journal* noted Burton's acknowledgement of the 'superior civilisation' of Celtic Scotland through the first millennium, easily absorbing all kinds of Norse invaders and their languages. It did also draw attention to Burton's presentation of the Battle of Harlaw (1411) in 'a very new and striking light' as illustrative of the alienation of Lowlanders and Highlanders. However, the writer passes over it quickly, and does not elaborate on Burton's notions of its significance as the turning back of a Celtic tide. Reviewers in Scottish papers such as the *Inverness Courier*, the *Banffshire Journal* and the *Dundee Advertiser* made no mention of his racial stereotypes and their significance. There is a brief nod in this direction in the *Chambers's Journal*'s 1870 review. But that is all.[64]

Burton had indeed emphasised that through much of the first millennium, it was the civilisation of the Celts that had reached 'far above' any other racial group. In the previous decade or two, in more specialist works, revision was already under way in the attention being paid to 'Celtic Scotland'. Under this title in the summer of 1873, a number of new or reissued editions of these publications were reviewed by J. C. Shairp, Principal of the United College at St Andrews, in the *Quarterly Review*. Significantly, though the *History* as a whole had been widely reviewed by this time, Shairp included Burton's first volume in the grouping. The other books were publications by Burton's close friends among the mid-century records scholars, including Joseph Robertson, as well as men Burton knew well from the Spalding Club and the Society of Antiquaries, like William Forbes Skene and Dr John Stuart.[65]

Shairp's article struck a note of admiration for the researches and revelations of these 'explorers', who were illuminating early Scottish

---

[64] William Burns, *The Scottish War of Independence: Its Antecedents and Effects*, 2 vols (Glasgow: James MacLehose, 1874), I, Appendix, Note II, pp. 485–6; [Anon], 'Scotland from Agricola's Invasion', *Chamb J* (1867), pp. 394–6; *Inv C*, 7 March 1867, p. 2; *Banf J*, 5 February 1867, p. 2; *Dund Adv*, 11 February 1867, p. 4; [Anon], 'Scotland from Agricola's Invasion', *Chamb J* (1870), p. 781.

[65] [J. C. Shairp], 'Celtic Scotland', *Q Rev* 135 (1873), 68–98.

history. If 'the first groundwork of Scottish history was Celtic' and the other elements 'additions intruded or inwrought at a later era', it was irrational to 'turn from all that is Celtic in language, usage, or tradition with disdain'. Even where, he pointed out, these scholars were probing and analysing the ethnological and linguistic roots of the Celtic-Scottish fables and origin myths, it had been to identify their roots in actual historical controversies and events, so establishing 'a residuum of fact'. And as he concluded the article, Shairp took aim at the Teuton supremacists: the new antiquarians and records scholars had not

> shared in the contempt, so common among the learned, for everything that pertains to the Gael. They have not turned from the Gaelic language as a barbarous jargon, nor looked down upon Celtic traditions, customs, laws, as unworthy of the notice of dignified historians[.]

Indeed, they had 'penetrated no inconsiderable way into the darkness of that great Celtic background, out of which Scottish history has come'.[66]

The irony was that it was respect for Burton's sceptical, scholarly and therefore credible reinstatement of significant sections of the first millennium that gave new meaning to the debate. He had provided a context within which Celtic history could be located and integrated, or reintegrated, within Scottish history as a whole. Shairp recognised this in his introductory remarks in the *Quarterly Review*. For a century and a half, since the work of Father Thomas Innes, the history of Celtic Scotland 'had been abandoned by historians' and left to the world of 'dryasdust' obsessives of the kind Scott had satirised in *The Antiquary*:

> But the appearance of Mr Hill Burton's History, five years ago, marked a new era. That he, no favourer of Celtic claims, no dreamer of antiquarian dreams, but hard-headed [. . .] should have devoted nearly the whole of his first volume to, we shall not say the history, but to the discussion of those abandoned centuries before Malcolm Canmore, – this fact of itself shows that the tide had turned.

Shairp urged on 'younger explorers' in Gaelic scholarship to build on the 'new era' that he saw as launched and to a degree validated in Burton's first volume: the previous decade had seen 'a decided recoil from the undiscriminating panegyric of the Anglo-Saxon, formerly so fashionable, and an awakening to the conviction that the Celt too has his virtues, his characteristics, and his traditions, which are worthy of our regard'.[67] Reading

---

[66] Ibid., pp. 72, 96–7.
[67] Shairp, 'Celtic Scotland', pp. 71, 97.

his *Quarterly Review* that summer, the *chef d'école* of Teutonist historiography may have wondered what he had done. To the nation's *longue durée*, he had not only added or recovered Prehistoric Scotland, Roman Scotland and Medieval Scotland, but incorporated at a foundational stage, 'Celtic Scotland'.[68]

There is no indication here of acquiescence in an overwhelming 'historiographic consensus' around Teutonist notions, which then functioned to limit Scottish historical consciousness; or in a consequent acceptance that 'race rather than nationhood came to shape the new grand narrative of the Scottish past'.[69] What Burton had produced, Teutonist or no, was very widely perceived as representing 'a new grand narrative of the Scottish past', but one exemplifying the *longue durée* of nationhood. The responses to the *History* in 1867–71 particularly in Scotland, though also in many publications in the Imperial capital, were not characterised predominantly by what some modern commentators have seen as a contemporary disestimation of pre-Union history. Through Burton's impartiality and 'completeness', the volumes had incorporated what many viewed as positive revelations on a series of aspects of the Scottish past hitherto devalorised or ignored, many of which could be related to contemporary Scottish social and cultural life. It was recognised that he had been able to rely on a great repository of new, validated source materials made available by 'enlightened antiquarians' and records scholars. Almost an entire millennium had been added to the earlier annals, sweeping aside Robertson's dismissal of anything before the eleventh century as of no value. At the other end, the work was perceived as recovering the continuity and significance of Scottish history in the early modern centuries. Although his account ended in 1748, there is little indication of, or emphasis on, the notion that Scottish history was thus drawn to a close. Indeed, in their reviews of his 1853 volumes, critics were prompted to address the need for a history of the nation from 1707 to their own time. The critical response to the completed work overwhelmingly welcomed the volumes as incorporating a much-extended timeframe and a range of cultural and institutional subject matter that had a recognisable relation to the contemporary nation; and so as constituting a national history with which the country could identify and of which it could be proud.

[68] See also Hutchison, *Industry, Reform and Empire*, though he views the historiographic contribution to 'the rehabilitation of Celtic Scotland' as attributable to 'eminent English historians of the era': pp. 156–7.
[69] Colin Kidd, 'Race, Empire, and the Limits of Nineteenth-Century Scottish Nationhood', *Historical Journal* 46, No. 4 (2003), 873–92 (pp. 884–8).

NEW PERSPECTIVES ON THE SCOTTISH PAST

And people were proud of it. What I have called the 'Romantic' or 'Gothic' or 'Theatrical' tropes would not have been as visible to contemporaries in the way it has been suggested they may be discerned today. However, many of the reviewers had some awareness of these themes, and they seem to have added to the perception of a unique and turbulent history, which the Scots were coming to really rather admire. While some with a convinced Whig perspective wrung their hands at the feudal barons or the sixteenth-century intrigues and murders, others saw a passionate adventure through which only a people like the Scots could have kept their feet and preserved their freedom, culture and independence.

A sense of the sheer verve of the national annals was certainly incorporated in the public assessments conveyed in publications widely read in Scotland, like *Chambers's Journal* and *Blackwood's Magazine*. They celebrated a national story, which encompassed periods of such incomparable adventure as Mary's reign, offering a narrative 'of twelve wonderful years, unparalleled in history for their plenitude of events, for their changes, their tragic scenes, the fierce strife of passions they had witnessed, and the wild, strong, criminal men whom they successively raised to power'. There may have been a 'melancholy' aspect to the story of the Stuart kings beset by ill fortune and fractious nobles; still it was 'the period sacred to romance', and nothing could be 'more remarkable than the story', so ultimately '[t]he tale is impressive and startling'.[70]

This tone of a new enthusiasm and some surprise at the dynamism and vitality of the Scottish past recurs in the private responses Burton received. After the publication of the first four volumes of the *History* in 1867 it had been made known that a further three would bring it to completion. By 1869–70, correspondents from across Scotland were writing anxiously to know when they would appear. Once the volumes were published, individuals welcomed the broader cultural aspects that Burton had incorporated in the earlier volumes, such as the history of architecture, including his dismissal of the 'stupid tradition' that the English architect Inigo Jones had been the architect of Heriot's Hospital in Edinburgh:

> It is one more example of those philosophers who would derive everything worth having from beyond the Tweed were it not for the stern logic of facts

---

[70] [Anon], 'Scotland from Agricola's Invasion', *Chamb J* (1870), p. 780; [Oliphant], 'History of Scotland', p. 331.

which (prove) [. . .] that after all our northern climate does sometimes produce such commodities as Architects, Poets etc to say nothing of Historians.

Others, like the essayist Andrew Boyd, found the volumes as compulsive as a fictional story:

> I kept them to read in my holiday in the Highlands: but instead of reading them with the leisurely progress becoming the dignity of History, I have torn through them like a novel, sitting up to all hours to do so. [. . .] I cannot suppose that your book will ever be superseded.[71]

Adam Dawson, a Whig entrepreneur and Provost of Linlithgow, had been one of those urging Burton on to complete the *History* 'of this gallant little country'. Once the final volumes appeared, he found them not only compulsive but transformative of his perception of the Scottish past. He had once remarked to the *Scotsman* editor Charles Maclaren, he told Burton, 'that with the exception of the heroic period the history of Scotland was to me a most disagreeable and uninviting subject'; however, he now found Burton's recently published fifth volume 'reads like a cunningly devised sensational fiction while you have made a plain story out of a perfect jumble', so that the reader

> [is led to] understand, be amused and instructed. As for me I only pretend to be a man of *average* common sense and in that position may be said to represent the bulk of the reading public. In so far as I can judge them for myself your history will be popular[.]

Dawson continued:

> [To bring] 10,000 people to read our history is no small matter – and an extraordinary story it is when handled as you have done it. I like your strokes of dry humour – they are in keeping with a Scottish historian [. . .]. It is astonishing to see the crop of men of metal that our little corner produced in these olden times – we are surely a peculiar people after all. Think too of the calm and business like way the Estates elected the Regents which you describe in a sentence.

Dawson ended by commenting that he had laid down the fifth volume with reluctance 'and hastened to resume it till the close'. Modern scholars may find Burton's delivery 'indigestible', and to modern taste at least some of the time it can appear convoluted, but the response of individual

---

[71] NLS MS 9398, fols 21, 48, 124, 149, 183, 198, 227. For the Reverend A. K. H. Boyd, see Thomas Cooper, ed., *Men of the Time: A Dictionary of Contemporaries [. . .]*, 8th edn (London: Routledge, 1872), p. 134.

readers confirms the evidence from the public reviewers that this was not generally the perception in his own day.[72]

The sense among these readers that here was a fascinating story that could be enjoyed almost like a novel, yet had the gravitas of a national history, echoes many of the published views already considered. These perspectives incorporate a concern to bring this new kind of history into relation – though not into opposition – with the previous handling of the Scottish past in fictional or semi-fictional guise, with its different romantic dimensions. A further instance of this effort of reconciliation appears in the *Scotsman*'s appreciation of the final volumes in 1870. For the reviewer, Burton's *History* had made available a kind of true romance. He had not sought to present or convince through a partisan presentation on religion or politics: the work was 'fascinating to those who read to be interested rather than instructed'. But the truths that emerged were 'more interesting than fiction, and in such truths Scottish history abounds'. Previous efforts had not been rigorous in sifting the evidence and so had failed 'either in getting belief as facts or giving pleasure as romances'. In the excessive focus on fiction there had been a failure to appreciate how the histories of nations 'show their impress even on the present aspect of the world'. The imaginary loves and adventures of the characters in novels had somehow become more interesting to 'the middle class multitude than the equally romantic loves and adventures of men and women who did exist, and whose acts become the causes [. . .] of great events'.[73]

There are various indications that the *History* was not only well received by influential figures across the denominational and political spectrum but that they shared their enthusiasm with the wider public, including associations of the young and of working men. In the spring of 1867, just after the first volumes appeared, James Moncrieff, the long-serving Lord Advocate and prominent Freechurchman, delivered a speech to the Edinburgh Young

---

[72] NLS MS 9398, fols 21, 118–19, 176–8, emphasis in original. For Adam Dawson, see *West Lothian Courier*, 11 October 1873, p. 4; Anderson, 'University History Teaching', p. 17; London's *Daily News* disapproved of colloquialisms, as did the *Aberdeen Journal*, though in general it assessed his style as 'clear and vigorous', and this was the typical view: *Daily News*, 19 April, 1867, p. 2; *Aber J*, 27 July 1870, p. 6; *Stand*, 21 October 1870, p. 2; *Exam*, 9 February 1867, p. 8 and 16 February 1867, p. 4; *Athen*, 3 September 1870, p. 301; *Sat Rev*, 30 March 1867, p. 404.

[73] *Sc*, 19 August 1870, p. 5.

Men's Christian Association that was widely reported in the newspapers. In support of one of his points, he appealed to the authority of the 'recent work by a very acute observer [. . .] I mean my friend Mr Hill Burton, in his very masterly history of Scotland'. At the same time the leading figure in the Scottish Episcopal Church, Edward Ramsay, wrote to Burton expressing his congratulations and his 'full assurance from the impressions received everywhere, that you have accomplished a *genuine standard history of your country*'.[74]

When the final volumes appeared in 1870, Principal John Tulloch, rising towards leadership in the Established Church, delivered a lecture at the opening of the Duncan Institute in Cupar, Fife. The new building had recently been endowed to provide accommodation for the local Mechanics' Institute. Tulloch's address was also widely carried by papers across the country. He urged his audience to pursue for self-improvement a suitable programme of reading. He recommended this include Robert Chambers' edition of Burns, partly because it shone 'many new lights into the history of the time, and the whole state of the Scottish mind and feeling, and social and religious civilisation in the end of the last century'. But for historical understanding, he particularly urged that his audience devote their winter study to 'Mr Burton's recent History of Scotland, marked as it is by so many supreme qualities of the historical mind'. It was critical, impartial, 'here and there glowing', and none 'could be said to know the History of Scotland as it ought to be known who has not turned to Mr Burton's pages'. He was confident that 'our working men and women' were quite up to the task and commended Burton's volumes 'to all of you, who wish to master the real character and complications of your country's history'.[75]

The earlier volumes had also been recommended to working men. In October 1867, it was reported that the library of the Mechanics' Institute in Linlithgow was soon to be supplemented by a large number of books suitable for winter reading among them: 'Mr Hill Burton's recently issued "History of Scotland", decidedly the best extant, and which no one really anxious to know the *true* history of his country,

---

[74] *Glasg H*, 17 April 1867, p. 6; NLS MS 9398, fol 162. Emphasis indicated by double underlining in original.
[75] *Fife H*, 15 December 1870, p.2; summaries of the report, including the recommended reading, were carried by a number of other papers: *Gr Adv*, 17 December 1870, p. 4; *Glasg H*, 15 December 1870, p.3; *Glasg Ev Cit*, 15 December 1870, p. 2; *Dund C*, 15 December 1870, p. 4.

weeded pretty clean of traditional rubbish and party *bias*, should fail to read.' Indeed, self-improvement associations of this kind seem, even without the prompting of the great, to have been increasingly interested in the nation's past. A year before the 1867 volumes appeared, Burton was approached by John Love on behalf of the Greenock Philosophical Society with a request that he contribute lectures 'on Early Scotch History – founded on the Records' to the society's forthcoming programme. Cosmo Innes, he advised, had done so in the previous year. The Society's interest in the early and medieval centuries and the new sources being uncovered, accords with that of many of the reviewers of the *History* once published:

> One important point would be to give our friends some satisfactory general idea of the character & extent of the State Papers and Records themselves [. . .].We are rather anxious to make Scotch History an element in our programme year by year; and it is of much consequence to us to begin well in the attempt.

Love promised Burton an audience of around 150 of 'the members and their wives and daughters'.[76] Better-off students than those in the Mechanics' Institutes may also have begun to take notice, even though Scottish history was not yet taught as a separate university subject. At the end of term in 1870, Burton's father-in law asked if Burton would escort his daughter to a reception for his students at Edinburgh, all of whom 'had imbibed a due respect for the Historian of Scotland': it would 'be very gracious of you, if you would take charge of your daughter and descend from your pedestal and help us with the *burschen*'.[77]

There was an expectation among Burton's correspondents at this time that the *History* was and would be popular amongst a range of 'ordinary readers'. This is unsurprising in the context of the history of publishing: in the decades after 1870, 'something happened to history and something happened to books. At the same time as the discipline was being made scholarly, quasi-scientific, and ultimately academic, the publishing business was flourishing', and responding to 'a reading public much better equipped with literacy and leisure than earlier generations'. In broadly the same period, there was a four-fold increase in book production and a halving of prices. Burton's volumes certainly reached large numbers among the reading public, as is borne out by Blackwood's ledgers. From the appearance of the first volumes

---

[76] *Falk H*, 10 October 1867, p. 2. Italics in original; NLS MS 9397, fols 99–100.
[77] NLS MS 9398, fols 163–4.

in 1867 through the 1870s (the decade that putatively saw the 'death' of Scottish history), around 25,000 individual volumes of the *History of Scotland* were sold. This would have been assisted by Blackwood's careful attention to marketing.[78]

Throughout the later nineteenth century, it was one of the firm's most profitable publications. In the Spring of 1897, nearly three decades after the work first appeared, the *Glasgow Herald* welcomed Blackwood's 'excellent popular reprint' of the *History*: it urged the publishers to correct 'occasional errors' in the later volumes 'in justice to the many readers who will doubtless hasten to possess themselves of this, the standard and classic history of Scotland [. . .].' Print runs of over five hundred eight-volume sets of the *History* continued every few years from the later 1880s to the end of the century and beyond. Indeed, of the 'popular' and cheaper 1897 edition welcomed by the *Herald* – twenty-eight shillings against the previous sixty-three shillings – over a thousand sets were printed. As the paper anticipated, they did indeed prove popular, with two-thirds sold within a year. The work was therefore available to a much wider social spectrum than could ever have gained access to the Scottish historical material published by the early to mid-century book clubs or to Tytler's volumes. The contrast with the likely spread and impact of Tytler's *History* a generation before is notable. At twelve shillings per volume, it was a publication intended for the few. The publisher, William Tait, seems to have tried to stimulate demand by halving the cost of a second edition to six shillings per volume, which then 'met with ready sale, the number taken by the Edinburgh trade, when it was subscribed, being no less than 184 copies, which was considered to be a great success in those days'.[79]

Some of the most celebratory notices of Burton's *History* appeared in publications like *Chambers's Journal* and the *Scotsman*, which had attained high levels of circulation. By 1870, *Chambers's* was selling

---

[78] Howsam, *Past into Print*, pp. xi, 26; the figure of 25,000 is my estimate from the records of print runs and sales in the Blackwood's Publication Ledgers: see NLS Blackwood's Collection, MS 30860, fols 344, 434; NLS MS 30861, fols 127, 156, 441. There were extensive press notices of the 1867 and 1870 volumes, both before and at publication.

[79] Finkelstein, *House of Blackwood*, Appendix 1, pp. 160–2; NLS MSS 30862, fol. 149; 30863, fol. 121; 30864, fols 186, 196; *Glasg H*, 25 March 1897, p. 8; James Bertram, *Some Memories of Books, Authors and Events* (London: Constable, 1893), pp. 41–2.

around 80,000 copies weekly across Britain, a significant percentage in Scotland; while the enterprising team led by Alexander Russel and J. R. Findlay (often supported by Burton) at the *Scotsman* had attained regular sales of 30,000 per issue. Large numbers of the Scottish reading public would therefore have read the ringing endorsement of Scottish history as the paper's reviewer drew his article to a close:

> The History of Scotland is written, and written so that it will never need to be re-written. Is it a history worthy of having been written? No man of any country can lay down these volumes without feeling that the history of the Scottish nation teaches by example as much as the history of many greater nations.[80]

THE PAST AS NATIONAL HISTORY

Earlier in the century, many educated Scots may have accepted the view that there was little to say about Scottish history before the reign of Alexander III (1249–86) and that it had ended in 1603, or at the latest 1707. Burton himself was comfortable that by his own time the Scottish polity whose growth he had traced had become 'fused into the great British Empire'. The conception that Scottish history ended with either the regal or parliamentary Union continued to be rehearsed in certain of the notices of Burton's *History* published outside Scotland. Commenting on one such review – in the *New York Times* – Andrew Newby has suggested that this 'encapsulates the prevalent discourse on Scottish identity by the 1870s'. The present study questions that view, but Newby did qualify his observation to the effect that this understanding was particularly strong in London 'and for many looking in from abroad through a London prism'. The perspective recurs in the most prestigious of the foreign notices of Burton's *History*, the lengthy article by Louis Étienne entitled '*Historiens Modernes de L'Écosse:* John Hill Burton', which was published in the *Revue des Deux Mondes* in the autumn of 1867. Étienne appears to view matters through that 'London prism': at the end of the day, England had 'annexed' Scotland, so that

---

[80] *Sc*, 19 August 1870, p. 5; for *Scotsman* circulation, see [Magnus Magnusson, Matthew J. Moulton, William R. Munro, Philip A. Stalker, David Terris et al.], *The Glorious Privilege: The History of the 'Scotsman'* (London: Nelson, 1967), p. 41; for *Chambers's Journal* circulation, see Lowell T. Frye, 'W. and R. Chambers', in *British Literary Publishing Houses, 1820–1880*, eds Patricia J. Anderson and Jonathan Rose (Detroit and London: Gale, 1991), 83–91 (p. 86).

Scottish historical *nationalité* had surely ended, and so 'l'étude en peut-être complète'.[81]

However, Étienne's *'peut-être'* is revealing since most of his highly complimentary essay recognised that Burton's volumes were replete with the *nationalité* whose extent previous Scottish historians had been unable to capture: Scott and Tytler had failed to answer the reproach that Augustin Thierry had directed at William Robertson – the failure to trace Scotland's *longue durée* and explain how Scotland had appeared fully constituted, armed and ready in the fourteenth century, 'une maturité subite':

> La nation écossaise existe et se reconnait bien avant le XIV siècle, quoiqu'elle ne parvienne à la libre disposition d' elle-même et a l'unité que longtemps après. C'est là réellement la pensée générale de l'ouvrage de M. Burton; là est l'opportunité de son livre. Le mouvement des nationalités provoque aujourd'hui la curiosité de tous les hommes qui pensent.

As this passage suggests, it was hardly possible at this time for 'thinking men' to approach a national history without reflecting on the contemporary fascination with nationality. In fact, Étienne's article repeatedly recognised 'l'objet de ce travail, la nationalité écossaise, qui est l'inspiration première du livre de M. Burton', and celebrated a new and fully credible account of Scottish history and nationality:

> Le patriotisme écossaise jaillissant du milieu de la poudre des archives et portant de nouvelles lumières dans l'obscurité du passé, c'est là ce qui nous a le plus frappé dans la lecture de cette histoire d'Écosse qui succède à tant d'autres et vient peut-être remplacer.[82]

Indeed, most commentators on the *History* were attuned to the fact that such a work must inevitably bring with it a focus and reflection on the country's contemporary 'nationality'. Even the London reviewers recognised this. Interestingly, despite Burton's Teutonist efforts, they noted that he had chosen to write the history as that of the geographical country and not on 'a mere ethnological basis'. One thought this had to do

---

[81] Burton, *HOS* (1873), I, p. viii; Andrew G. Newby, '"A Mere Geographical Expression?" Scotland and Scottish Identity, c. 1890–1914', in *Region and State in Nineteenth-Century Europe: Nation-Building, Regional Identities and Separatism*, eds Joost Augusteijn and Eric Storm. (Basingstoke: Palgrave Macmillan, 2012), pp. 149–67 (p. 149); Étienne, *'Historiens Modernes'*, p. 222: 'L'Angleterre s'annexa l'Écosse comme l'Écosse s'était annexe les highlands[.]'
[82] Étienne, *'Historiens Modernes'*, pp. 209, 221–2.

with the fact that contemporary Scottish identity was caught in uncertain territory, 'not quite a nation' and yet 'something more than a province'. This helped to explain the 'completeness' reflected in Burton's unusual attention to prehistory, architecture, legal traditions and the like: 'Does not this ever-conscious feeling of nationality lead a man who studies the history of his country at all to study it in a more complete way, to look at it in all its aspects, to make it his business to find out all that he can about everything that concerns it?' The *London Quarterly Review* recognised the potential relevance of Burton's volumes in the context of the rise of contemporary European nationalisms. Burton had observed that in the fourteenth century it was small, defiant, freedom-loving peoples like the Belgians, the Swiss and the Scots who had kept the Norman conquerors, as Burton put it, 'beyond the gate'. It was an age, the reviewer noted 'when nationalities were just beginning to show themselves; and therefore its history is specially interesting now, when this same question of nationalities has once more come to the front'.[83]

Burton's *History* did in fact incorporate most of the characteristics of the national histories which were produced in the course of the nineteenth century throughout Europe, both for existing nation states and for nations which, for the moment at least, were subsumed in multi-national states and empires. These works fashioned the 'master narratives' that created or reinforced national historical consciousness, strengthened the nation's contemporary sense of identity and in many of the 'stateless nations' and nations within multi-national entities played a central role in the ultimate assertion of separate statehood at varying intervals over the following century. A magisterial comparative study, composed by Stephan Berger with Christoph Conrad, has recently identified the typical features associated with the texts of European national histories in the nineteenth century. This section considers Burton's *History* in relation to these attributes.[84]

Many of those who composed such works aspired to a 'literary' construction of the national story and reflected this aim in their narrative style. This had a great deal to do with the influence of Walter Scott. After Scott, throughout Europe, '[n]ovelists, dramatists and poets [...] all served historians as models of how to craft a gripping narrative', so that many sought to increase their allure to the wider public 'by adopting a

---

[83] [Anon], 'The History of Scotland', *BQ* 46 (1867), 214–17 (p. 214); *Sat Rev*, 6 April 1867, p. 437; [Anon], 'Burton's History', *LQ* (1867–8), p. 310.
[84] Berger with Conrad, *Past as History*.

literary style'. Since this 'transdisciplinary dialogue' involved playwrights as well as novelists, history 'was increasingly put on stage, as dramatists turned to the past in order to promote the nation'. Historians frequently felt the need to narrate the national annals 'in a dramatic fashion which would engulf the reader and make him, as well as the historian, part and parcel of the seamless web of the past'.[85]

At times in Burton's volumes, there are what appear to be incompatible or even contradictory tendencies: on the one hand showing empathetic interest and being intrigued by the difference in past times, in the 'spirit' and 'manners' of former ages; and on the other, periodic efforts to explain historical features in ways that include allusions to current or recent events (in the process helping to sustain that sense of a national continuity which many reviewers recognised). However, this is less a contradiction than a further indication of the extent to which Burton shared the *mentalité* of the historians of his time. Many nineteenth-century historians, in the decades following the French revolution, a 'post-revolutionary and modernising world' that had discarded the past, 'also longed for that past, searching for continuities and similarities between the past and the present'. Yet it was also 'part and parcel of that inner tension of Romanticism's attitude towards the past that Romantics also often emphasised the difference between past and present'.[86]

A concern to incorporate recognisable elements relating to language and linguistics in the national traditions was also characteristic of romantic history: '[t]he search for a codified national language and for authentic national literary canons was part and parcel of nationalising historiographies'. Although Scotland had no unifying spoken language, Burton did reflect national 'voices' with which most of his readers could identify. He incorporated vernacular Scots and the 'second language' of Presbyterian religiosity in ways that Patrick Fraser had looked for in vain in P. F. Tytler, whose neglect of the Scottish medieval and Renaissance poets had incorporated nothing 'of their language and of ours'. Closely related to vernacular language and literature in the construction of national narratives was folklore: attention to folk poetry 'swept like a tidal wave across the continent, and folklore studies established itself as a subject between history, literature and archaeology'. Reviewers perceived that Burton's treatment of popular social *mores*, ballads, superstitions and vernacular culture, demonstrated that he was not just a compiler of

---

[85] Ibid., pp. 88–90, 100.
[86] Berger with Conrad, *Past as History*, p. 96.

events, but had looked below the surface to reflect 'national life and character'; and quoted his own celebration of the social significance of the vernacular tradition even above high literature, 'among a people with a nationality and a history of their own'.[87]

At the same time in the fine arts, particularly painting, there was a close relation between the historians' 'master narratives' and history-painters' choice of scenes for their works. In both nation states and nations still located in multinational structures, history paintings 'depicted mythical and "real" events from the nation's past, glorifying the nation's achievements, sufferings and heroic deeds'. Although Burton could be sceptical on popular tourist-romanticism, he made sure that iconic scenes his readers knew, from the depictions of Greyfriars in 'Edinburgh landscape art' to the oft-painted Fast Castle (and its resonance with scenes in Scott), were given their place. More generally, he went out of his way to ensure that episodes well known in contemporary Scottish art, such as the murders of Archbishop Sharp and Rizzio, the encounters of Mary and Knox, or the martyrdom of Brown of Priesthill, were recounted with their 'picturesque' potential and associations intact.[88]

Not unrelated to this sensibility, throughout Europe, Berger and Conrad traced how 'national narratives were fascinated with the nation's ruins'. Burton was attuned to such fascination from an early stage in life, but it was intensified by his years-long involvement with Blackwoods' *Baronial and Ecclesiastical Architecture of Scotland*. Many reviewers were struck by the attention he gave to Scottish architectural traditions as well as to other physical remains like the sculptured stones, presented as a set of remarkable survivals almost unique to Scotland. This engagement was also closely related to his broader interest in what was emerging in its modern sense as archaeology. It is likely that his realisation of the increasing validity of the subject (as well as the roles taken in its local development by close friends) encouraged his extensive treatment of the first millennium, in effect rescuing Scottish claims to ancient nationhood from William Robertson's dismissal of the fabled 'pretensions to antiquity'. Now, 'in an age of nationalism, existing and emerging nation states needed physical proof of their antiquity. Archaeology was a useful science in this respect and it became fundamental to the national imagination in many parts of Europe.'[89] This was nowhere

---

[87] Ibid., pp. 92–3; *Exam*, 15 October 1870, p. 660; Burton, HOS (1873), VII, p. 87.
[88] Berger with Conrad, *Past as History*, p. 92; see above, pp. 125–6, 149–51, 175–7, 186–7.
[89] Robertson, *History of Scotland*, I, p. 2; Berger with Conrad, *Past as History*, pp. 93, 95.

more so than in parts of Scandinavia, particularly Denmark and Norway, whose scholars and national collections Burton and his friends in the Scottish Society of Antiquaries admired and sought to emulate. As we have seen in his *Blackwood's* reviews of works by Daniel Wilson and others, Burton publicised the need for what, from the early 1850s, Wilson had urged should be a National Archaeological Museum for Scotland, comparable to the institutions established in continental capitals as well as London.

In accord with the increasing interest and scholarship devoted to early history and archaeology, Burton not only restored in what was regarded as a critically credible form almost an entire first millennium to the national annals, but provided a much-extended medieval era, which was portrayed as prosperous and advanced in areas such as urban and legal/constitutional development. This relied heavily on the remarkable labours of the records scholars and in particular Cosmo Innes. It is true that both Burton and Innes interpreted the extensive new source material as confirming Scotland's early teutonic roots. However, as we have seen, the reviewers and other commentators on the *History* did not dwell on this aspect. They were much more struck by the fact of the restoration of a valorised Scottish medieval world, centuries that the eighteenth-century historians had dismissed as characterised by unremitting feudal strife and socio-political backwardness. In this too, Burton's *History* accorded with comparable works of national history-writing throughout Europe: '[t]he longue durée was important for national history, and hence historians could not avoid the problem of beginnings. They concentrated on the middle-ages as an important foundational moment for national histories.' In the perception of many commentators, Burton's work had extended Scotland's *longue durée* considerably further back (with appropriate cautions), but his use of the work of the book clubs and records scholars mirrored exactly the new foundations made available across the continent for national histories: 'Source editions of medieval texts were published to underpin claims to national greatness [. . .]. Across Europe, historians were using philology to re-edit medieval texts, an activity in line with Romanticism's vogue for the middle-ages more generally.'[90]

As characteristics of national histories, the elements discussed above were particularly prominent in some European nations in the first half of the century in the high 'Romantic age', so to an extent it might be said that Scotland was coming a little late to this central means of reinforcing national consciousness. However, this would be to forget that it had been

---

[90] Berger with Conrad, *Past as History*, pp. 113–15.

to a large extent Scottish history that had been the subject of the original romantic historical 'master narrative'. Through Scott, as Berger and Conrad observed, 'Scottish history became the object of attention for millions of readers outside the borders of Scotland, contributing to an unprecedented transnational reception of the construction of a national history'. It is not difficult to trace in many of Burton's writings a drawn-out, critical engagement or dialogue with Scott. The interactions of history and literature were intimate and complex, but a national historical narrative rooted in works of fiction, however widely admired, was never going to be enough. Critics welcomed a work intending 'to supersede by real history the romance which in Scotland has hitherto gone by that name', bringing continuity and coherence to a national history that had 'hitherto been little more than a string of romantic incidents – even Principal Robertson being as uncritical as the author of Waverley himself'.[91]

It has been suggested that in Scotland, by the time history was becoming established as a university subject in the last quarter of the century, professionalisation and the focus on constitutional development 'had driven a wedge between "scientific" history and the study (often inspired by Sir Walter Scott) of such expressions of national identity and continuity as landscapes, ancient buildings, historic families, balladry, popular traditions, and other phenomena rooted in locality'.[92] In the case of Burton's *History*, just the opposite can be argued. As already described, there is a distinct narrative pattern to the work in which, for each of the major epochs covered, chapters are incorporated that address the 'condition of the nation'. These passages are very much concerned with 'expressions of national identity and continuity' such as the national tradition in architecture, a uniquely rich balladry, folk traditions, university characteristics, literary achievements in vernacular Scots and Scottish Latinity and so on. Much of the rest of the work is devoted to a narrative of 'what happened', in which Burton does manifest something of the focus on political and constitutional issues characteristic of Whig historiography. However, there too, as has been argued above, Burton's account reflects a range of aspects of the Scottish cultural world of his time incorporating many of the elements that Scott had implicitly constructed as a kind of template for national histories.

---

[91] Berger with Conrad, *Past as History*, p. 88; [Anon], 'Burton's History', *LQ* (1870), p. 332.
[92] Anderson, 'University History Teaching', p. 7.

In these ways, Burton's *History* can be seen as managing to integrate the two principal, and to an extent competing, approaches to the construction of national histories at this time – the 'étatist', focusing on the political and constitutional development of states, and the 'history of the people' or social history. He had previously expressed admiration for both Hume and Macaulay as harbingers of the need for historians to give greater attention to the history of the people and their forms of cultural expression, rather than focus exclusively on elite political institutions. As late as 1858, introducing his own *Domestic Annals of Scotland* (and echoing Fraser's critique of P. F. Tytler ten years before) Robert Chambers had lamented that history had 'in a great measure confined itself to political transactions and personages, and usually says little of the people'. He regretted that in spite of his own effort to record popular traditions in the pages that followed, no very coherent narrative could emerge from 'these details, broken up and disjointed as they often are'.[93]

Burton was able to incorporate a range of elements of 'people's history', yet at the same time to avoid any 'wedge' between this and modernising notions of history since, crucially, he was also perceived to have secured throughout his volumes the additional characteristic aspired to across Europe as the *sine qua non* of a credible national story in the second half of the century: *Wissenschaft* – scientificity – had developed chiefly in the German lands but was now almost universally viewed as the central requirement for authentic history.[94] A consistent theme running through the responses to Burton's volumes celebrated its exemplification of 'the painstaking research of the nineteenth century'. Put in more literary terms by the novelist Margaret Oliphant, it demonstrated how the 'historical Muse' was now better described as 'the science of history', which, as exemplified in Burton's work, had 'come to a new stage of development' and was 'altogether an invention of modern times'. As the second half of the century progressed, and especially from the 1870s when Burton's *History* was published in final form, 'the subject's scientific credentials went hand in hand with the nationalisation of history'. In some places, this was closely associated with the professionalisation of historical scholarship in universities and academic institutes. This was not yet the case in Scotland where, after Innes's departure, both at Edinburgh and in the

---

[93] Berger with Conrad, *Past as History*, pp. 111, 173–5; Robert Chambers, *Domestic Annals of Scotland: from the Reformation to the Revolution*, 2 vols (Edinburgh: Chambers, 1858), I, p. v.
[94] Berger with Conrad, *Past as History*, pp. 140–3, 145–8.

other Scottish universities, the evolution of academic posts in history has been described as characterised by conventional Whig constitutional history and largely English-focused.[95] However, the generation and impact of Burton's volumes confirms the assessment that 'developments outside the university continued to be influential'. The contribution to national identity that the Scottish reading public drew from their history did not rely on its presence and standing within academic institutions.[96]

A further prominent aspect of Burton's historical endeavour is relevant here. Both in the earlier publication *The Scot Abroad*, and in his ultimate *History*, Burton sought to portray prominent figures and events in the Scottish past in a way that highlighted their relevance to and influence on European-wide developments. This internationalising characteristic seems counter-intuitive when considered in relation to processes centred on the reconstruction of a nation's own *longue durée*. In reality the aspiration for a 'transnational' influence and significance was a recurrent feature in many of the efforts to constitute or reconstitute national history made elsewhere in nineteenth-century Europe: in their survey of such developments across the continent, Berger and Conrad described how 'all national history strove to demonstrate belonging to Europe, setting the benchmarks for Europe, being in the vanguard of European developments or explaining [. . .] lack of Europeanness'. Of course, for Burton, Scotland's transnationality was much bound up with its destined role in the development of the Empire. Nevertheless, his attention to the nation's prominent and even 'pivotal' role at significant junctures in the cultural and political history of Europe provided a balancing perspective. Commentators on the *History* were attuned to this aspect of Burton's narrative. For instance, one recognised that his account of the conditions surrounding the Battle of Langside (1568) demonstrated that it had 'settled the fate of Scotland, affected the future of England, and had its influence over all Europe', while others admired his elucidation of the connections between Scottish Protestantism and the French Huguenots. More broadly, the *Times* reviewer admired how the *History* had 'described and set in a clear light an unexplored but important subject, the international relations of France and Scotland from the 14th to the 16th centuries'.[97]

---

[95] [Anon], 'Burton's History', *BQ* (1867), p. 214; [Anon], 'Burton's History', *LQ* (1867–8), p. 285; *Exam*, 15 October 1870, p. 660; [Oliphant], 'History of Scotland', p. 317; Anderson, 'University History Teaching', pp. 2, 13–16, 19.
[96] Berger with Conrad, *Past as History*, p. 150.
[97] Ibid., pp. 214–15; *Exam*, 8 October 1870, p. 644; *Aber J*, 27 July 1870, p. 6; *Glasg H*, 6 October 1870, p. 2; *Times*, 22 April 1867, p. 9; see above pp. 88–94.

The aspiration for European transnational legitimacy extended to relations among the scholars themselves. It seems clear that Burton and his associates shared this reflex. It was exemplified in the scholarly friendships, exchange visits and 'corresponding' or honorary memberships of the SSA that characterised relations with the 'Northern Archaeologists', such as the Danes C. J. Thomsen and J. J. A. Worsaae, and the Norwegian historian P. A. Munch. Similar relations sustained over decades characterised the involvement of the Book Club men, with European scholars like Alexandre Teulet and Francisque Michel. A further illustration of such connections, both in terms of personal relations and of common historiographic purpose can be found in Burton's interaction with the Swiss–French historian Albert Rilliet.[98]

Nowhere in Europe at this time was it more important to reconstruct a national history traced through origins that had a firm 'scientific' basis than in Switzerland. The new Swiss state established after the 1848 revolutions had more in common with the constitution forced upon it by Napoleon in 1798 than with the medieval alliance of cantons. Still, popular belief cleaved to the origins of the nation as rooted in that medieval concord, around which had accreted the traditions of the oath sworn on the *Rütli* meadow, and the rebellion against Habsburg tyranny led by William Tell. However, as in Scotland 'nineteenth-century research' was subjecting the old stories to sceptical scrutiny in works like Rilliet's *Origines de la Confédération Suisse: Histoire et Légende*, published in 1868. Burton contributed a laudatory article on Rilliet's book to the *Edinburgh Review* in January 1869, which he commenced by observing how a 'legendary period' was typical of all national histories not subject to 'strict criticism': so, for instance, if a community had offered resistance to the 'tyrannous interference of a powerful neighbour', it would soon be associated with the heroic leadership of 'some Arminius, or William Tell, or Wallace'.[99]

---

[98] Berger with Conrad, *Past as History*, pp. 211, 363–4; Ash, '"A fine genial hearty band"', pp. 98, 108–9.

[99] Guy P. Marchal, 'Medievalism, the Politics of Memory and Swiss National Identity', in *The Uses of the Middle Ages in Modern European States: History, Nationhood and the Search for Origins*. Writing the Nation Series, eds R. J. W. Evans and Guy P. Marchal (Basingstoke: Palgrave Macmillan, 2015), 197–220 (pp. 197–200); Albert Rilliet, *Les Origines de la Confédération Suisse: Histoire et Légende* (Geneva and Bâle: H. George, 1868); [John Hill Burton], 'The Legend of Tell and Rütli', *ER* 129 (1869), 65–79 (p. 65).

Rilliet wrote letters of appreciation to Burton for his positive review. In them, he acknowledged Burton as a fellow traveller in the business of using documented evidence and critical judgement in re-examining the national annals: his own work he suggested was 'dans quelques points n'est pas sans analogie avec celui qui avait les origines de l'histoire d'Écosse pour objet', and he particularly welcomed the approbation of a historian 'qui a étudié et discuté lui-même avec une science si sûre et un jugement si sagace les annales de son propre pays'. There were indeed similarities. Burton had raised a sceptical eyebrow at even the most revered of popular Scottish liberation heroes, noting at one point in his passages on Wallace that there were similarities in the way he was traditionally portrayed to the tales of Robin Hood. However, in his review Burton had also emphasised that Rilliet's job was only half done. The Swiss historian had struck down the stories and images of Tell's bowmanship, the splitting of the apple and the slaying of the tyrannous Gessler, but Burton ended by urging that having 'cleared away the rubbish, let him go on and reconstruct the history of Switzerland' and so 'trace the growth' of the oldest federal government in the world.[100]

What the Swiss comparison brings out very clearly is the extent to which the influence of history and historians on national identity and national historical consciousness is necessarily a two-way process: the public reception or 'consumption' of the historical narrative inevitably involves a mediation that produces something new and sometimes unexpected. Burton almost certainly thought that he was sending out a liberal, Whig-Teutonist understanding of Scotland's story and to an extent he was, though as has been argued above, this understanding fails to detect much else in the *History*. However, the last thing Burton intended was, for example, to stimulate critical thinking about the Union or to raise up 'Celtic Scotland' as central to the nation's origins and character. In Switzerland, a comparable liberal conception of the national past did not go unchallenged and its ultimate impact and significance were moulded by its public reception:

> This becomes plain once we move beyond the realm of intellectual discourse to take account of how historians' messages were publicly received. It then becomes apparent that a concept like 'invented tradition', which assumes that ideologies diffuse more or less unhindered from those that produce them

---

[100] NLS MS 9398, fols 31–4; Burton, *HOS* (1873), II, pp. 75–6; [Burton], 'Legend of Tell', pp. 78–9; on less iconoclastic associations of Tell and Wallace in Scotland in the previous decades, see Coleman, *Remembering the Past*, pp. 69–73.

to the public at large, cannot do justice to the often protracted gestation of particular conceptions of the nation.[101]

Just as Burton had urged, Rilliet's work was indeed followed up in Switzerland by 'monumental works of national historiography'. They were produced by a group of prominent liberal historians with modernising views on the 'correct' approach to history not far divorced from those of the Scottish historian, and in an environment in which a liberal elite was promoting the establishment of national historical institutions. These at first placed a confident emphasis on the legend-busting, 'scientific' approach and some, associated with Wilhelm Oeschli in Zurich, pursued a frankly 'positivist orientation'. However, during the 1870s, the prominent liberal historian Karl Hilty began to row back from a too-severe scepticism: an excessively arid presentation swept entirely clear of popular conceptions ran the risk of undermining 'the sense of national history' among the public especially the young. Subsequently, another of the most influential liberal historians, Karl Dändliker, while in general defending the new methodological approach 'also maintained that the new fetishism of the document had had the negative side-effect of creating a rift between "the people" and "its historians"'. For Oliver Zimmer, drawing on the terms of Pierre Nora, this resulted in an effort to encompass and to a degree reconcile 'history' and 'memory', leading to a 'synthesis of the two competing visions of the national past', a synthesis that served Swiss historical consciousness for the ensuing century.[102]

Burton may be seen, consciously or otherwise, to have anticipated the need for such an accommodation. He certainly viewed as 'quixotic' the obsessive enthusiasm for historical accuracy, which he observed in source scholars like Teulet, whose efforts he otherwise acknowledged as beneficial. At the same time, he sought to incorporate a range of subjects concerning which his remarkably broad participation in the social and cultural world of early to mid-century Scotland had prepared him. Based on such experience, he adopted an almost instinctual inclusiveness about material on which traditional Whig historians may have looked with disdain. It was a reflex probably much assisted by the fact that he remained unconstrained by the methodologically strict academic professionalisation that at first enthused the liberal Swiss scholars. The general response to

---

[101] Oliver Zimmer, 'Competing Memories of the Nation: Liberal Historians and the Reconstruction of the Swiss Past 1870–1900', *Past & Present* 168 (2000), 194–226 (p. 217).
[102] Ibid., pp. 216–20.

the *History*, particularly in Scotland, suggests that his approach allowed him to short-circuit the element of 'competition' – between 'scientific' and 'people's history' – that Zimmer identified as preceding the production of a 'syncretic' historical narrative for Switzerland. As we have seen, Burton managed in one way or another to incorporate many of the stories and legends relating to iconic events in the popular memory of the Scottish past, like the tale of Rizzio, the murder of Archbishop Sharp, the Wigton Martyrs and so on, as well as those surrounding the likes of Wallace, Bruce, Knox and Mary, figures who acted as the reference points for so many of the anniversary celebrations and public 'commemorations' that had punctuated the earlier decades. Prized icons and events, drawn episodically from 'the lucky-dip of the nation's past', now took their place in a continuous and coherent national history, which was widely perceived to display the valorising 'scientific' credentials of the nineteenth century.[103]

It has been argued that the aspiration in Switzerland to construct, or reconstruct, a coherent national history was a response partly to the dislocating trauma and conflict of the 1848 revolutions out of which the new Swiss state was born, but also to a series of internal and external dangers associated with rapid industrialisation and threats from foreign powers between the 1850s and 1870. There is a great deal in John Hill Burton's experience and writings that speaks of a scarcely suppressed sense of anxiety over the potential for social crisis and conflict, as well the recurring threats from abroad. This was partly rooted in concerns for what industrialisation might bring in its wake for established social and economic structures, concerns well-rehearsed in the debates in political economy with which he was familiar. Framing such anxiety in both intellectual and socio-political terms was the legacy of the French Revolution, which continued to impact many aspects of European culture throughout the first half of the nineteenth century, and this preoccupation is evident in many of Burton's literary asides. Throughout Europe, there was a response that sought reassurance in the past and in historical compositions of a characteristic kind, for which Berger has coined the term 'historism' (as distinct from historicism):

> One important reaction to this crisis was historism, which sought to provide reassurance in the form of organic historical development and authentic national character. Whilst the relationship between historism and Romanticism was not always straightforward, it is arguably their rejection of mechanistic

---

[103] Burton, *Scot Abroad*, I, pp. 159–60, footnote; Zimmer, 'Competing Memories', p. 217.

explanations of historical change, their organicism, their developmentalism, their penchant for naturalistic explanations, their idealism and their concern with authenticity and the agency of the individual (including the individual nation) that connects both throughout much of the first half of the nineteenth century.[104]

Burton was familiar with the concept of 'organic historical development'. For one thing, the valorisation of evolutionary rather than mechanistic and sudden change was fundamental to arguments advanced in British political thought since the later eighteenth century that he fully endorsed: writers like the Irish political philosopher Edmund Burke and the Scottish Whig historian Sir James MacIntosh had commended the incremental development of governmental institutions, which thus became 'adapted' to their society and 'national character'. Such thinking was in part a response to the Revolution in France, though it also had roots in the 'historical sociology' of the Scottish Enlightenment. Burton summarised this element in the thought of Burke and MacIntosh in the formulation 'systems of government (or at other times, 'constitutions') are not made – they grow' – a phrase that he used approvingly throughout his life. It has been argued that such thinking, combined with the contemporary interest in ethnological science, underscored belief in the notion of Britain as 'an organic Union' of 'the two Englands' and that Burton and his teutonism exemplified this. There is no doubt that some Scottish intellectuals adopted these perceptions. However, as we have seen, Burton's Teutonist ideas had limited contemporary appeal and were soon subject to doubt and criticism.[105]

There is however a good deal of organicism both in the language and conceptualisation used by Burton in his approach to history particularly his national *History* and in the response to it. But it was, almost by definition, primarily centred on the Scottish nation, not the British Union. And it was organicism for the nineteenth century, couched in terms of contemporary developments in the sciences and expressing a broader, more holistic conception of the emergence and career – the

---

[104] Marchal, 'Swiss National Identity', p. 201; Berger with Conrad, *Past as History*, p. 96.

[105] NLS MS 9430, fols 3, 115; Burton, *Emigrant's Manual*, p. 76; [John Hill Burton], 'Guizot's History of France', *ER* 140 (1874), 201–28 (p. 206); James MacIntosh, *A Discourse on the Study of the Law of Nature and of Nations; [. . .]*, 2nd edn (London: Cadell, 1799), pp. 28–9, 51–2; Kidd, *Unionisms*, pp. 134–38, 151–69; see above, pp. 228–33.

longue durée – of nations. An organicist reflex in Burton himself was hardly surprising in view of his exposure at a formative stage in his early life to the new thinking circulating in Edinburgh radical circles in the third and fourth decades of the century. This was the period when he had arrived in the Scottish capital and had been swept up in the enthusiasm for reform, cemented by the close relations he developed with his group of radical friends. At that time, radical circles had been infused with the early thinking on biological evolution developed by the French naturalists Jean-Baptiste Lamarck and Étienne Geoffroy. Their ideas had been carried home by Scottish students and doctors augmenting their Edinburgh medical and scientific education with study in Paris.[106] One of these was Dr Andrew Combe and such French thinking certainly influenced his brother George, and the rest of the self-styled 'modernisers' who gathered around George Combe in this period. Burton's exposure to organicist principles must have been increased through his engagement with the Combe circle in the mid-to-late 1830s – the point at which Combe's *Constitution of Man*, with its philosophy founded on the primacy of organic natural laws, took off in sales and influence – as well as in the following years by the proto-evolutionist ideas expounded by their mutual friend Robert Chambers.[107]

Such thinking accorded with the contemporary exploration of the processes of growth, development and disease in the agricultural, medico-physiological and biological sciences, partly in response to the challenges faced by industrial society over food production, epidemic disease and industrial waste. Interest and concern on how these ideas could illuminate and help to control contemporary social and economic upheaval carried over into debates on appropriate responses in social policy. The developing 'sanitary science' – public health – in the debates and campaigns around which Burton was much involved, touched on all of these issues. Holistic conceptions of a unity of organic 'design' in nature resonated with advocates of reform in what many considered the most critical issue in political economy in the 1830s and 1840s, the establishment of Free Trade – in the campaign for which Burton again played an active part – and Combe's *Constitution* 'became the foundation text of the free trade movement'.[108]

---

[106] Adrian Desmond, *The Politics of Evolution: Morphology, Medicine, and Reform in Radical London* (Chicago: University of Chicago Press, 1989), pp. 41–6, 58–81, 174–80.
[107] Stack, *Victoria's Skull*, pp. 86–9; see above, pp. 45–6.
[108] Stack, *Nature and Artifice*, p. 185.

Burton's predilection for organic analogies is exemplified in many passages of his mid-century writings on political economy. In these works, his conceptions of social and economic processes are often expressed in terms of the natural world, and of organic growth and change.[109] A perspective that viewed societal development in these terms inevitably had implications for history. Intellectual influences from elsewhere in continental Europe and complementary to those emerging from France helped to make the connection: Scottish reformers like his old friend John Stuart Blackie, who shared Burton's educational background and admired the same contemporary writers, 'were influenced by the emphasis in German idealist thought on the 'organic' nature of nations and their historic embodiment in ancient but continually evolving institutions and traditions'.[110] In the same period, on the other side of the ideological divide, the writings of the Blackwood's stalwart, J. G. Lockhart, were heavily influenced by Schiller and Friedrich Schlegel, who had presented historical composition as a holistic endeavour, which, through appreciation of the nation's literature, could 'reconstitute a fragmented national identity [. . .] reintegrating the vital, totalizing bond between nation and psyche'.[111]

In the preface to his 1873 edition, Burton indicated that he had perceived the opportunity to mould the new 'materials' that the source editions and records scholars had revealed as an holistic endeavour: he did not have in mind mere adjustments to what had previously existed but rather a 'great effort completely to interpret the past of Scotland to the world', and to 'arrange its several parts into a systematic whole'. Using similar language years before in a review of one of P. F. Tytler's volumes, at the time when organicism was rife in Edinburgh radical circles, Burton had lamented Scotland's surprising 'national want' of a coherent historical narrative:

> In historical literature, Scotland has taken the lead of every other European country. This makes it not a little remarkable, that no continuous and complete national history had been attempted until very recently. The contributions of Robertson, Pinkerton, Laing, Hume, and we may add to the list, McCrie, Cook, and others, refer chiefly to insulated periods, more or less interesting; and allowing for the prejudices and predilections of some of the writers, they all form either valuable portions, or amusing fragments of the Scottish annals.

---

[109] See Burton, *Political Economy*, pp. 90, 112, 245, 252–3; Burton, *Emigrant's Manual* [Introductory Essay], pp. 60, 62, 72, 74, 76.
[110] Anderson and Wallace, 'Universities and National Identity', p. 271; NLS MS 9392, fols 137–8; NLS MS 9394, fols 68–9.
[111] Duncan, *Scott's Shadow*, pp. 47–8, 57–8, 61.

What was needed was a work that would fashion 'a great whole, resting on sure foundations, complete in all its parts, and harmonious in its proportions'. In the event, Tytler too would provide only a 'valuable portion' and be judged to have shown too many of his own 'prejudices and predilections'.[112]

Burton was quite conscious that what he had done for Scotland represented a contemporary historical form, which other nations should cultivate. In his 1874 review of Guizot's complete history of France from 'les temps les plus reculés' to 1789, Burton lamented 'our own poverty in the literature of completed histories when measured with the wealth of other nations'. He commended the effort in Guizot's previous works to 'trace the growth' of 'French nationality' and institutions back to their roots in the old Empire, and now admired even more 'a full history where all parts, great and small, demand their proper place, and must have it'. In the course of the article, he drew comparison between cultivative and social or institutional 'growths'; and between developments in biological science – 'the examination of animal organisms [. . .] even to the algae in the gutter' – and 'the examination of the rise and progress of communities and empires'. And he commended Guizot's 'favourite doctrine of the adaptability of institutions to the nature of a people'. The most remarkable quality in the work was 'a unity and harmony in the narrative as it sweeps through events that in feebler hands would stand separate and alone'.[113]

In the previous decades Burton's notices of the new source editions and other publications on the Scottish past had rehearsed in similarly holistic terms the opportunity that was thus presented and was in danger of being missed. His 1856 review of Teulet's *Papiers d'État* expressed concern that 'no one had come forward to perform the synthetic function' and weave together the many fresh, newly illuminated materials to show 'how, in short, Scotland became Scotland'. He had earlier used the same metaphoric conception of synthesis in an 1851 review of Daniel Wilson's *Annals*: even the modern neo-antiquarians, whose approach had excised the tales of the 'monkish chroniclers' from

---

[112] Burton, *HOS* (1873), I, p. vii; [John Hill Burton], 'History of Scotland,–VOL. V. By Patrick F. Tytler, ESQ. F.A.S.', *Tait's* 1 n.s. (1834), 521–7 (p. 521). The *Wellesley Index* has Burton as 'probable' author: he had certainly developed a close friendship with William Tait and reviewed all of Tytler's subsequent volumes for *Tait's*.

[113] [Burton], 'Guizot's History of France', pp. 201–3, 206, 208, 222.

history, worked by 'groping and analysing' but it was the role of the narrative historian to fashion a substitute – '[t]he historian's operation is synthetic – he begins at the beginning, putting together the materials collected for him'.[114]

Many of the responses to Burton's *History* reflect a consensus that here was a significant re-presentation of the Scottish past and one that would supersede previous fragmented accounts. Commentators described the achievement using terms that recognised a new and substantial revision: the work was 'the first complete and judicial history of his country'; he had 'not merely written, he has recast the History of Scotland'; and particularly he had provided the nation with a holistic account of the past that was greater than the sum of its parts: '[I]f to write a scholarly, trustworthy, and vigorous history which gathers up into an organic whole, the results of all previous investigations [. . .] be a worthy national service, as great as it is rare, Mr Burton has achieved it [. . .]. We cannot hope for a history more complete.' Other reviewers in both Scotland and London highlighted his equable attention to different parts of the *History*, with the result that he 'treats his subject as a whole with a deeper insight'.[115]

Commentators in both the Tory *Blackwood's* and the Whig *Scotsman* reflected this organicist teleology, the conception of a people and nation developing over time and in hostile conditions, eventuating in the present, its 'independence' intact. The 1867 *Blackwood's* reviewer discerned an arresting vision emerging from those early centuries in the first millennium and developing continuously down to the present:

> a curious shadow, as of another great personage on the scene, is present through all those troublous chapters [. . .] the great body of the Scottish people, slowly forming, growing, taking shape and force; a people tenacious of all its ancient attachments and hatreds, immovable in its independence, loyal and faithful to its historic career. Nothing can be more remarkable than this apparition[.]

The *Scotsman* celebrated the completed work in comparable teleological terms of continuity, and a growing identity through time, an identity that was still 'moving on':

> No Scotchman 'whose blood is warm within him' but must feel it grow warmer as he reads how much was suffered, and dared, and done by his ancestors through so many troubled generations [. . .]. And where, in the history of the world, shall we find a nation so small stubbornly maintaining its

---

[114] Burton, 'France and Scotland', p. 290; Burton, 'Vestiges', p. 660.
[115] *Daily News*, 19 April 1867, p. 2; [Anon], 'History of Scotland', *BQ* (1867), pp. 214, 217; [Tulloch], 'Burton's History', p. 794.

independence against powerful enemies, through centuries both of deadly war and of ensnaring intrigue – even in her deepest straits as jealous and quick of quarrel as the most potent monarchies – in her internal affairs, struggling fiercely, after the varying fashions of each age, against the oppression of whatever sought to exalt itself as lord – and then, when peace, and honour, and security were won, and the days of the sword had waned, moving on, before the strongest, in the march of arts and industry? [116]

It has been argued that '[t]hroughout the eighteenth and nineteenth centuries Scottish history was generally presented as a narrative of defective state formation', and that 'a negativity about Scotland's pre-1707 history as an independent state was one of the principle justifications of Union'.[117] The characteristics of Burton's *History* and the highly positive responses it was accorded – not infrequently associated with valedictions for those eighteenth- and early nineteenth-century efforts – suggest that this perception of the nation's past was no longer predominant. Perhaps this did, ultimately, help to remove 'one of the principal justifications of Union'. The immediate consequence at the height of the imperial project could never credibly have been a lost nationalist reflex, at least in the sense of a drive for independence. It is of course as unwise to search for late twentieth-century Scottish nationalism in the mid-to-late nineteenth century as to search for late-twentieth century unionism, or its avatars, in earlier centuries. Nevertheless, it is clear that attitudes to the Scottish past, including – indeed particularly – the pre-Union past, were changing radically.

Burton's *History of Scotland* and the widespread welcome it received, both within the nation and internationally, is incompatible with the view that Scottish history suffered a mortal decline, that there was some kind of atypical, catastrophic failure of national historical confidence in the second half of the nineteenth century. On the contrary, the country produced, and welcomed, a national narrative that incorporated the full range of characteristics typifying the national histories produced around the same period across Europe. These were produced in existing nation states (and, with less success, empires) but most critically by and for re-emergent nations that – for the time being – were still incorporated in multinational states.

---

[116] [Oliphant], 'History of Scotland', p. 331; *Sc*, 19 August 1870, p. 5. London reviewers also perceived, in Burton's account, 'a whole people [. . .] rapidly growing up' in wealth, culture 'and in stubborn devotion to its peculiar form of Christianity'; and, from the medieval centuries, 'we find the germs of the institutions developed throughout [Scotland's] subsequent history'. [Anon], 'Burton's History', *LQ* (1871), p. 338; *Times*, 22 April 1867, p. 9.
[117] Kidd, *Unionisms*, pp. 145, 148.

9

History and Heritage: The Revival of Scottish National Identity

THE PRESENT STUDY SET OUT with a combined purpose of reappraising the achievements of John Hill Burton and of revising current perceptions of Scottish historical consciousness as the nineteenth century advanced. Central to both of these aims has been a detailed re-examination of Burton's multi-volume *History of Scotland* and of the highly positive reception it was accorded. In a single volume seeking to address both reappraisals it has not been possible to provide a full intellectual biography or as much detail on his life as might be desirable. It is to be hoped that sufficient indication has been given to prompt further consideration of the broad spectrum of intellectual activity in which he engaged, particularly in the first half of his adult life, as a scholar of Bentham and of Hume and as a contributor to debates on social policy and political economy. The impact of his early immersion in utilitarian thinking on one prominent aspect of his historiography has been addressed more fully.

In what little attention he does attract among scholars, Burton is portrayed in rather one-dimensional terms as a Whig-Teutonist historian, and this has functioned to obscure a full appreciation of the significance of his work. That is, he is viewed as simply and derivatively rehearsing a standard historiographic interpretation that had been widely adopted in the period and become almost hegemonic, so his work has faded into the background as just another exemplar of a common narrative. There are many passages in his *History* that do reflect Whig-Teutonist assumptions. However, the biographical approach that has been followed has aimed to alert the reader to a more complex picture.

His responses to intense life experiences, whether inspiring or traumatic, have been analysed in some detail seeking to form an impression of his underlying cultural, psychological and emotional reflexes. They reveal Burton, for all his subsequent utilitarian 'practicalism' – which was real enough – as a figure deeply influenced by the sensibility of the Picturesque and the emerging forms of the Romantic imagination. It comes as no surprise that the 'picturesque eye' and the tropes of romance recur in his work. Early immersed in Romantic literature and displaying a romantic subjectivity cleaving to wilderness, he was also attuned to the terrors that Nature could engender, whether in an aesthetic response to actual dangers in the 'sublime' landscape or to associations borne of his knowledge of the supernatural in folklore. In public life, his wide-ranging social and cultural experience was imbued with a sense of the Scottish past, captured and conveyed in imagist and performative terms in painting, or on the history-stage. At the same time, it reinforced his otherworldly sensibility by exposing him to the 'gothic' horrors and fears that fascinated post-Enlightenment Edinburgh and were exploited by the writers and publishers he knew well. Equipped with this richer and more varied understanding of the man, of his emotional responses, cultural experience and social relations, it has been argued that with a little effort one can uncover and recognise a range of other dimensions to his historical *œuvre* and particularly his multi-volume *History of Scotland*. The response of critics and of much of the Scottish reading public suggests they recognised the elements he incorporated in the work as constituting the past as a national history with which they could identify.

In the second half of the nineteenth century there is evidence that Scottish identity was ceasing to be so dependent on the nation's place in the British Union or even on in its role in the British Empire. No doubt for many, identification with the idea of Britain, forged in the Napoleonic Wars and refreshed in the Crimea, remained strong. Yet from the later 1840s and early 1850s, doubts had begun to break the surface on the benefits to Scotland of the way the Union state was evolving. At the same time a renewed sense of Scottish identity began to form, founded on a new attitude to the Scottish past. In the years around the mid-century the lawyerly Whig elite in Edinburgh, drawn to Burton's sociability as well as his efforts to support reform, became increasingly impressed by his literary works. This began with the *Life of Hume* (1846) but soon extended to his publications on Scottish history in periodical articles and in book form, beginning with his two early volumes in 1853. We have seen that, from different ideological standpoints, the authors of reviews in prominent periodicals grasped at these 1853 volumes as a means of turning a spotlight back on the 1707 Union, and on how the supposed guarantees it offered regarding Scottish institutions, not least the Scottish Church, had been betrayed. It is difficult to read these extensive articles and other commentary at the time and miss the sense of anxiety about, and the determination to reassert, Scottish national identity expressed in terms which resist the interpretation that anything less than national identity was at stake.

In his public life it is the sheer diversity of the social and cultural *milieux* Burton frequented that appears exceptional. Among other consequences, this led to his participation in and exposure to developments within the Scottish middle and upper class that cumulatively represented a new attitude to the Scottish past. Across the middle decades of the century many members of the elite groups appear to have become convinced that a proper discharge of their leadership role should include support for a variety of efforts at reclamation of the national past. This appears to have been a reflex shared across otherwise deep divisions, whether in politics or religious confession. As we have seen, this led to ambitious ventures by prestigious publishing houses promoting the history of Scottish architecture and antiquities; to senior lawyers and academics patronising and expanding the Book Club publishing of medieval and early modern source texts; to a reinvigoration of the Society of Antiquaries under a senior judge supported by leading scholars and lawyers; and to the transnational activities of leading book clubs in bringing to light Scottish sources in European archives. The variety of Burton's personal relationships and associational activities meant that he was directly involved in almost all these initiatives. Similar activities were sustained through the remainder of the century. There is little indication in all of this of decline in historical consciousness or a lack of confidence in the nation's past.

It is notable that much of this began or was accelerated in the period when there arose an increasing concern at the manner in which assimilationist policies seemed to be abolishing or centralising Scottish institutions. It hardly seems coincidental that, commencing at that time and continuing to the end of the century, the Scottish elites ensured the establishment of a new set of institutions housed in mostly new and grandiloquent buildings whose purpose was to celebrate the nation's heritage. As we have seen, renewed pressure to establish a National Antiquities museum had its origins in that period of mid-century unease and from the early 1850s was doggedly promoted by the reinvigorated SSA. In the same period, the foundation stone of the National Gallery of Scotland was laid in 1850 and the imposing 'Greek temple' designed to house it by the Edinburgh architect William Playfair opened in 1859. In that decade too, planning commenced on the Industrial Museum of Scotland which would focus on natural history, geology, technology and the decorative arts, and by 1866 would be located near the centre of Edinburgh in another new building with a monumental, this time Italian-Renaissance façade.[1] The transfer of the art collection to its new home provided the opportunity for the national antiquities collection to secure much improved accommodation in Playfair's equally imposing Royal Institution building, which stood adjacent to the new National Gallery on Princes Street. In 1895 (by which time the antiquities collection was no longer confined to prehistory), continued pressure as well as the large number of visitors the historical museum attracted, secured it official recognition as the National Museum of Antiquities of Scotland and joint occupancy of the striking new building on Queen Street which was completed in 1889 to house the Scottish National Portrait Gallery.[2]

These institutions were established to publicise and display the nation's history and cultural heritage, whether expressed in genre paintings, which depicted dramatic and iconic scenes from national history; in collections of portraits of the nation's heroes and battles; or in collections of artefacts and antiquities, as well as more recent technological achievements, which attested to the nation's ancient origins and continuity through time. Recent scholarship has demonstrated that such 'assemblages' of national history museums and art museums, housed in prestigious buildings and located in fairly close proximity within a national capital, became characteristic across Europe as a means of asserting and 'constituting' national identity.[3] Although these institutions were promoted and secured by elite groups, they represented one of the means by which the national past could be conveyed to a mass audience.

---

[1] Sheila Watson, 'National Museums in Scotland', in *Building National Museums in Europe 1750–2010. Conference proceedings from EuNaMus, European National Museums: Identity Politics, the Uses of the Past and the European Citizen*, EuNaMus Report No 1, eds Peter Aronsson and Gabriella Elgenius (Linköping University Electronic Press, 2011), 747–77 (pp. 747–9, 756–60).

[2] R. B. K. Stevenson, 'The Museum, its Beginnings and its Development. Part II: The National Museum to 1954', in A. S. Bell, ed., *The Scottish Antiquarian Tradition: Essays to mark the bicentenary of the Society of Antiquaries of Scotland 1780–1980* (Edinburgh: John Donald, 1981), 142–209 (pp. 143–53, 172–3).

[3] Gabriella Elgenius, 'National Museums as National Symbols', in Peter Aronsson and Gabriella Elgenius, eds, *National Museums and Nation-Building in Europe 1750–2010: Mobilization and Legitimacy, Continuity and Change* (Abingdon: Routledge, 2015), 145–66 (pp. 145–6); Peter Aronsson, 'National Museums as Cultural Constitutions', in Aronson and Elgenius, *National Museums*, 167–99 (pp. 174–6).

The historiographic interpretation outlined at the beginning of this book remains highly influential. The perspectives of many of the writers considered there form the basis of the summation arrived at by the editors of the recent *Oxford Handbook of Modern Scottish History* (2012). Nineteenth-century Scotland, they maintained, failed to attain the 'historiographic revolution' through which nations elsewhere in Europe had asserted national identity through celebration of the nation's past. Only much later, with the critique of Whig historiography by English historians like Namier and Butterfield could the perception of the Scottish past escape 'a narrative of defective and inadequate development'. This had its origins, the editors continued – in an analysis unchanged from that of Marinell Ash forty years earlier – in Walter Scott's 'dramatic and colourful tales', which had directed interest in the Scottish past 'into the intellectual dead end of "historical kailyards" and romantic appendages'. The present study recognises Scott's influence, not in these negative terms but as one component – though a highly important one, as has been recognised in its influence on national history-writing throughout Europe – in the formation of Burton's national history of Scotland.[4]

In his study of Sir Walter Scott, Ian Duncan observed that in modern times, historians in particular had clung to 'disparaging characterisations of the Waverley novels as tools of a factitious "invention of Scotland"', a delusional substitution of romance for real history'.[5] Certainly the derogatory references to 'historical kailyards', 'Highlandism' and 'tartan monsters' made by historians considering Scottish historical consciousness in the later nineteenth century bear the hallmarks of the thinking outlined in *The Invention of Tradition*, the influential collection edited by Eric Hobsbawm and Trevor Ranger in 1983; and perhaps particularly Hugh Trevor-Roper's contribution contending that Scottish national identity had been manufactured in the nineteenth century from a fabricated 'highland tradition'.[6] The debates of the early 1980s involving various theorists of nationalism cannot be pursued in detail here, though Benedict Anderson's observation on another of those thinkers, Ernest Gellner, might more often be kept in mind: 'Gellner is so anxious to show

---

[4] T. M. Devine and Jenny Wormald, 'Introduction', in *Oxford Handbook of Modern Scottish History*, eds Devine and Wormald, 1–15 (pp. 1–4, 10).
[5] Duncan, *Scott's Shadow*, p. xiii.
[6] Hugh Trevor-Roper, 'The Invention of Tradition: The Highland Tradition of Scotland', in *The Invention of Tradition*, eds Eric Hobsbawm and Terence Ranger (Cambridge: Cambridge University Press, 1983), pp. 15–41.

that nationalism masquerades under false pretences that he assimilates "invention" to "fabrication" and "falsity", rather than to "imagining" and "creation".' On the situation in Scotland, Anderson himself seemed to rely largely on the analysis of Tom Nairn: in advance of the rise of nationalism in Europe, the Scottish middle classes and intellectuals had already abandoned the country for the high road to London or the opportunities of Empire.[7] Thinking of this kind has obscured what actually happened in Scotland. However, Anderson's own ideas on the formation of 'nation-ness' in the nineteenth century accord with the present study in a number of important respects.

First, he realised at an early point the importance of the nation's *longue durée*: Anderson argued that the assurance of national historical continuity filled the void left by the collapse of religious certainties in the face of Enlightenment scepticism, but it was therefore essential that the nation must 'always loom out of an immemorial past'. He recognised too the potential role of museums in the presentation or manipulation of national identity – though on this issue his analysis focused chiefly in developments in colonial and post-colonial lands. Finally, and centrally for Anderson, he traced the crucial agency of the growth of 'print capitalism' and the opportunities it provided for the sense of membership of a shared national identity among people 'who will never know their fellow-members'. This accelerated in the nineteenth century as the 'membership' of national 'imagined communities' expanded with the increased reach of print media founded on an unprecedented progress in technology and communications.[8]

Elsewhere in Europe, where nations aspired to independence at this time, Anderson identified middle-class elites engaging with a range of 'producers for the print market' of the kind able to convey and define the nation's cultural difference – lexicographers, writers, folklorists, philologists and so on.[9] For Anderson the significance of this centred on the assertion of vernacular language as a 'language-of-state' in the nationalist movements that ensued. This was not of course applicable to Scotland (though the country did participate in what he termed the 'golden age of vernacularizing

---

[7] Benedict Anderson, *Imagined Communities: Reflections on the Origin and Spread of Nationalism*, revised edn (London: Verso, 1991), pp. 6, 90; Nairn, *Break-Up*, pp. 123–5.
[8] Anderson, *Imagined Communities*, pp. 6, 11, 36, 178–85.
[9] Ibid., pp. 71–2, 74–6, 78–80.

lexicographers', as well as related efforts in the reclamation of vernacular culture[10]). Nevertheless, the 'coalitions' of 'middle strata' to be found collaborating in the assertion of national identity elsewhere in Europe accord closely with the social make-up of the middling elites whose members we have seen involved in the recovery, publication and exhibition of the Scottish national past. They had not all left for London or India. The fact that such groups were disinterested in political independence should not obscure their increasing support for the same efforts at reappraisal and reclamation of the national past that occurred in many other European nations seeking to assert national identity – and expressing their support in ways that reached out beyond the elites. In the 1870s and 1880s, when Blackwood's coffers benefited from large print runs of Burton's national *History*, approaching 120,000 people per annum were visiting the Museum of Antiquities on the principal thoroughfare of Edinburgh. Through its imposing portals, broad swathes of the population were beginning, to paraphrase Tom Nairn, to be invited into history.[11]

In the mass expansion of 'print capitalism' in the nineteenth century, Scotland played a central part, as is evidenced in Burton's own experience. For many decades, he exploited the opportunities presented by the 'publishing revolution' that began in the country around 1830. It brought an explosion of newspapers, journals, periodicals and books of every sort, and extended from the increasingly national and nationally named *Scotsman* newspaper to the Edinburgh-based weeklies and monthlies, many of which were fully or partially devoted to Scottish material. Often highly astute in commercial as well as cultural terms, leading Scottish publishers began to appear centre stage. It comes as no surprise that among the gentry, academics, lawyers and businessmen with whom Burton collaborated and who supported his own historical efforts, John Blackwood loomed large. The role played by Blackwood in promoting and supporting the publication of periodical articles and books bearing directly on Scottish history and antiquities has been

---

[10] John Jamieson's *Etymological Dictionary of the Scottish Language [. . .]* (Edinburgh: Creech/Tait, 1808/1825) was a groundbreaking work in historical lexicography in general and became widely popular in Scotland as a 'national icon' and a valuable repository of vernacular culture – as Burton himself had anticipated: Susan Rennie, 'The First Scottish "National" Dictionary: [. . .]', in *The Whole World in a Book: Dictionaries in the Nineteenth Century*, eds Sarah Ogilvie and Gabriella Safran (Oxford: Oxford University Press, 2020), pp. 110–30; Burton, *HOS* (1873), III, p. 423, footnote 1.

[11] Stevenson, 'The Museum, its Beginnings', p. 156; Nairn, *Break-Up*, p. 340.

described. It included his business acumen in 'managing' authors as well as devising effective pricing and marketing strategies. This complemented and supported the broader cultural influence of what David Finkelstein has identified as Blackwood's literary 'ecumene', and its significance has been recognised in the preceding chapters.

In his book *Scott's Shadow*, Ian Duncan proceeded to a more insightful analysis of Walter Scott and his influence than that reflected in some recent histories, partly based on the argument that at the root of Scott's endeavour had been the continuing impact of David Hume's thought on Scotland in the early decades of the nineteenth century: 'it was Hume who provided the philosophical justification for Scott's combination of history and romance. The Humean trajectory of Enlightenment traces a sceptical dismantling of the metaphysical foundations of reality and their replacement with a sentimental investment in 'common life'. This may be seen, ultimately, to have drawn into history a whole range of previously excluded subject matter. In any case, Duncan went on to illustrate how Humean scepticism deepened the cultural divide in post-Enlightenment Edinburgh between modernising Whig political economy and the Blackwoodian emotive and ethnological reaction exemplified in works like the *Noctes Ambrosianae* and J. G. Lockhart's *Peter's Letters to his Kinsfolk*.[12] It is notable how far Burton's own social and intellectual trajectory mirrors this analysis, from his early and sustained admiration for Humean scepticism; to his extensive engagement with Whig political economy; and in different phases of his life exposure to the Blackwoodian cultural world, first as a youth in what has been termed above the 'northern *Noctes*', then later in his absorption in John Blackwood's sphere of influence. Interestingly, Lockhart had appealed to history as 'the discipline that can unite the severed faculties' of intellect and feeling into which he believed Hume's thought had split the nation's cultural identity. Burton's life, and his *History* can be viewed as managing to span what had appeared an unbridgeable cultural divide earlier in the century.[13]

The present study has traced the remarkable range of socio-political endeavours and cultural engagements that prepared John Hill Burton to compose a national history in ways which resonated across Scottish society from the elite groups to most literary critics, but also to a much broader reading public. Besides the reappraisal of his national history per se, it has been argued that greater attention should be paid to its

---

[12] Duncan, *Scott's Shadow*, pp. xiii, 29.
[13] Ibid., pp. 61–5.

enthusiastic reception across that broad swathe of opinion as evidencing a growing historical identity centred on the Scottish nation. He was enabled to compose the work and elicit this response partly because of the decades-long effort in the collection and classification of historical evidence produced by book clubs, records scholars and publishers: in each of these spheres Scotland matched and, in some cases, outperformed similar efforts being pursued across Europe. Validated by a reputation for impartiality – which extended to the critical sphere of ecclesiastical history – and for adherence to 'the science of history' founded on 'the painstaking research of the nineteenth century', his account of the nation's past incorporated and expressed apparently disparate elements of the culture he shared with his readership from hard-headed social and political practicalism to romantic sensibility, from gothic *frissons* to the 'National Drama'. What resulted for many observers was a new and holistic conception, a historiographic perspective on the nation's past, generated from and for the second half of the nineteenth century.

It is beyond the scope of the present work to assess what impact Burton's *History* and its reception may have had in other respects and beyond the period covered here. From the critique of W. L. Mathieson at the beginning of the twentieth century, it might be assumed that any influence on the development of Scottish history as an academic discipline was negligible. Still, in Dauvit Broun's recent reassessment of the achievements of Peter Hume Brown, there are significant elements that recall Burton's work. Broun noted that Hume Brown's *History of Scotland* (1902–9) was accorded an 'unprecedented profile' in Prothero's 'Cambridge Historical Series' as the only national history allowed to extend before the modern era beginning with the Romans, and so the longest, stretching to three volumes: but it was not Hume Brown who had established Scotland's *longue durée*. The admiration for Hume Brown's achieving a 'balanced and impartial' approach and his 'appreciation of the European dimensions of whatever aspect of Scottish history he was engaged in' echoes the accolades for Burton's work decades earlier.[14] The influence of Burton's work on Hume Brown and his 'self-confident vision of a Scottish past', and on other Scottish historians of his time, merits examination.

In addition, it has been increasingly recognised that socio-cultural forms other than academic or 'scientific' history come to constitute 'collective memory' and contribute to the historical identity of communities, including national communities. One of these involves an

---

[14] Broun, 'Forgotten Anniversary', pp. 272–4, 277, 280.

ongoing dialogue between history and literature. Although Burton was admired partly because his account superseded some of Walter Scott's presentations, that dialogue resumed with the substantial influence that Hill Burton's historical work had on Robert Louis Stevenson. Burton's *History* was a set text on the course of Law and History that Stevenson took at Edinburgh in 1875 in preparation for his calling as an advocate. At the time he also obtained Burton's *Criminal Trials in Scotland*. His copy of the *History* remained with him throughout his life, and he carried it to Samoa. By 1880 his interest had grown to a point where he consulted Burton on his intention to write a history of Scotland around the time of the Union: 'An old idea, first started while I was reading your history of Scotland, has just been revived over your Queen Anne, which I am in the heart of, with sincere pleasure.'[15]

His correspondence with his brother at the time suggests that he was drawn to a number of themes to which Burton had given particular prominence. Although he did not write a formal history, it has recently been suggested that Stevenson's absorption of such themes, and the ways in which they were incorporated in his writings, carried the history within the novels and conveyed significant aspects of Scottish history with a new or renewed empathy: 'the material and the intellectual resources for Kidnapped and David Balfour' – which certainly included Burton's publications – 'were reconstituted as hidden texts within the novel'. Even where Burton was himself unsympathetic to aspects of Scottish history, Stevenson could absorb the material and convey the issues with a quite different and more positive emphasis. For instance, in developing the characteristics of Alan Breck Stewart in *Kidnapped*, Stevenson 'subverts the image of the uncivilized Highlander' from rapacious cattle thief to someone 'calculated and deliberate' in pursuing the path he must take; and more generally the MacGregors' predatory activities are qualified in the context of the long history that Burton had outlined of government judicial vengeance against recalcitrant clans through 'letters of fire and sword'.[16]

Similarly, as we have seen, Burton provided readers of his *History* with a detailed signposting to the martyrology of the covenanters, a

---

[15] Barry Menikoff, *Narrating Scotland: The Imagination of Robert Louis Stevenson* (Columbia, SC: South Carolina Press, 2005), pp. 13–14, 87–8; NLS MS 9983, fols 57–9.
[16] Menikoff, *Narrating Scotland*, pp. 3, 19, 87–8, 104, 122–3; John Hill Burton, *Criminal Trials in Scotland*, 2 vols (London: Chapman and Hall, 1852) I, pp. 8–11; Burton, HOS (1853), I, pp. 157–8, 173–8; Burton, HOS (1873), VII, pp. 412–14.

literature for which Stevenson (like John Buchan) developed a particular fascination. In the sequel to *Kidnapped*, while David Balfour is held captive on the Bass Rock, and despite the overall rootedness of the story in Jacobitism and the Highlands, through the 'interpolated story' of Tod Lapraik, Stevenson 'deftly moves his whole text back to the late seventeenth century and the persecution of the covenanters'. Just before he is ferried to the Bass, David conceives the 'panoramic sweep of Scottish history embedded' in the ruined battlements along the East Lothian coast and once held in the old prison, 'a place full of history', imagines that he 'could have heard the pious sound of psalms out of the martyrs' dungeons'.[17]

The novelist was of course also 'drawn to elements of terror and violence, [. . .] a master at creating fear', an enthusiasm most obviously evidenced in his *Strange Case of Dr Jekyll and Mr Hyde* (1886). It has been argued above that the trope of 'the double', whether figures caught in a Mephisthophelean pact or as 'divided self' and *doppelgänger*, recur in Burton's writings, particularly his *History*. Transformations are traced, bringing individuals, originally godly or chivalrous, to extreme and evil acts that are quite 'out of character'. For these episodes, Burton relied heavily on the material gathered by Robert Wodrow, as well as James Kirkton's *Secret History* (edited by Kirkpatrick Sharpe). Stevenson used both sources in his early work, and Burton's prominent use and admiration for these works can only have reinforced Stevenson's preoccupation with such supernatural themes.[18]

In the course of the nineteenth century, besides literature, a range of other cultural forms were coming to represent and strengthen the historical identity of national communities. It has been argued above that Burton's *History* was accorded a positive reception partly because he had gone beyond the political-constitutional focus of traditional history and incorporated a range of elements of 'the history of the people', such as antiquities and architectural traditions, vernacular language, popular literature and folklore. This was partly founded on his respect for particular previous historians. At an early stage he expressed his admiration for Hume as 'the first to add to a mere narrative of events, an inquiry into the progress of the people, and of their arts, literature, manners, and general social condition', but he added that this had been taken significantly further in the nineteenth century by figures such as

---

[17] Menikoff, *Narrating Scotland*, pp. 172–3, 181–4, 188–9; Robert Louis Stevenson, *Catriona: A Sequel to 'Kidnapped'* (London: Cassell, 1893), pp. 156–7, 170–82.
[18] Menikoff, *Narrating Scotland*, p. 63; see pp. 154–9, 169–70.

Francois Guizot. As already described, Burton's admiration for the French historian was elaborated in his review of the initial volumes of Guizot's *L'Histoire de France* for the *Edinburgh Review*.[19]

However, *le moment Guizot* is now also recognised as marking 'the birth of heritage' or, in French, of *le patrimoine* – that sense of historical identity that developed around the conservation and appropriate display of the surviving antiquities and monuments of the nation's past. As a minister in Louis Philippe's 'July Monarchy' (1830–48), Guizot initiated a number of measures to promote the study and conservation of France's historical records, monuments and architectural treasures in order to demonstrate the nation's continuity through history: '[t]he conservation of the past thus formed part of the intellectual strategy of the Nation-State.' As a historian, he reflected such concerns in his work on the *longue durée* of French national history and in his conviction that the physical survivals of the nation's past offered a key to understanding its social development – for example he argued that the form of the *château* explained a range of features of the French medieval world.[20] This perspective was echoed in Burton's repeated assertion that 'the most enduring testimony to the social habits of early times is architecture'. Since Burton had clearly read Guizot by the mid-1840s, it is appropriate that this observation comes from one of his subsequent articles on France and Scotland. Indeed, *le moment Guizot* seems, more broadly, to have much in common with the increasing support of the Scottish elites for establishing the 'assemblage' of national history museums and art museums; with the convictions and efforts of Burton and his associates in their recording, classification and publishing of original texts, documentary facsimiles, architectural traditions and archaeological antiquities; and subsequently with Burton's effort at incorporating such elements into his own national history.[21]

Further consideration of the impact of Burton's historical *œuvre*, including the national *History*, on subsequent histories, on literary culture and on the emergence of the collective memory of *le patrimoine* may prove fruitful.

---

[19] See p. 256; Burton, *Life of Hume*, II, pp. 129–30.
[20] Dominique Poulot and Richard Wigley, 'The Birth of Heritage: le moment Guizot', *Oxford Art Journal* 11 (1988), 40–56 (pp. 41–2, 44–50).
[21] [Burton], 'France and Scotland', p. 320; *HOS* (1873) III, p. 427 and VIII, p. 540; it is notable that the laudatory Introduction to the twenty-first century edition of 'Billings' was contributed by the Chief Curator of the National Trust for Scotland. See pp. 77–8.

Epilogue

IN THE VOLUMINOUS CORRESPONDENCE surviving in the Burton archive, it is seldom that Victorian formality gives way in his correspondents' salutations to the familiar 'my dear John'. On one occasion it is used by an old friend at the time his first wife died; but otherwise, its regular use is confined chiefly to letters from his mother and sister. He remained closely bound to his nuclear family, his mother and sister Mary, for over half his life. In the only period they were parted – when he came to study and qualify in Edinburgh – Eliza kept him well provisioned with favourite provender, including 'Whisky, Butter, Gingerbread' and always around August a sufficiency of ripe gooseberries, a favourite through life. As for almost all in his time, the early death of close relations was a regular occurrence: as a boy of ten he lost his father and a short time after his first marriage, his young wife; a child of his second marriage died in infancy; and his closest friends were lost in middle age. A number of his male relations, including a brother, went east to find fortune and never returned: he later wrote that he well understood 'how dear we pay for India'.[1]

In his interactions with his friends among the newspapermen he enjoyed exchanging the sarcastic, mock-aggressive conversational barbs known in Scots as 'flyting'; one at least who came to know him in his later years thought him rather caustic and self-important. However, in general he was, within the constraints and according to the values of a middle-class economic liberal of his time, a kindly and generous man. He loved to walk, and this trait is one that this study has traced as rooted

---

[1] Katherine Burton, 'Memoir', pp. xl–xlii; NLS MS 9413, fol. 13; NLS MS 4257, fol. 125.

in a cleaving to romantic subjectivity; but it might be added that he also avoided riding or coach travel because he could never stand to see an animal whipped. His attitude to providing state assistance for the able-bodied poor was harsh from a modern viewpoint; on the other hand, he took a prominent, unremunerated role, in times when he himself had no secure income, to raise pauper children out of the cycle of poverty through the development of 'industrial' schooling. There is good evidence, for all his lecturing the working classes on the need to live within their means, that he did not manage money well, and the sale of the prized library of 'the Book-Hunter' late in life was almost certainly due to straitened circumstances, if not actual debt. This placed his second wife in a difficult position, and probably coloured the frank and critical picture she painted in her *Memoir* of her husband.[2]

Yet for most of their time at Craig House, Kate recalled a happy family life in a home that was loved 'as much as any home ever was loved'. Burton bought a small pony and trap, which allowed them in summer to make trips to the coast at Portobello to swim. There was a good deal of warmth and consideration in his familial relations through most of his life. He supported and encouraged the education of his children, male and female, and though Kate thought he did not 'manage' children well, he certainly loved them. He clearly felt deeply the loss of the infant girl who had died and been interred at Dalmeny, the family's move to the coast unable to prevent her decline; he was insistent that when his time came, he was to be buried beside her.[3]

And there indeed he lies, under a simple stone on the edge of the parish churchyard overlooking the Forth, together at the last with the only child he lost and eschewing forever the company of Jeffrey, Cockburn and the other Whig grandees, ostentatiously at rest in the New Town's Dean Cemetery, beneath their elaborate and monumental tombs.

---

[2] Hedderwick, *Backward Glances*, p. 107; Charles A. Cooper, *An Editor's Retrospect: Fifty Years of Newspaper Work* (London: Macmillan, 1896), pp. 319–24; NLS MS 4243, fol. 223; NLS MS 4403, fols 92–3; Masson, *Edinburgh Sketches*, pp. 380–3.

[3] Katherine Burton, 'Memoir', pp. lxvi, lvi.

Bibliography

MANUSCRIPT SOURCES

National Library of Scotland

Burton Archive: Mss 9391–5; 9398; 9402–3; 9406–7; 9409; 9412–13; 9415–16; 9418; 9426; 9428–9; 9430; 9445; 9983.

Blackwood Papers: Mss 4101; 4115; 4122; 4129; 4136; 4146; 4158; 4168; 4179; 4196; 4207; 4218; 4230; 4243; 4257; 4259; 4272; 4287; 4315; 4329; 4356; 4372; 4387; 4403.

Blackwood Ledgers: Mss 30860–30864.

NE.20.f.13: The first of two volumes described as 'Newspaper Cuttings of articles mainly by James and John Grant on Scottish Grievances under centralised government and on the formation and progress of the National Association of Scottish Rights; newspaper cuttings of the meetings of the Association with some of its publications and pamphlets' (1852–6).

PRIMARY PRINTED SOURCES

Aikman, James, *The History of Scotland, Translated from the Latin of George Buchanan; with Notes and a Continuation to the Present Time*, 6 vols (Edinburgh: Thomas Ireland, 1829).

Allardyce, Alexander, ed., *Letters from and to Charles Kirkpatrick Sharpe, Esq.*, 2 vols (Edinburgh: Blackwood, 1888).

[Allen, William Francis], 'Burton's History of Scotland', *The Nation* 19 (1874).

Anderson, Peter John, ed., *Fasti Academiae Mariscallanae Aberdonensis: [. . .]*, 3 vols (Aberdeen: Spalding Club, 1898).

[Anon], *A Collection of the Dying Testimonies of some Holy and Pious Christians [. . .]* (Kilmarnock: Calderwood, 1806).

[Anon], *A Directory for the City of Aberdeen and its Vicinity: 1829–30* (Aberdeen: Gordon, 1829).

[Anon], 'Memorabilia of the Month', *Aber M* 2 (1832).

[Anon], 'Burton's Life of David Hume', *Tait's* 13 n.s. (1846).

[Anon], *Catalogue of the highly interesting and valuable Collection [. . .] of the late Charles Kirkpatrick Sharpe [. . .]* (Edinburgh: Constable, 1851).
[Anon], *Catalogue of the Extensive and Valuable Library [. . .] and a portion of the Cabinet of Pictures of the late Charles Kirkpatrick Sharpe* (Edinburgh: Constable, 1852).
[Anon], *Address to the People of Scotland and Statement of Grievances* (Edinburgh: Johnstone and Hunter, 1853).
[Anon], 'The History of Scotland from the Revolution to the Extinction of the Last Jacobite Insurrection', *Ecl R* n.s. 7 (1854).
[Anon], 'The History of Scotland', *BQ* 46 (1867).
[Anon], 'Scotland from Agricola's Invasion to 1688', *Chamb J*, Series 4 v.4 (15 June 1867).
[Anon], 'Burton's History of Scotland', *LQ* 29 (1867–8).
[Anon], 'Scotland from Agricola's Invasion to 1688', *Chamb J*, Series 4 v.7 (1870).
[Anon], 'Burton's History of Scotland', *LQ* 35 (1871).
[Anon], 'Biographical Sketch', in Patrick Fraser Tytler, *The History of Scotland from the Accession of Alexander III. To the Union*, Vol. I (Edinburgh: Nimmo, 1882).
[Anon], 'Biographical Memoir', in Joseph Robertson, *Scottish Abbeys and Cathedrals* (Aberdeen: Wyllie, 1891).
[Anon], *General Index and Index of Illustrations to the Proceedings of the Society of Antiquaries of Scotland, Vols I–XXIV* (Edinburgh: SSA/Neill, 1892).
[Anon], *Original Letters relating to the Ecclesiastical Affairs of Scotland* (Edinburgh: Bannatyne Club, 1851).
[Aytoun, William Edmonston], 'Scotland since the Union', *BM* 74 (1853).
Baillie, Robert, *The Letters and Journals of Robert Baillie, A.M. [. . .]*, ed. David Laing, 3 vols (Edinburgh: Bannatyne Club/R. Ogle, 1841–2).
Bentham, Jeremy, *The Works of Jeremy Bentham, Now First Collected; under the Superintendence of his Executor, John Bowring*, 11 vols (Edinburgh: William Tait, 1838–43).
Bertram, James, *Some Memories of Books, Authors and Events* (London: Constable, 1893).
Billings, Robert William, *The Baronial and Ecclesiastical Antiquities of Scotland*, 4 vols (Edinburgh: Blackwood, 1845–52).
Boswell, James, *The Journal of a Tour to the Hebrides, with Samuel Johnson, LLD*, 3rd edn (London: Dilly, 1786).
Brodie, George, *A History of the British Empire, From the Accession of Charles I. to the Restoration; [. . .]*, 4 vols (Edinburgh: Bell & Bradfute, 1822).
Brown, Thomas, *Inquiry into the Relation of Cause and Effect*, 3rd edn (Edinburgh: Constable, 1818).
Brown, Thomas, *Lectures on the Philosophy of the Human Mind*, 4 vols (Edinburgh: Tait, 1820).
Burke, Edmund, *A Philosophical Enquiry into the Origin of our Ideas of the Sublime and Beautiful* (London: Dodsley, 1757).

[Burnett, George], 'Burton's History of Scotland: Celtic Scotland and Feudal Scotland', *MM* 16 (1867).
Burns, William, *The Scottish War of Independence: Its Antecedents and Effects*, 2 vols (Glasgow: James MacLehose, 1874).
[Burton, John Hill], 'Sayings and Doings in the Modern Athens: No. 1', *Aber M* 1 (1831).
[——], 'Sayings and Doings in the Modern Athens: No. 2', *Aber M* 2 (1832).
[——], 'Pitcairn's Criminal Trials in Scotland', *W Rev* 19 (1833).
[——], 'History of Scotland (Vol. V) By Patrick F. Tytler, Esq. F.A.S.', *Tait's* 1 n.s. (1834).
[——], 'Witchcraft in Scotland', *Tait's* 3 n.s. (1836).
[——], 'Tytler's History of Scotland (Vol. VI)', *Tait's* 4 n.s. (1837).
——, *A Manual of the Law of Scotland* (Edinburgh: Oliver & Boyd, 1839).
[——], 'Tytler's History of Scotland' (Vol. VII), *Tait's* 7 n.s. (1840).
[——], 'Tytler's History of Scotland' (Vol. VIII), *Tait's* 9 n.s. (1842).
——, ed., *Benthamiana, or, Select Extracts from the Works of Jeremy Bentham. With An Outline Of His Opinions on the Principle Subjects Discussed in his Works* (Edinburgh: William Tait, 1843).
——, *Introduction to the Study of the Works of Jeremy Bentham, by John Hill Burton, Advocate, One of the Editors of the Collected Edition* (Edinburgh: William Tait, 1843).
[——], 'Tytler's History of Scotland' (Vol. IX), *Tait's* 11 n.s. (1844).
——, *Life and Correspondence of David Hume: [. . .]*, 2 vols (Edinburgh: William Tait, 1846).
——, *Lives of Simon Lord Lovat, and Duncan Forbes of Culloden: From Original Sources* (London: Chapman and Hall, 1847).
[——], 'Celtic Clearings – Free Sites – Highland Passes', *ER* 86 (1847).
——, ed., *Letters of Eminent Persons Addressed to David Hume* (Edinburgh: Blackwood, 1849).
——, ed., *The Darien Papers: Being a Selection of Original Letters and Official Documents Relating to the Establishment of a Colony at Darien by the Company of Scotland Trading to Africa and the Indies, 1695–1700* (Edinburgh: Bannatyne Club, 1849).
——, *Political and Social Economy: Its Practical Application* (Edinburgh: Chambers, 1849).
[——], 'Sanitary Reform', *ER* 91 (1849–50).
[——], 'Baronial and Ecclesiastical Antiquities of Scotland', *BM* 68 (1850).
[——], 'Vestiges of the Ancient Inhabitants of Scotland', *BM* 69 (1851).
[——], 'The New Zealanders', *BM* 70 (1851).
——, *The Emigrant's Manual: Emigration in its Practical Application to Individuals and Communities* (Edinburgh: Chambers, 1851).
——, *Criminal Trials in Scotland*, 2 vols (London: Chapman and Hall, 1852).
[——], *Political Economy, for Use in Schools, and for Private Instruction. Chambers's Educational Course* (Edinburgh: Chambers, 1852).
[——], 'Ferguson the Plotter', *BM* 71 (1852).

——, *History of Scotland from the Revolution to the Extinction of the Last Jacobite Insurrection, 1689–1748*, 2 vols (London: Longmans, 1853).
[——], 'The Romans in Scotland', *BM* 74 (1853).
[——], 'Student Life in Scotland', *BM* 76 (1854).
[——], *Report on the Arrestment of Wages [. . .]* (London: House of Commons, 1854).
——, *Communism, From the Eighth Edition of the Encyclopedia Britannica* (Edinburgh: Neill & Company, 1854).
[——], 'France and Scotland', *NBR* 24 (1856).
[——], 'The Scot Abroad: The Man of Letters', *BM* 79 (1856).
[——], 'The Scot Abroad: The Man of Council', *BM* 80 (1856).
[——], 'The Scot Abroad: The Man of Art', *BM* 80 (1856).
[——], 'The Sculptured Stones of Scotland' *BM* 81 (1857).
[——], 'Our Convicts – Past and Present', *BM* 83 (1858).
[——], 'The Ballad Poetry of Scotland and of Ireland', BM 84 (1858).
[——], 'The Soldier and the Surgeon', *BM* 84 (1858).
[——], 'Mephitis and the Antidote', *BM* 85 (1859).
[——], 'The French on Queen Mary', *BM* 86 (1859).
——, ed., *The Autobiography of Dr. Alexander Carlyle of Inveresk 1722–1805* (Bristol: Thoemmes, 1990).
——, *The Book-Hunter etc.* (Blackwood, Edinburgh, 1862).
[——], 'The Scot in France', *BM* 92 (1862).
[——], 'The Frank in Scotland', *BM* 93 (1863).
——, *The Cairngorm Mountains* (Edinburgh and London: Blackwood, 1864).
——, *The Scot Abroad*, 2 vols (Edinburgh and London: Blackwood, 1864).
——, *A History of Scotland from Agricola's Invasion to the Revolution of 1688*, 7 vols (Edinburgh: Blackwood, 1867–70).
[——], 'The Legend of Tell and Rütli', *ER* 129 (1869).
[——], 'Veitch's Memoir of Hamilton', *ER* 131 (1870).
——, *The History of Scotland: From Agricola's Invasion to the Extinction of the Last Jacobite Insurrection, A New Edition Revised in Eight Volumes* (Edinburgh: Blackwood, 1873).
[——], 'Guizot's History of France', *ER* 140 (1874).
——, 'Life of Professor W. Spalding', in William Spalding, *A Letter on Shakespere's Authorship of The Two Noble Kinsmen*, new edn (London: Trübner, 1876).
——, *A History of the Reign of Queen Anne*, 3 vols (Edinburgh: Blackwood, 1880).
Burton, J. H. and Laing, David, eds, *Jacobite correspondence of the Atholl family, during the rebellion, M.DCC.XLV–M.DCC.XLVI. From the originals in the possession of James Erskine of Aberdona* (Edinburgh: Abbotsford Club, 1840).
Burton, Katherine, 'Memoir of the Author', in John Hill Burton, *The Book-Hunter*, new edn (Edinburgh: Blackwood, 1882).
Calderwood, David, *The History of the Kirk of Scotland*, ed. Reverend Thomas Thomson, 8 vols (Edinburgh: Wodrow Society, 1842–9).

Chambers, Robert, *Domestic Annals of Scotland: from the Reformation to the Revolution*, 2 vols (Edinburgh: Chambers, 1858).
——, *Vestiges of the Natural History of Creation and Other Evolutionary Writings*, ed. James A. Secord (Chicago: University of Chicago Press, 1994).
C[hambers], W[illiam], 'The Two Cities', *Chamb J* 9 n.s. (1848).
Chéruel, A, *Marie Stuart et Catherine de Médicis: Étude Historique sur les Relations de la France et de l'Écosse dans la Seconde Moitié du XVIe Siècle* (Paris: Hachette, 1858).
Combe, George, *The Constitution of Man considered in Relation to External Objects* (Edinburgh: Anderson, 1828).
Cockburn, Henry, *Life of Lord Jeffrey: with a Selection of his Correspondence*, 2 vols (Edinburgh: Black, 1852).
Cooper, Charles A., *An Editor's Retrospect: Fifty Years of Newspaper Work* (London: Macmillan, 1896).
Cooper, Thomas, ed., *Men of the Time: A Dictionary of Contemporaries [. . .]*, 8th edn (London: Routledge, 1872).
Cordiner, Charles, *Remarkable Ruins, and Romantic Prospects, of North Britain, with Ancient Monuments, and Singular Subjects of Natural History: the Engravings by Peter Mazell* (London: Mazell, 1788–95).
Crowe, Catherine, *The Seeress of Prevorst: Being Revelations Concerning the Inner-Life of Man, and the Inter-Diffusion of a World of Spirits in The One We Inhabit* (London: Moore, 1845).
Catherine Crowe, *The Night Side of Nature; Or, Ghosts and Ghost Seers*, 2 vols (London: Newby, 1848).
Dalrymple, David, *Annals of Scotland, from the Accession of Malcolm III to the Accession of the House of Stewart* (Edinburgh and London: Murray, 1776–9).
[Dalyell, J. G.], ed., *The Chronicles of Scotland, by Robert Lindsay of Pitscottie [. . .]*, 2 vols (Edinburgh: Constable, 1814).
De Foe, Daniel, *The History of the Union between England and Scotland, With A Collection of Original Papers Relating Thereto* (London: John Stockdale, 1786).
[Dennistoun, James], 'Burton's History of Scotland, from 1689 to 1748', *ER* 100 (1854).
Dove, P. Edward, *Romanism, Rationalism, and Protestantism, Viewed Historically in Relation to National Freedom and National Welfare* (Edinburgh: Shepherd and Elliot, 1855).
[Empson, William], 'Life and Correspondence of David Hume', *ER* 85 (1847).
Étienne, Louis, 'Historiens Modernes De L'Écosse: John Hill Burton', *Revue des Deux Mondes* 71 (1867).
[Fagan, H. S.], 'Burton's History of Scotland', *BQ* 53 (1871).
Findlay, John Ritchie, 'Personal Recollections', in *De Quincey and his Friends: [. . .]*, ed. Hogg (London: Samson Low, 1895).
[Fraser, Patrick], 'Tytler's History of Scotland', *NBR* 3 (1845).
[Fraser, Patrick], 'Mary Stuart and Her Times', *NBR* 4 (1845).

Fraser, Patrick, *Tytler's History of Scotland Examined* (Edinburgh: W. P. Kennedy, 1848).
[Froude, J. A.], 'History of Scotland, from the Revolution to the Extinction of the Last Jacobite Insurrection', *Fraser's Magazine* 48 (1853).
Galt, John, *The Provost* (Edinburgh: Foulis, 1913).
——, *The Spaewife; A Tale of the Scottish Chronicles*, 3 vols (Edinburgh: Oliver & Boyd, 1823).
Gordon, Mary, *'Christopher North': A Memoir of John Wilson compiled from Family Papers and Other Sources*, 2 vols (Edinburgh: Edmonston and Douglas, 1862).
Gow, Harry, ed., *Scotland Since the Union: Being a Reprint of an Article in 'Blackwood's Magazine' for September, 1853 By the Late William Edmonston Aytoun* (Perth: Cowan, 1891).
[Grant (née MacVicar), Anne], *Essays on the Superstitions of the Highlanders of Scotland: [. . .]*, 2 vols (London: Longman, 1811).
Grierson, J. M., *Records of the Scottish Volunteer Force* (Edinburgh and London: Blackwood, 1909).
Grub, George, ed., *Illustrations of the Topography and Antiquities of the Shires of Aberdeen and Banff: The First Volume*, 4 vols (Aberdeen: Spalding Club, 1869).
Guizot, Francois, *L'Histoire de France, depuis les temps les plus reculés jusqu'en 1789 [. . .]*, 5 vols (Paris: Hatchette, 1872–6).
Hedderwick, James, *Backward Glances: or, some Personal Recollections* (Edinburgh: Blackwood, 1891).
Hillyard, Brian, 'Moir, George', *Oxford DNB*.
Hogg, James, *The Private Memoirs and Confessions of a Justified Sinner*, ed. David Groves (Edinburgh: Canongate, 2008).
Hogg, James, ed., *De Quincey and his Friends: [. . .]* (London: Samson Low, 1895).
Storey, Graham, Tillotson, Katherine Mary, and Easson, Angus, eds, *The Letters of Charles Dickens: Volume Seven 1853–55*, Pilgrim Edition (Oxford: Clarendon, 1993).
Howell, T. B., ed., *A Complete Collection of State Trials [. . .]*, 34 vols (London: Longman, 1816–28).
Innes, Cosmo, ed., *The Acts of the Parliament of Scotland, I*, AD MC.XXIV–AD M.CCCC.XXIII (London: House of Commons, 1844).
——, ed., *Origines Parochiales Scotiae: The Antiquities Ecclesiastical and Territorial of the Parishes of Scotland*, 3 vols (Edinburgh: Lizars, 1851–5).
——, ed., *Fasti Aberdonenses: Selections from the Records of the University and King's College of Aberdeen 1494–1854* (Aberdeen: Spalding Club, 1854).
——, ed., *Munimenta Alme Universitatis Glasguensis: Records of the University of Glasgow From Its Foundation Till 1727*, 4 vols (Glasgow: Maitland Club, 1854).
——, *Scotland in the Middle Ages: Sketches of Early Scotch History and Social Progress* (Edinburgh: Edmonston and Douglas, 1860).

——, *Sketches of Early Scotch History and Social Progress: [. . .]* (Edinburgh: Edmonston and Douglas, 1861).
——, ed., *Facsimiles of the national manuscripts of Scotland: selected under the direction of the Right Honourable Sir William Gibson-Craig. Bart, Lord Clerk Register of Scotland and photozincographed by command of Her Majesty Queen Victoria*, 3 vols (Southampton: Ordnance Survey Office, 1867–72).
Irvine, Christopher, *Medicina Magnetica: or, The rare and wonderful Art of Curing by Sympathy: [. . .]* (Edinburgh, n.p., 1656).
Irving, David, *The History of Scotish [sic] Poetry by David Irving, LL.D.*, ed. John Aitken Carlyle, MD (Edinburgh: Edmonston and Douglas, 1861).
Jamieson, John, *An Etymological Dictionary of the Scottish Language: [. . .] and Supplement [. . .]* (Edinburgh: Creech/Tait, 1808/1825).
Japp, Alexander, 'Thomas De Quincey: His Friends and Associates', in *De Quincey and his Friends: [. . .]*, ed. James Hogg (London: Samson Low, 1895).
Kirkton, James, *The Secret and True History of the Church of Scotland, [. . .]*, ed. Charles Kirkpatrick Sharpe (Edinburgh: Ballantyne, 1817).
Knight, Richard Payne, *An Analytical Inquiry into the Principles of Taste* (London: Payne, 1805).
Knox, John, *The Works of John Knox*, ed. David Laing, 6 vols (Edinburgh: Bannatyne Club, 1846–64).
Laing, David, ed., *Select Remains of the Ancient Popular Poetry of Scotland* (Edinburgh: Laing, 1822).
——, ed., *A Compendious Edition of Psalms and Spiritual Songs, commonly known as 'The Gude and Godlie Ballates'* (Edinburgh: Paterson, 1868).
Laing, Malcolm, *The History of Scotland, from The Union of the Crowns [. . .]*, 2 vols (London: Cadell and Davies, 1800).
[Lake, William C.], 'Life and Correspondence of David Hume', *Q Rev* 78 (1846).
[Lancaster, Henry Hill], 'Burton's History of Scotland', *ER* 126 (1867).
[——], 'Burton's History of Scotland: Vols V, VI, VII', *ER* 134 (1871).
Lauder, Thomas Dick, *The Great Floods of August, 1829, in the Province of Moray and Adjoining Districts* (Elgin: Stewart, 1830).
[Laughton, J. K.], 'Burton's Reign of Queen Anne', *ER* 151 (1880).
Law, Robert, *Memorialls [sic]; or, The Memorable Things that fell out within this Island of Brittain [sic] from 1638 to 1684*, ed. Charles Kirkpatrick Sharpe (Edinburgh: Constable, 1818).
[Macaulay, Thomas Babington], 'History', *ER* 47 (1828).
MacGibbon, David, and Ross, Thomas, *The Castellated and Domestic Architecture of Scotland from the Twelfth to the Eighteenth Century*, 5 vols (Edinburgh: David Douglas, 1887–92).
MacIntosh, James, *A Discourse on the Study of the Law of Nature and of Nations; [. . .]*, 2nd edn (London: Cadell, 1799).
Maidment, James, *Scotish [sic] Ballads and Songs: Historical and Traditionary*, 2 vols (Edinburgh: Paterson, 1868).
Marshal, Ebenezer, *A History of the Union of Scotland and England* (Edinburgh: Peter Hill, 1799).

[Masson, David], 'The Union with England and Scottish Nationality', *NBR* 21 (1854).
——, *Edinburgh Sketches and Memories* (Edinburgh: Black, 1892).
——, *Memories of Two Cities: Edinburgh and Aberdeen* (Edinburgh: Oliphant, Anderson and Ferrier, 1911).
Michel, Francisque, ed., *Le Roman des Aventures de Fregus par Guillaume Le Clerc, Trouvère Du Treizième Siècle* (Edinburgh: Abbotsford Club, 1841).
——, *Les Écossais en France Les Francais en Écosse*, 2 vols (London: Trübner, 1862).
[Moir, George], 'Demonology and Witchcraft', *FQR* 6 (1830).
[Moncrieff, James], 'Life and Correspondence of David Hume', *NBR* 7 (1847).
Neaves, Charles, 'Opening Address', in *Proceedings of the Society of Antiquaries of Scotland,* III (Edinburgh: Neill, 1862).
[Oliphant, Margaret], 'The History of Scotland', *BM* 101 (1867).
[——], 'The Reign of Queen Anne', *BM* 127 (1880).
Pitcairn, Robert, *Criminal Trials in Scotland [. . .]*, 3 vols (Edinburgh: Bannatyne Club, 1833).
Porter, Mrs Gerald, *Annals of a Publishing House: John Blackwood* (Edinburgh and London: William Blackwood, 1898).
Rait, R. S., *The Universities of Aberdeen: A History* (Aberdeen: Bisset, 1895).
Rilliet, Albert, *Les Origines de la Confédération Suisse: Histoire et Légende* (Geneva and Bâle: H. George, 1868).
[R. N.], 'Life and Correspondence of David Hume', *W Rev* 46 (1846–7).
Robertson, William, *The History of Scotland during the Reigns of Queen Mary and of King James VI. till his Accession to the Crown of England [. . .]*, 15th edn, 3 vols (London: Cadell, 1797).
Rousseau, Jean-Jacques, *Émile*, transl. Barbara Foxley (London: Dent, 1993).
Row, John, *The History of the Kirk of Scotland [. . .]* (Edinburgh: Wodrow Society, 1842).
Scott, Walter, ed., *The Works of John Dryden*, 18 vols (London: Miller, 1808).
——, 'Introduction to a Legend of the Wars of Montrose', in *Introductions and Notes from The Magnum Opus: Waverley to A Legend of the Wars of Montrose*. The Edinburgh Edition of the Waverley Novels, eds J. H. Alexander with P. D. Garside and Claire Lamont (Edinburgh: Edinburgh University Press, 2012).
[——], 'Tytler's History of Scotland', *Q Rev* 41 (1829).
——, *Letters on Demonology and Witchcraft Addressed to J. G. Lockhart, Esq.* (London: John Murray, 1830).
——, *The Poetical Works of Sir Walter Scott*, ed. J. Logie Robertson, MA (London: Henry Frowde, 1894).
——, *The Tale of Old Mortality*, ed. Douglas Mack. The Edinburgh Edition of the Waverley Novels (Edinburgh: Edinburgh University Press, 1993).
——, *The Bride of Lammermoor*, ed. J. H. Alexander. The Edinburgh Edition of the Waverley Novels (Edinburgh: Edinburgh University Press, 1995).
[Shairp, J. C.], 'Celtic Scotland', *Q Rev* 135 (1873).

Shields, Michael, *Faithful Contendings displayed; [. . .] and kept in record by Mr Michael Shields* (Glasgow: John Bryce, 1780).
Smiles, Samuel, *Self-Help, With Illustrations of Character and Conduct* (London: Murray, 1859).
[Spalding, William], 'Recent Shakespearian Literature', *ER* 71 (1840).
[——], 'White's Scottish Historical Dramas', *ER* 84 (1846).
Stephen, William, *History of the Queen's Rifle Volunteer Brigade* (Edinburgh: Blackwood, 1881).
Stevenson, Robert Louis, *Catriona: A Sequel to 'Kidnapped'* (London: Cassell, 1893).
——, *Strange Case of Dr Jekyll and Mr Hyde* (London: Longman, 1886).
Stewart, Dugald, *Philosophical Essays* (Edinburgh: Constable, 1816).
Struthers, John, *The History of Scotland from The Union to the Abolition of the Heritable Jurisdictions in 1748*, 2 vols (Edinburgh: Blackie Fullarton, 1827).
Stuart, John, *Sculptured Stones of Scotland*, 2 vols (Aberdeen: Spalding Club, 1856–67).
Stuart, Robert, *Caledonia Romana: A Descriptive Account of the Roman Antiquities of Scotland*, 2nd edn, revised by David Thomson (Edinburgh: Sutherland and Knox, 1852).
[Teulet, Jean Baptiste Alexandre Théodore], ed., *Inventaire chronologique des documents relatifs à l'histoire d'Écosse conservés aux archives Du Royaume à Paris* (Edinburgh: Abbotsford Club, 1839).
——, *Papiers d'État, pièces et documents inédits ou peu connus relatifs à l'histoire d'Écosse au seizième siècle, tirés des bibliothèques et des archives de France, et publiés pour le Bannatyne-Club d'Edimbourg*, 3 vols (Edinburgh: Bannatyne Club, 1851–60).
Thomson, Thomas, ed., *The Acts of the Parliaments of Scotland II–XI* (London: House of Commons, 1814–24).
——, ed., *The Acts of the Lords Auditors of Causes and Complaints: AD M.CCCC.LXVI–AD M.CCCC.XCIV* (London, House of Commons, 1839).
——, ed., *The Acts of the Lords of Council in Civil Causes, AD M.CCCC.LXXVIII–AD M.CCCC.XCV* (London: House of Commons, 1839).
[Tucker, Thomas], *Report by Thomas Tucker upon the settlement of the revenues of excise and customs in Scotland, AD MDCLVI* (Edinburgh: Bannatyne Club, 1824).
[Tulloch, John], 'Burton's History of Scotland: Concluding Volumes', *BM* 109 (1871).
Turner, James, *Memoirs of his own Life and Times* (Edinburgh: Bannatyne Club, 1829).
Tytler, Patrick Fraser, *The History of Scotland from the Accession of Alexander III. To the Union*, 4 vols (Edinburgh: William Nimmo, 1882).
Veitch, John, *Memoir of Sir William Hamilton, Bart.: Professor of Logic and Metaphysics in the University of Edinburgh* (Edinburgh: Blackwood, 1869).

Wilson, Daniel, *The Archaeology and Prehistoric Annals of Scotland* (Edinburgh: Sutherland and Knox, 1851).
——, 'Anniversary Address', in *Proceedings of the Society of Antiquaries of Scotland: Sessions MDCCCL–MDCCCLIV* I (Edinburgh: Neill, 1855).
Wodrow, Robert, *The History of the Sufferings of the Church of Scotland [. . .]*, ed. the Reverend Robert Burns, 4 vols (Glasgow: Blackie, 1829–35).
——, *Analecta: or, Materials for a History of Remarkable Providences [. . .]*, 3 vols (Glasgow: Maitland Club, 1842–3).
Wright, Thomas, *The History of Scotland; from the Earliest Period to the Present Time*, 3 vols (London: London Printing Company, 1873–4).

SECONDARY PRINTED SOURCES

Alexander, J. H. et al., eds, *Introductions and Notes from The Magnum Opus:[. . .]* (Edinburgh: Edinburgh University Press, 2012).
Anderson, Benedict, *Imagined Communities: Reflections on the Origin and Spread of Nationalism*, revised edn (London: Verso, 1991).
Anderson, Robert, 'University History Teaching, National Identity and Unionism in Scotland, 1862–1914', *SHR* 91 (2012).
Anderson, Robert and Stuart Wallace, 'The Universities and National Identity in the Long Nineteenth Century c. 1830–1914', in *The Edinburgh History of Education in Scotland*, eds Robert Anderson, Mark Freeman and Lindsay Paterson (Edinburgh: Edinburgh University Press, 2015).
Anon, revised by John Cunliffe, 'Dove, Patrick Edward (1815–73), political theorist', in *ODNB*.
Aronsson, Peter, 'National Museums as Cultural Constitutions', in *National Museums and Nation-Building in Europe 1750–2010: Mobilization and Legitimacy, Continuity and Change*, ed. Peter Aronsson and Gabriella Elgenius (Abingdon: Routledge, 2015).
Aronsson, Peter and Elgenius, Gabriella, eds, *National Museums and Nation-Building in Europe 1750–2010: Mobilization and Legitimacy, Continuity and Change* (Abingdon: Routledge, 2015).
Ash, Marinell, *The Strange Death of Scottish History* (Edinburgh: Ramsay Head Press, 1980).
——, '"A Fine Genial Hearty Band": David Laing, Daniel Wilson and Scottish Archaeology', in *The Scottish Antiquarian Tradition: Essays to mark the bicentenary of the Society of Antiquaries of Scotland and its Museum, 1780–1980*, ed. A. S. Bell (Edinburgh: John Donald, 1981).
Barker, G. F. R., revised by H. J. Spencer, 'Rutherfurd [formerly Greenfield], Andrew, Lord Rutherfurd (1791–1854), judge and politician', in *ODNB*.
Bell, Alan, 'Cockburn in his correspondence', in *Lord Cockburn: A Bicentenary Commemoration, 1779–1979* (Edinburgh: Scottish Academic Press, 1979).
Bell, Barbara, 'The Nineteenth Century', in *A History of Scottish Theatre*, ed. Bill Findlay (Edinburgh: Polygon, 1998).

Berger, Stefan, with Conrad, Christoph, *The Past as History: National Identity and Historical Consciousness in Modern Europe* (Basingstoke: Palgrave Macmillan, 2015).
Boase, G. C., revised by Christopher Lloyd, 'Dennistoun, James, of Dennistoun', in *ODNB*.
Bolton, H. Philip, *Scott Dramatized* (London: Mansell, 1992).
Briggs, Asa, *Victorian People: A Reassessment of Persons and Themes, 1851–67* (Chicago: University of Chicago Press, 1972).
Broun, Dauvit, 'A Forgotten Anniversary: Hume Brown's History of Scotland, 1911', in *Writing a Small Nation's Past: Wales in Comparative Perspective, 1850–1950*, eds Neil Evans and Huw Pryce (Farnham: Ashgate, 2013).
Burnett, L. Andersson and Newby, A. G., 'Unionist Nationalism and the National Museum of Scotland, c. 1847–1866', in *Making National Museums: Setting the Frames*, eds P. Aronsson and M. Hillström (Linköping University Electronic Press, 2007).
Burns, J. H., 'Bentham and the Scots', *Journal of Bentham Studies* 7 (2004).
Patrick Cadell, 'Sharpe, Charles Kirkpatrick', in *ODNB*.
Cameron, Ewan A., *Impaled upon a Thistle: Scotland since 1880*. The New Edinburgh History of Scotland, Vol. 10 (Edinburgh: Edinburgh University Press, 2010).
Cameron, Kenneth J., 'William Weir and the Origins of the "Manchester League" in Scotland, 1833–39', *SHR* 58 (1979).
Caw, James L., *Scottish Painting Past and Present, 1620–1908* (Edinburgh: Jack, 1908).
Coleman, James J., *Remembering the Past in Nineteenth-Century Scotland: Commemoration, Nationality and Memory* (Edinburgh: Edinburgh University Press, 2014).
Craig, Cairns, *The Wealth of the Nation: Scotland, Culture and Independence* (Edinburgh: Edinburgh University Press, 2018).
——, 'Scott's Staging of the Nation', *Studies in Romanticism* 40 (2001).
Davie, George Elder, *The Democratic Intellect: Scotland and her Universities in the Nineteenth Century*, 3rd edn, ed. Murdo Macdonald (Edinburgh: Edinburgh University Press, 2013).
Debus, Allen G., *Chemistry and Medical Debate: Van Helmont to Boerhaave* (Canton: Watson, 2001).
De Laperrière, Charles Baile, ed., *The Royal Scottish Academy Exhibitors 1826–1990 [. . .]*, 4 vols (Calne: Hilmarton Manor Press, 1991).
De Quincey, Thomas, 'A Postscript to "On Murder Considered as One of the Fine Arts"', in *De Quincey on Murder*, ed. Robert Morrison (Oxford: Oxford University Press, 2009).
Desmond, Adrian, *The Politics of Evolution: Morphology, Medicine, and Reform in Radical London* (Chicago: University of Chicago Press, 1989).
Devine, Thomas Martin, *The Scottish Nation: A Modern History* (London: Penguin, 2012).

Devine, T. M., and Wormald, Jenny, 'Introduction', in *The Oxford Handbook of Modern Scottish History*, eds Devine and Wormald (Oxford: Oxford University Press, 2012).

Dixon, Thomas, *From Passions to Emotions: The Creation of a Secular Psychological Category* (Cambridge: Cambridge University Press, 2003).

Dixon, Thomas, 'Revolting against Reid: The Philosophy of Thomas Brown', in *Scottish Philosophy in the Nineteenth and Twentieth Centuries*, ed. Gordon Graham (Oxford: Oxford University Press, 2015),

Dugdale, Eric, 'Philoctetes', in *Brill's Companion to the Reception of Sophocles*, eds Rosanna Lauriola and Kyriakos N. Demetriou (Leiden: Brill, 2017).

Duncan, Ian, *Scott's Shadow: The Novel in Romantic Edinburgh*. Literature in History Series (Princeton: Princeton University Press, 2007).

Elgenius, Gabriella, 'National Museums as National Symbols', in *National Museums and Nation-Building in Europe 1750–2010: Mobilization and Legitimacy, Continuity and Change*, eds Peter Aronsson and Gabriella Elgenius (Abingdon: Routledge, 2015).

Esterhammer, Angela, 'John Galt's Fictional and Performative Worlds', in *The Edinburgh Companion to Scottish Romanticism*, ed. Murray Pittock (Edinburgh: Edinburgh University Press, 2011).

Ewan, Elizabeth, Innes, Sue, Reynolds, Sian and Pipes, Rose, *The Biographical Dictionary of Scottish Women: From the Earliest Times to 2004* (Edinburgh: Edinburgh University Press, 2006).

Ferguson, William, *Scotland 1689 to the Present*. Edinburgh History of Scotland IV (Edinburgh: Oliver & Boyd, 1968).

Ferguson, William, *The Identity of the Scottish Nation: An Historic Quest* (Edinburgh: Edinburgh University Press, 1998).

Findlay, Bill, ed., *A History of Scottish Theatre* (Edinburgh: Polygon, 1998).

Finkelstein, David, *The House of Blackwood: Author–Publisher Relations in the Victorian Era* (University Park: Pennsylvania State University Press, 2002).

Finlay, Richard J., *A Partnership for Good?: Scottish Politics and the Union since 1880* (Edinburgh: John Donald, 1997).

Fraser, W. Hamish, 'The Press', in *Aberdeen 1800–2000: A New History*, eds W. Hamish Fraser and Clive H. Lee (East Linton: Tuckwell Press, 2000).

Fry, Michael, *Patronage and Principle: A Political History of Scotland* (Aberdeen: Aberdeen University Press, 1991)

——, 'The Whig Interpretation of Scottish History', in *The Manufacture of Scottish History*, eds Ian Donnachie and Christopher Whatley. Determinations Series (Edinburgh: Polygon, 1992).

——, 'Burton, John Hill', in *ODNB*.

——, *A New Race of Men: Scotland 1815–1914* (Edinburgh: Birlinn, 2013).

Frye, Lowell T., 'W. and R. Chambers', in *British Literary Publishing Houses, 1820–1880*, eds Patricia J. Anderson and Jonathan Rose (Detroit and London: Gale, 1991).

Garbin, Lidia, '"Not fit to tie his brogues": Shakespeare and Scott', in *Shakespeare and Scotland*, eds Willy Maley and Andrew Murphy (Manchester: Manchester University Press, 2004).

Gauld, Alan, 'Colquhoun, John Campbell', *ODNB*.

Goudie, Lachlan, *The Story of Scottish Art* (London: Thames and Hudson, 2020).

Gow, Ian, 'Introduction', in *The Baronial and Ecclesiastical Antiquities of Scotland: Illustrated by Robert William Billings, Architect*, 2 vols (Edinburgh: Birlinn, 2008).

Graham, Gordon, 'Scottish Philosophy after the Enlightenment', in *Scottish Philosophy in the Nineteenth and Twentieth Centuries*, ed. Gordon Graham (Oxford: Oxford University Press, 2015).

Griffiths, Trevor, and Morton, Graeme, 'Introduction', in *The History of Everyday Life in Scotland, 1800–1900*, eds Trevor Griffiths and Graeme Morton (Edinburgh: Edinburgh University Press, 2010).

Hanham, H. J., *Scottish Nationalism* (London: Faber, 1969).

——, 'Editor's Introduction', in Henry Thomas Buckle, *On Scotland and the Scotch Intellect* (Chicago: University of Chicago Press, 1970).

Hay, Denys, 'The Historiographers Royal in England and Scotland', *SHR* 30 (1951).

Hill, Richard J., *Picturing Scotland through the Waverley Novels: Walter Scott and the Origins of the Victorian Illustrated Novel* (Abingdon: Routledge, 2016).

Hornstein, Katie, 'Just Violence: Jacques Callot's Grandes Misères et Malheurs de la Guerre', *Bulletin: The University of Michigan Museums of Art and Archaeology* 16 (2005).

Houghton, Walter E., ed., *The Wellesley Index to Victorian Periodicals: 1824–1900*, 5 vols (Toronto: University of Toronto Press, 1966).

Howsam, Leslie, *Past into Print: The Publishing of History in Britain, 1850–1950* (London: British Library, 2009).

Hutchison, I. C. G., *Industry, Reform and Empire: Scotland, 1790–1880*. New Edinburgh History of Scotland, Vol. 9 (Edinburgh: Edinburgh University Press, 2020).

——, *A Political History of Scotland, 1832–1924: Parties, Elections, and Issues* (Edinburgh, John Donald, 2003).

Irwin, David and Francina, *Scottish Painters at Home and Abroad: 1700–1900* (London: Faber, 1975).

Jessop, T. E., 'Some Misunderstandings of Hume', in *Hume*, ed. V. C. Chappell. Modern Studies in Philosophy series (London: Macmillan, 1966).

Johnson, Christopher, 'Historical Note', in Walter Scott, *The Abbot*, ed. Christopher Johnson (Edinburgh: Edinburgh University Press, 2000).

Jones, Catherine, 'History and Historiography', in *The Edinburgh Companion to Sir Walter Scott*, ed. Fiona Robertson (Edinburgh: Edinburgh University Press, 2012).

Jones, Naomi Lloyd, 'Liberalism, Scottish Nationalism and the Home Rule Crisis, c. 1886–93', *EHR* 129 (2014).
Kennedy, James C., 'Religion, Nation and European Representations of the Past', in *The Contested Nation: Ethnicity, Class, Religion and Gender in National Histories*, eds Stephan Berger and Chris Lorenz. Writing the Nation Series (Basingstoke: Palgrave Macmillan, 2008).
Kidd, Colin, *Subverting Scotland's Past: Scottish Whig Historians and the Creation of an Anglo-British Identity, 1689–c. 1830* (Cambridge: Cambridge University Press, 1993).
——, 'Race, Empire, and the Limits of Nineteenth-Century Scottish Nationhood', *Historical Journal* 46, No. 4 (2003).
——, 'The Strange Death of Scottish History Revisited: Constructions of the Past in Scotland, c. 1790–1914', *SHR* 86 (2007).
——, *Union and Unionisms: Political Thought in Scotland, 1500–2000* (Cambridge: Cambridge University Press, 2008)
Kromm, Jane, *The Art of Frenzy: Public Madness in the Visual Culture of Europe, 1500–1850* (London: Continuum, 2002).
McCracken-Flesher, Caroline, 'Walter Scott's Romanticism: A Theory of Performance', in *The Edinburgh Companion to Scottish Romanticism*, ed. Murray Pittock (Edinburgh: Edinburgh University Press, 2011).
MacDonald, Catriona M. M., 'Gender and Nationhood in Modern Scottish Historiography', in *The Oxford Handbook of Modern Scottish History*, eds T. M. Devine and Jenny Wormald (Oxford: Oxford University Press, 2012),
McGann, Jerome J., 'Walter Scott's Romantic Postmodernity', in *Scotland and the Borders of Romanticism* eds Leith Davis, Ian Duncan and Janet Sorensen (Cambridge: Cambridge University Press, 2004).
Mackie, Peter, 'The Foundation of the United Industrial School of Edinburgh: "A Bold Experiment"', *Innes Review* 39 (1988).
Macleod, Emma Vincent, 'Craig, Sir James Gibson, first baronet', *ODNB*.
Macmillan, Duncan, *Scottish Art: 1460–1990* (Edinburgh: Mainstream, 1990).
[Magnusson, Magnus, Moulton, Matthew J., Munro, William R., Stalker, Philip A., Terris, David et al.], *The Glorious Privilege: The History of the 'Scotsman'* (London: Nelson, 1967).
Marchal, Guy P., 'Medievalism, the Politics of Memory and Swiss National Identity', in *The Uses of the Middle Ages in Modern European States: History, Nationhood and the Search for Origins*, eds R. J. W. Evans and Guy P. Marchal. Writing the Nation Series (Basingstoke: Palgrave Macmillan, 2015).
Marsden, Richard, *Cosmo Innes and the Defence of Scotland's Past* c. 1825–75 (Farnham: Ashgate, 2014).
Mathieson, W. L., 'Hill Burton in Error', *SHR* I (1903).
Maver, Irene, 'Leisure and Culture: The Nineteenth Century', in *Aberdeen 1800–2000: A New History*, eds Hamish Fraser and Clive H. Lee (East Linton: Tuckwell Press, 2000).

Menikoff, Barry, *Narrating Scotland: The Imagination of Robert Louis Stevenson* (Columbia, SC: South Carolina Press, 2005).
Alison Milbank, 'Calvinist and Covenanter Gothic', in *Scottish Gothic: An Edinburgh Companion*, eds Carol Margaret Davison and Monica Germanà (Edinburgh: Edinburgh University Press, 2017).
Millar, A. H., revised by Robert Shiels, 'Neaves, Charles, Lord Neaves', in *ODNB*.
Millar, Gordon F., 'Murray, Sir John Archibald, Lord Murray', in *ODNB*.
Morrison, John, *Painting the Nation: Identity and Nationalism in Scottish Painting, 1800–1920* (Edinburgh: Edinburgh University Press, 2003).
Morrison, Robert, ed., *Thomas De Quincey on Murder* (Oxford: Oxford University Press, 2009).
——, *The English Opium-Eater: A Biography of Thomas De Quincey* (London: Weidenfeld and Nicolson, 2009).
Morrison, Robert, and Baldrick, Chris, eds, *Tales of Terror from Blackwood's Magazine* (Oxford: Oxford University Press, 1995).
Morton, Graeme, *Unionist Nationalism: Governing Urban Scotland, 1830–1860* (East Linton: Tuckwell Press, 1999).
——, 'Scotland is Britain: The Union and Unionist-Nationalism, 1807–1907', *Journal of Irish and Scottish Studies* 1 (2008).
——, 'Identity Out of Place', in *A History of Everyday Life in Nineteenth-Century Scotland, 1800 to 1900*, eds Trevor Griffiths and Graeme Morton (Edinburgh: Edinburgh University Press, 2010).
Mosch, Jan, 'Introduction', in *History and Drama: The Pan-European Tradition*, eds Joachim Kupper, Jan Mosch and Elena Penskaya (Boston: De Gruyter, 2019).
Murison, David, 'The Two Languages in Scott', in *Scott's Mind and Art*, ed. A. N. Jeffares (Edinburgh: Oliver and Boyd, 1969).
Nairn, Tom, *The Break-Up of Britain* (London: New Left Books, 1977).
Newby, Andrew G., '"A Mere Geographical Expression?" Scotland and Scottish Identity, c. 1890–1914', in *Region and State in Nineteenth-Century Europe: Nation-Building, Regional Identities and Separatism*, eds Joost Augusteijn and Eric Storm (Basingstoke: Palgrave Macmillan, 2012).
Page, Frederick, ed., *Byron: Poetical Works* (Oxford: Oxford University Press, 1970).
Paterson, Lindsay, *The Autonomy of Modern Scotland* (Edinburgh: Edinburgh University Press, 1994).
Perkins, Pam, 'Tait, William', in *ODNB*.
Pickard, Willis, *The Member for Scotland: A Life of Duncan Maclaren* (Edinburgh: John Donald, 2011).
Pittock, Murray, *Scottish Nationality* (Basingstoke: Palgrave, 2001).
Poulot, Dominique, and Wigley, Richard, 'The Birth of Heritage: le moment Guizot', *Oxford Art Journal* 11 (1988).
Rennie, Susan, 'The First Scottish "National" Dictionary: [. . .]', in *The Whole World in a Book: Dictionaries in the Nineteenth Century*, eds Sarah Ogilvie and Gabriella Safran (Oxford: Oxford University Press, 2020).

Rhodes, Neil, 'Shakespeare at St Andrews: Origins and Growth of a Tradition', in *Launch-Site for English Studies: Three Centuries of Literary Studies at the University of St Andrews*, ed. Robert Crawford (St Andrews: Verse, 1997).

Rigney, Ann, *The Afterlives of Walter Scott: Memory on the Move* (Oxford: Oxford University Press, 2017).

Robertson, Fiona, 'Gothic Scott', in *Scottish Gothic: An Edinburgh Companion*, eds Carol Margaret Davison and Monica Germanà (Edinburgh: Edinburgh University Press, 2017).

Royle, Trevor, *Crimea: The Great Crimean War 1854–1856* (London: Little, Brown, 1999).

Scott, W. W., 'Lindsay, Robert of Pitscottie', in *ODNB*.

Simcox, Geoffrey, 'The Wild Man's Return: The Enclosed Vision of Rousseau's Discourses', in *The Wild Man Within: An Image in Western Thought from the Renaissance to Romanticism*, eds Edward Dudley and Maximillian E. Novak (Pittsburgh: University of Pittsburgh Press, 1972).

Smith, Charles J., *Historic South Edinburgh*, 2 vols (Edinburgh: Charles Skilton, 1979).

Smith, G. G., revised by Sondra Miley Cooney, 'Masson, David Mather', in *ODNB*.

Smith, John S., 'The Growth of the City', in *Aberdeen 1800–2000: A New History*, eds W. Hamish Fraser and Clive H. Lee (East Linton: Tuckwell Press, 2000).

Stack, David, *Nature and Artifice: The Life and Thought of Thomas Hodgskin (1787–1869)* (Woodbridge: Royal Historical Society, 1998).

——, *Queen Victoria's Skull: George Combe and the Mid-Victorian Mind* (London: Hambledon Continuum, 2008).

Stevenson, R. B. K., 'The Museum, its Beginnings and its Development. Part II: The National Museum to 1954', in *The Scottish Antiquarian Tradition: Essays to mark the bicentenary of the Society of Antiquaries of Scotland 1780–1980*, ed. A. S. Bell (Edinburgh: John Donald, 1981).

Stewart-Robertson, J. C., 'Brown, Thomas', in *ODNB*.

Thomas, William, ed., *The Journals of Thomas Babington Macaulay*, 5 vols (London: Pickering and Chatto, 2008).

Thompson, Michael Welman, 'Wright, Thomas', in *ODNB*.

Townsend, Dabney, 'The Picturesque', *Journal of Aesthetics and Art Criticism* 55 (1997).

——, 'Dugald Stewart on Beauty and Taste', *The Monist*, 90 (2007).

Trevor-Roper, Hugh, 'The Invention of Tradition: The Highland Tradition of Scotland', in *The Invention of Tradition*, eds Eric Hobsbawm and Terence Ranger (Cambridge: Cambridge University Press, 1983).

Tyrrell, Alex, 'The Earl of Eglinton, Scottish Conservatism, and the National Association for the Vindication of Scottish Rights', *Historical Journal* 53 (2010).

Van Wyhe, John, 'Introduction', in *Combe's Constitution of Man considered in Relation to External Objects and Nineteenth-Century Responses*, ed. John van Whye, 3 vols (Bristol: Thoemmes, 2004).

Watkins, M. G., revised by Douglas Brown, 'James Grant', in ODNB.
Watson, Sheila, 'National Museums in Scotland', in *Building National Museums in Europe 1750–2010. Conference proceedings from EuNaMus, European National Museums: Identity Politics, the Uses of the Past and the European Citizen*, EuNaMus Report No. 1, eds Peter Aronsson and Gabriella Elgenius (Linköping University Electronic Press, 2011).
White, Hayden, 'The Forms of Wildness: Archaeology of an Idea', in *The Wild Man Within: An Image in Western Thought from the Renaissance to Romanticism*, eds Edward Dudley and Maximillian E. Novak (Pittsburgh: University of Pittsburgh Press, 1972).
Wyhe, John Van, ed., *Combe's Constitution of Man considered in Relation to External Objects and Nineteenth-Century Responses*, 3 vols (Bristol: Thoemmes, 2004).
——, 'Introduction', in Combe's *Constitution of Man considered in Relation to External Objects and Nineteenth-Century Responses*, Vol. 1, ed. Van Wyhe (Bristol: Thoemmes, 2004).
Wilkes, Joanne, 'Crowe [née Stevens], Catherine Ann', in ODNB.
Wilson, Claudine I., 'Francisque Michel and His Scottish Friends', *The Modern Language Review* 30 (1935).
Withrington, D. J., 'Aberdeen Antiquaries: the Founding of the Spalding Club in 1839', *Aberdeen University Review* 44 (1971).
Womersley, D. J., 'The Historical Writings of William Robertson', *Journal of the History of Ideas* 47 (1986).
Yeoman, L. A., 'Wodrow, Robert', in ODNB.
Zimmer, Oliver, 'Competing Memories of the Nation: Liberal Historians and the Reconstruction of the Swiss Past 1870–1900', *Past & Present* 168 (2000).

Web References

https//artuk.org/discover/artworks/the-signing-of-the-national-covenant-in-greyfriars-kirkyard-edinburgh-93072
https://dbcs.rutgers.edu/all-scholars/8508-allen-william-francis
www.ep.liu.se/ecp_home
http://hdl.handle.net/2027/spo.0054307.0016.102
https://www.nationalgalleries.org/search/artist/rev-john-thomson
https://www.nationalgalleries.org/search/artist/david-scott
https//www.nationalgalleries.org/search/artist/sir-william-allan
https//www.nationalgalleries.org/art-and-artists/134942/john-knox-admonishing-mary-queen-of-scots
https//www.nationalgalleries.org/art-and-artists/4837/porteous-mob

Index

Abbot, The (drama), 185
Abbot, The (Scott), 24, 121
Abbotsford Club, 1, 70, 88
Abercrombie, James, Lord
    Dunfermline, 47–8
Aberdeen, 27, 28, 33, 34, 42, 43, 44,
    119, 137, 150, 184, 223
  Gallowgate, 27
  Union Street, 35
Aberdeen Magazine, 33–4, 143
Aberdeen Herald, 49
Aberdeenshire, 29, 34, 64, 81, 161
Aberdeen University, 82; *see also*
    Marischal College
Absalom and Achitophel (Dryden),
    157
Acta Auditorum, 63
Acta Dominorum Consilii, 63
*Acts of the Parliaments of Scotland
    (APS)*, 74, 85–6, 222, 224
Act of Security, 207
Adams, James, 49
Adamson, Robert, 189
'Address to the People of Scotland,
    and Statement of Grievances'
    (NAVSR), 203
Admiral of Scotland, 153
*Adventures of Susan Hopley, or,
    Circumstantial Evidence,
    The* (Crowe), 53

Advocates' Company, Volunteer Rifle
    Militia, 66
Advocates Library, 23, 44, 50, 71, 130,
    146
Aesthetic theory, 29, 30, 37–41
Africa, 63–4
African explorers, 63
Agamemnon, the, 227
Aikman, James, 21, 199
Alexander III (of Scotland), 21, 218,
    219, 230, 240
Alison, Archibald, 31
Allan, William, Sir, 55, 56, 186–7, 192
Allen, William Francis, 215
Alma, the, 66
Alpine explorations, 60–1
Alps, 60–2
America, 59, 215, 217
Analecta (Wodrow), 157, 159–60, 168
'Ancient League' with France, 92, 93
Anderson, Benedict, 263–4
Anderson, Robert, 12
Anderson, Rowand, Sir 77
Anglican circumstances, 143
Anglo-Danish population of the
    Lothians, 231
Anglo-Saxon, 232
Anglo-Saxon Chronicle, 148
Anglo-Scottish Union, 103, 195, 212;
    see also Union of 1707

Annals (Wilson), 256
Annals of Scotland (Dalrymple), 21
Anti-christ(s), 131, 165
Anti-Corn Law League, 44
antiquarian (ism), 20, 40, 52, 69, 70, 72–3, 79–80, 90, 98, 144–5, 232–3
  and national history, 80–1
  and romanticism, 102
  see also Scottish Society of Antiquaries
Antiquary, The (Scott), 79, 232
APS (*Acts of the Parliaments of Scotland*), 62–3, 153–5; *see also* Scottish constitutional history
Aquinas, Thomas, 91
Arbroath (abbey), 84
archaeology, 72–3, 81–2, 161, 217, 243–5
Archaeology and Prehistoric Annals of Scotland (Wilson), 79
architecture, 270; *see also* Scottish architecture
Argyle, Earl of, 120
Argus (newspaper), 44, 49
Aristotle, 106
Arminius, 249
Arthur, 118
'Arthurian romance', 118–19
Ash, Marinell, 8–9, 11–12, 14, 16, 18, 263
assimilationist assumptions, 212–13, 213n35, 261–2
associationist theory, 30–2, 41
Athenaeum, 193
Attic tragedy, 185
'Augustan age of Scotland', 110
Australasia
  indigenous peoples, 68
'Author of Waverley', 115, 138, 145, 246; *see also* Scott, Walter, Sir
Autobiography (Alexander Carlyle), 110
Aytoun, William Edmonston, 23, 76, 200, 211

Bacon, Francis, 101
Baillie, Robert, 124
Balfour, James, of Pilrig, 108
Balfour, John, of Burley, 16
ballads 18, 23, 26, 29, 34, 44, 73, 122, 173, 225; *see also* Scots language; Scottish vernacular culture of Aberdeenshire, 161, 220
Ballads of Scotland, The (Aytoun), 130, 220
Baltic, 84
Bannatyne Club, 1, 51, 64, 70, 74, 88, 124, 151
Bannockburn (battle of), 202, 230
Barbour (John), 129
Baronial and Ecclesiastical Antiquities of Scotland (Billings), 77, 244
Bass Rock, 269
Beaton, David, Cardinal, 176
Beaton, James, Archbishop, 124
Beattie, James, 30–1
Beautiful, the, 37–8, 40
Beccaria (Cesare), 106
Begg, Rev. James, 210–11
Belgians, the, 242
Belhaven, John Hamilton, Lord, 205
Bellenden, Adam, Bishop of Dunblane, 124
Bellenden, John, 127
Ben Macdui, 62
Bentham, Jeremy, 1, 44, 57, 104–6, 108–11, 259
Benthamiana (Burton), 105
Benthamite(s), 104, 111; *see also* Philosophic Radicals
Berger, Stephan, 242–52
Bernese *Oberland*, 61
'Billings', 82, 220; *see also Baronial and Ecclesiastical Antiquities of Scotland*
Billings, Robert William, 76–7
Black, Adam, 47
Blackie, John Stuart, 33, 255

Blackwood, John, 63, 69, 74, 81, 96, 197, 214, 220–1
  support for Burton's *History*, 75–6
Blackwood, Mary, 75
Blackwood's Magazine, 1, 25, 33, 43, 54, 60, 62, 67, 73, 75, 82, 88, 95, 200, 214–15, 221, 234, 257
  and 'terror fiction', 161, 166
  Burton's reviews for, 152–3
Blackwood's publishing house, 2, 77, 239, 271
  publishing strategy, 221
  author-reader 'ecumene', 221, 266
  ledgers, 238
Blackwood, Robert, 75, 76
Blackwood, William, 63
Blake, William, 56
Blind Harry, 129
Board of Trade, 112
Boece, Hector, 17, 98, 119, 128, 147
Bologna, 88
'Bonnie Dundee', 21; *see also* Graham, John of Claverhouse
book clubs, 1, 3, 8, 23, 52, 70–1, 76–7, 88–9, 95–6, 124, 131, 144–5, 159, 206, 239, 245, 261, 267
'Book Club men', 81, 249
  interaction with European scholars, 88–9, 249–50
  see also book clubs
Book-Hunter, The (Burton), 1, 52, 54, 73, 79, 81, 144
Border hills, 59
Border Minstrelsy (Scott), 161
Boswell (James), 141
Bothwell (castle), 84
Bower, Walter, 98
Bowes (Robert), 117
Bowring, Sir John, 44, 104
Boyd, Andrew, 235
Bride of Lammermoor, The (drama), 185
Bride of Lammermoor, The (Scott Lauder), 187
Bride of Lammermoor, The (Scott), 105, 114, 149, 162
Bridge of Tummel, 36
British Empire, 5–6, 7, 15, 63, 67, 75, 195, 217, 248, 260, 264
British civil wars, 170
British Isles, 100
British legislature, 205–6
British state, 208, 298
British Union, 253, 260; *see also* Great Britain
Brodie, George, 9, 10, 21
Broun, Dauvit, 267
Brown, John, of Priesthill, 151, 244
Brown, Thomas, 31–2
Brown, Peter Hume, 211, 267
Bruce, Robert (King of Scots), 5, 7, 118–19, 178, 252
Bruis, The (Barbour), 119
Buchan, John, 269
Buchanan, George, 21, 29, 82, 91, 98, 101, 125, 128, 225
Buckle, Henry Thomas, 8, 10–11, 216, 223
Burke, Edmund, 40, 253
Burkeian aesthetic, 38, 40, 62
Burnett, George, 215, 224, 230
Burns, J. H., 109
Burns, Robert, 5, 7, 43, 23
  son of, 129
Burns, William, 230–1
Burton, Eliza, 59, 271; *see also* Paton, Elizabeth (Eliza)
Burton, John Hill, 6–8, 15, 18, 21, 22
  Book Club activities, 70–1
  character, 42, 271–2
  contemporary reputation, 193–4
  early education, 28–9
  early literary and intellectual circles, 33–4, 42–6
  familiarity with vernacular culture, 28–9, 138, 243–4, 265n10

influenced by Romantic literature
  and historiography, 137–43
  particularly Walter Scott, 128,
  137–8, 139, 144, 148, 151, 158,
  169, 192, 242–3, 246
influence on Robert Louis
  Stevenson, 267–9
later reputation, 2
principal publications on political
  economy, 111–12
radicalism, 44–6, 110–11
role in reform campaigns, 49, 65–7,
  110–12
role in the Society of Antiquaries,
  71–2
scholar of Bentham and Hume,
  31–2, 104–10
sensibility of the Picturesque, 34–42,
  143
subject matter of Blackwood
  publications, 76
Burton, Katherine (Kate), 59, 65, 66, 272
Burton, Mary, 28, 271
Burton, William Kinninmont, 28
Butterfield, Herbert, Sir, 263
Byron (George Gordon), Lord, 39

Cadyow Castle (Scott), 121
Cairngorm mountains, 27, 61–2, 63, 161
Cairngorm Mountains, The (Burton),
  60–2
Cairn o' Mount, 37
Calder Lynn, 37–8
Calderwood, David, 131
Caledonia Romana (Stuart), 79
Callander, 37–8
Callot, Jacques, 150, 170
'Calvinist and Covenanter Gothic'
  (Milbank), 170
Calvinist theology, 130
Cambridge Historical Series, 267
Cameron, Ewan, 11
Cameronian(s), 131
Carberry Hill (battle of), 93
Carlyle, Alexander, 110

Carlyle, Thomas, 11
Carmichael, William, 157
Carruthers, Robert, 47, 49
Cassandra, 52
Castelnau (Michel), Sieur de
  Mauvissière, 93
Castle Campbell, 37, 120
Castle of Towie, 122
Catholic League, 178
Cavalier troopers, 157
Cecil, William, Baron Burghley, 181
Celts/Celtic, 9, 19, 81, 204
  barbarism, 199
  civilisation, 229
  controversy on Scotland's racial
    origins, 100, 230–2
  mythology, 147
  origins of Picts, 98
  tales of the hero-kings, 118
'Celtic Scotland' (Shairp), 231
Chalmers, George, 9, 98
Chadwick, Edwin, 44, 66–7, 104–5,
  110–12
Chambers, Robert, 9, 44, 45–6, 159,
  237, 247, 254
Chambers, William, 198, 212
Chambers's Edinburgh Journal, 198,
  234, 239–40
*Chambers's Universal Biography of
  Eminent Scotsmen*, 44
Charlemagne, 91
Charles I (of Great Britain), 124, 180,
  182, 223
Charles II (of Great Britain), 13,
  153
Charles V (of Spain), 93
Chatham dockyard, 211
Chéruel, Pierre-Adolphe, 93
Chief Curator of the National Trust,
  77, 270n 21
Childe Harold (Byron), 39
Christomathea (Bentham), 105
'Christopher North', 33; *see also*
  Wilson, John
Clyde (river), 159, 230

Cockburn, Henry, Lord, 47–9, 56, 57, 65, 197–8, 272
Coldingham (abbey), 84
Coleman, James, 12–15, 211
Coleridge, Samuel Taylor, 33
Coliseum, 39
Collected Works (Bentham), 1, 44
Colquhoun, John, 164, 167
Combe, Cecilia, 45
Combe 'set', 45, 56
Combe, Andrew, Dr, 45, 254
Combe, George, 45–6, 56, 254
Commissioner Lauderdale, 182
'Communism' (Burton), 65
Compendious Edition of Psalms and Spiritual Songs [. . .] (Laing), 130
Complaynt of Scotland, The (Anon), 129
Confessions (Hogg), 169
conjectural history, 11, 99
Conrad, Christoph, 242–8
Conservative, 33, 47
Constable (publishers), 127
Constitution of Man (Combe), 46, 254
Continental museums, 72
Cook, John, 255
Cooper (Antony Ashley), Earl of Shaftesbury, 158
Corn Laws, 44
Corrieyairack Pass, 36
Cortes, Hernan, 68
Countess of Buchan, 118–19
Court of Chancery, 112
Court of Session, 16, 47, 80
  Principal Clerk of, 64
Covenant/covenanters, 13, 16, 132–4, 136, 156, 159, 170, 177, 182, 225, 268–9; *see also* National Covenant
Cox, Robert, 45
Craig, Cairns, 15
Craig House, 63, 69, 71, 75, 194, 271
Craiglockhart Hill, 56, 69, 194
Crimean War, 66–7, 260

Criminal Trials (Pitcairn), 162
Criminal Trials in Scotland (Burton), 268
Cromwell, Oliver, Lord Protector, 136
Cromwellian
  conquest of Scotland, 19
  Commonwealth, 102
  union 103
  general, 150
Crowe, Catherine, 45, 51–4, 167–8, 173
'culture of Blackwood', 220–1
Cunninghame, John, Lord, 48, 197
Cunninghame, Nina, Lady, 48
Cupar (Fife), 237

Dacre, Thomas, Lord, 124
Daily News (newspaper), 49
Dalgetty, Dugald, *Rittmeister*, 151
Dalmeny, 272
Dalrymple, David, Lord Hailes, 21, 22, 140
Dändliker, Karl, 251
Danish/Danes, 249
  archaeologists, 80; *see also* Museum of Antiquities in Copenhagen
Dante (Alighieri), 165
Darien Papers, The (Burton), 1, 70
Darien Scheme, 195, 201, 206–7
Dark Continent, 63
David II (of Scotland), 116
David Balfour (Stevenson), 268
Davie, G. E., 5–6, 11–12
Dawson, Adam, 235
Dean Cemetery, 272
Dean of the Faculty of Advocates, 16
Deans, Jeannie, 130
Death of John Brown of Priesthill (Duncan), 188
Death-Song of Lodbroc, The, 147
Defoe, Daniel, 199
De Quincey, Thomas, 43, 51, 53–5, 62, 165–8, 169, 172–3
Denmark, 245

Dennistoun, James, of Dennistoun, 56, 206
Derby, Lord, 80
Detectio (Buchanan), 153
Devine, T. M. (Thomas Martin), Sir, 5, 7
Dickens, Charles, 53
Die Seherin von Prevorst (Kerner), 167
Dirleton (castle), 84
Disruption, the, 13–14, 109, 205–6, 212
Doane, Richard, 105
Domestic Annals of Scotland (Chambers), 247
Don (river), 27
Don Quixote (Cervantes), 68
doppelgänger, 156, 167, 269
'Doric, the', 28; *see also* Scots Language
Douglas, Gavin, 18
Douglas, James, Earl of Morton, 117, 176, 228
Douglas, Willy, 121
Dove, Patrick Edward, 210–11
Dr Dryasdust, 125, 224
Drumclog (battle of), 133
Drury Lane, 181
Duke of Châtellerault, 120; *see also* Hamilton, James, Earl of Arran
Dunbar (battle of), 136
Dunbar (castle), 120
Dunbar, William, 18, 130
Duncan, Ian, 263, 266
Duncan Institute, 237
Duncan, Thomas, 187
'Dundas Despotism', 47
Dundee, 51, 150, 223
  Thester Row, 150
Dunfermline (abbey), 84
Dunottar Castle, 151
Duns Scotus, John, 90
Druid(ism), 21, 98, 216
Drummond, James, 188
Drummond, Margaret, Lady 174
Dyce, 27

East Lothian coast, 268
Eastwood, 159–60
Edinburgh, 41, 43, 44, 45, 53, 54, 65, 68, 104, 163, 184, 192, 223
  Burgh Muir, 69
  Caledonian (theatre), 185
  Castle, 69, 155
  Darnaway Street, 168
  Grassmarket, 42, 188
  Greyfriars' Churchyard, 177, 188, 225, 244
  Hermitage of Braid, 194
  Keir Street, 69
  landscape-art, 177, 188, 244
  Lauriston Place, 66, 69
  Manor Place, 43
  Mary's Place, Stockbridge, 56
  Morningside, 69
  New Town, 42, 69, 272
  Old Town, 42, 69
  polite society, 51, 54, 55
  political world, 197–8
  post-Enlightenment, 161, 164–5, 260, 266
  Princes Street, 42, 262
  Princes Street Gardens, 51
  Queen Street, 262
  radical circles, 175–6
  Theatre Royal, 185
  theatrical *tableaux,* 189
  West Port, 42
Edinburgh Blackwoodians, 34
Edinburgh Castle (Nasmyth), 188
Edinburgh Philosophical Institution, 211
Edinburgh Review, 48, 66, 184, 194, 200, 215, 223, 228
Edinburgh Shakspearian [*sic*] Club, 184
Edinburgh University, 33, 42
  Professor of Civil/Constitutional History, 65
  Professor of Moral Philosophy, 33
  Professor of Rhetoric and Belles-Lettres, 24, 200, 203
  Philosophy chair, 146
  Course of Law and History, 268

Edinburgh Young Men's Christian Association, 236–7
Edward I (of England), 99–100, 103, 118, 177
Effie (Deans), 131
'Eglinton Tournament', 210
Eleanor (Queen of England), 119, 177
Elgin Cathedral, 35, 39, 40
Elgin Chapter House, 76
Elizabeth I (of England), 117, 178, 180
Elizabethan courts, 117
Elizabethan state, 122–3, 181
Ellen's Isle, 37
Emerson, Ralph Waldo, 172
Emigrant's Manual, The (Burton), 111
Émile (J.-J. Rousseau), 28
Encyclopaedia Britannica (Eighth Edition), 65
England, 22, 56, 69, 85, 86, 110, 123–4, 128, 147, 178, 195, 215, 222, 240
  its history an 'unbroken evolution', 10
English Bible, 130
English
  architect, 234
  constitutional liberties, 223
  historiography, 228
  national character, 196, 202
  law, 197
  universities, 82
English statesmen, 50, 205, 223
Enlightenment, 15, 23, 83, 144
  scepticism, 264, 266
  see also Scottish Enlightenment
Enquiry concerning the Principles of Morals (Hume), 108
Entrance of Prince Charles into Edinburgh after the Battle of Prestonpans (Duncan), 55
Episcopalian(ism), 16, 17, 64, 71, 83, 156, 169, 182
Essays (Hume), 106
Established Church of Scotland, 109, 237; *see also* Scottish Church, Presbyterian(ism)

Estates (of Scotland), 9, 86, 102, 222, 235; *see also* Scottish constitutional history; Scottish Law/legal system
Étienne, Louis, 240
Etymology, 98
Ethno-symbolism, 7
Europe(an), 15, 22, 25, 64, 65, 73, 76, 77, 87–94, 153, 170, 201, 213, 229, 252, 255, 258
  archives, 88–90, 96, 261
  constituents of national identity: national histories, 242–6, 248–9; history and art museums, 262; middling elites, print capitalism and vernacular culture, 264–6; *see also* Scottish national identity
  rise of nationalisms, 208, 212, 242
  universities tradition, 82, 88, 221
  influence of Franco-Scottish Alliance, 76, 88
Euston Station, 68
Examiner (newspaper), 49

Faculty of Advocates, 16
Fahn, the, 62
Fair Maid of Perth, The (Scott Lauder), 187
Fast Castle, 149–50, 244
Fast Castle from Below (Thomson), 149–50
Fates, the, 104
Faustian relation, 155, 158
Ferguson, Robert, 'the Plotter', 153–4, 158–9
Ferguson, William, 19, 209
Fettercairn, 147, 161
Fife peasants, 157
Findhorn (river), 39
Findlay, John Ritchie, 45, 48–9, 54, 165, 240
Finella, 147, 161
Fingal, 118
Finkelstein, David, 221, 266
Finlay, Richard J., 5, 7

'First Covenant', 131, 133; see also Covenant/covenanters
'Fitzpatrick Smart', 52; see also Sharpe, Charles Kirkpatrick
Fletcher, Andrew, of Saltoun, 103–4, 201–2
Flodden (battle of), 93, 123, 148, 164
folklore, 5, 24, 73, 170, 243–4, 260, 269; see also Scottish vernacular culture; superstitions; ballads
fourth estate, 49
Fontblanque, Albany, 49
Forbes, Duncan, of Culloden, 1, 70, 159
Fordun, John of, 98, 147
Forster, John, 49
Fort Augustus, 36
Forth (Firth of), 69, 120, 136, 149, 230, 272
Fortingall, 36
Fortunes of Nigel, The (drama), 185
Fortunes of Nigel, The (Scott), 142, 185
Fotheringhay, 180, 190
Foundation Stone (of National Gallery), 56, 261
Foyers (river), 38
France, 45, 58, 66, 91, 119, 215, 270
  Franco-Scottish alliance, 76; see also 'Ancient League' with France
Francis II (of France), 93
Fraser, Patrick, Lord, 16–19, 24, 243
Fraser, Simon, Lord Lovat, 70, 159
Free Church of Scotland, 11, 16, 203
Freechurchman, 236
Freeman, Edward, 76, 194
Free Trade, 49, 254
French
  Encyclopaedism, 110
  Huguenots, 248
  knights, 88, 153
  medieval world, 270
  nationality, 256
  naturalist thinkers, 254
  records scholars, 88–94
  Revolution, 243, 252–3

Froissart (Jean), 123, 174
Froude, James Antony, 135, 144, 156–7, 194, 207, 226–7
Fry, Michael, 8, 10

Gaelic, 126, 230
  language, 232
  scholarship, 161
Gaels, 126, 230
Galt, John, 25, 115, 138–9, 162–3, 170
Gaul, 104
Geddes, Patrick, 11
Gellner, Ernest, 263
General Assembly of 1638, 177, 223
General Board of Health, 66–7
Geoffroy, Étienne, 254
Gerard, Alexander, 29, 31
German
  idealist thought, 255
  legend of 'bottle imp', 158
  phrenological theory, 45
  psycho-spiritualist writers, 167
  romantic literature, 24–5
  romantic movement, 164
German lands, 247
Gibbon (Edward), 113
Gibson-Craig, J. T., 64
Gibson-Craig, James, Sir, 48
Gibson-Craig, William, Sir, 197
Gillies, R. P., 43
Glasgow, 159
  Cathedral, 177, 223, 225
  Theatre Royal, 191
  University, 82
Glasgow Argus, 44, 49
Glasgow Citizen, 49
Glen Lui, 62
Glorious Revolution (of 1689), 12, 133, 151, 183
Godolphin's gold, 104
Goethe (Johann Wolfgang von), 167
Goodall, William, 98
Gordons, 122

Gothic
  architecture, 84–5
  church of the Friary (Edinburgh), 177
  literary traditions, 24–5, 149–50, 157, 161–70; see also 'Calvinist and Covenanter Gothic'
  Scottish, 162
  sculptors, 172
  see also Supernatural, the
Gow, Ian, 77
Gowrie Conspiracy, 25, 148–9, 175, 176, 178, 185, 226
Graeme, Roland, 121
Graham, H. G., 10
Graham, James, Marquis of Montrose, 21, 150, 225
Graham, John, of Claverhouse, Viscount Dundee, 21, 151
Graham, Robert, Sir, 152, 162
Grand Cyrus, 52
Grandholm House, 27–8
Grant, Ann, of Laggan, 36, 39
Grant, James (antiquarian), 98
Grant, James (novelist), 200, 210–11
Grant, John, 200
Great Britain, 72, 201, 204
  as 'organic Union', 174
  idea of, 260
Great Moray Floods, 35, 58
Green, J. R., 76
Greek (language), 30
Greek tragedy, 227
Greenock Philosophical Society, 238
Grey Mare's Tail, 59
Grindelwald, 61
Grub, George, 33, 70
Guizot, Francois, 194, 270
Guy Mannering (drama), 185
Guy Mannering (Scott Lauder), 187

Habsburg tyranny, 172
Hamilton, James, of Bothwellhaugh, 121, 225
Hamilton, James, Earl of Arran, 117, 183
Hamilton, John, Lord Belhaven, 205
Hamilton, Robert, 133
Hamilton, William, Sir, 43–6, 57, 163–4, 167, 211
  his inner circle, 43–4, 171, 173
Hanham, H. J., 203
Hanse(atic), 84, 91
Harlaw, battle of, 231
Harz (mountains), 147
Heart of Midlothian, The (drama), 185
Heart of Midlothian, The (Scott), 130
Heart of Midlothian, The (Scott Lauder), 187
Hedderwick, James, 45, 49, 55
Henrician state, 123
Henry VIII (of England), 128, 129
Henryson (Robert), 130
Hepburn, James, Earl of Bothwell, 120, 153–5, 175, 179
Heriot's Hospital, 42, 69, 234
Heritage
  national cultural, 161–2, 270
  of sculptured stones, 81
  of the 'second language of Scotland', 130
  Scottish medieval, 83
  see also Scottish national identity
Hickson, W. E., 111
Highlands (of Scotland), 18, 35, 58, 61, 119, 126, 235, 269
Highlandism, 5, 7, 60, 263
Highland mania, 230; see also Highlandism
Highlanders, 152, 201, 231, 268
Hill, D. O., 189
Hilty, Karl, 251
'Historian of France, the', 194; see also Guizot, Francois
'Historian of Scotland, the', 194, 238; see also Burton, John Hill
Historie and Chronicles of Scotland (Pitscottie), 127
'Historiens Modernes de L'Écosse: John Hill Burton' (Étienne), 240
Historiographer Royal for Scotland, 193

historiography, 106–7
　modern, of nineteenth-century Scotland, 5–15, 263
　nineteenth-century whig, 10–11, 15, 19, 22, 79, 199, 228–9, 234, 246, 248, 259; *see also* teutonism
　nineteenth-century presbyterian, 12–15, 211
　nineteenth-century romantic, 22–3, 137–45, 236, 242–54
　see also national histories; history of the people
History of Civilization in England: On Scotland and the Scotch Intellect (Buckle), 8, 10
History of England (Hume), 18, 107
History of England (Macaulay), 22, 69, 194, 227
History of the Kirk (Calderwood), 131
History of the Kirk (Row), 131
history of the people, 18–19, 107, 142, 247, 269
history of publishing, 238
History of the Reformation in Scotland (Knox), 124–5, 128, 131–2
History of the Reign of Queen Anne, A (Burton), 193, 268
　reception, 194
History of Scotland (Hume Brown), 267
History of Scotland (Pinkerton), 128
History of Scotland (Robertson), 21, 233, 244
History of Scotland (Struthers), 21
History of Scotland (Tytler), 6, 8, 16–19, 21, 139–40, 216, 217, 219, 239, 243, 255
History of Scotland from Agricola's Invasion to the Extinction of the Last Jacobite Insurrection (Burton), 2–3, 26, 60, 69, 75, 81–3, 96, 106–7, 112–14, 232, 266–7
　as gothic history, 146–60
　as national history, 240–58
　as utilitarian history, 100–4
　as romantic history, 115–37
　as theatre, 174–84
　contemporary reception, 3–4, 19–20, 214–40
　later influence of, 267–70
　narrative structure, 220
　re-assessment of medieval Scotland, 76, 83–8
　Scotland's European-wide significance, 76, 89–94, 248
　use of continental records, 92–4
History of Scotland from Agricola's Invasion to the Revolution (Burton), 2, 75, 234
History of Scotland from the Revolution to the Extinction of the Last Jacobite Insurrection (1689–1748) (Burton), 2, 50, 102, 260–1
　contemporary reception, 4, 195–207
History of Scotish [sic] Poetry (Irving), 130
History of the Sufferings of the Church [. . .] (Wodrow), 132, 134, 159
History of the Union between Scotland and England [. . .] (Defoe), 199
Hogarth (William), 40
Hogg, James, 25, 43, 62, 170
Hogg, James (son of the novelist), 53, 165
Holland, 91
Homeric literature, 118
Home Secretaries, 197
Hood, Robin, 250
Household Words, 53
Howard, Thomas, Duke of Norfolk, 181
Hubert, Nicholas, 175
Hume, Baron David, 106
Hume, David, 1, 18, 30–2, 106–10, 113, 140, 141–2, 190, 247, 255, 259, 266, 269
Hume Brown, Peter, 10, 211, 267
Hundred Years War, 91, 93

Huntly, 35
Huntly Castle, 76
Hutcheson, Francis, 108
Hutchison, I. G. C., 209
Hyde, Edward, Earl of Clarendon, 141–2

impartiality, 14, 16, 18, 24, 26, 106, 216–17, 226, 227, 233, 267
Imperial capital, 232; see also London
Imperial project, 177; see also British Empire
India, 265, 271
Indian Mutiny, 66–7
Indian 'race', 67
Industrial Museum of Scotland, 261
'industrial' schooling, 49, 272
Inkerman, 66
Innes, Cosmo, 23, 59, 64–5, 69, 70–4, 82, 83–4, 85, 86, 89, 95, 144, 217, 221
Innes, Father Thomas, 232
Introduction to the Study of the Works of Jeremy Bentham (Burton), 105
'invented tradition', 250
Invention of Tradition, The (Hobsbawm and Ranger), 263
Inverness, 35
Inverness Courier, 49
Iona, 81
Ireland, 151
Irish Home Rule, 212
Irvine, Christopher, 163
Irving, David, 88
Italian-Renaissance façade, 261
Italy, 188

Jacobean courts, 117
    pageants, 181–2
Jacobite Correspondence of the Atholl Family (Burton), 1
Jacobite/Jacobitism, 10, 14, 70, 159, 269
    Risings, 144, 195–6, 199, 206–7

James II (of Great Britain), 108, 112, 128, 153, 158, 183
James I (of Scotland), 85, 127, 148, 152, 162
James II (of Scotland), 97
James III (of Scotland), 116
James IV (of Scotland), 123, 128, 148, 174, 175
James V (of Scotland), 128, 185
James VI (of Scotland), 21, 22, 25, 69, 101, 117, 120, 132, 148–9, 176, 183, 185
Jamieson, John, 23, 146
Jason, 179
Jedburgh (abbey), 84
Jeffrey, Francis, Lord, 31, 46, 47, 51, 54, 57, 62, 272
Johnston, Arthur, 29
'July Monarchy', 270
Jones, Inigo, 234
Jungfrau, 61
Junior Lord of the Treasury, 197
'Justice to Scotland', 72, 200, 202, 208

kailyards, 'historical', 8, 11, 263
Kames (Henry Home), Lord, 31, 38
'Kant's 'Metaphysic of Ethics', 43
Kelso (abbey), 84–5
Kenilworth, 117
Kerner, Justinus, 167
Kidd, Colin, 8, 12, 13, 19, 203, 212
Kidnapped (Stevenson), 268–9
Kildrummie (castle), 84
Killin, 37–8
Killing Times, 25, 133, 151, 156, 170
King John (Shakespeare), 180
Kinneil, 120
Kircher, Athanasius, 171
Kirkcaldy, William, Sir, of Grange, 126, 155–6, 158
Knight, Richard Payne, 30, 32, 38, 40
Knight, William, 30

Knox Admonishing Mary Queen of Scots (Allan), 186
Knox, John, 16–18, 125–6, 156, 175, 176, 186, 225, 228, 244, 252

Lady of the Lake, The (Scott), 37, 38, 148
Laggan, 38–9
Laing, David, 52, 70, 73, 88
Laing, Malcolm, 9, 21, 22, 199, 255
Lake Poets, 33, 43
Lamarck, Jean-Baptiste, 254
Lancaster, Henry Hill, 215–16, 218, 223, 225
Langside (battle of), 109, 156, 171, 225, 248
Lapraik, Tod, 269
Lasswade, 54, 165
Latin, 29, 30
 civilisation, 100
Laud, William, Archbishop, 156, 182
Lauder, David, Captain, 50
Lauder, Isabella, 50–1, 58–9, 60, 64
Lauder, Robert Scott, 55, 187–8
Lauterbrunnen, 61
Le Croc (Philibert du), 93
Lectures on the Philosophy of the Human Mind (Brown), 31
le moment Guizot, 270; see also Heritage
Legend of the Wars of Montrose (Scott), 151
Les Écossais en France, Les Français en Écosse (Michel), 89
Les Grandes Misères de la Guerre (Callot), 150; see also Miseries of War
'Les Tableaux Vivans', 132; see also theatrical *tableaux*
Leith, 149
Leslie, John, Bishop, 181
Leslie, David, General, 136
Letters and Journals (Baillie), 131

Letters of Eminent Persons addressed to David Hume (Burton), 110
Letters on Demonology (Scott), 162
L'Histoire de France (Guizot), 194, 256, 270
Life and Correspondence of David Hume (Burton), 50, 106–10, 260
 reception, 109–10
Liberal hegemony, 5
Life of Jeffrey (Cockburn), 56
Lindsay, David, Sir, 18, 130
Lindsay, Robert, of Pitscottie, 127–8, 148, 153
Linlithgow, 237
Lives of Simon Lord Lovat, and Duncan Forbes of Culloden: From Original Sources (Burton), 1
Lloyd-Jones, Naomi, 209–10
Loch Avon, 62
Lochearnhead, 38, 39
Loch Katrine, 37, 62
Lochleven Castle, 120, 121, 125, 225
Loch Lubnaig, 40
Loch Ness, 35
Loch Tay, 36–8
Lockhart, J. G., 33, 43, 192, 255
Logan, Robert, of Restalrig, 149
London, 29, 45, 49, 55, 59, 76, 182–3, 195–7, 240, 245, 264–5
Long Parliament, 141, 223
Lord Advocate, 47–8, 50, 77, 197, 202, 236
Lords of the Articles, 86; see also Estates of Scotland
Lords of the Congregation, 94
Lord of the Isles, 116
Lord Provost (of Edinburgh), 45
Louis Phillipe (King of France), 58, 270
Love, John, 238
Lowland Scots, 126, 231

Macaulay, Hannah, 68
Macaulay, Margaret, 68

Macaulay, Thomas Babington, Lord, 10, 68–9, 113, 140–3, 194, 247
Macbeth, 25, 147
Macbeth (Shakespeare), 147
McCrie, Thomas, 255
McCrie, Thomas (the younger), 16
McCulloch, J. R., 111
MacDonald, Catriona, 12
Macdonald, Laurence, 42
Machiavelli, 155
Mackintosh, Charles Rennie, 11
Mackintosh, James, 10
Mackintosh, Sir James, 253
MacGibbon (David) and Ross (Thomas), 78
MacGregors' predatory activities, 268
Maclaren, Charles, 45, 55, 56, 235
McLaren, Duncan, 45, 47, 197, 211
MacMillan, Alexander, 76
Macmillan's Magazine, 215
Macpherson (James), 118
Magus Muir, 25, 156
Maidment, James, 122
Maitland Club, 74, 82, 87, 157
Maitland, William, of Lethington, 101, 155–6, 158, 180, 225
'makars', medieval Scots, 23
Malcolm III (of Scotland), 100; see also Malcolm Canmore
Malcolm Canmore, king of Scots, 218, 230, 232
Manfred (Byron), 39
Manichean view, 170
Manual of the Law of Scotland (Burton), 1, 47
Manufacture of Scottish History, The, 10
Marischal College, 29, 31–3, 39
  Professor of Natural History, 30
Marmion (Scott), 128, 161
Marquis of Hamilton, 124
Marsden, Richard, 23, 83
Marshal, Rev. Ebenezer, 199

Mary Stuart, Queen of Scots, 14, 17, 21, 22, 93–4, 117, 121–2, 125–6, 129, 132, 153–6, 175, 178–81, 190, 216, 225, 227–8, 234, 244, 252; *see also* Queen Mary
Mary Queen of Scots Receiving the Warrant of her Execution (D. Scott), 187
Masson, David, 29, 30, 52, 203, 211
Mathieson, W. L., 2, 267
Maule, Fox, 197
Mazzini, Giuseppe, 211
Mechanics' Institute, 237–8
Medea, The (Euripides), 179
Medici, Catherine de, 93
Melrose Abbey, 76, 86
Melville, Andrew, 132
Melvin, James, 29
Memoir (Katherine Burton), 272
Memoirs (of his Own Life and Times) (Turner), 151
Memorialls (Law), 168
Mephistopheles, 156
Mephistolean pact, 269
Michel, Francisque, 88–9, 91–2, 217, 249
Mill, John Stuart, 105, 111
'Miseries of War' (Callot), 170
Mitchell, James, 157, 169
'Modern Athens', 55; *see also* Edinburgh
Moir, George, 24–5, 43, 164
Monadhliath range, 36
Monastery, The (Scott), 24
Moncrieff, James, Lord, 48, 236
Monk, George, General, 150
Monkbarns, Laird of, 98, 230
Monmouth conspiracy, 158
Montgomerie, Archibald, Earl of Eglinton, 210–11
Montgomery Plot, 154
Moral Philosophy, 26, 27, 30–1, 33, 42
Morayshire, 35
Morton, Graeme, 5, 7, 207–8

Munch, P. A., 249
Murison, David, 130–1
Murray, Erskine, of Aberdona, 44
Murray, James Archibald, Lord, 47, 49, 51, 57, 77, 197
Murder of Archbishop Sharp, The (Allan), 186
Murder of Rizzio, The (Allan), 186
Museum of Antiquities in Copenhagen, 99

Nairn, Tom, 5–7, 11–12, 264
Namier, Lewis, Sir, 263
Napoleon I (of France), 58, 249
Napoleonic Wars, 260
Nasmyth, Alexander, 185
Nation, The, 214
'National Archaeological Museum for Scotland', 72, 80, 245; *see also* National Museum of Antiquities of Scotland
National Association for the Vindication of Scottish Rights (NAVSR), 200, 208–13
  President of, 146
  see also Scottish Rights Association; 'Justice to Scotland'
National Covenant (1638), 127, 131, 156, 182, 188; *see also* Covenant/covenanters
National Drama, the, 25, 185–7, 191–2, 267
National Education, 49, 67
National Gallery (of Scotland), 56, 261–2
national histories
  characteristics across Europe, 242–9
  of France, 194, 270
  of Scotland: changing expectations of, 18–22; new perspectives on, 214–40, 257–8
  of Switzerland 250–2
  as non-sectarian narrative, 15
  see also History of the people

nationalism, 6, 34, 209–12
  recent theorists of, 263–4
  see also Scottish nationality; Scottish national identity
National Manners, 80–1, 142
National Manuscripts of Scotland, 82
National Museum of Antiquities of Scotland, 261–2, 265
Nature, 29, 37, 39–40, 46, 60, 260
  design in, 254
  and Rousseau, 28, 59–60
Neaves, Charles, Lord, 80
Neville's Cross (battle of), 116
Newby, Andrew, 240
New Race of Men, A (Fry), 10–11
Newry, 151
New Statistical Account, 74
New York, 214
New York Times (newspaper), 240
'New Zealanders', 67
Nightingale, Florence, 66
Night Side of Nature, The (Crowe), 167
Nile (river), 63
Noble Savage, 59, 64; *see also* savage, conceptions of
Noctes Ambrosianae, 33–4, 43, 266
Nora, Pierre, 251
Norman(s), 87, 100, 230, 242
  fortresses, 84
  Conquest, 231
Norse, 231
  Sagas, 118, 146
  mythology, 146–7
  Eddas, 147
North British Review, 200, 203
North Sea, 153
'Northern archaeologists', 99, 249; *see also* Scandinavian scholars
Norway, 245
Norwegian historian, 249

Ochil Hills, 37, 120
Oeschli, Wilhelm, 251

Oedipus, the, 227
Old Mortality (Scott), 16, 142, 151, 169
Old Statistical Account, 74
Oldbuck, Jonathan, 20
Oliphant, Margaret, 214, 222, 226, 228, 229, 247
On Murder Considered as One of the Fine Arts (De Quincey), 166
organicism
  and historical development, 252–4
  and Edinburgh radicals, 254
Original Letters relating to the Ecclesiastical Affairs of Scotland (Anon), 124
Origines de la Confédération Suisse: Histoire et Légende (Rilliet), 249
Origines Parochiales Scotiae (Innes), 74
Orygynale Cronikil of Scotland (Wynton), 98
Ossian (Macpherson), 47, 62
Ossianic literature, 118
Otterburn (battle of), 123
Oxbridge history chairs, 193
Oxford Handbook of Modern Scottish History (Devine and Wormauld), 263

pantomime, 181–2
Papiers d'Etat (Teulet), 89, 256
Paris, 59, 88, 178, 254
Parliament Hall (Edinburgh), 50
'Passive Obedience' (Hume), 108
Paterson, Lindsay, 5
Paton, Elizabeth (Eliza), 27–8; *see also* Burton, Eliza
Paton, John, 28
Patriots (party), 104
'people's history', 247, 252; *see also* history of the people
Perth, 37, 163
Perthshire Militia, 50
Peter's Letters to his Kinsfolk (Lockhart), 34, 266

Philip II (of Spain), 90
Philosophical Enquiry (Burke), 38
Philosophical Essays (Stewart), 40
'Philosophic Radicals', 111
photozincography, 71
Phrenology, 45–6
Phrenological Journal, 45
Pict(ish), 216, 219, 230
  language, 21, 98
  mythology, 147
Picturesque, the, 26, 37, 38–40, 125, 135, 140, 143, 224, 260
Pinkerton, John, 22, 98, 219, 255
Pitcairn, Robert, 162
Pizarro (Francisco), 68
Playfair, William, 261–2
Political and Social Economy: Its Practical Application (Burton), 111
political economy, 1, 65, 68, 111–12
Political Economy for Use in Schools and Private Education (Burton), 111
Poor Law reform, 49
Porteous Mob, The (Drummond), 188
Portobello, 51, 272
post-Enlightenment Scotland
  crisis of, 171
Postscript (to On Murder Considered as One of the Fine Arts) (De Quincey), 166
'Prehistory', 150, 217
Prehistoric Scotland, 76, 233
Pre-Raphaelite Brotherhood, 56
Presbyterian(ism), 13–14, 16, 17, 24, 25, 83, 131–2, 136, 176, 206, 243
  ministers, 133, 176
Pre-Reformation world, 83
pre-Union past (of Scotland), 8–9, 224, 257
Priestley (Joseph), 106
Pro Bono Publico Club, 30
'Prophet, the', 105, 111; *see also* Bentham, Jeremy

Prothero (George), 267
proto-evolutionist ideas, 254
Provost of Linlithgow, 237
Provost Pawkie, 139
Provost, The (Galt), 138–9
Punch (journal), 200

Queen Margaret (wife of Malcolm III), 100
Queen Mary, 69, 90, 101, 119–21, 176, 186; *see also* Mary Stuart, Queen of Scots
Quentin Durward (Scott Lauder), 187

Radical(ism), 44–5, 57, 87, 254
'Raid of Ruthven', 132, 175, 183, 225
Ramsay, John, Sir, 178
Ramsey, Edward, Dean, 10, 237
Randolph, Thomas, 180
Ranke (Leopold), von, 194
Rational of Evidence (Bentham), 105
records scholars(hip), 3, 8, 22, 23, 26, 33, 51, 83, 85, 88, 124, 131, 143–5, 232–3, 245
Reeve, Henry, 194, 223
Reformation, 13, 16, 19, 85, 86, 125, 129, 134–5, 206, 216, 220, 222
Reform Bills, 44, 205
Reform campaigns, 49
Regal Union, 195
Regents/Regencies, 175, 235
Regent Morton, 101; *see also* Douglas, James, Earl of Morton
Regent Murray, 119–20, 121, 175, 223, 225; *see also* Stewart, James, Earl of Murray
Regent Murray Shot by Hamilton of Bothwellhaugh, The (Allan), 186
Register House, 71, 219
Reid, Thomas, 30–1, 163
Remarkable Ruins, and Romantic Prospects, of North Britain (Cordiner), 39
Renaissance poets, 129

Report on Army Sanitary Conditions, 50
Rerum Scoticarum historia (Buchanan), 98
Restoration, the, 69, 151, 156, 182
Revolutions of 1848, 252
Revue des Deux Mondes, 214
Rhine, 39
Rhymer, 163; *see also* Thomas of Ercildoune
Rilliet, Albert, 249–50
Ritchie, John, 45, 48
Ritson, Joseph, 98, 219
Rizzio, David, 16, 18, 120, 125, 175–6, 244, 252
Rob Roy (drama), 185, 192
Robert II (of Scotland), 222
Roberts, David, 186
Robertson, Joseph, 33–4, 37, 70–3, 82, 89, 95, 144, 161–2, 217, 219, 221, 231
Robertson, William, 21, 22, 93, 113, 140, 148–9, 190, 219, 232, 244, 255
Roger, Rev. Charles, 132
Roman Empire, 68
Roman period (in Scotland), 219
Romantic Age, 224, 245
Romantic literature, 85, 102, 155, 179
Romanticism
  changed attitudes to the past, 243; *see also* historiography, romantic
  generates 'historism', 252
  vogue for the Middle Ages, 245
Romantic sensibility, 24, 35, 37, 60, 144, 260
Romeo and Juliet (Shakespeare), 185
Rousseau, Jean-Jacques, 28, 59, 64
Roxburgh (siege of), 97
Royal Burghs, 84
Royal Institution, 55, 72, 143, 262
Royal Scottish Academy, 55–6, 171–2, 187
Royal Society of Edinburgh, 106
Ruddiman, Thomas, 29

'Rudolphi affair', 177
Russel, Alexander, 49, 240
Russel, James, 168, 186
Russell, John, Lord, 197
Russia, 91
Rutherfurd, Andrew, Lord, 48, 77, 197
Ruthven family, 149
Ruthven, John, Earl of Gowrie, 25, 148, 178
Ruthven, Patrick, Lord, 176, 228
Ruthven, William, Earl of Gowrie, 133
Rütli meadow, 249
Ryehouse Plot, 153, 158

Sadler, Ralph, Sir, 180
Samoa, 268
St Andrews, 110
   Archbishop, 156
   University, 191, 231
St Jerome, 147
Sanitary Reform, 38, 51
'Sanitary Report' (Chadwick), 110, 112
'sanitary science', 67, 254
Sanquhar Declaration, 13
savage, the, Victorian conceptions of, 62–4; *see also* 'Noble Savage'
Saxon(s), 68, 104, 229–30
   origins of the nation, 100, 230
   racial qualities of Lowlanders, 9
   see also teutonism
Scandinavian scholars, 99, 217, 245; *see also* 'northern archaeologists'
Schegel, Friedrich, 255
Schiller (Friedrich), 255
'Scientific' history, 247, 251–2
Scot Abroad, The (Burton), 1, 92, 221, 248
Scotch novels, the 224
Scotland in the Middle Ages (Innes), 73
Scotland
   Post-Enlightenment, 120
Scotichronicon (Bower), 98
Scotish (sic) Ballads and Songs (Maidment), 130

'Scotland since the Union' (Aytoun), 200, 211
Scotorum historia (Boece), 98
Scots language, 18, 23, 28, 126–30, 146, 148, 153, 243
Scots Dictionary (Jamieson), 23, 146, 162, 265n10
Scotsman (newspaper), 45, 48–9, 55, 56, 239–40, 257, 265
Scott Centenary, 192
Scott, David, 51, 56, 170–3, 187
Scott, William Bell, 56
Scott, Walter, Sir, 8, 16, 17, 34, 37, 40, 52, 60, 62, 64, 115, 117, 120–2, 128, 137, 139–40, 148–9, 151, 158, 225, 246, 263
   and antiquarianism, 20, 144–5
   encouragement of P. F. Tytler, 15, 19, 139–40
   viewed as unable to articulate Scottish nationality, 13
   influence on theatre and painting, 25–6, 185–9, 191–2
   influence on historical composition, 22, 24, 141, 242–3, 245–6, 266
   popularises 'Scottish Gothic', 162, 169–70
   see also Burton, John Hill; historiography, romantic; history of the people
Scotticisms, 23
Scottish Academy of Painting, Sculpture and Architecture, 171
Scottish architecture, 26, 84–5, 220, 222, 234–5, 244, 261
   as national style, 77, 78–9
   baronial and ecclesiastical, 69, 76–8
   castellated and domestic, 78–9
   source for national history, 79
Scottish Burgh Records Society, 71
'Scottish Canova', 42; *see also* Macdonald, Laurence
Scottish Church, 203–4, 260; *see also* Established Church of Scotland

Scottish Common Sense Philosophy, 30–1, 163
Scottish constitutional history 26, 34, 74, 86, 222–4; *see also* Scottish Law/legal system
Scottish Diaspora, 15
Scottish Enlightenment, 6, 8, 11, 29, 31, 56, 110, 163, 224, 253
Scottish Episcopal Church, 237; *see also* Episcopalian(ism)
Scottish Estates, 182, 223; *see also* Estates (of Scotland)
Scottish grievances
  after 1707, 195–6
  in mid-nineteenth century, 196–8, 200–7
  see also Scottish Rights movement; 'Justice to Scotland'
Scottish Historical Review, 2
Scottish Home Rule Association (SHRA), 209–10
Scottish Latinity, 29, 82, 91, 246
Scottish Law/legal system, 9, 85–7, 202
  Code of the Burgher Corporations, 85
  assimilation with English, 197–8
  and the Union Treaty, 141
  see also Scottish constitutional history; *Manual of the Law of Scotland*
Scottish medieval and Renaisssance poets, 243
Scottish medieval world, 223, 245
Scottish Merlin, 118; *see also* Thomas of Ercildoune
Scottish middle classes, 208, 264
Scottish Nation, The (Devine), 5
Scottish national identity, 2–5, 7, 12–14, 206, 210, 212–13, 240–2, 246, 248, 250
  as Anglo-British, 9, 19, 22
  as presbyterian, 13
  revival of, 260–70
  see also Scottish nationality
Scottish national institutions, 202, 204, 212n33, 260–1

Scottish National Portrait Gallery, 262
Scottish nationalism, modern, 6, 203, 211, 258
Scottish nationality, 10, 12–13, 72–3, 90, 196, 201–2, 204, 206, 211, 222, 241–2
  Celtic influence, 229–33
  see also Scottish national identity
Scottish peasantry, 153
Scottish people, the, 210, 242, 257
Scottish Parliament, 103, 201, 223
  origins, 85
  see also Estates of Scotland
Scottish Prison Board, 1, 65, 112
Scottish Philosophy, the, 110
Scottish publishers, 3, 55, 75–6, 96, 265, 267
Scottish reading public, 2–3, 73, 221
Scottish Reformation, 13, 94, 129, 131, 176; *see also* Reformation
Scottish Rights movement, 4, 7, 205, 73n25, 207–13; *see also* National Association for the Vindication of Scottish Rights (NAVSR)
Scottish Society of Antiquaries (SSA), 71–3, 80, 99, 231, 245, 249, 261; *see also* antiquarian(ism)
Scottish Solicitor General, 48, 80
Scottish Universities, 6, 12, 26, 82, 88, 203, 221–2, 248; *see also* Aberdeen University; Edinburgh University; Glasgow University
Scottish vernacular culture, 23, 121, 130, 138, 160, 173, 243–4, 246, 264–5
  of the North-East, 28–9
  see also ballads; folklore; Scots language; superstitions
Scottish Wars of Independence, 63, 66, 124, 152
Scott's Shadow (Duncan), 266
Sculptured stones, 81–2, 161, 244
Sculptured Stones of Scotland (Stuart), 81, 221

Scutari, 66
Seceder churches, 132
Secession of 1734, 206
'Second Confession of Faith', 133
'second language of Scotland', 130–5, 243
Secret and True History of the Church of Scotland, The (Kirkton), 118, 168–9
Secretary of State for Scotland, 50, 196, 202
Secretary to the Scottish Prisons Board, 7, 49
sectarianism/ anti-sectarianism, 14, 26, 49
Seeress of Prevorst, The (Kerner), 117
Select Remains of the Ancient Popular Poetry of Scotland (Laing), 130
Self-Help, With Illustrations of Character and Conduct (Smiles), 113
Semple, J. W., 43
Shairp, J. C., Principal, 231–3
Sharp, James, Archbishop, 25, 156–8, 168–9, 182, 225, 226–7, 244, 252
Sharpe, Charles Kirkpatrick, 51–5, 159, 168–9, 170, 172–3, 186, 187
Shakespearean dramas, 187
Shakespeare, William, 43, 147, 184–5, 189, 191
Sheriff of Moray, 64
Signet library, 50
Signing of the National Covenant in Greyfriars' Kirkyard (Allan), 188
Simpson, J. Y., 72, 217
Sir Tristrem, 118
Skelton, John, 194
Skene, William Forbes, 70, 231
Sketches of Early Scotch History and Social Progress (Innes), 73, 95, 136
Smiles, Samuel, 113–14
Smith, Adam, 111
Smith, Antony D., 7

Smith, Thomas Southwood, 105
Smith, William Robertson, 11
Society of Writers, 33–4, 43, 137, 141
Solemn League and Covenant, 177; *see also* National Covenant
Spaewife, The (Galt), 162–3
Spalding Club, 64, 70, 74, 81, 82, 87, 231
Spalding, William, 33, 56, 171, 184–5, 187, 191
Spanish archives, 90, 96
Spanish Empire, 68
Speaker of the House of Commons, 47–8
Speke, John Hanning, 63–4
Spirit of the Storm, The (D. Scott), 172
Spottiswood Society, 70
State Paper Office, 18, 129
State Papers, 122–3, 238
State Trials, 157
Staubbach cataract, 61
Staunton, 130
Stevenson, Robert Louis, 11, 170, 268–9
Stewart, Alan Breck, 268
Stewart, Dugald, 31–2, 38, 40–1, 163
Stewart, Henry, Lord Darnley, 119, 120, 125, 128, 153, 175, 178–9
Stewart, James, Earl of Murray, 17–18, 132, 228; *see also* Regent Murray
Stewart, Mathew, Earl of Lennox, 228
Stewart, Walter, Earl of Atholl, 163
Stirlingshire, 146
Strange Case of Dr Jekyll and Mr Hyde (Stevenson), 269
Strange Death of Scottish History, The (Ash), 8, 12
Struan, 36
Stuart, John, Dr. 70–2, 81, 217, 231
Stuart, Robert, 79
Struthers, John, 21, 199
Stuarts (dynasty), 74, 106, 133, 153, 234
'Student Life in Scotland' (Burton), 82, 221

Sublime, the, 37–8, 62
Subverting Scotland's Past (Kidd), 8
Supernatural, the, 24–5, 53, 62, 146–50, 152–3, 156–7, 159–65, 167–8, 226–7
superstitions, 34, 138, 160, 162, 168, 172, 220, 243; *see also* folklore; Scottish vernacular culture; Supernatural
Susannah and the Elders, 52–3
Sweden, 91
Swiss, the, 242
Switzerland, 249–2
　constitution of 1798, 249
　historical consciousness, 251
　liberal historians, 251
　post-1848 State, 249

Tait's Edinburgh Magazine, 44–5, 54, 70, 140
Tait, William, 44, 54, 57, 104, 106, 239
Tales of a Grandfather (Scott), 128
Tales of Demonology and Witchcraft (Scott), 24
Tasmania, 68
Taste, 35–41, 85, 177
Tell, William, 249
'Ten years controversy', 205
Teulet, Alexandre, 88–94, 217, 249, 251
Teutonism, 19, 79, 81, 86, 100, 126, 195, 201, 203–4, 228–33, 245, 253, 259; *see also* historiography – nineteenth-century whig
theatrical *tableaux*, 186, 188–9
'The Elfin Knight', 131
'The Original Contract' (Hume), 108
'The Man of Council' (Burton), 91
'The Resurrection on the Day of the Crucifixion (D. Scott), 172
'The Scot Abroad' (Burton), 91
'The Union with England and Scottish Nationality' (Masson), 203
'The Whig Interpretation of Scottish History' (Fry), 10

Thierry, Augustin, 241
Thirty Years War, 150–1, 170
Thomas of Ercildoune, 118, 164
'Thomas Papaverius', 54; *see also* De Quincey, Thomas
Thomsen, C. J., 249
Thomson, John, 149–50
Thomson, Thomas, 52, 64, 70, 73, 85, 88
Three Estates, The (Lindsay), 129
Throckmorton, Nicolas, Sir, 180
Times (newspaper), 200, 228–9
Tory (ism), 10, 33, 43, 54, 137, 257
Tour to the Hebrides (Boswell), 39
tourism, 37, 39–40, 60
Traitor's Gate, The (D. Scott), 171
Treatise (Hume), 107–8
Treaty of Union, 50, 104, 202, 207, 210; *see also* Union of 1707
Trevor-Roper, Hugh, 263
Trossachs, 37, 60
Trustees' Academy, 187
Tucker, Thomas, 102
Tulloch, John, Principal, 215, 216, 237
Turnbull, W. B. D., 88
Turner, Sir James, 151
Tweed (river), 129, 234
'Two Englands, the', 253
Two Noble Kinsmen, The (Shakespeare), 184
Tytler, Patrick Fraser, 6, 8, 15–19, 24, 43, 93, 127, 139–40, 148–9, 189–90, 192, 226, 247, 256

Undersecretary for Scottish affairs, 197
Union of the Crowns, 117; *see also* regal Union
Union of 1707, 4, 5, 7, 102–4, 195, 198–209, 212–13, 250, 258, 268
unionist-nationalism, 5, 7, 208, 213
　'counter-discourse' to, 210
University College, London, 203
University of Wisconsin, 215
'Unrecorded Ages', 99, 218

utilitarian(ism), 3, 104–11, 113, 259–60
Utopianism, 103

Vestiges of Creation (Chambers), 46
Victorian(s), 63
  central state, 110
  formality, 271
  imagination, 64
  middle class, 58
  novel, 165
  scientific discovery and reportage, 63
  values, 7, 60, 113
Victorian political nation, 19
Viscounts Melville, 47
Volunteer Rifle Militia, 66

Walker, Patrick, 151
Wallace, William, 5, 7, 177–8, 230, 249–50, 252
Wardour, Sir Arthur, 20, 98, 230
War of Scottish Independence (Burns), 230–1
Wars of Scottish Independence, 85, 90, 91, 177, 220
Waterloo, 58
Waverley (Scott), 144
Waverley novels, 128, 189, 192, 263
Waverley (station), 68
Weir, William, 44, 49, 104
Westminster, 47, 198
Westminster Review, 44, 70, 109, 111
Whig(s), 10, 11, 23, 33, 62, 64, 77, 104, 197–8, 235
  elite, 47–51, 56, 57, 163, 260
  political economy, 34, 266

Whitaker, John, 98
Wigton Martyrs, 136, 151, 227, 252
Wilkie, David, 187–8
wild man/the Wild Man, 59–60, 62, 64; *see also* savage, Victorian conceptions of
Williams, John, 166–7, 169
Wilson, Daniel, 72–3, 80, 161, 217, 245
Wilson, John, 33, 42–4, 60, 62
Wishart, George, 125
Wissenschaft, 247; *see also* 'Scientific' history
'Witchcraft in Scotland' (Burton), 162
'Wizard of the North', 161; *see also* Scott, Walter, Sir
Wodrow, Robert, 132, 151, 157, 159–60, 269
Wolf's Crag, 149
Wollstonecraft, Mary, 28
Wolsey, Thomas, Cardinal, 123–4, 180
Wood, Andrew, Sir, 128
Worcester, 150
Wordsworthian enthusiasm, 36
Wordsworth, William, 33, 62
Works (Bentham), 104
Works (Dryden), 158
Worsaae, J. J. A., 249
Wringhim, Robert, 169
Wynton, Andrew, 98, 129, 147–8

Xenitean empire, 15

Zauber-Bibliothek (C. G. Horst), 24–5
Zimmer, Oliver, 251–2

EU representative:
Easy Access System Europe
Mustamäe tee 50, 10621 Tallinn, Estonia
Gpsr.requests@easproject.com

www.ingramcontent.com/pod-product-compliance
Lightning Source LLC
Chambersburg PA
CBHW052045220426
43663CB00012B/2453